Encyclopedia of Japanese American Internment

Encyclopedia of Japanese American Internment

GARY Y. OKIHIRO, EDITOR

 GREENWOOD

AN IMPRINT OF ABC-CLIO, LLC
Santa Barbara, California • Denver, Colorado • Oxford, England

Library of Congress Cataloging-in-Publication Data

Encyclopedia of Japanese American internment / Gary Y. Okihiro, Editor.
     pages cm
   Includes bibliographical references and index.
   ISBN 978-0-313-39915-2 (hardcopy : alk. paper) — ISBN 978-0-313-39916-9
(ebook)   1. Japanese Americans—Evacuation and relocation, 1942–1945—
Encyclopedias.   2. World War, 1939–1945—Japanese Americans—Encyclopedias.
3. Japanese Americans—Biography—Encyclopedias.   I. Okihiro, Gary Y., 1945– editor.
   D769.8.A6E64   2013
   940.53'1773—dc23   2013000311

ISBN: 978-0-313-39915-2
EISBN: 978-0-313-39916-9

17 16 15 14 13   1 2 3 4 5

This book is also available on the World Wide Web as an eBook.
Visit www.abc-clio.com for details.

Greenwood
An Imprint of ABC-CLIO, LLC

ABC-CLIO, LLC
130 Cremona Drive, P.O. Box 1911
Santa Barbara, California 93116-1911

This book is printed on acid-free paper ∞

Manufactured in the United States of America

Contents

Camps, Centers, and Prisons

Primary Documents

x   **CONTENTS**

Introduction

Gary Y. Okihiro

Encyclopedia of Japanese American Internment is about the forced removal and confinement of some 120,000 Japanese Americans during World War II. On February 19, 1942, 10 weeks after Japan's attack on Pearl Harbor, President Franklin D. Roosevelt signed Executive Order 9066, which authorized the mass exclusion and detention on the basis of "military necessity." In fact, as the government knew, Japanese Americans were completely innocent of espionage or sabotage, including the Pearl Harbor disaster, and two-thirds of them were U.S. citizens while the rest could not become citizens by law. They were profiled on the basis of race, not as individuals as is guaranteed by the U.S. Constitution, for their alleged association with Japan and the "Japanese race." The United States declared war against Germany and Italy, but German and Italian Americans, by contrast, were spared the treatment given to Japanese Americans.

This *Encyclopedia* is organized around biographies of leading figures in the internment experience, like President Roosevelt, significant events and acts, like Pearl Harbor and Executive Order 9066, and the various detention camps and centers that held Japanese Americans until their release. Finally, a chronology highlights the sequence of events, primary documents allow readers to learn from firsthand accounts, and a bibliography of secondary works facilitates additional research on the subject of Japanese American internment.

[*In this narrative history of the Japanese American internment experience, italicized words and terms, except for book titles, are discussed in the sections that follow.*]

Narrative History

This story actually begins long before President Roosevelt's Executive Order. It starts around the mid-19th century when the United States dispatched to Japan an armed flotilla "to drive by force," in the words of the expedition's leader, Commodore Matthew C. Perry, the overmatched Japanese into opening its doors to U.S. trade and influence (Heine, 3, 4). That invasive entering wedge of U.S. military and commercial interests led to sweeping changes in Japan and to Japanese labor migrations to Hawai'i and the U.S. continent.

The first government-contract recruits to work in sugar were brought to Hawai'i in 1868, and an additional 29,000 arrived between 1885 and 1894. About 125,000 came to the islands as free migrants from 1894 to 1908, when the Gentlemen's Agreement between Japan and the United States halted the further migration of male laborers. Women were a mere 9 percent of Hawai'i's Japanese in 1890, but they increased to 22 percent in 1900, 31 percent in 1910, and 41 percent in

1920. About 27,440 Japanese migrated to the U.S. continent between 1891 and 1900 to work mainly in agriculture, and 42,457 between 1901 and 1907, along with about 38,000 who remigrated from Hawai'i to the continent. Women constituted only 4 percent of the U.S. continental Japanese in 1900, but they rose to 13 percent in 1910, and 35 percent in 1920. Most of that increase was due to the migration of so-called "picture brides," who escaped the restrictions of the Gentlemen's Agreement.

Originally welcomed, indeed recruited, for their labor, Japanese Americans posed a problem to their employers when they struck for higher wages and improved working conditions. Thus, in 1920, when some 8,300 Japanese, Filipino, Puerto Rican, and other sugar plantation workers on the island of O'ahu demanded higher wages for men and women, an eight-hour day, paid maternity leave for women, and better health-care and recreational facilities, the planters cast that multiracial, democratic action as "an attempt on the part of the Japanese to obtain control of the sugar industry" and as "a dark conspiracy to Japanize this American territory." A federal commission sent to investigate Hawai'i's labor situation after the strike warned of the "menace of alien domination," and military intelligence concluded that Japan had embarked upon a global race war by orchestrating its nationals abroad, notably Buddhist and Shinto priests, Japanese-language school teachers, newspaper owners and editors, radical labor leaders, and pliant workers to advance its imperial ambitions (Okihiro, 70–81, 94–97, 100–01, 108–11).

The Bureau of Investigation, forerunner of the *Federal Bureau of Invesitgation (FBI),* predicted a year after the 1920 strike that the rising tide of color would soon swamp the white race not only in California but also the entire Pacific Coast, and stated that "it was the determined purpose of Japan to amalgamate the entire colored races of the world against the Nordic or white race, with Japan at the head of the coalition, for the purpose of wrestling away the supremacy of the white race and placing such supremacy in the colored peoples under the dominion of Japan" (Okihiro, 116–17). Such exaggerations matched the most lurid *yellow peril* fantasies being churned out for the public by journalists, writers, and filmmakers of the time with no firm basis (Daniels, 1970; Marchetti).

The advance legions in that momentous clash, Japanese Americans, comprised a significant proportion of the population of Hawai'i, about 43 percent in 1920, but they totaled a mere 111,000 of some 106 million souls on the U.S. continent. And their reliance upon Japan to bolster their slender ranks was tenuous at best. For instance, in 1909, when the Higher Wages Association and some 7,000 Japanese American workers from all major O'ahu plantations went on a four-month strike for full equality in the workplace, Japan's consul general, as "a representative of the Japanese Emperor," ordered the strikers to return to their jobs. He reprimanded them for damaging relations with their employers, and accused them of being disloyal to Japan's emperor (Okihiro, 51). In reality, the strikers, by disobeying Japan's consul general, were acting in a very American way in exercising their right to strike and demanding a living wage to support themselves and their children. Their intention was to build futures in the United States as Americans and not in Japan.

During the 1930s, U.S. intelligence expanded its surveillance network and refined its plans to quarantine the alleged Japanese contagion. In the midst of those preparations, President *Franklin D. Roosevelt* wrote an astonishing note to the military in Washington, D.C. dated August 10, 1936: "Has the local Joint Planning Committee (Hawaii) any recommendation to make? One obvious thought occurs to me—that every Japanese citizen or non-citizen on the Island of Oahu who meets these Japanese ships or has any connection with their officers or men should be secretly but definitely identified and his or her name placed on a special list of those who would be the first to be placed in a *concentration camp* in the event of trouble" (Okihiro, 173–74).

The president's query and obvious thought had been prompted by a report from Hawai'i that discussed the arrival of Japanese naval vessels in Hawaiian waters and the entertainment of their officers and men by local Japanese Americans, all legal and very public events. But in the eyes of U.S. strategists and the president, those encounters held national security consequences largely because, as put by a bureau report, "it is said, and no doubt with considerable truth, that every Japanese in the United States who can read and write is a member of the Japanese intelligence system" (Okihiro, 128). That assumption was untrue but the president, unwilling to be caught unprepared, pressed the military and the acting navy secretary, "what arrangements and plans have been made relative to concentration camps in the Hawaiian Islands for dangerous or undesirable aliens or citizens in the event of [a] national emergency?" (Okihiro, 174).

In response, the acting secretary of war informed Roosevelt that the *Army* had established a Service Command in Hawai'i, which linked the military with territorial forces such as the National Guard, police, and other civilian organizations for "the control of the civil population and the prevention of sabotage, of civil disturbances, or of local uprisings" of "potentially hostile Japanese." And the military reassured the president: "It is a routine matter for those responsible for military intelligence to maintain lists of suspects, who will normally be the first to be interned under the operation of the Joint Defense Plan, Hawaiian Theater, in the event of war." But it underscored the necessity for continued vigilance, and urged that the total resources of government, in addition to those of the army and *Navy*, be pooled for a common effort against the anticipated danger (Okihiro, 174–75).

While military and civilian intelligence disagreed over the potential for sabotage among Hawai'i's Japanese Americans, they agreed that the people's loyalty to the United States could be compelled by interning their leaders. Thus, on the eve of Pearl Harbor, both military intelligence and the FBI maintained lists of Japanese American "suspects," in reality community leaders, for a program of selective detention. That strategy was especially important for Hawai'i where Japanese American labor was essential for the territory's economy, and accordingly the military's concern was, as put by the army's chief planner, "to guarantee security to the islands and still maintain economic stability as well as adherence to the democratic principles of American government." The army rejected as impractical and destructive of the islands' industries the mass removal and detention of Hawai'i's Japanese Americans, despite the president's insistence upon, seconded by his navy secretary, that course of action well into 1942 (Okihiro, 183; Daniels, 1981, 72–73).

Instead, the military's plan for Hawai'i, at least since 1923, was *martial law* to guarantee absolute power justified by an imagined Japanese peril. Military rule was swift and sure and neatly bypassed the democratic principles of American government; it could impose its program of selective detention and labor controls as well as restrictions over freedoms of speech, religion, and movement, and it inspired fear and thus obedience. "Fear of severe punishment," an Army document declared, "is the greatest deterrent to commission of crime." "It is certain," the author claimed, "that many persons who might have been tempted to give aid, support or comfort to our enemy were deterred from so doing by the severity and the promptness with which punishment was meted out by the Provost Courts operating under the martial-law regime." Hawai'i's civilian governor added, "internment of all suspected enemy aliens was the only safe course to put the 'fear of god' in the hearts of those who would assist the enemy" (Okihiro, 211–12).

That "day of infamy," December 7, 1941, marked the entry of the United States into World War II and a pivotal moment for Japanese Americans, that day when Japan attacked *Pearl Harbor*. As smoke still rose from the wreckage of America's Pacific Fleet, martial law was declared in Hawai'i, and squads of FBI agents, military police, and local law enforcement officers knocked on the doors of persons listed on index cards for apprehension in Hawai'i and on the *"ABC" list* along the West Coast. Within two days, there were 1,291 Japanese, 865 *Germans,* and 147 *Italians* in custody in the islands and on the U.S. continent (Christgau; Fox; DiStasi).

Thus it was that in the conduct of a war waged for white supremacy, according to U.S. planners, against imperial Japan, some 120,000 Japanese Americans were forcibly and summarily removed from their homes and placed in concentration camps for the war's duration. They were not accused of any crime other than the presumed fact of their "race." One drop of "Japanese blood" justified that racial profiling, according to the U.S. government. As the general in charge of the defense of the West Coast explained: "The Japanese race is an enemy race and while many second and third generation Japanese born on United States soil, possessed of United States citizenship, have become 'Americanized,' the racial strains are undiluted." The *Los Angeles Times* added: "A viper is nonetheless a viper wherever the egg is hatched—so a Japanese-American, born of Japanese parents—grows up to be a Japanese, not an American" (Armor and Wright, 38, 43–44).

Japanese American community leaders, like the newspaper publisher *Yasutaro Soga,* found themselves in Honolulu's immigration station after having been suddenly taken from their homes and families without charges. There, soldiers with bayonets ordered them around contemptuously and threatened to kill them if they resisted or took a false step. So despite their intense anger, Soga and his fellow internees had to restrain themselves or "we would have died . . . a dog's death from the thrust of his bayonet" (Okihiro, 212–13). The treatment given to those men at the immigration station was brutal as if in retribution for Japan's devastating attack on Pearl Harbor. And yet, their captors knew, the men had not been selected because they had participated in the destruction of the U.S. Pacific Fleet. Military and

Despite their government betrayal of their citizenship rights, these children pledge their allegiance to the flag at Weill Public School in San Francisco, April 1942. (Library of Congress)

civilian inquiries into the Pearl Harbor disaster completely exonerated Hawai'i's Japanese Americans. Rather, they received this special treatment of humiliation and abuse because they were leaders of the Japanese American community.

On the U.S. continent, 12-year-old Donald Nakahata lived with his sister, mother and father, aunt, and grandfather in San Francisco. His father, a newspaperman, left on December 7 or 8 to help Japanese Americans in nearby San Jose. "And I walked him to the bus stop," remembered Nakahata. "We went down Pine Street down to Fillmore to the number 22 streetcar, . . . and [he] took the train to San Jose. And that was the last time I saw him." In San Jose, Nakahata's father was spirited away, held at a detention station in San Francisco, and sent to several camps reserved for Japanese American leaders. "Dad was gone, and we just heard from him a little," said Nakahata sadly. "We have a few letters from him. And you know, I have no feeling if I look at them now. He apparently suffered several more strokes in various camps. But I know he was in *Fort Sill,* Oklahoma, and *Camp Livingston,* Louisiana, and I think he died in *Bismarck,* North Dakota. It's really kind of sad if you think about it, that I don't know where he died" (Tateishi, 32–35).

Yoshiaki Fukuda, a Konko church minister in San Francisco, was apprehended on December 7. "Although we were not informed of our destination," Fukuda recalled, "it was rumored that we were heading for *Missoula*, Montana. There were many leaders of the Japanese community aboard our train. . . . The view outside was blocked by shades on the windows, and we were watched constantly by sentries with bayoneted rifles who stood on either end of the coach. The door to the lavatory was kept open in order to prevent our escape or suicide. A gloomy atmosphere prevailed on the train. Much of this was attributable to the fact that we had been forced to leave our families and jobs with little or no warning. In addition, there were fears that we were being taken to be executed" (Fukuda, 7–8).

Like Fukuda, 45-year-old Ichiro Shimoda, a gardener from Los Angeles, was taken from his family on December 7. On the train to the Missoula detention camp, he attempted suicide by biting off his tongue. Others restrained him by putting a piece of wood between his jaws. Shimoda, a friend reported, worried over the fate of his wife and family back in Los Angeles, and was thus depressed. At Missoula, Shimoda tried to asphyxiate himself, and, transferred to Fort Sill in March 1942, he climbed the inner fence of the camp and was shot to death by a guard. According to the FBI report: "One Jap became mildly insane and was placed in the Fort Sill Army Hospital. [He] . . . attempted an escape on May 13, 1942 at 7:20 A.M. He climbed the first fence, ran down the runway between the fencing, one hundred feet and started to climb the second, when he was shot and killed by two shots, one entering the back of his head. The guard had given him several verbal warnings" (Kashima, 54).

A consequence of those arbitrary and swift removals and detentions was the fear anticipated by the military and civilian planners. In Seattle, Christian minister Daisuke Kitagawa remembered visiting the families of those who had been interned. "In no time," he wrote, "the whole community was thoroughly panic-stricken; every male lived in anticipation of arrest by the FBI, and every household endured each day in fear and trembling. Most Japanese, including at least one clergyman, were so afraid of being marked by association with those who had been taken away that they hesitated to visit the wives and children of the victims. Much of that fear can be attributed to the rumors, rampant in the community," Kitagawa reasoned, "about the grounds for those arrests, about the treatment the detainees were getting, and about their probable imprisonment for the duration of the war. No rational explanation could set their minds at ease" (Kitagawa, 41).

Across Honolulu harbor, within clear view of the immigration station, was *Sand Island*, a flat, desolate piece of land that at one time served as a quarantine station for the thousands of migrants who landed in Hawai'i. Similar to that intention of the health officials, the army sought to isolate the leaders from the rest of Hawai'i's people by transforming the station into a concentration camp. Called "prisoners of war" and later "merely detainees" by the camp commander, the captives were strip-searched, forced outside into the pouring rain, and in the gathering darkness, ordered to erect the tents that housed them (Okihiro, 215, 217).

Sand Island's terror worked on both the body and mind. Strip searches were a common feature designed to peel off the outer defenses and expose the private parts. Citing that indignity, an internee exclaimed: "They stripped us down and even checked the anus. We were completely naked. Not even undershorts." Another described how guards holding rifles lined a group up against a wall and threatened to shoot them if they refused to do as they were told. "With that threat," he remarked, "there was no need to say anything more."

The island was physically taxing. "A dust wind kept blowing almost every day in December," reported Yasutaro Soga, "and the night air was shivering cold." When it rained, the camp flooded, the tents leaked, and the cots, set on bare ground, frequently stood in huge pools of water. As a result, the internees' bedding, clothing, and supplies were constantly damp from the rain and daytime humidity. "The boss [camp commander] there made us, us men, really cry," recalled Kaetsu Furuya. "It was February and it was rainy—the rain would come down from the mountains and this boss would make us stand in the rain, practically naked, in our undershirt and underpants" (Okihiro, 217, 218).

One of those who stood in the rain that day was Kokubo Takara of Kaua'i. After about a month in a military prison in *Wailua* where a one-gallon can served as the men's toilet and where, because of the infestation, "we all got swollen faces from mosquito bites," Takara and 26 others were shipped to Honolulu's immigration station and from there to Sand Island. After having been forced to stand in the rain, Takara caught a cold, and was constipated for a week without any medication. "We had no medicine or means of helping him, so he died," lamented his friend, Furuya. His body was returned to Kaua'i for burial but because all of the island's Buddhist priests had been interned, there was no one to conduct the funeral service. A priest had to be released from Sand Island for that purpose, after which he returned to resume his detention (Okihiro, 218).

Women internees were kept separate from men and, unlike the men, were racially integrated. At least 18 Japanese and about 10 German and Italian women were interned on Sand Island. The camp commander's wife served as matron. Like the men internees, Japanese American women were held because they were leaders who were often connected with Shintoism or Buddhism. But there were also women like Tsuta Yamane who was interned apparently because she defended her husband as he was being arrested, and Umeno Harada, wife of Yoshio Harada who harbored a downed Japanese pilot on *Ni'ihau* after the Pearl Harbor attack and was killed along with the pilot upon their discovery. Harada was separated from her three young children, placed in solitary confinement, watched constantly by armed guards, and was handcuffed whenever she was taken her from her cell to the interrogation room. In protest, Harada refused to eat for five days. Her keepers summoned a minister to rekindle in her a desire to live. She eventually ended up on Sand Island (Okihiro, 220–21).

The FBI picked up Take Uchida and her husband, Setsuzo, in the early morning of December 8, 1941, in Idaho Falls, Idaho, because they were Japanese-language schoolteachers. "We were taken to the Seattle Immigration office immediately," she recalled. "We were not given a chance to store our belongings or furniture—just enough time to finish breakfast." From Seattle, her husband was sent to Bismarck,

North Dakota while Uchida remained in Seattle until April 1942, when she was transferred to the *Federal Women's Penitentiary* in Seagoville, Texas. There she joined other Japanese American internees, women and children, hostages from Peru, Panama, and Hawai'i. "Most of the ladies were schoolteachers and the educated wives of influential businessmen engaged in business with Japan," Uchida explained (Uchida, 31). The *Latin American Japanese* were in U.S. internment camps mainly because of pressure from the U.S. government, which intended to use them as hostages to exchange for U.S. prisoners of war in the Pacific theater (Gardiner; Higashide; Kikumura-Yano).

Wives of interned men had to cope with maintaining households on their own. In Hawai'i, when Dan Nishikawa was taken away, Grace was left with a seven-year-old son, a frozen bank account, and unemployment, having been forced to leave her job. Without an income and with a son to support, Nishikawa sold all of her furniture and appliances at greatly reduced prices for money to buy food, and she gave away their entire hothouse of nearly 500 orchid plants, some costing as much as $125 each, for $25. She eventually had to leave her home because of poverty. Her health suffered from the strain of coping. "I became very ill," she said. "I went from one doctor to another, but they say there's nothing wrong. It's just nerves. I couldn't eat . . . it lasted for how many weeks, I don't remember. Even if I didn't eat for a few days, I just didn't get hungry. It was just like morning sickness; when you look at food, you just don't feel like eating" (Hazama and Komeiji, 138).

On February 17, 1942, two days before President Roosevelt signed the Executive Order that authorized the mass removal of all Japanese Americans along the West Coast, 172 Sand Island internees were told that they would be shipped to concentration camps on the U.S. continent. Upon hearing that, Yasutaro Soga testified, most "no longer cared about their future because they were in despair," and even the strongest willed among them broke down and cried. On the early morning of February 20, military trucks escorted by jeeps with machine gun mounts sped the internees through the back gate of the immigration station, past family members who had come to catch a glimpse of their husbands, fathers, brothers, and sons. On board the *Ulysses Grant,* the hostages were hustled below deck for the one-week voyage to Angel Island in San Francisco Bay (Okihiro 224).

Throughout the spring and summer of 1942, Hawai'i's internees were scattered across the U.S. continent, and by 1946, traces of the islands' Japanese Americans could be found at Angel Island and *Tule Lake* (California), *Camp McCoy* (Wisconsin), *Camp Forrest* (Tennessee), *Camp Livingston* (Louisiana), *Camp Shelby* (Mississippi), Fort Sill (Oklahoma), Fort Missoula (Montana), *Lordsburg* and *Santa Fe* (New Mexico), *Crystal City* and *Seagoville* (Texas), *Jerome* (Arkansas), and *Topaz* (Utah). Altogether, between 1942 and 1945, 1,875 Japanese Americans from Hawai'i made the crossing to concentration camps on the continent. An additional 1,466 Japanese Americans were held in camps in the islands. Those camps included Sand Island and *Honouliuli* on the island of O'ahu, but also prisons and special camps on the islands of Kaua'i, *Maui,* and *Hawai'i.*

While the nation prepared to defend democracy against the threat of fascism abroad, its leaders authorized and conducted undemocratic actions at home in violation of constitutional guarantees and freedoms. Secretary of War *Henry L. Stimson* reportedly received from the president, on the afternoon of February 11, 1942, instructions to "go ahead and do anything you think necessary . . . if it involves citizens, we will take care of them too. He says there will probably be some repercussions, but it has got to be dictated by *military necessity,* but as he puts it, 'Be as reasonable as you can'" (Daniels, 1981, 65).

The fate of Japanese Americans on the continent was accordingly scripted by that fiction of "military necessity," and the military, in particular the army's *Western Defense Command* headquartered in San Francisco, was responsible for implementing the order of the president. Indeed, Roosevelt signed on February 19, 1942, *Executive Order 9066,* which gave to the military power to designate areas from which "any and all persons may be excluded" and to provide for such persons "transportation, food, shelter, and other accommodations as may be necessary . . . to accomplish the purpose of this order."

Five days before EO 9066, an impatient Navy secretary *Frank Knox* served eviction notices to Japanese American residents of Terminal Island in the port of Los Angeles giving them a month to vacate their homes. The islanders, mainly cannery workers and fishermen, were prime targets because adjacent to their community was the Long Beach Naval Station and the fishermen knew the coastal waters and had boats equipped with short wave radios. Many of the men had been taken away in FBI sweeps shortly after Pearl Harbor during which "the families huddled together sorrowing and weeping," as Virginia Swanson, a Baptist missionary on the island, described it (Girdner and Loftis, 112).

Suddenly and unexpectedly, contrary to that first directive, on February 25, 1942, the Navy posted new notices that ordered Japanese Americans to vacate their homes within two days. "Near-panic swept the community," wrote *Bill Hosokawa,* "particularly those where the family head was in custody. Word spread quickly and human vultures in the guise of used-furniture dealers descended on the island. They drove up and down the streets in trucks offering $5 for a nearly new washing machine, $10 for refrigerators" (Hosokawa, 310). A nisei volunteer who helped the islanders pack recalled: "The women cried awful. . . . Some of them smashed their stuff, broke it up, right before the buyers' eyes because they offered such ridiculous prices" (Girdner and Loftis, 112–13).

"The volunteers with trucks worked all night," Swanson reported. "The people had to go, ready or not. Some had to be pulled forcibly from their homes. They were afraid they were going to be handed over to a firing squad. Why should they have believed me," she asked, "telling them to get into trucks with strangers?" At the Forsyth School, one of the reception centers prepared by whites and Japanese Americans, Esther Rhoads was among the volunteers. "All afternoon trucks and Japanese kept coming," she wrote to her friend. "They were tired and dazed as a result of the sudden exodus. . . . We have old men over seventy—retired fishermen whom the FBI considered ineffective, and we have little children—one baby a year old . . . practically no men between thirty-five and sixty-five, as they all are interned. . . . Where are these people to go?" she asked poignantly. "There are many Japanese with young leaders able to face pioneer life, but those who have come to

Grandfather and grandson, Manzanar concentration camp. (National Park Service)

our hostels represent a group too old or too young to stand the rigors of beginning all over again" (Girdner and Loftis, 113). Terminal Island was just a dress rehearsal for the mass eviction and confinement program that would soon follow.

Those World War II government-sanctioned forced removals in Hawai'i and along the West Coast had precedents in U.S. history. President Andrew Jackson's particular hatred of American Indians and their expulsion from the South come to mind, when thousands of Choctaws, Creeks, Chickasaws, and Cherokees walked and died along the Trail of Tears to the Great American Desert to settle on land deemed unfit for white habitation. Other deserts and barren lands, many on or bordering Indian reservations, awaited Japanese Americans about 100 years later, and, with his experience as director of the *War Relocation Authority,* the government bureaucracy that administered the World War II concentration camps for Japanese Americans, *Dillon S. Myer* became the head of the Bureau of Indian Affairs where he launched a program of Indian removal and assimilation called "termination" (Myer; Drinnon).

Other native peoples, the Unangan or Aleuts, when Japan launched an attack on the Aleutian and Pribilof islands in the summer of 1942, "were relocated [by the U.S.] to abandoned facilities in southeastern Alaska and exposed to a bitter climate and epidemics of disease without adequate protection or medical care." There, in the words of a U.S. government commission, "they fell victim to an extraordinarily high death rate, losing many of the elders who sustained their culture." And while the U.S. government held the Aleuts in detention in southeastern Alaska, its military pillaged and ransacked their homes in the islands. Those forced removals, the commission concluded, along with the slow and inconsiderate *resettlement* thereafter, sadly followed the historical pattern of "official indifference which so many Native American groups have experienced . . ." (*Personal Justice Denied,* 318–19).

Not all of America's peoples believed or followed their leaders. The *San Francisco Chronicle,* for instance, a paper with a long history of anti-Japanese animus, editorialized two days after the Pearl Harbor disaster: "The roundup of Japanese citizens in various parts of the country . . . is not a call for volunteer spy hunters to go into action. Neither is it a reason to lift an eyebrow at a Japanese, whether American-born or not. . . . There is no excuse to wound the sensibilities of any persons in America by showing suspicion or prejudice. That, if anything, is a help to fifth column spirit. An American-born Nazi would like nothing better than to set the dogs of prejudice on a first-class American Japanese" (Grodzins, 380).

And religious groups, amidst the apprehension of Japanese American leaders, issued calls for vigilance but also charity. On December 8, 1941, the presidents of the Federal Council of the Churches of Christ in America, the Foreign Missions Conference of North America, and the Home Missions Council of North America released a joint statement: "Under the strain of the moment, Americans will be tempted to express their resentment against the action of Japan's government by recriminations against the Japanese people who are in our midst," they wrote. "Let us remember that many of these people are loyal, patriotic American citizens and that others, though Japanese subjects, have been utterly opposed to their nation's acts against our nation. It is incumbent upon us to demonstrate a discipline which, while carefully observing the precautions necessary to national safety, has no place for vindictiveness" (Matsumoto, 10).

Whites, as church members and individuals, heeded the call for distinguishing between the enemy without and the neighbor within. In Seattle, whites called on Japanese American homes to affirm their belief in the patriotism of the interned man and his family, they tracked the whereabouts of the internees to reassure their families, and they assisted issei (first-generation Japanese Americans) with frozen bank accounts and disrupted businesses. Race hatred had not trickled from the top down to all of America's people. Their faith in Japanese Americans and in the presumption of innocence unless proven guilty was vindicated by a comprehensive report by an Army Board of Inquiry into the Pearl Harbor disaster. The Board found that among Japanese Americans "no single instance of sabotage occurred . . . up to December 7," and "in no case was there any instance of misbehavior, despite a very exhaustive investigation being made constantly by the FBI, and by G-2 [army intelligence], as well as by Naval Intelligence" (Okihiro, 228).

In March 1942, Lieutenant General *John L. DeWitt,* head of the army's Western Defense Command and in charge of implementing Roosevelt's Executive Order, issued proclamations that divided up the command into a "prohibited zone," essentially the coast and a strip along the Mexican border, and a "restricted zone," a larger area contiguous to the former. Although the restrictions applied to German and Italian aliens, they fell upon "any person of Japanese Ancestry" who were advised to move "voluntarily" inland away from the prohibited zone. Perhaps as many as 9,000, Japanese Americans tried unsuccessfully to comply with the army's suggestion. "Those who attempted to cross into the interior states ran into all kinds of trouble," a government report noted. "Some were turned back by armed posses at the border of Nevada; others were clapped into jail and held overnight by panicky local peace officers; nearly all had difficulty in buying gasoline; many were greeted by 'No Japs Wanted' signs on the main streets of interior communities; and a few were threatened, or felt that they were threatened, with possibilities of mob violence." The interior states refused to become California's "dumping ground" (Daniels, 1981, 83–84).

DeWitt's first proclamations designated restricted zones, established a curfew for enemy aliens, and prohibited all Japanese Americans from leaving parts of Washington, Oregon, California, and Arizona, where most of them on the continent lived, but they did not order any removals or confinement. On March 24, 1942, the general issued a Civilian Exclusion Order that departed from his earlier proclamations and became a model for all other exclusion orders that effected the complete removal of Japanese Americans from the West Coast. The target of his experiment was the several hundred Japanese Americans who farmed on Bainbridge Island in Puget Sound, near Seattle and at the approach to Bremerton Naval Yard. Soldiers dressed in battle fatigues tacked up the notices, "Instructions to All Persons of Japanese Ancestry," on the island's utility poles, at the post office, and at the ferry landing. The Bainbridge Japanese Americans, mostly berry and truck farmers, had six days to close their farms, settle their affairs, and pack their possessions.

Bill Hosokawa described the "raw, overcast day" of March 30. "Although the Japanese had been given less than a week in which to settle their affairs and pack," he wrote, "they began to gather at the assembly point long before the designated hour, each of the fifty-four families carrying only the meager items authorized by the Army—bedding, linens, toilet articles, extra clothing, enamel plates and eating utensils. All else, the possessions collected over a lifetime, had to be stored with friends, delivered to a government warehouse, sold or abandoned. Farms developed over decades were leased or simply left to be overgrown by weeds" (Hosokawa, 308–9). Armed soldiers directed the people onto a ferryboat, from which they viewed, some for the last time, their island home. In Seattle, a train took the islanders to California. "What impressed me most was their silence," wrote Thomas R. Bodine of the Bainbridge Islanders as they boarded the train. "No one said anything. No one did anything" (Girdner and Loftis, 134). The train creaked out of the station, and headed south for *Manzanar.*

Following the Bainbridge precedent, the army and its civilian agency the *Wartime Civil Control Administration* (WCCA) swept southward, forcibly evicting all Japanese Americans living in California and parts of Washington, Oregon, and Arizona. By August 1942, the deed was done. "We were herded onto the train just like cattle and swine," recalled Misuyo Nakamura. "I do not recall much conversation between the Japanese" (Tamura, 168). "All I can remember is its being so dirty and rattly, miserable and cold," Kathleen Shimada said of the train ride to *Pinedale Assembly Center.* "Day wasn't bad, but at night we had to sleep in the chairs, just sitting with the blanket we had with us, frightened and depressed. The whole thing was just miserable. I was bitter then for being uprooted from my home and taken off. We didn't know where we were going. . . . The future is pretty bleak when you are uprooted from your home, not knowing where to go . . ." His vision blurred by tears, Shuji Kimura saw a lifetime of labor pass before his eyes. "The train began to go faster and the berry rows, the rhubarb, the lettuce fields, the pea fields began to slip past our window like a panorama," he recalled. "My throat hurt, but I couldn't take my eyes from the family fields and pastures slipping so quickly away" (Girdner and Loftis, 139–40, 142).

A few Japanese Americans refused to go quietly. In April 1942, before the eviction notices were posted, *Mary Asaba Ventura,* a nisei (second-generation Japanese American) married to a Filipino American and a Seattle resident, challenged in court the military curfew orders that infringed unreasonably, she held, upon her rights as a loyal citizen. A federal judge denied her petition, trivializing her claim as "some technical right of [a] petitioning wife to defeat the military needs in this vital area during this extraordinary time." A fellow Seattle nisei, *Gordon Hirabayashi,* deliberately refused to comply with the curfew orders to test its constitutionality and failed to report for *evacuation.* He was jailed for five months before his trial, where he was found guilty on both counts by the same judge who had heard the earlier Ventura case. Hood River, Oregon native *Minoru Yasui,* like Hirabayashi, purposefully violated the curfew order to challenge its legality, and was found guilty and sentenced to a year's imprisonment of which more than nine months were spent in solitary confinement. *Fred Korematsu* of Oakland, California, tried to evade his forced removal, and was found guilty of violating the military exclusion order. The U.S. Supreme Court eventually heard the *Hirabayashi* and *Korematsu* cases, and its judgments rendered against them formed the legal pillars that upheld the entire program of mass removal and detention (Irons).

More than a violation of civil liberties, the government's actions sought to deny Japanese Americans their dignity and essential humanity. Registered and given numbers after waiting in long lines, the nameless were herded onto trucks, buses, and trains like cattle and swine. They were dumped in makeshift "assembly centers," often county fairgrounds and horse racetracks, made wards of their government that arbitrarily stripped them of their rights and possessions, told them nothing about their destinations, and even denied them their futures. Japanese Americans knew that their victimization was by reason of their race, deemed inferior and repugnant, and self-hatred and loathing might have been nurtured by that startling recognition. One's face and culture might have required, thus, denial and erasure. That was the heart of the matter, for Japanese Americans in Hawai'i and on the U.S. continent.

"We went to the stable, *Tanforan Assembly Center,*" Osuke Takizawa recalled. "It was terrible. The government moved the horses out and put us in. The stable stunk awfully. I felt miserable, but I couldn't do anything. It was like a prison, guards on duty all the time, and there was barbed wire all around us. We really worried about our future. I just gave up." Added his wife, Sadae, "Though I was tired, I couldn't sleep because of the bad smell. . . . It was hell. Everybody felt lonely and anxious about the future. In a word, we were confused. Deep down we felt anger. It was a melancholy, complex feeling." Her husband admitted: "I was all mixed-up. We couldn't do anything about the orders from the U.S. government. I just lived from day to day without any purpose. I felt empty. . . . I frittered away every day. I don't remember anything much. . . . I just felt vacant" (Sarasohn, 183–84).

Pinedale Assembly Center near Fresno, called by the internees" hell's acre," was unbearably hot. Temperatures soared to 120 degrees in the shade. "It was a terribly hot place to live," Hatsumi Nishimoto recalled. "It was so hot that when we put our hands on the bedstead, the paint would come off! To relieve the pressure of the heat, some people soaked sheets in water and hung them overhead." Others threw water on the concrete floor and lay there as the water evaporated. Besides the heat and tight and uncomfortable sleeping quarters, Tei Endow reported that there was no privacy in the barracks that had flimsy or no walls and in the toilets that stood in a long row without partitions. And the meals, remembered Miyoshi Noyori, often consisted of strange and unappetizing foods and combinations that left one hungry after eating (Tamura, 173–76).

To regain a measure of dignity, women pinned up curtains and propped up boards for privacy in the communal toilets, and despite knowing that Tanforan was a temporary shelter, volunteers planned a pond and park. They transplanted trees and shrubs around swampy ground that became a pond, and created islands and built a bridge and designed a promenade. When the park opened on August 2, 1942, North Lake "was a great joy to the residents and presented new material for the artists," a grateful *Miné Okubo* reported. "In the morning sunlight and at sunset it added great beauty to the bleak barracks" (Okubo, 99). Still, after some time at Pinedale, nine- or ten-year-old Louie Tomita looked up and said, "'Pa, go home, go home. I like to go home.' I can't say nothing—maybe someday go home," was his father's hopeful, uncertain reply (Tamura, 176).

From assembly centers like *Puyallup* (Washington), *Portland* (Oregon), Tanforan, *Marysville, Sacramento, Stockton, Turlock, Merced, Salinas,* Pinedale, *Fresno, Tulare,* Santa Anita, and *Pomona* (California), and *Camp Myer* (Arizona), the exiles were transplanted to the 10 concentration camps run by the successor to the WCCA, the War Relocation Authority (WRA): *Tule Lake* and Manzanar (California), *Minidoka* (Idaho), *Topaz* (Utah), *Poston* and *Gila River* (Arizona), *Heart Mountain* (Wyoming), *Amache* (Granada, Colorado), and *Rohwer* and *Jerome* (Arkansas).

Located some 200 miles northeast of Los Angeles, Manzanar, or "apple orchard," was named by the 18th-century Spanish invaders to the valley. The Sierras, topped by Mt. Whitney at its highest point, dominated the visual and emotional landscape. One always felt the mountains' presence. In the clear, desert sky, spread out over 560 acres row upon row of flimsy tar paper barracks, spare and drab, extended in straight lines that converged where the earth met the sky. "When we got to Manzanar," recalled Yuri Tateishi, "it was getting dark and we were given numbers first. We went to the mess hall, and I remember the first meal we were given in those tin plates and tin cups. It was canned wieners and canned spinach. It was all the food we had, and then after finishing that we were taken to our barracks. It was dark and trenches were here and there. You'd fall in and get up and finally got to the barracks. The floors were boarded, but they were about a quarter to a half inch apart, and the next morning you could see the ground below." Haruko Niwa remembered: "The next morning, the first morning in Manzanar, when I woke up and saw what Manzanar looked like, I just cried. And then I saw the mountain, the high Sierra Mountain, just like my native country's mountain, and I just cried, that's all. I couldn't think about anything" (Tateishi, 24–25, 29).

The government rubbed salt in the open wound of racism by requiring Japanese Americans to prove their merit and worth by serving in the U.S. armed forces. "The Army recruiting team came into Manzanar around the early part of 1943," Frank Chuman recalled. "We had a big meeting in this mess hall of all persons eligible for military duty with two white soldiers and a person of Japanese ancestry, and this guy was trying to persuade us all to volunteer for the Army, and I'm not too sure whether I got up and spoke back to him or whether I said it in my own mind, but I said, 'Why should we fight for the United States Government as soldiers, when the United States Government distrusts us? Why do they now want us to serve when they consider us to be disloyal? Why do they want us to serve when they have taken us out of our homes and schools and businesses? It doesn't make sense, and so far as I'm concerned I'm not going to do anything . . . until the United States Government does something to remedy this unjust situation'" (Tateishi, 230–31).

The *Fair Play Committee* at Heart Mountain concentration camp, begun by Hawaii-born *Kiyoshi Okamoto* to protest against injustices, attracted large and eager audiences after Secretary of War *Henry L. Stimson* announced on January 20, 1944, that the nisei, formerly classed as "aliens not acceptable to the armed forces," would be subject to the draft. In a bulletin to the camp community, the committee declared: "We . . . are not afraid to go to war—we are not afraid to risk our lives for our country. We would gladly sacrifice our lives to protect and uphold the principles and ideals of our country as set forth in the Constitution and the Bill of Rights, for on its inviolability depends the freedom, liberty, justice, and protection of all people including Japanese-Americans and all other minority groups." Instead of those protections, the committee noted, "without any hearings, without due process of law . . . without any charges filed against us, without any evidence of wrongdoing on our part, one hundred and ten thousand innocent people were kicked out of their homes, literally uprooted from where they have lived for the greater part of their lives, and herded like dangerous criminals into concentration camps with barb wire fencing and military police guarding it" (Emi, 43–44).

To make an example, the government charged 63 of them and seven members of the Fair Play Committee's executive council with draft evasion and conspiracy to violate the law. The trial judge, Blake Kennedy, addressed the defendants as "you Jap boys," and after finding the 63 guilty and sentencing them to three years' imprisonment, the judge assailed the men's loyalty: "If they are truly loyal American citizens," he wrote, "they should . . . embrace the opportunity to discharge the duties of citizens by offering themselves in the cause of our National defense." As for the seven leaders, Kennedy found them all guilty and sentenced them to four years in *Leavenworth Federal Penitentiary*. After the war, an appeals court overturned those convictions, and on Christmas Eve, 1947, President Harry Truman granted a presidential pardon to all draft resisters, including the nisei (Muller).

Meanwhile, just as principled, patriotic, and heroic were nisei who volunteered and later were drafted to fight against fascism but also for their futures and those of their families. After Pearl Harbor, Hawai'i's military governor dismissed the 137 Japanese Americans who served in the Territorial Guard, and nisei soldiers in the National Guard were disarmed. Despite that obvious distrust, those disallowed from the Territorial Guard formed themselves into a volunteer labor battalion called the *Varsity Victory Volunteers* to "set out to fight a twofold fight for tolerance and justice," in the words of a prominent member. In May 1942, the military governor endorsed the formation of a segregated unit of mainly Japanese Americans, and in June, 1,432 men of the newly created Provisional Battalion set sail for the U.S. continent. In Oakland, they were hustled onto trains that took them into the interior, and at its destination, *Camp McCoy,* Wisconsin, where the men trained to die for democracy in the shadow of an internment camp that held some of the leaders of their community (Okihiro, 255).

The men of the renamed *100th Infantry Battalion* confronted other indignities before facing their country's enemies. They marched and trained with wooden guns until their commanders could trust them with firearms, white soldiers taunted them by calling them "Japs," and some of them were chosen to play the enemy on Cat Island, Mississippi. Because of the belief that "Japs" emitted a peculiar body odor that trained dogs could sniff, nisei soldiers were ordered to hide in the island's cover and wait for the dogs to find them. "Most of us were transferred to Cat Island to pollute the island where the dogs were with the smell of 'Jap' blood," Yasuo Takata recalled. "Later results showed that this did not make any difference. . . . Each dog trainer sent his dog out to find us. When the dog spotted us, the trainer would fire a shot and we would drop dead with a piece of meat . . . in front of our necks. The dog would eat the meat and lick our face. We didn't smell Japanese. We were Americans. Even a dog knew that!" (Okihiro, 255–56).

In the end, about 26,000 Japanese American men and women served in the U.S. armed forces during World War II: in the 100th, composed mainly of men from Hawai'i; the *442nd Regimental Combat Team* composed of nisei from the concentration camps; those in the *Military Intelligence Service* and Office of Strategic Services, who fought in the Pacific war; and women who served in the *Women's Army Corps*. The 100th and 442nd were among the most decorated and most decimated units of the war, garnering 18,143 individual citations, and suffering casualty rates of 680 deaths, 67 missing, and 9,486 receiving Purple Hearts (Tanaka, 112, 143, 146). "If you look at the 442nd boys," said Shig Doi, a veteran, "don't look at their faces, look at their bodies. Then you'll find out how much they've suffered" (Tateishi, 161).

Of their sacrifice, President Harry Truman told the thinned ranks of soldiers of the 100th and 442nd assembled on the White House lawn in 1946: "You fought for the free nations of the world . . . you fought not only the enemy, you fought prejudice—and you won. Keep up that fight . . . continue to win—make this great Republic stand for what the Constitution says it stands for: 'the welfare of all the people, all the time.'" Spark Matsunaga, veteran of the 100th and later U.S. senator from Hawai'i, elaborated upon that continuing struggle and its responsibilities: "If we the living, the beneficiaries of their sacrifice are truly intent upon showing our gratitude, we must do more than gather together for speechmaking and perfunctory ceremonies. We must undertake to carry on the unfinished work which they so nobly advanced. The fight against prejudice is not confined to the battlefield, alone. It is still here and with us now." And, he concluded, "So long as a single member of our citizenry is denied the use of public facilities and denied the right to earn a decent living because, and solely because of the color of his skin, we who 'fought against prejudice and won' ought not to sit idly by and tolerate the perpetuation of injustices" (Tanaka, 167, 170–71).

Nonetheless, even the gallantry of the nisei soldier could not fully restore the losses sustained by a people judged guilty by reason of race. For how did the deaths of Ichiro Shimoda and James Wakasa, both shot and killed by guards at the fence, make the United States safe for democracy? Wakasa was a 63-year-old issei bachelor who was shot by a sentry with a single bullet to the heart as he took his evening stroll at Topaz concentration camp (Taylor, 136–46). Or how was justice served by the unnecessary death of a mother who, after giving birth, fell into a coma? Because of the poorly equipped camp hospital, she suffered for about 10 days before her husband asked to put out of her misery. "The doctor said we had nothing here to offer her," an attending nurse testified, "and if that's the wishes of the family, then he'll go along with it." And so the next day, the husband and four young children stood by their mother's bedside. "There was a teaspoon there with some water in it, and the father told each child to give the mother a sip of water, and after the last child gave the sip of water, the father did the same thing. . . . That was it. That was it. Right away the oxygen tent was removed and she just went to sleep." Haunted by that death, the nurse reflected years later, "But I still feel that if we were not in camp, that there might have been some other treatment" (Tateishi, 149–50).

And what about the psychological impacts of the concentration camps on those interned and also on their children? (Nagata; Fugita and Fernandez). What were some of those costs? Powerlessness, inferiority, and self-hatred were some of the lessons taught by the experience, along with an imposed silence because of the fear that it could happen again. Ben Takeshita recalled his feelings upon first learning about his older brother's ordeal at the Tule Lake camp, a long closeted family secret. Targeted as a troublemaker, he was held and questioned for three days, and "they got to a point where they said, 'Okay, we're going to take you out.' And it was obvious that he was going before a firing squad with MPs ready with rifles. He was asked if he wanted a cigarette; he said no. . . . You want a blindfold? . . . No. They said, 'Stand up here,' and they went as far as saying, 'Ready, aim, fire,' and pulling the trigger, but the rifles had no bullets. They just went click." "I really got mad listening to it," exclaimed Takeshita, "because the torture that he must have gone through . . . . I mean it's like the German camps. Torturing people for the sake of trying to get them to break down or something" (Tateishi, 247).

Despite President Truman's acknowledgement that racism was undemocratic, an unrepentant government pursued the "repatriation" of Japanese Americans to a defeated and occupied Japan long after the war's end. San Francisco attorney *Wayne M. Collins* argued from 1945 to 1968 that the 5,766 Japanese Americans who renounced their U.S. citizenship during the war did so under duress and thus their action had no legal validity. "You can no more resign citizenship in time of war than you can resign from the human race," declared an indignant Collins about Public Law 405, an extraordinary measure passed by Congress in July 1944 to allow citizenship renunciation and supported by some who saw it as a way to rid the United States permanently of its "Japanese problem." Collins, almost single-handedly, managed to restore the U.S. citizenship of all but a few hundred (Girdner and Loftis, 441–49). Still, the fact that the U.S. House of Representatives passed as late as May 7, 1945, HR 384, authorizing the "repatriation" of native-born women who had lost their U.S. citizenship by marrying "aliens ineligible to citizenship" (issei), and that the government sought repatriation over two decades after the war's end reveals a government determined to follow the same path of racism that justified the original violation of civil liberties.

And Japanese Americans remained in the concentration and internment camps long after "military necessity" seemed credible and even after the war ended on September 2, 1945, when over 44,000 were still in those camps. Although groups of Japanese Americans were gradually released to work in vital industries, to serve in the military, and to attend colleges and universities, the last camp closed on March 1946 when Tule Lake expelled its last Japanese American.

Miné Okubo remembered her departure from Topaz as "plowing through the red tape, through the madness of packing again," and attending seminars on how to make friends and how to behave in the outside world. On the day of her release, she received a train ticket and $25 plus $3 a day for meals while traveling, and a booklet, *When You Leave the Relocation Center,* courtesy of the WRA. For too many, the losses of a lifetime were reduced to a train ticket, an allowance, and instructions on how to act in a democracy; for all, the journey was a new beginning. "I looked at the crowd at the gate," continued Okubo. "Only the very old or very young were left. . . . I swallowed a lump in my throat as I waved good-by to them. . . . I relived momentarily the sorrows and the joys of my whole evacuation experience, until the barracks faded away into the distance. My thoughts shifted from the past to the future" (Okubo, 207–9).

The U.S. government passed in 1950, over President Truman's veto, the *Internal Security Act,* Title II of which enabled the attorney general to apprehend and place in detention camps, without the rights of due process or trial by jury, any person suspected of "probably" engaging in espionage or sabotage. The act, passed during the Cold War, was intended to contain the menace of communism. One of its sponsors but a critic of Title II called it a program for "establishing concentration camps into which people might be put without benefit of trial, but merely by executive fiat . . . simply by an assumption, mind you, that an individual might be thinking about engaging in espionage or sabotage." Accordingly, from 1952 to 1957 when funding ended, the justice department maintained six concentration camps, including Tule Lake, which held Japanese Americans just six years earlier. Some 10 years after funds ran out but with Title II still the law of the land, the chairman of the *House Un-American Activities Committee* resurrected the provision because, he said, "black militants have essentially declared war on the United States, and therefore they lose all constitutional rights and should be imprisoned in detention camps" (Chuman, 327–29). Alert to the injustice and danger of Title II, Japanese Americans, as the past victims of American concentration camps, led a repeal effort, joined by African Americans and civil libertarians, which succeeded on September 1971 (Okamura, Takasugi, Kanno, Uno, 71–111).

The Title II repeal effort was a part of the unfinished business of the World War II concentration camps, along with the *redress and reparations* campaign that followed (*Personal Justice Denied;* Hohri; Takezawa; Maki, Kitano, Berthold; Shimabukuru). As noted astutely by *Edison Uno,* the Title II repeal campaign was an effort by the Japanese American community to come to terms with a shameful past by acting as Americans with the full rights of citizenship. Japanese Americans, he declared, were held in physical and psychological concentration camps for too long. Further, he added, that acting out enabled a clearer sense of that group's place in the United States and a realization of its common ground with other oppressed minorities, including Native Americans who "for generations have been victims of the original American concentration camps which exist to this very day." And the social ills of poverty, hunger, disease, unemployment, mid-education, and racism "contribute towards the psychological concentration camps which continue to repress human beings as man practices his inhumanity to man. It is wrong to say 'it can't happen again,'" he predicted (Uno, 111).

Sadly, Edison Uno's warning has fallen upon deaf ears, and the past haunts the nation still. Prodded mainly by Japanese Americans, Congress passed the *Civil Liberties Act* of 1988, which issued a formal apology, presidential pardons for those who resisted the eviction and detention orders, recommendations that government agencies restore to Japanese American employees lost status or entitlements because of the wartime actions, and financial redress to Japanese American individuals and communities, $20,000 to each survivor and the creation of a community fund to educate the American public about the experience. Never again, the act's sponsors intended through redress and education, will racism justify government infringements of civil liberties. However, just 13 years later, Congress passed the U.S.A. Patriot Act of 2001 under which racial and religious profiling enables a secret and arbitrary government-sponsored program of registration, expulsion, and indefinite detention.

"I am the wife of Albert Kurihara who cannot be here today due to a stroke he suffered last week," Mary Kurihara explained to the presidential commission that resulted in the Civil Liberties Act of 1988. "My husband is now in the hospital, but he still really wanted to testify. Albert has asked me to deliver his testimony." Kurihara was born in Hawai'i, and was sent to Santa Anita and Poston during the war. "I remember having to stay at the dirty horse stables at Santa Anita," he noted. "I remember thinking, 'Am I a human being? Why are we being treated like this?' Santa Anita stunk like hell." From Poston, he was "released" to do hard labor, "work which no one else wanted to do," and even after the war, "I was treated like an enemy by other Americans. They were hostile, and I had a very hard time finding any job. . . . This was the treatment they gave to an American citizen!" he exclaimed. "I think back about my younger brother, Dan, who was in the 442nd Regiment. In combat to defend his American native land, Dan suffered a bullet wound that damaged one-fourth of his head and caused him to lose an eye. I think back about what happened to my cousin, Joe. He was a World War I veteran and very proud to be an American. . . . Joe was never the same after camp. Once a very happy person, Joe became very bitter and very unhappy. . . . Every time I think about Dan or Joe, it makes me so angry. Sometimes I want to tell this government to go to hell. This government can never repay all the people who suffered. But, this should not be an excuse for token apologies. I hope this country will never forget what happened," Kurihara concluded, "and do what it can to make sure that future generations will never forget" (Kurihara, 63–64).

References

Armor, John and Peter Wright. *Manzanar.* New York: Times Books, 1988.

Christgau, John. *"Enemies": World War II Alien Internment.* Ames: Iowa State University Press, 1985.

Chuman, Frank F. *The Bamboo People: The Law and Japanese-Americans.* Del Mar, CA: Publishers, Inc., 1976.

Daniels, Roger. *Concentration Camps: North America, Japanese in the United States and Canada during World War II.* Malabar, FL: Robert E. Krieger, 1981.

Daniels, Roger. *The Politics of Prejudice.* New York: Atheneum, 1970.

DiStasi, Lawrence (Ed.). *Una Storia Segreta: The Secret History of Italian American Evacuation and Internment during World War II.* Berkeley: Heyday Books, 2001.

Drinnon, Richard. *Keeper of Concentration Camps: Dillon S. Myer and American Racism.* Berkeley: University of California Press, 1987.

Emi, Frank Seishi. "Draft Resistance at the Heart Mountain Concentration Camp and the Fair Play Committee," in *Frontiers of Asian American Studies: Writing, Research, and Commentary,* edited by Gail M. Nomura et al. Pullman: Washington State University Press, 1989.

Fox, Stephen. *The Unknown Internment: An Oral History of the Relocation of Italian Americans during World War II.* Boston: Twayne, 1990.

Fugita, Stephen S. and Marilyn Fernandez. *Altered Lives, Enduring Community: Japanese Americans Remember Their World War II Incarceration.* Seattle: University of Washington Press, 2004.

Fukuda, Yoshiaki. *My Six Years of Internment: An Issei's Struggle for Justice.* San Francisco: Konko Church of San Francisco, 1990.

Gardiner, C. Harvey. *Pawns in a Triangle of Hate: The Peruvian Japanese and the United States.* Seattle: University of Washington Press, 1981.

Girdner, Audrie and Anne Loftis. *The Great Betrayal: The Evacuation of the Japanese-Americans during World War II.* London: Macmillan, 1969.

Grodzins, Morton. *Americans Betrayed: Politics and the Japanese Evacuation.* Chicago: University of Chicago Press, 1949.

Hazama, Dorothy Ochiai and Jane Okamoto Komeiji. *Okage Sama De: The Japanese of Hawai'i*. Honolulu: Bess Press, 1986.

Heine, William. *With Perry to Japan: A Memoir,* translated by Frederic Trautmann. Honolulu: University of Hawaii Press, 1990.

Higashide, Seiichi. *Adios to Tears: The Memoirs of a Japanese-Peruvian Internee in U.S. Concentration Camps.* Honolulu: E&E Kudo, 1993.

Hohri, William Minoru. *Repairing America: An Account of the Movement for Japanese-American Redress.* Pullman: Washington State University Press, 1984.

Hosokawa, Bill. *Nisei: The Quiet Americans.* New York: William Morrow, 1969.

Irons, Peter. *Justice at War: The Story of the Japanese American Internment.* New York: Oxford University Press, 1983.

Kashima, Tetsuden. "American Mistreatment of Internees during World War II: Enemy Alien Japanese," in *Japanese Americans: From Relocation to Redress,* rev. ed., edited by Roger Daniels, Sandra C. Taylor, and Harry H. L. Kitano. Seattle: University of Washington Press, 1991.

Kikumura-Yano, Akemi (Ed.). *Encyclopedia of Japanese Descendants in the Americas: An Illustrated History of the Nikkei.* Walnut Creek, CA: AltaMira Press, 2002.

Kitagawa, Daisuke. *Issei and Nisei: The Internment Years.* New York: Seabury Press, 1967.

Kurihara, Albert. "The Commission on Wartime Relocation and Internment of Civilians: Selected Testimonies from the Los Angeles and San Francisco Hearings," *Amerasia Journal* 8:2 (1981).

Maki, Mitchell T., Harry H. L. Kitano, and S. Megan Berthold. *Achieving the Impossible Dream: How Japanese Americans Obtained Redress.* Urbana: University of Illinois Press, 1999.

Marchetti, Gina. *Romance and the "Yellow Peril": Race, Sex, and Discursive Strategies in Hollywood Fiction.* Berkeley: University of California Press, 1993.

Matsumoto, Toru. *Beyond Prejudice: A Story of the Church and Japanese Americans.* New York: Friendship Press, 1946.

Muller, Eric L. *Free to Die for Their Country: The Story of the Japanese American Draft Resisters in World War II.* Chicago: University of Chicago Press, 2001.

Myer, Dillon S. *Uprooted Americans: The Japanese Americans and the War Relocation Authority during World War II.* Tucson: University of Arizona Press, 1971.

Nagata, Donna K. *Legacy of Injustice: Exploring the Cross-Generational Impact of the Japanese American Internment.* New York: Plenum Press, 1993.

Okamura, Raymond, Robert Takasugi, Hiroshi Kanno, and Edison Uno. "Campaign to Repeal the Emergency Detention Act," *Amerasia Journal* 2:2 (Fall) (1974): 71–111.

Okihiro, Gary Y. *Cane Fires: The Anti-Japanese Movement in Hawaii, 1865–1945.* Philadelphia: Temple University Press, 1991.

Okubo, Miné. *Citizen 13660.* New York: Columbia University Press, 1946.

Personal Justice Denied. Report of the Commission on Wartime Relocation and Internment of Civilians. Washington, D.C.: Government Printing Office, 1982.

Sarasohn, Eileen Sunada. *The Issei: Portrait of a Pioneer: An Oral History.* Palo Alto, CA: Pacific Books, 1983.

Shimabukuro, Robert Sadamu. *Born in Seattle: The Campaign for Japanese American Redress.* Seattle: University of Washington Press, 2001.

Takezawa, Yasuko I. *Breaking the Silence: Redress and Japanese American Ethnicity.* Ithaca, NY: Cornell University Press, 1995.

Tamura, Linda. *The Hood River Issei: An Oral History of Japanese Settlers in Oregon's Hood River Valley.* Urbana: University of Illinois Press, 1993.

Tanaka, Chester. *Go for Broke: A Pictorial History of the Japanese American 100th Infantry Battalion and the 442nd Regimental Combat Team.* Richmond, CA: Go for Broke, Inc., 1982.

Tateishi, John. *And Justice for All: An Oral History of the Japanese American Detention Camps.* New York: Random House, 1984.

Taylor, Sandra C. *Jewel of the Desert: Japanese American Internment at Topaz.* Berkeley: University of California Press, 1993.

Uchida, Take. "An Issei Internee's Experiences," in *Japanese Americans: From Relocation to Redress,* rev. ed., edited by Roger Daniels, Sandra C. Taylor, and Harry H. L. Kitano. Seattle: University of Washington Press, 1991.

Uno, Edison. "Therapeutic and Educational Benefits (a Commentary)," *Amerasia Journal* 2:2 (Fall) (1974): 109–11.

Chronology

[N.B. This chronology includes Japanese Americans, Asian Americans, and other peoples of color to show the connections and commonalities among Asian Americans and other peoples of color in U.S. history.]

1607	Jamestown
1658	Asian slaves taken to Africa's Cape of Good Hope
1760s	Filipino Manilamen establish communities near New Orleans
1773	Boston Tea Party
1776	American Declaration of Independence
1778	British Captain James Cook places Hawai'i on European maps
1783	Treaty of Paris; Great Britain recognizes American independence
1784	*Empress of China* leaves New York harbor for China
1787	U.S. Constitution adopted
1789	George Washington becomes president; Bill of Rights adopted by Congress
1790	Nationality Act limits naturalization to "free white persons"
1790s	Asian Indians settle on the East Coast
1794	first Chinese arrive in Hawai'i
1795	Kamehameha I conquers all of Hawai'i except Kau'ai
1802	Tze-Chun Wong, a Chinese, begins producing sugar in Hawai'i
1809	Hawaiians Opukahaia and Hopu arrive in New England via an American ship; Opukahaia enrolls at Yale
1810	Kau'ai comes under Kamehameha's kingdom uniting all the islands
1819	Kamehameha dies; Ka'ahumanu, one of Kamehameha's wives and the kingdom's kuhina nui (executive officer), breaks and ends the kapu (taboo) system
1820	New England missionaries arrive in Hawai'i
1820s	Chinese settle in New York City and on the East Coast

1835	American William Hooper establishes Koloa sugar plantation on Kau'ai
1838	South Asian indentures arrive in British Guiana
1839	Opium War begins
1840	Hawaiian constitution establishes a constitutional monarchy and institutes property rights
1842	Treaty of Nanking ends Opium War
1844	U.S. and China sign first treaty
1845	Hawaiians petition Kamehameha III against foreign political and economic dominance
1847	Chinese students, including Yung Wing, arrive in the United States
1848	gold discovered in California prompting Gold Rush;
	Treaty of Guadalupe Hidalgo;
	Great Mahele in Hawai'i privatizes land and disburses it; aliens allowed to lease property
1850	California imposes Foreign Miners' Tax;
	Hawai'i passes Masters and Servants Act; Royal Hawaiian Agricultural Society established to recruit plantation workers; aliens allowed to purchase property
1852	Chinese contract laborers arrive in Hawai'i
1853	U.S. Commodore Matthew C. Perry "opens" Japan to the West
1854	*People v. Hall* by California's supreme court rules that Chinese cannot testify for or against whites in court;
	United States and Japan sign the Treaty of Kanagawa formalizing relations
1857	San Francisco opens a segregated school for Chinese children;
	Dred Scott v. Sanford, U.S. Supreme Court rules that slaves are property
1858	California passes a law barring entry to Chinese and "Mongolians"
1861	Civil War begins
1865	Central Pacific Railroad recruits Chinese workers for the transcontinental railroad;
	Hawaiian Board of Immigration sends a labor agent to recruit Chinese laborers for the kingdom's sugar plantations;
	Civil War ends;
	Thirteenth Amendment abolishing slavery ratified
1866	Japanese students, sent by their government, study at Rutgers University

1867	2,000 Chinese Central Pacific Railroad workers strike for a week;
	Congress passes a plan of Reconstruction for the South;
	Chinese, some from Cuba, work the sugar fields of Louisiana to supplement African American labor
1868	U.S. and China sign Burlingame-Seward Treaty recognizing the right of free migration to citizens of both countries;
	149 Japanese, the *gannenmono,* recruited for Hawai'i's plantations;
	Fourteenth Amendment ratified, conferring citizenship on the basis of birth and equal protection
1869	completion of the transcontinental railroad;
	Japanese establish the Wakamatsu Tea and Silk Colony in California
1870	California passes a law against the importation of Chinese, Japanese, and "Mongolian" women for prostitution;
	Chinese railroad workers in Texas sue company for failure to pay wages;
	Chinese brought from California to North Adams, Massachusetts to break a strike of white shoe workers;
	Fifteenth Amendment ratified, guaranteeing the rights of citizens to vote regardless of race, color, or previous condition of servitude;
	Congress extends naturalization to Africans
1871	Los Angeles riot against Chinese leaving 21 dead
1872	Chinese allowed to testify in California's courts for or against Whites
1875	Page Law bars entry to Chinese, Japanese, and "Mongolian" prostitutes, felons, and contract laborers
1876	Reciprocity Treaty signed by the United States and Hawaiian kingdom providing for duty-free sugar imports from the islands;
	Korea and Japan sign the Treaty of Kanghwa opening Korea to trade
1877	Reconstruction ends
1878	*In re Ah Yup,* a California circuit court rules that the Chinese are ineligible for naturalized citizenship;
	United States gains treaty rights for a base at Pago Pago, Samoa
1879	California adopts its second constitution that discriminates against Chinese in employment and housing, later declared unconstitutional by a U.S. circuit court

1880	United States and China sign treaty allowing the United States to limit but not prohibit Chinese immigration;
	California passes Section 69 of its Civil Code that prohibits marriage between whites and "Mongolians, Negroes, mulattoes and persons of mixed blood";
	anti-Chinese riot in Denver destroys homes and businesses
1882	Chinese Exclusion Act prohibits Chinese laborers entry for 10 years;
	United States and Korea sign first treaty allowing for Korean immigration
1883	Yu Kil-jun, a member of a Korean diplomatic mission to the United States, remains in America to study in Massachusetts
1884	Joseph and Mary Tape sue the San Francisco school board over segregated schools;
	Korean political refugees, including Suh Jae-p'il (Philip Jaisohn), arrive in the United States after the reform movement's failure in Korea
1885	Rock Springs, Wyoming anti-Chinese riot leaves 28 dead;
	Japanese government-sponsored contract workers arrive in Hawai'i
1886	*Yick Wo v. Hopkins,* U.S. Supreme Court rules that laws with unequal impacts on different groups is discriminatory;
	Chinese expulsions from Tacoma, Seattle, Alaska and other places in the West;
	Hawai'i ends Chinese immigration
1887	Chinese gold miners attacked by whites in Hell's Canyon on the Idaho-Oregon border leaving 31 dead;
	United States and Hawai'i renew the Reciprocity Treaty and the kingdom cedes the use of Pearl Harbor to the U.S. Navy;
	Hawaiian constitution forced on Kalakaua curtails power of monarchy
1888	Scott Act renders 20,000 Chinese reentry certificates null and void
1890	United States ends Hawai'i's favored status in sugar trade
1892	Geary Act renews the 1882 Chinese Exclusion Act for another ten years and requires all Chinese to register
1893	San Francisco school board orders then rescinds order to Japanese children to attend the segregated Chinese school;
	American-led coup topples the Hawaiian kingdom and deposes the queen, Lili'uokalani; its leaders declare a provisional government and seek U.S. annexation
1894	Republic of Hawai'i declared;

	In re Saito, Japanese declared ineligible for naturalized citizenship by a U.S. circuit court in Massachusetts
1895	Hawaiian Sugar Planters' Association (HSPA) formed;
	Native Sons of the Golden State (later the Chinese American Citizens Alliance), a civil rights organization, founded in San Francisco
1896	*Plessy v. Ferguson,* the U.S. Supreme Court establishes the "separate but equal" doctrine and thereby upholds segregation
1898	*Wong Kim Ark v. U.S.,* the U.S. Supreme Court rules that Chinese cannot be stripped of their citizenship;
	United States annexes Hawai'i, the Philippines, and Guam;
	Korean merchants arrive in Honolulu
1899	United States declares an "open door" policy toward China;
	American-Filipino war begins;
	United States establishes a protectorate over American Samoa
1900	Organic Act makes all U.S. laws applicable to Hawai'i, ending contract labor and prompting a series of strikes by Japanese plantation workers;
	health officials burn Honolulu's Chinatown and quarantine about 7,000 Chinese, Japanese, and Hawaiians to camps for several months;
	bubonic plague scare in San Francisco leads to Chinatown quarantine and the mass inoculation of the city's Chinese and Japanese;
	Japanese Association of American founded in San Francisco as a civil rights organization
1901	five Korean laborers arrive in Hawai'i;
	United States appoints a civilian government in the Philippines
1902	Chinese labor exclusion renewed for another 10 years;
	HSPA sends recruiter to Korea, who sends groups of workers to Hawai'i;
	New People's Association formed to unify Korean Americans for Korea's independence;
	American-Filipino war declared at an end, resulting in 4,300 American and over 50,000 Filipino deaths
1903	1,500 Japanese and Mexican sugar beet workers strike in Oxnard, California, and form the Japanese Mexican Labor Association;
	102 Korean migrants arrive in Hawai'i;
	Friendship Association founded in San Francisco for the promotion of mutual aid among Korean Americans

	(in 1905, changed its name to the Mutual Cooperation Federation);
	Filipino students, the *pensionados,* arrive in the United States
1904	Chinese labor exclusion made indefinite;
	Punjabi Sikhs arrive in British Columbia;
	250 Korean workers hired on Waialua sugar plantation on the island of O'ahu to break a strike of Japanese laborers
1905	Chinese Americans support boycott of U.S. goods in China;
	San Francisco school board resolves to segregate Japanese children;
	Korean emigration ends;
	Korean Episcopal and Methodist churches in Honolulu dedicated;
	Asiatic Exclusion League formed in San Francisco;
	California amends Section 60 of its Civil Code to forbid marriage between whites and "Mongolians"
1906	anti-Asian riot in Vancouver;
	San Francisco earthquake and fire destroys U.S. immigration records;
	San Francisco school board orders the segregation of Japanese children;
	Korean government and businesses send money to Koreans in San Francisco who suffered losses from the earthquake and fire;
	Presbyterian mission and later church established in Los Angeles for Korean Americans;
	15 Filipino workers, recruited by the HSPA, arrive in Hawai'i
1907	President Theodore Roosevelt issues an executive order prohibiting Japanese remigration to the United States from Hawai'i, Mexico, and Canada;
	San Francisco school board rescinds its segregation of Japanese children;
	San Francisco riot against Japanese;
	United States and Japan sign Gentlemen's Agreement whereby Japan agrees to restrict labor migration to the United States;
	Filipino laborers, 188 men, 20 women, and 2 children, arrive in Hawai'i;
	Asian Indians expelled from Bellingham, Washington
1908	Canada restricts Asian Indian immigration by requiring continuous passage from nation of birth to Canada;

Asian Indians expelled from Live Oak, California;

an American employee of Japan's foreign office is shot and killed by a Korean American in San Francisco;

Korean Women's Association established in San Francisco

1909   7,000 Japanese sugar plantation workers on O'ahu strike for four months;

Korean National Association formed from a merger of the Mutual Cooperation Federation and the United Federation

1910   California restricts Asian Indian immigration by administrative procedures;

Japanese picture brides arrive;

Korean picture brides arrive;

Japan formally annexes Korea

1911   Pablo Manlapit forms the Filipino Higher Wages Association in Hawai'i

1912   Sikhs in California establish the Khalsa Diwan

1913   California passes the Alien Land Law prohibiting "aliens ineligible to citizenship" from buying land or leasing it for more than three years;

Sikhs in Washington and Oregon establish the Hindustani Association, and Asian Indians in California found the revolutionary Ghadar Party;

Korean farm workers are expelled from Hemet, California;

Korean Women's Association organized in Honolulu

1914   *Komagata Maru,* a ship chartered by Gurdit Singh to test Canada's restrictive immigration law, denied landing in Vancouver;

Korean National Association sends money to Koreans suffering from famine in China

1915   Chinese American Citizens Alliance founded from the Native Sons of the Golden State

1917   Arizona passes an alien land law;

Immigration Act passed by the U.S. Congress declares a "barred zone" from whence no immigrants can come; the Act adds West, South, and Southeast Asians to the list of excluded Asians

1918   Asians who served in the U.S. military during World War I allowed the right of naturalization

1919   Japanese in Hawai'i form the Federation of Japanese Labor;

Women's Friendship Association formed by Korean women in Los Angeles to promote friendship among Korean Americans, to boycott Japanese goods, and to send funds to the Korean independence movement;

	Korean Women's Patriotic League founded in California to unite all Korean women's organizations in North America
1920	8,300 Japanese and Filipino sugar plantation workers on O'ahu strike for six months;
	Hawaiian Rehabilitation Act creates the Hawaiian Homes Commission;
	California amends its 1913 Alien Land Law to restrict rents;
	Nineteenth Amendment ratified, guaranteeing the right to vote regardless of sex
1921	Japanese farm workers expelled from Turlock, California;
	Washington and Louisiana pass alien land laws;
	Japan halts passports to picture brides
1922	*Takao Ozawa v. U.S.,* the U.S. Supreme Court affirms that Japanese are ineligible for naturalization;
	New Mexico passes an alien land law;
	Cable Act by the U.S. Congress takes away U.S. citizenship from women who marry "aliens ineligible to citizenship"
1923	*U.S. v. Bhagat Singh Thind,* the U.S. Supreme Court rules that Asian Indians are ineligible for naturalization;
	Idaho, Montana, and Oregon pass alien land laws;
	American Loyalty League of Fresno, California founded (later became the Japanese American Citizens League);
	California denies Japanese sharecropping rights;
	Terrace v. Thompson, the U.S. Supreme Court upholds alien land laws
1924	Immigration Act by the U.S. Congress excludes virtually all Asians;
	about 9,000 Filipino sugar plantation workers strike in Hawai'i over an 11-month period
1925	Filipino Federation of America formed;
	In re. Toyota, the U.S. Supreme Court rules Filipinos, except those who served in the U.S. military for three years, are ineligible for citizenship; Kansas passes an alien land law;
	Korean Americans send money to Korea for flood and famine relief
1927	*Gong Lum v. Rice,* the U.S. Supreme Court upholds racial segregation in schools and reaffirms the "separate but equal" doctrine;
	U.S. Supreme Court rules that government control of Japanese language schools in Hawai'i is unconstitutional on a challenge filed by the schools

1928	Filipino farm workers expelled from Dryden and warned to leave town at Wenatchee, Washington
1929	Japanese American Citizens League formed;
	stock market crash and the onset of the Great Depression
1930	anti-Filipino riot in Watsonville, California; a Filipino rooming house in California's Imperial Valley and the office of the Filipino Federation of America in Stockton are bombed
1931	U.S. Congress amends the Cable Act to allow naturalization to women who were citizens by birth;
	Japan invades Manchuria
1932	Congress passes the Hawes-Cutting Act that named Filipinos as aliens ineligible to citizenship and established an immigration quota of 100 Filipinos each year
1933	Filipino field workers in Salinas, California, refuse to work in protest against growers who failed to deliver on their promised wages; Filipino Labor Union organizes;
	California's Court of Appeals rules in favor of Salvador Roldan's petition to marry a white woman because Filipinos are Malays and not Mongolians prompting the state legislature to amend its anti-miscegenation law to include Malays;
	Mexican berry pickers strike against Japanese growers in El Monte, California;
	Chinese Hand Laundry Alliance formed in New York City
1934	Tydings-McDuffie Act by the U.S. Congress establishes a timeline for Philippine independence and reduces Filipino immigration to 50 persons per year;
	Filipino farm workers strike in Salinas Valley and walkout in Santa Maria and Lompoc valleys, California; Whites expel Filipino workers from Turlock, California
1935	Filipino Repatriation Act provides free transportation for indigent Filipino Americans to the Philippines;
	an act of Congress grants naturalization to U.S. veterans of World War I who were before the war aliens ineligible to citizenship (under this act, several Chinese, Filipino, and Japanese American veterans of World War I became U.S. citizens)
1936	American Federation of Labor grants charter to a Filipino-Mexican farm workers union;
	Mexican, Japanese, and Filipino celery workers strike against Japanese growers in Venice, California;
	Cable Act is repealed
1937	white vigilantes expel striking Filipino workers in Yakima Valley, Washington;

	Filipino Repatriation Act extended to December 31, 1938
1938	150 Chinese women garment workers strike for three months against the Chinese-American owned National Dollar Stores;
	dockworkers strike in Hilo, Hawai'i, and in a union march in support of the strikers fifty are wounded by the police
1939	Filipino asparagus workers strike against growers in Stockton and Sacramento, California and form the Filipino Agricultural Workers Union;
	the second Filipino Repatriation Act signed into law
1940	American Federation of Labor charters the Filipino Federated Agricultural Laborers Association;
	Filipino American repatriation ends
1941	Japan attacks Pearl Harbor; United States declares war;
	military in Hawai'i declares martial law;
	Japanese Americans interned in Department of Justice camps;
	Public Law 360 allows Filipinos to serve in the U.S. army
1942	President Franklin D. Roosevelt signs Executive Order 9066 that begins the mass removal and detention of Japanese Americans on the West Coast;
	Congress passes Public Law 503 to impose sanctions for violations of Executive Order 9066;
	National Student Relocation Council formed to assist nisei students continue their college education;
	resistance movements at Poston and Manzanar concentration camps;
	Minoru Yasui tests the army's curfew and loses in Portland federal district court;
	Chinese, Filipino, Japanese, and Korean Americans support the American war effort as soldiers and through national defense bond drives
1943	U.S. Congress repeals all Chinese exclusion laws and establishes a quota of 105 persons per year on Chinese immigration, and allows Chinese naturalization;
	Yasui, U.S. Supreme Court affirms Minoru Yasui's conviction *Hirabayashi*, U.S. Supreme Court rules on Gordon Hirabayashi's appeal and affirms his conviction of violating the army's curfew
1944	resistance movements at Tule Lake concentration camp and martial law imposed, and draft resistance at other camps;

Ex parte Endo, U.S. Supreme Court rules that Mitsuye Endo and other "loyal" U.S. citizens must be released from the concentration camps;

Korematsu, U.S. Supreme Court decides that Fred Korematsu's exclusion and detention were constitutional

1945   United States drops atomic bombs on Hiroshima and Nagasaki; World War II ends;

Korea is divided temporarily at the 38th parallel;

U.S. Supreme Court rules Filipinos are not aliens but nationals and are thus not susceptible to the various laws against aliens

1946   Luce-Celler Act confers naturalization rights and small immigration quotas to Asian Indians and Filipinos;

Philippine Rehabilitation Act allows Filipino students to study in the United States;

the Philippines wins its independence;

U.S. Congress allows Chinese wives of American citizens to immigrate on a nonquota basis;

Tule Lake concentration camp closes; the last shipment of "disloyals" sent to Japan as "repatriates"

1947   U.S. Congress amends the 1945 War Brides Act to allow Chinese American veterans to bring their brides to the United States;

Aiko and John Reinecke, alleged communists, lose their jobs in Hawai'i;

India gains its independence

1948   *Oyama v. California,* the U.S. Supreme Court declares California's alien land laws unconstitutional;

Japanese American Evacuation Claims Act enables federal restitutions for financial losses suffered in the mass removal and detention;

Republic of Korea declared with Syngman Rhee, American educated and based, becomes its first president;

Burma gains its independence;

U.S. Supreme Court rules that California's antimiscegenation law is unconstitutional

1949   Mao Zedong announces the People's Republic of China; Chiang Kai-shek flees to Taiwan and declares the Republic of China 5,000 highly educated Chinese granted refugee status in the United States from communist China;

Indonesia wins its independence;

Iva Toguri d'Aquino, allegedly "Tokyo Rose," sentenced to 10 years in prison for treason

1950	Internal Security Act allows for detention camps for those suspected of posing national security threats;
	Korean War begins;
	United States recognizes the French puppet government in Viet Nam and sends it military and economic aid;
	Organic Act confers U.S. citizenship on the inhabitants of Guam
1952	McCarran-Walter Act, repressive of those classed as communists, grants naturalization and an annual immigration quota of 185 to Japanese
1953	armistice ends Korean War;
	Laos becomes independent;
	Hawai'i Seven, charged with conspiring to overthrow the U.S. government by force are convicted (this conviction was overturned on appeal in 1958)
1954	Viet Minh forces defeat the French at Dien Bien Phu;
	Geneva Accords divides Viet Nam along the 17th parallel, promises elections in 1955 to reunite the country, and grants independence to Cambodia;
	Brown v. Board of Education, the U.S. Supreme Court ends "separate but equal" and educational segregation;
	Democrats gain control Hawai'i's legislature
1955	Rosa Parks and the Montgomery, Alabama bus boycott inspire a civil rights movement
1956	Dalip Singh Saund wins in California to become the first Asian American elected to Congress;
	United States supports the South Vietnamese regime's refusal to hold free elections as specified by the Geneva Accords and sends military and economic aid
1959	Hawai'i becomes the 50th state
1964	Civil Rights Act prohibits racial discrimination in public accommodations, federally funded programs, and public and private employment;
	Congress passes the Gulf of Tonkin Resolution allowing the president to escalate American military involvement in Viet Nam;
	Patsy Takemoto Mink wins in Hawai'i and is the first Asian American woman elected to Congress
1965	Immigration Act abandons national origins as the basis for establishing quotas for a hemispheric formula along with preferences for certain classes of immigrants;
	Voting Rights Act forbids racial discrimination in voting;
	Delano, California grape strike of Mexicans and Filipinos;

	riot in the Watts section of Los Angeles, leaving 34 dead;
	Malcolm X assassinated
1967	riot in Detroit leaves 43 dead
1968	Tet offensive begins, yielding little military advantage to the communists but great political and psychological gains for the antiwar movement;
	students at San Francisco State College form the Third World Liberation Front and strike for ethnic studies;
	Martin Luther King, Jr. assassinated
1969	students at the University of California, Berkeley form the Third World Liberation Front and strike for ethnic studies;
	United States pursues Vietnamization of its war and reduces its military presence
1970	United States expands its war into Cambodia;
	Kokua Kalama formed
1971	Title II, the detention camp measure, of the 1950 Internal Security Act repealed
1972	Aboriginal Lands of Hawaiian Ancestry formed;
	Congress passes the Equal Rights Amendment, providing equal rights to women
1973	United States and North Viet Nam sign the cease-fire Paris Accords;
	Organization of Chinese Americans established in Washington, D.C.;
	American Indian Movement members occupy Wounded Knee, South Dakota to press for reforms;
	Roe v. Wade, the U.S. Supreme court legalizes abortion based on the right to privacy
1974	*Lau v. Nichols,* the U.S. Supreme court rules for bilingual education;
	'Ohana O Hawai'i formed
1975	North Vietnamese troops enter Saigon and end the civil war;
	more than 130,000 refugees from Viet Nam, Cambodia, and Laos enter the U.S. fleeing communist governments;
	Congress passes the Indochina Migration and Refugee Assistance Act;
	Voting Rights Act of 1965 amended to include language minorities within the Act's purview
1976	Health Professionals Education Assistance Act reduces the immigration of foreign physicians and health professionals;
	President Gerald Ford rescinds Executive Order 9066;
	Protect Kaho'olawe 'Ohana formed

1977	President Gerald Ford pardons Iva Toguri, the so-called "Tokyo Rose"
1978	"boat people" flee Viet Nam;
	Office of Hawaiian Affairs established by the state to promote the interests of native Hawaiians
1979	United States and People's Republic of China re-establish diplomatic relations
1980	Refugee Act systematizes the admission of refugees to the United States;
	Commission on Wartime Relocation and Internment of Civilians formed
1982	Vincent Chin murdered in Detroit;
	Equal Rights Amendment dies for lack of ratification by the states
1983	Commission on the Wartime Relocation and Internment of Civilians issues its report and recommends redress and reparations to Japanese Americans;
	Native Hawaiians Study Commission appointed by Congress, and recommends against Hawaiian reparations
1984	*Korematsu,* the 1944 U.S. Supreme Court ruling, is vacated and his conviction reversed
1986	Immigration Reform and Control Act creates an amnesty program for undocumented immigrants and installs employer sanctions;
	John Waihee becomes Hawai'i's governor and is the first Hawaiian to be elected to that office
1987	Navroze Mody killed in Jersey City, New Jersey;
	Constitutional Convention for a Hawaiian Nation meets and drafts a constitution
1988	Civil Rights Act, offering redress and reparations to Japanese Americans, passed by Congress and signed by President Ronald Reagan;
	Hirabayashi, the 1943 U.S. Supreme Court ruling, is vacated and his conviction reversed
	Amerasian Homecoming Act allows Vietnamese children of American fathers the right to immigrate to the United States.
1989	Jim (Ming Hai) Loo killed in Raleigh, North Carolina;
	massacre of Asian American schoolchildren in Stockton, California by a gunman who killed five and wounded 20;
	China's government suppresses student uprising at Tiananmen Square;
	Communist governments collapse throughout eastern Europe

1990	murder of Hung Truong in Houston, Texas;
	bombing of Kaho'olawe suspended
1992	Los Angeles riots in which Korean American businesses, in particular, were targeted resulting in losses of over $350 million
1993	Congress passes a joint resolution, signed by President Bill Clinton, apologizing for America's role in the 1893 overthrow of Queen Lili'uokalani
1994	California passes Proposition 187 that denies rights and government services to undocumented immigrants
1996	Illegal Immigration Reform and Immigrant Responsibility Act curtails the rights of undocumented immigrants to receive federal entitlements, limits due process for political asylum applicants, and increases enforcement of immigration laws;
	California passes Proposition 209 that eliminates governmental affirmative action programs
1999	FBI arrests Chinese American scientist Wen Ho Lee and charges him with mishandling restricted nuclear data at the Los Alamos National Laboratory
2000	U.S. Justice and Interior departments release a draft report recommending sovereignty for Hawaiians;
	President Bill Clinton signs Executive Order 13125 establishing the president's Commission on Asian Americans and Pacific Islanders to improve the quality of life for those groups

ENCYCLOPEDIA ENTRIES

"ABC" LIST

The "ABC" List refers a system of classification used by U.S. counterintelligence agencies to identify individuals of Japanese descent who were suspected of anti-American activities in the years leading up to and following Japan's involvement in World War II. The list was comprised of over 2,000 individuals in Hawai'i and on the U.S. continent who were ultimately investigated and apprehended for what institutions such as the Federal Bureau of Investigation (FBI) and the Office of Naval Intelligence (ONI) saw as behaviors that threatened American safety.

Although the forcible removal and confinement of some 120,000 Japanese Americans is often thought of in relation to the Executive Order 9066 signed by President Franklin Roosevelt in 1942, the "ABC" List is important because it authorized the round up and detainment of targeted persons prior to that order, particularly in the days immediately following Japan's attack on Pearl Harbor. In addition, the singling out of Japanese American business and cultural leaders on the "ABC" List points to the ways that Japanese culture was targeted under the guise of national security.

The development of the "ABC" List has its roots in Japan's invasion of Manchuria in 1931. As the United States saw it, Japan's move to occupy Manchuria and its subsequent invasion of China interfered with its own plans for imperial expansion and an "open door" policy with China. As a result, the U.S. State Department and the U.S. Navy began preparing for an inevitable war with Japan. As part of their planning, U.S. intelligence agencies began to seriously consider what it would mean to have Japanese Americans living in the United States in the midst of an impending war with Japan. In particular, the FBI and the ONI began fearing that Japanese living on the West Coast and in Hawai'i would commit sabotage, spy, or provide information to the Japanese. In order to assuage those fears, both agencies began collecting names of individuals who they believed posed a threat to national security. By 1941, and with the United States and Japan inching closer and closer to war, the FBI and the ONI combined their list of potential suspects and created what became the "ABC" List.

It is important to note that the fears and anxieties that prompted the creation of the "ABC" List were almost completely unfounded. Japanese living in the United States, in Hawai'i and on the West Coast, were not engaged in any covert or subversive anti-American activities. The "ABC" List grouped individuals into three categories. Group A was considered to be "known and dangerous" threats that demanded immediate and close observation, and were to be immediately seized and detained at the onset of war with Japan. Importantly, this group was largely made up of first-generation (issei) males who were fisherman, owned successful farming ventures, or led and participated in local Japanese cultural and religious organizations. That the targeted individuals were highly successful farmers and community leaders, with the exception of fishermen who allegedly knew the coastal waters, shows how the efforts of counterintelligence agencies went beyond their stated goal of protecting the United States, and instead waged a war on the community, culture, and economic success of Japanese Americans. Those who comprised the B group were identified as "potentially dangerous," and group C were those who were believed to be operating on the margins of any anti-American activities. Groups B and C were largely made up of newspaper editors, active members of the community, Japanese language teachers, and instructors in martial arts. Thus while the list was formed under the guise of national security, the list ultimately worked to target anyone who showed any ties to Japanese culture and the Japanese American community.

Moreover, an erroneous and racist view held by many in the intelligence community was that Japanese Americans, being communal people, would not pose any risk without their leaders. Accordingly, unable to penetrate Japanese American communities and organizations, military and civilian intelligence agencies simply chose to single out the leaders. It was also clear, especially in Hawai'i, that making an example of Japanese American leaders by removing and confining them was designed to inspire fear, and with it obedience, among the masses of Japanese Americans.

Although the "ABC" List authorized the investigation of Japanese by counterintelligence agencies and the arrest of those classified in the A group immediately following the bombing of Pearl Harbor on December 7, 1941, *all* individuals on the list were ordered by the president to be arrested and detained.

Autumn Womack

Reference

Irons, Peter (Ed.). *Justice Delayed: The Record of the Japanese American Internment Cases.* Middletown, CT: Wesleyan University Press, 1989.

AISO, JOHN F. (1909–1987)

Born in Burbank, California, Aiso was during World War II the director of the U.S. Army Military Intelligence Service Language School (MISLS) that trained mainly nisei Japanese-language experts necessary for the war effort in the Pacific theater. Aiso was also an Asian American pioneer in the legal profession, serving as a judge in California. He was the first Japanese American judge on the U.S. continent.

Aiso grew up in Hollywood where he attended school and was a brilliant student. From his youth, Aiso encountered racism. White barbers refused to cut his hair, and he recalled a day when he boarded a streetcar and sat next to a white woman who elbowed him and declared loudly, "No Jap is going to sit next to me!" White schoolmates at Grant Grammar School in Hollywood taunted Aiso and other Asian Americans, bullied them, and called them names. At LeConte Junior High School, Aiso ran for and won the presidency of the student body, but white parents protested at mass meetings, saying: "No child of mine is going to be under a Jap" (Ichinokuchi, 5). Because of parental pressure, the principal gave in and suspended student government until after Aiso graduated.

At Hollywood High School, Aiso joined the Reserve Officers' Training Corps (ROTC) program and received military training. He distinguished himself on the school's debating team, and won an oratorical contest on the Constitution but the principal pressured him to decline the award because, he said, white parents would be angry if a Japanese American represented the school. Aiso graduated from high school at the age of 16, went to Japan to study the Japanese language for 10 months, and returned to enter Brown University, which had offered Aiso admission and a scholarship through the intervention of Japan's ambassador in Washington, D.C. He graduated with honors in economics and went on to Harvard Law School. He received his law degree in 1934.

After passing New York's bar examination, Aiso practiced law in New York City in a Wall Street firm. On the invitation of a Japanese banker, he went to Tokyo to study Japanese legal terminology. He secured a job in China, working for the British-American Tobacco Company, and after three years, largely because of his hepatitis, Aiso returned to the United States. He was drafted into the army in December 1940, and was selected to join other nisei at the military's fledgling Japanese-language school. Because of the army's exclusion orders, the school moved from San Francisco, California, to Camp Savage, Minnesota, and when that camp became too small, the school moved to nearby Camp Snelling. The school expanded from Japanese-language instruction to the teaching of Chinese and Korean.

The army promoted Aiso from instructor to the director of the MISLS, and he earned the rank of major. The school reached its peak in October 1945, and its some 6,000 graduates translated enemy documents, maps, and battle plans, interrogated Japanese prisoners, and undertook intelligence work. After the war, they translated for the Occupation forces in Japan. Their work hastened the war's end, and facilitated Japan's transition to democracy. Aiso urged the U.S. Occupation government to stress educational reform and to provide wage labor for the ordinary man "to earn, as a free man, a decent living for himself and his family" (Ichinokuchi, 21).

After his return from military duty in 1947, Aiso practiced law in California, and in 1952 was appointed commissioner of the Los Angeles superior court. A year later, he became a judge of the Los Angeles municipal court, and then, of the Los Angeles county superior court. In 1968, California's governor appointed Aiso an associate justice to the California court of appeals for the second appellate district where he remained until his retirement in 1972.

Japan's government decorated Aiso with its Third Class Order of the Rising Sun in 1984, and the following year at the awards banquet, Aiso thanked the Japanese government for the honor and said: "We Nisei and our offspring are making our contributions as American citizens to the political experiment which is the United States of America. For our unique position in Japanese-American and world history, we Nisei are indebted as no other generation to our Issei parents who migrated from Japan to the United States. They were imbued with adventurous aspirations and permeated with the integrity of character so characteristic of heritage from such parents, which we have found to be an indispensable factor in making us exemplary American citizens" (Ichinokuchi, 27–28).

Aiso died in 1987 at the hands of a mugger.

Gary Y. Okihiro

Reference

Ichinokuchi, Tad. *John Aiso and the M.I.S.: Japanese American Soldiers in the Military Intelligence Service, World War II.* Los Angeles: MIS Club of Southern California, 1988.

AMERICAN CIVIL LIBERTIES UNION

Founded in 1920, the American Civil Liberties Union (ACLU) is a nonpartisan organization established, from its mission statement, "to defend and preserve the individual rights and liberties guaranteed to every person in this country by the Constitution and laws of the United States." At first, defense of those rights involved mainly freedom of speech, but that broadened as social movements for group rights arose in opposition to racism and sexism that treated persons as collectives and not as individuals as required by the nation's laws and legal structure.

Roger Baldwin, one of the three founders of the ACLU and its director during World War II, compiled an ambivalent record regarding Japanese Americans. While disturbingly group-specific and not individually based in violation of individual civil liberties, the government's mass removal and detention of Japanese Americans was based upon the doctrine of "military necessity." Baldwin and the ACLU, accordingly, acceded to that authority and reluctantly supported the action, urging Japanese American compliance. Likewise, when Kiyoshi Okamoto, Heart Mountain's Fair Play Committee leader, asked Baldwin for ACLU's legal representation to defend draft resisters, the ACLU head declined, saying the dissidents had "a strong moral case" but they had "no legal case at all." Those who advise others to resist military service, he wrote, "are not within their rights and must expect severe treatment" (Daniels, 272). The ACLU failed to support Gordon Hirabayashi when he refused to abide by the military curfew for "enemy aliens."

At the same time, A. L. Wirin, a southern California ACLU attorney, took on the case of the seven Fair Play Committee leaders, including Okamoto. Wirin lost, but he broke with the ACLU leadership in his stand. However, in the case of Fred Korematsu before the U.S. Supreme Court in 1944, the ACLU submitted an amicus curiae or friend of the court brief, which focused on "whether or not a citizen of the United States may, because he is of Japanese ancestry, be confined in barbed-wire stockades . . . actually concentration camps" (Daniels, 277). The ACLU also joined the U.S. Supreme Court case of Mitsuye Endo by submitting a brief in her support. In it, the ACLU contended the government had no right to hold a citizen against whom no charges had been made, segregation and detention of citizens on the basis of race or ancestry was unconstitutional, and Endo, held involuntarily and without due process, bore no obligation to obey War Relocation Authority regulations and was thus entitled to release.

Although the Supreme Court agreed that Endo was unjustly detained and thus ordered her release, bringing to an end the forcible detention of loyal citizens, the court failed to condemn the government's curtailment of civil liberties during times of war. In fact, its *Hirabayashi, Korematsu,* and *Endo* decisions affirmed the military powers of the state by agreeing that citizens must concede to that authority even at the expense of individual rights and liberties. The ACLU acceded to that ruling by expressing satisfaction with the Supreme Court's *Endo* ruling.

Gary Y. Okihiro

Reference

Daniels, Roger. *Asian America: Chinese and Japanese in the United States since 1850.* Seattle: University of Washington Press, 1988.

AMERICAN FRIENDS SERVICE COMMITTEE

Founded in 1917 as an affiliated organization of the Religious Society of Friends (the Quakers), the American Friends Service Committee (AFSC) worked for peace and social justice in the United States and world. During World War I, the AFSC assisted conscientious objectors with the draft, and provided them with spiritual guidance and support. The AFSC helped in the European relief effort, collecting clothes, food, and supplies for displaced and impoverished persons as a consequence of the war. From its headquarters in Philadelphia, the AFSC shipped materials to France, and after the war, worked in Austria, Germany, Poland, and Russia setting up kitchens to feed the hungry and assisting with orphans and victims of famine and disease.

During World War II, the AFSC helped refugees escape from Nazi Germany, and provided relief to children and refugees from Spain and France. The AFSC took up the cause of Japanese American education on May 5, 1942, when Milton Eisenhower, director of the War Relocation Authority (WRA), asked the AFSC's executive secretary, Clarence Pickett, to build a national program for the relocation of nisei students. The AFSC was already involved in supporting Japanese American students on the West Coast, so Pickett readily accepted the challenge.

The program had wide support. Even assistant secretary of war, John McCloy, an ardent defender of the mass removal and detention, wrote to Pickett after Eisenhower informed him of the project of nisei student relocation. "I take great pleasure in advising you that I am in complete sympathy with the suggestions made by Mr. Eisenhower in his letter to you," declared McCloy. "Anything that can legitimately be done to compensate loyal citizens of Japanese ancestry for the dislocation to which they have been subjected, by reason of military necessity, has our full approval. In particular," McCloy continued, "the suggestion for the establishment of a committee of distinguished educators to work out a program of university education in other parts of the country for Japanese-American citizens evacuated from the Pacific Coast meets with my hearty approval" (Okihiro, 37).

With that assurance, Pickett invited prominent educators, church leaders, and representatives from the Young Men's Christian Association (YMCA) and Young Women's Christian Association (YWCA), the AFSC, and Japanese American Citizens League to a meeting in Chicago on May 29, 1942. In all, 46 attended the meeting. The members, according to a digest of the proceedings, were told there were some 2,300 college and university students in the WRA concentration camps, about two-thirds men and one-third women, and that these were "among the best students in the colleges they have left" (Okihiro, 37). Because their forced removal and confinement had been "a terrific wrench," it was important these students be informed of an orderly procedure that might make it possible for them to obtain permits to attend institutions outside the restricted areas. The Chicago meeting ended by establishing the National Student Relocation Council headed by Robbins Barstow, president of Hartford Seminary. In March 1943, the council was renamed the National Japanese American Student Relocation Council, and was moved from San Francisco to Philadelphia.

The AFSC and Student Relocation Council maintained close ties. Key figures in the Student Relocation Council were Quakers and members of the AFSC, and AFSC regional chapters performed the work of the Student Relocation Council in their areas of the country. Staffers in Philadelphia corresponded with colleges and universities, advised Japanese American students in the camps and on campuses, and left for the field to recruit college students in the WRA concentration camps and resolve problems in communities in which those students were placed. AFSC branches, like its Midwest branch, led coalitions of churches, government agencies, private charities, the YMCA and YWCA, and nisei volunteers to place and support Japanese American students in their areas. Those students needed help with transportation from the camps to the campuses, housing, employment and financial advice, and personal counseling.

An example was the AFSC's Marjorie Hyer, peace section secretary for the AFSC's Middle Atlantic states. Hyer visited colleges in her region to solicit their interest in accepting nisei students, and reported her findings to the Student Relocation Council. Thomas Bodine attended Quaker schools, and in 1941 he received a draft deferment to work with the AFSC in Philadelphia. When the war broke out, the AFSC sent Bodine to Seattle to help Japanese Americans who were being arrested, placed under curfew, and excluded from restricted zones. In June 1942, the AFSC dispatched him to San Francisco to work on nisei student relocation. Bodine eventually became the West Coast director, and he followed the office when it moved to Philadelphia in March 1943. He visited the concentration camps to recruit students, and wrote from a camp to the Friends (Quakers) of his Germantown, Pennsylvania, meeting in May 1943. "Outside my window I can see the barbed wire fence and the armed guards sitting up in the watch towers. . . . I sense the evacuee's feelings of confinement, his feeling of being locked up without trial when he has committed no crime, the feeling that his country—his America—no longer considers him American. These feelings hurt. I feel for the older people, all of whom came to America more than 20 years ago. . . . These older people lived here most of their lives. They have loved America. They have helped build America. And like so many other immigrants, they have watched their children become real Americans." It "hurts," he continued, to talk to college-age youth who are uncertain about their future. "It hurts to be here . . ." (Okihiro, 131–32).

The American Friends Service Committee and especially Quakers played a central role in enabling thousands of Japanese American students to continue their education in the midst of wartime and the concentration camps.

Gary Y. Okihiro

Reference

Okihiro, Gary Y. *Storied Lives: Japanese American Students and World War II*. Seattle: University of Washington Press, 1999.

ANTI-ASIAN MOVEMENT

Historians widely understand the World War II concentration camps as a culmination of the anti-Asian movement. Most believe the anti-Chinese movement led to the anti-Japanese movement, which led to the forced, mass removal and confinement. Some hold that politicians, from California's delegation to Congress to President Franklin Roosevelt, were the principal movers behind this World War II policy. Others believe economic interests, such as white growers, shippers, and commercial enterprises, saw the war as a prime opportunity to get rid of their competition, Japanese American farmers. Still others contend that patriotic and white supremacist organizations like the American Legion and Native Sons and Daughters of the Golden West lobbied for Japanese American exclusion. Those interpretations depend upon an idea that policy, such as Roosevelt's Executive Order 9066 and Public Law 503, is responsive to and derives from public opinion and attitudes that elect politicians and shape their law-making.

Briefly, the anti-Asian movement, as exhibited in the anti-Chinese and anti-Japanese movements, involved immigration laws that restricted Asian migration, statutes like the alien land laws, racially segregated schools, city ordinances that discriminated against Asian businesses, and segregated housing and occupations, riots against and murders and expulsions of Asians, and everyday racist practices. Those are the conventional depictions of what historians have called the anti-Asian movement.

If placed, however, within the broader context of U.S. history especially the position of nonwhite peoples, a pattern emerges. The English colonies that began what became the United States considered American Indians, the original guardians of the land, as foreign nations for treaty and war making. What the colonists wanted was the land of the indigenous peoples. Virginia colony, run as a business from London, imported European indentured servants to supply labor to farm mainly tobacco at first, and from 1819 began replacing those indentures with Africans held in bondage. Cultivating tobacco, rice, and later cotton, Africans provided the labor the colony's rulers needed to plant and harvest green gold from American Indian lands. Asians and Mexicans supplied the labor, like Africans in the South, to tend the fields in Hawai'i and the Southwest. African, Asian, and Mexican Americans were in the United States because they were useful as laborers.

The anti-Asian movement, from that perspective, involved the exploitation of Asian labor. In that way, immigration laws, alien land laws, segregated schools, and so forth were the means by which to control that labor. Accordingly, recruiters in China and India during the 19th century sought laborers for the plantations of the tropical band, and the Chinese Exclusion Act (1882) prohibited entry into the United States to Chinese workers, not businessmen or students. The alien land laws were designed to stop the upward mobility of Asians or "aliens ineligible to citizenship," and segregated, inferior education directed children back into labor and not into the professions. What made Asian migrants particularly valuable to employers, in light of the Civil War and freedom for enslaved African Americans who could vote, was the fact that Asian migrants could not become U.S. citizens. They fell under the Naturalization Act (1790), which stipulated that only free white persons could become naturalized citizens. As noncitizens, Asians had few rights and were thus easily controlled and removed as mere workers; they were "best abused." A leader of the Hawaiian sugar planters called Asian workers "like cattle on the range" (Okihiro, 17).

Asian workers, nonetheless, were not mere passive pawns for exploitation. They organized and fought back. They formed unions, struck for higher wages and better working conditions, and resisted their exploitation in everyday activities such as breaking tools that belonged to the planters. In turn, their employers struck back. They expelled strikers from their homes, hired vigilantes to harass and intimidate the workers, and replaced them with another, more docile and less expensive group. In that way, Japanese replaced Chinese, Koreans were hired to break Japanese-led strikes, and Filipinos were recruited to displace Japanese. That pattern resulted in waves of labor migration beginning with the Chinese, then Japanese, Korean, and Filipino. South Asians provided another source of labor mainly along the West Coast. And when Asian labor was no longer desirable, Mexicans worked alongside and then replaced Asians in the fields.

Still, the problem for the nation's rulers was the "Oriental problem" caused by the birth of the second generation. Asian workers did not return to Asia after their exclusion (Asian exclusion laws limited entry to workers, in sequence, from China, Japan and Korea, India, and the Philippines), but instead formed families and settled in the United States. Their children, under the Constitution's Fourteenth Amendment, were U.S. citizens having been born on American soil. They comprised the "Oriental problem" or problem of molding them into worthy citizens. "Americanization" was the answer, involving mainly the public schools as a way to assimilate Asian students but also to wean them away from their parents who remained, by law, aliens. That became especially acute in the case of Japanese Americans during World War II.

Japanese American workers became a "problem" when they organized strikes against Hawai'i's sugar planters, especially the 1920 strike. Intelligence services, civilian and military, took interest in the "Japanese problem," citing their disruption of the sugar industry, the islands' principal economic base, as a matter of national security. And when their children, the nisei, came of age during the 1920s and 1930s, "Americanization" efforts were directed at them, hoping to steer them away from their parents, the issei, who were considered to be loyal to Japan and toward "useful" labor as field workers and not as professionals.

Martial law and internment in Hawai'i and concentration and internment camps on the continent were instruments of racial segregation, separating Japanese Americans from other Americans. One drop of "Japanese blood" made them susceptible to government-sponsored removal and confinement. The War Relocation Authority (WRA), the administrators of the concentration camps, favored nisei citizens over issei aliens with the intention of "Americanizing" and assimilating the second generation by facilitating their education, including college education outside the camps, and offering them employment in the fields and factories beyond the barbed wire fences. Other nisei forced laborers were the men and women who served in the U.S. military to prove their loyalty in blood. At the same time, those opportunities for education, work, and military service provided openings for Japanese American claims on the promise of full equality as guaranteed by the Constitution.

The anti-Asian movement oppressed and exploited Asian Americans, but Asian Americans complied with and resisted those designs and thereby became agents of change or history.

Gary Y. Okihiro

Reference

Okihiro, Gary Y. *Cane Fires: The Anti-Japanese Movement in Hawaii, 1865–1945*. Philadelphia: Temple University Press, 1991.

B

BENDETSEN, KARL R. (1907–1989)

Born in Washington State, Karl Bendetsen pursued his education at Stanford University, from where he received an undergraduate degree in 1929 and a law degree in 1932. He joined the Officers Reserve Corps, and in 1934 opened a law office in his hometown of Aberdeen, Washington. He rose rapidly in rank when he was appointed to the office of the Army's judge advocate general, becoming captain in 1940, then major the following year, and colonel in 1942. While serving as head of the Aliens Division of the army's provost marshal general office, Bendetsen played a key role in designing and implementing the plan for the mass removal and confinement of Japanese Americans.

The provost marshal general's office sent Bendetsen to Lieutenant General John DeWitt's Western Defense Command to assist DeWitt on matters concerning "enemy aliens." Shortly after his arrival, Bendetsen drew up plans that became DeWitt's policy regarding "enemy aliens." It called for the immediate registration of all "enemy aliens" and their photographing and fingerprinting to set up a "pass and permit system" to regulate their movement. On January 4, 1942, DeWitt called a meeting at his headquarters to consider the problem of his military command. "We are at war and this area—eight states—has been designated as a theater of operations. I have approximately 240,000 men at my disposal. . . . [There are] approximately 288,000 enemy aliens . . . which we have to watch. . . . I have little confidence that the enemy aliens are law-abiding or loyal in any sense of the word. Some of them yes; many, no. Particularly the Japanese. I have no confidence in their loyalty whatsoever. I am speaking now of the native born Japanese—117,000—and 42,000 in California alone" (Daniels, 1981, 45–46).

Employing Bendetsen's plan, DeWitt designated prohibited zones, excluding enemy aliens from 86 Category A zones, and maintaining tight controls over enemy aliens in eight Category B zones on a pass and permit system. In late January 1942, the Justice Department announced and administered the plan, and Tom C. Clark was appointed coordinator of the Alien Enemy Control Program within the Western Defense Command.

Not content with that program, which affected only about 7,000 enemy aliens and less than 3,000 Japanese Americans, Bendetsen and DeWitt met to work on a more comprehensive scheme that would include all Japanese Americans within the Western Defense Command. Bendetsen summarized DeWitt's view to him on January 29, 1942. "As I understand it, . . . you are of the opinion that there will have to be an evacuation on the west coast, not only of Japanese aliens but also of Japanese citizens, that is, you would include citizens along with alien enemies . . ."

DeWitt affirmed that synopsis, and Bendetsen urged the general to take a leadership position in securing the Western Defense Command.

Back in Washington, D.C., Bendetsen was instrumental in changing assistant secretary of war John McCloy's mind on the matter. McCloy believed the exclusion zones were sufficient to handle "enemy aliens," but Bendetsen convinced him of the necessity of a mass "evacuation" of Japanese Americans. McCloy's change of mind was crucial because he was a major figure in the government's decision for mass removal. Bendetsen returned to DeWitt's headquarters where on February 11, 1942, he received McCloy's assurance that the president would authorize the military to "do anything you think necessary," including enemy aliens and U.S. citizens but "it has got to be dictated by military necessity . . ." Bendetsen then helped DeWitt to draft what the general called "the plan that Mr. McCloy wanted me to submit" (Daniels, 1981, 65).

Before the Commission on Wartime Relocation and Internment of Civilians in 1981, Bendetsen claimed he, as a soldier, was just following orders when previously he had boasted he had "conceived method, formulated details and directed evacuation of 120,000 persons of Japanese ancestry from military areas" (Daniels, 1988, 337). The historical record shows Bendetsen, the lawyer, to have been instrumental in DeWitt's military assessment of the situation of "enemy aliens" within his command, and he led, not followed, in the policy to remove and confine some 120,000 Japanese Americans from the West Coast.

Gary Y. Okihiro

References

Daniels, Roger. *Asian America: Chinese and Japanese in the United States since 1850*. Seattle: University of Washington Press, 1988.
Daniels, Roger. *Concentration Camps: North America: Japanese in the United States and Canada during World War II*. Malabar, FL: Robert E. Krieger, 1981.

BIDDLE, FRANCIS B. (1886–1968)

Born in Paris, France, Francis B. Biddle descended from a privileged family with strong ties to the Republican Party. He graduated from Harvard College and Harvard Law School, clerked with Supreme Court Justice Oliver Wendell Holmes, and worked for 23 years in corporate law in Philadelphia. After switching to the Democratic Party, Biddle chaired the National Labor Board from 1934 to 1946. From 1941 to 1945, Biddle served as President Franklin Roosevelt's attorney general. In that position, Biddle was a reluctant, though compliant participant in the government's mass removal and confinement of Japanese Americans.

Biddle's Justice Department oversaw the Federal Bureau of Investigation (FBI), which investigated Japanese Americans before and during World War II, and Justice was responsible for the aliens and hence "enemy alien" programs. The military, accordingly, had to work with Justice in handling "enemy aliens" within its Western Defense Command. The command's head, Lieutenant General John DeWitt, was frustrated by Biddle's reluctance to hand over control of the "enemy aliens" program, which was a central feature of the army's desire for prohibited zones and restrictions on the movement of "enemy aliens." Although Biddle reached out to assistant secretary of war John McCloy to agree on a common alien-control program, he ignored DeWitt's request for a compulsory registration program and insisted that FBI authorize military searches for contraband only when there was "reasonable or probable cause."

However, the War Department and military persisted, and by January 1942, Biddle conceded the registration of "enemy aliens" was a military measure, and he relinquished to the army the ability to establish restricted areas from which "enemy aliens" could be excluded. More problematic was Biddle's agreement for warrantless searches conducted by the army, eroding Fourth Amendment rights, of which the attorney general was fully aware. "Probable cause," Biddle wrote to DeWitt, was established simply on the grounds that an "alien enemy is resident in such premises." That is, an alien enemy's residence can be searched without a warrant simply because that alien lived on that premises. Still, not wanting to tarnish his pledge to defend the Constitution, Biddle promised DeWitt, "under no circumstances will the Department of Justice conduct mass raids on alien enemies" (Irons, 35).

Biddle called a meeting on February 1, 1942, with representatives from the War Department and military to state clearly his position on the campaign for the mass removal of Japanese Americans. At the meeting, the attorney general declared his department "will have nothing whatsoever to do with any interference with citizens, whether they are Japanese or not." The military shot back, "Mr. Biddle, do you mean to tell me that if the Army, the men on the ground, determine it is a military necessity to move citizens, Jap citizens, that you won't help us." Biddle responded with a prepared statement, which he hoped the War Department would sign, indicating the FBI had investigated Japanese Americans and found "no substantial evidence of planned sabotage by any alien," and thus, the Justice Department agreed that the military situation "does not at this time require the removal of American citizens of the Japanese race" (Irons, 44). The War Department declined to sign, and the meeting concluded in disagreement.

While the War Department and military pressed for authority to remove all Japanese Americans from the West Coast, Biddle subscribed to the FBI's assessment and belief that the roundup of the "ABC" list had effectively neutralized any national security threat. But he left the door open for the military to enter into what was a Justice Department matter when he admitted to a senate committee, "The military must determine the risk and undertake the responsibility for evacuation of citizens of Japanese descent . . ." (Irons, 52).

Troubled by the pressure for mass "evacuation," Biddle arranged a lunch meeting with the president on February 7, 1942. During the luncheon, Biddle, from his notes, "discussed at length with him the Japanese situation" and told the president that the FBI thought a mass removal was unnecessary. To sway the president, Biddle added, such a move was politically risky, especially involving German and Italian Americans. Roosevelt gave his attorney general little support when he told Biddle he was "fully aware of the dreadful risk of Fifth Column [internal subversion] retaliation in case of a raid" (Irons, 53).

Unhappy, Biddle consulted with a team of attorneys outside the Justice Department. Their report argued for constitutional guarantees but noted "military necessity" in times of national peril required a resolution "in favor of action to preserve the national safety" (Irons, 54). Although the attorneys, by their own testimony, opposed the mass removal of Japanese Americans, Biddle read it as an endorsement of the action. At the same time, he remained skeptical of the need for "evacuation" and complained that the Justice Department was ill equipped to deal with a mass removal. Biddle, thus, favored transferring the responsibility to the military and War Department since its justification rested upon military necessity.

Secretary of War Henry Stimson tried to avoid the responsibility tossed his way by the attorney general. He doubted the constitutionality of a plan targeting a group based upon their racial characteristics and believed the removal of some 120,000 persons was beyond the military's capacity. Stimson, however, faced pressures from McCloy and DeWitt in his own department and from politicians, so he deferred to the president the decision for mass evacuation. "Is the President willing to authorize us to move Japanese citizens as well as aliens from restricted zones?" he asked McCloy and the army chief of staff, General Mark Clark, on February 11, 1942.

That afternoon, Stimson called the president to settle the question, which he answered in broad terms. "Proceed," Roosevelt directed Stimson, in the direction he thought best, but he wanted the matter resolved as soon as possible. In turn, he promised he would back up Stimson's actions with an executive order, giving the War Department the authority Biddle was so eager to relinquish. McCloy relayed that message to the Western Defense Command that the president supported its plans for the mass removal of Japanese Americans as long as it was "dictated by military necessity" with the admonishment, "be as reasonable as you can." Thus began the mass removal and confinement of Japanese Americans.

With Japanese Americans in concentration camps, Biddle and his Justice Department drafted what became the Denationalization Act (1944) that led to the loss of U.S. citizenship for 5,589 Japanese Americans. At the same time, Biddle, as a civil libertarian, expressed regret over the government's treatment of Japanese Americans during the war. "We should never have moved the Japanese from their homes and their work," he was quoted as saying in September 1944. "It was un-American, unconstitutional and un-Christian" (Weglyn, 114). And years later, Biddle testified before Congress in favor of the Japanese American Claims Act (1948), and served as an advisor to the American Civil Liberties Union.

Gary Y. Okihiro

References

Irons, Peter. *Justice at War.* New York: Oxford University Press, 1983.
Weglyn, Michi. *Years of Infamy: The Untold Story of America's Concentration Camps.* New York: William Morrow, 1976.

CIVIL LIBERTIES ACT (1988)

The Civil Liberties Act of 1988 was an outcome of the Commission on Wartime Relocation and Internment of Civilians (CWRIC), which issued its report in 1982 and recommendations the following year. The CWRIC's fifth recommendation was for Congress to appropriate $1.5 billion "to provide personal redress to those who were excluded" as well as to fund "research and public educational activities" to inform Americans of the wartime Japanese American experience and of "similar events." The sole CWRIC member to dissent from the personal redress recommendation was Daniel Lundgren, the commission's cochair.

It took more than five years for the Congress to enact the Civil Liberties Act, which began as a bill submitted by Congressman Norman Mineta, a Japanese American from San Jose, California, and Senator Alan Simpson of Wyoming. A majority of Democrats voted for the bill, while a majority of Republicans voted against it. President Ronald Reagan signed the act into law on August 10, 1988.

President Ronald Reagan, despite his initial opposition, signs the 1988 Civil Liberties Act that authorized redress and reparations for the internment of Japanese Americans during World War II. (Ronald Reagan Library)

The Civil Liberties Act agreed that the mass removal and confinement of Japanese Americans during the war was based on "race prejudice, war hysteria, and a failure of political leadership." The act provided for payments of $20,000 to Japanese Americans who were held in government detention camps during World War II. The act also made restitution to Aleut residents of the Pribilof and Aleutian Islands for injustices suffered and unreasonable hardships endured as a result of the military's expulsion of them from their homes, and for personal and community property destroyed by U.S. forces during the war.

The act did not compensate Japanese mainly from Peru but also from Mexico, Central America, Latin America, and the Caribbean who were held in U.S. detention camps. In 1996, Carmen Mochizuki filed a lawsuit, and won a settlement of $5,000 per person from the remaining funds of the Civil Liberties Act. Some 145 Japanese from Latin America received $5,000 each as a result. In 1999, the attorney general approved additional monies to pay reparations to other claimants.

Gary Y. Okihiro

COLLINS, WAYNE M. (1900-1974)

Born in Sacramento, California, Wayne M. Collins received his law degree from San Francisco Law School. Collins practiced law in San Francisco, and was especially dedicated to defending civil liberties. That interest led him to the forced removal and detention of Japanese Americans, and he was among the first to learn of the Justice Department's plan to deport from America the U.S. Japanese Americans who had, under the Denationalization Act (1944), renounced their citizenship. On July 14, 1945, President Harry Truman signed Proclamation Number 2655, which, under the Alien Enemy Act (1798), authorized the attorney general to remove from the United States interned "enemy aliens" considered to be "dangerous to the public peace and safety of the United States because they have adhered to . . . enemy governments . . ." (Collins, 110).

Determined to stop the government from "repatriating" those Japanese Americans because of the injustices of the concentration camps and loss of U.S. citizenship, Collins visited Japanese Americans held in Tule Lake, California, Bismarck, North Dakota, Santa Fe, New Mexico, and Crystal City, Texas. He worked ceaselessly, admitting, "I was frightened stiff that if I was not able to be in my office every day early and late that the government might attempt to remove all of them to Japan" (Collins, 111). His devotion and energy buoyed the spirits of Japanese American renunciants (those who had filed to renounce their U.S. citizenship) and confirmed his fanaticism to government officials.

Collins was known for his work on the U.S. Supreme Court cases, *Hirabayashi*, *Korematsu,* and *Endo*. The American Civil Liberties Union (ACLU) appointed Collins to represent Fred Korematsu in his test case of the mass "evacuation" in June 1942. Korematsu's trial began in September of that year in San Francisco before federal judge Martin Welsh, a member of the Native Sons of the Golden West, a racist organization with particular animus toward Asians and Japanese Americans.

Welsh chose to go on vacation, and Adolphus St. Sure replaced him. Korematsu impressed St. Sure with his demeanor and testimony. Still, the judge denied Collins's motion for acquittal, and found Korematsu guilty of violating the military's exclusion order and gave him a five-year probationary sentence.

When Collins asked to appeal the judge's decision, St. Sure set bail at $2,500, which the ACLU posted. Korematsu was free, but a military policeman in the courtroom grabbed Korematsu and insisted he had orders to take him back to Tanforan assembly center. "I was supposed to be free to go," recalled Korematsu, "but the MP got all excited. He wasn't going to let me out on the street and he pulled a gun on me and said he's not going to let me go. The judge was all excited, he didn't know what to do" (Irons, 154). The judge offered to raise the bail, which the ACLU agreed to post. At that point, St. Sure relented to military authority, and allowed the MP to take Korematsu into custody. The episode pitted civilian against military authority, and exemplified the erosion of democracy under a regime of military necessity.

On February 19, 1943, on the anniversary of Executive Order 9066, Collins and Korematsu appeared in the court of appeals to file an appeal to the Supreme Court. The Supreme Court ruled on *Korematsu* on December 18, 1944, upholding his conviction by a six-to-three margin. When Collins took up the case of Japanese American renunciants, accordingly, both Japanese Americans and the government knew about him. In fact, in July 1944, St. Sure dispatched Collins to Tule Lake to resolve an issue involving the camp's stockade because of his reputation. While at the Tule Lake camp, Collins learned about Japanese American renunciation and the government's plan to send them to Japan. Collins was outraged, exclaiming, "That's ridiculous! You can no more resign citizenship in time of war than you can resign from the human race" (Collins, 113).

Japanese American parents were afraid their children would be sent to Japan, having lost their U.S. citizenship. Collins told them he believed the Denationalization Act was unconstitutional so he advised them to write to the U.S. attorney general and other government officials to explain that renunciation took place in an environment of duress and coercion. He wrote sample letters, and his advice and letter-writing campaign generated wide interest. Between August and September 1945, Tule Lake's renunciants organized to regain their citizenship. Especially after Japan's surrender on August 14, 1945, they sought legal representation to help them, but no attorney, except Collins, offered assistance.

The renunciants formed the Tule Lake Defense Committee, and in September 1945, the committee hired Collins as their sole attorney with the nominal support of the Northern California ACLU. Because each case had to be handled individually, Collins tried to slow down the government effort to deport the renunciants as a group. He began a letter-writing campaign among renunciants who requested the rescinding of their renunciation supported by letters from family and friends. On October 10, 1945, Tule Lake moved from the War Relocation Authority (WRA) to the Justice Department, which managed aliens and referred to Tule Lake's renunciants as "native American aliens." Those would be "repatriated" to Japan, together with their families, whether citizens or aliens, who wanted to accompany them.

Collins sued to prevent the Justice Department from carrying out its plan. He filed suit on November 13, 1945, two days before the first ship was to sail from San Francisco. The suit asked that renunciants be set free, the deportation orders be rescinded, the renunciations be declared void, and the plaintiffs be considered U.S. citizens. Collins filed for habeas corpus and obtained a court order preventing the mass deportation but keeping the renunciants in government internment camps. To avoid the prospect of years of litigation and millions of dollars in legal fees, the Justice Department agreed on December 1945 to hold mitigation hearings for those who did not want to be deported to Japan, including renunciants and aliens.

The hearings were held between January 7 and April 1, 1946 for 3,161 in Tule Lake and 25 in Bismarck and Santa Fe who applied for a hearing of their cases. Only 107 renunciants at Tule Lake failed to ask for a hearing. The Justice Department disallowed attorneys or witnesses at the hearings, and after their completion, announced that 449 renunciants would be deported to Japan. Most of those to be departed appealed the ruling, and Collins and the Tule Lake Defense Committee urged another letter-writing campaign. The government closed Tule Lake on March 28, 1946, and shipped the camp's Japanese Americans to Crystal City, Texas, and Seabrook Farms, New Jersey. Some of those were released en route, and others gained their freedom upon reaching their destinations. Of the 3,186 total renunciants, 2,780 were released unconditionally. The United States succeeded in sending some 6,200 Japanese Americans from Tule Lake and Justice Department internment camps to Japan, and of that number about 1,800 to 2,000 were renunciants. Among the 4,406 shipped to Japan from Tule Lake were 1,767 U.S. citizens who had not renounced, including over a thousand children under 10 years old and another 679 teenagers who left with their parents. Those who succeeded in remaining in the United States were indebted, in large part, to the untiring efforts of Wayne M. Collins.

Gary Y. Okihiro

References

Collins, Donald E. *Native American Aliens: Disloyalty and the Renunciation of Citizenship by Japanese Americans during World War II*. Westport, CT: Greenwood Press, 1985.
Irons, Peter. *Justice at War*. New York: Oxford University Press, 1983.

COMMISSION ON WARTIME RELOCATION AND INTERNMENT OF CIVILIANS

The redress and reparations movement, begun by students, activists, and the Japanese American Citizens League (JACL), together with pilgrimages to Manzanar and other concentration camps, led to a change in attitude among Japanese Americans regarding the World War II concentration camps. Prior to the 1970s, most Japanese Americans believed their wartime experience was better forgotten and remain buried in the past. Most felt ashamed by their victimization, and were uncertain about their standing as U.S. citizens. The redress and reparations movement, however, changed that attitude by allowing Japanese Americans to claim their rights as U.S. citizens.

Those claims led to President Gerald Ford's Presidential Proclamation 4417, which formally revoked the wartime Executive Order 9066 that enabled the mass, forcible removal and confinement of Japanese Americans along the West Coast. Ford's Proclamation came on February 19, 1976, the 34th anniversary of EO 9066 and in the year of the nation's celebration of its 200th anniversary. In this "honest reckoning," Ford declared, we must remember "our national mistakes as well as our national achievements." We now know, the president continued, "not only was the evacuation wrong, but Japanese Americans were and are loyal Americans" (Daniels, 331).

In 1970, the JACL passed the first of several resolutions calling on the government to acknowledge "the worst mistakes of World War II." Edison Uno, an activist and delegate, proposed that the JACL begin a movement for redress and reparations. A year later, Uno joined in the JACL's successful campaign to repeal Title II of the Internal Security Act (1950), which directed the Justice Department to establish concentration camps for persons suspected of engaging in "or probably will conspire with others to engage in, acts of espionage or sabotage." After Uno's untimely death, Clifford Uyeda chaired the JACL national committee on redress, and at the JACL national convention in 1978, the committee proposed a plan for redress or monetary compensation for the wartime losses and Uyeda was elected national president of JACL. John Tateishi headed the JACL's redress committee, and while other redress activists sought redress through the courts and the Congress, the JACL supported the establishment of a commission to investigate whether the U.S. government had committed a wrong against Japanese Americans during World War II.

President Jimmy Carter and the leaders of Congress named and appointed the Commission on Wartime Relocation and Internment of Civilians (CWRIC) in 1980. The commission's seven original members were Joan Bernstein, chair and former general counsel of the Department of Housing and Urban Development; Daniel Lundgren, vice-chair and congressman; Edward Brooke, a former U.S. senator; Arthur Flemming, chair of the Civil Rights Commission; Arthur Goldberg, a former Supreme Court justice; Hugh Mitchell, a former U.S. senator; and William Marutani, a federal judge and the only Japanese American on the panel. Later, Ishmael Gromoff, a Russian Orthodox priest and Robert Drinan, a Jesuit priest, were added to the commission.

The commission held hearings in Washington, D.C. and other cities around the country. Those hearings galvanized Japanese Americans, requiring many who had suppressed memories of the camps to come to terms with that dark past. The hearings allowed formerly silenced victims to speak publicly for the first time about the traumas and losses inflicted upon them by their government. Those testimonies, along with those by officials who had supervised the removal and detention, were overwhelmingly in favor of redress or an apology from the government and were critical of the loss of civil liberties. A few, notably Karl

Bendetsen and John McCloy, continued to justify their actions during the war on the basis of "military necessity." Abe Fortas, at the time undersecretary of the Interior Department and supervisor of the War Relocation Authority after February 1944, expressed the majority view: "I believe that the mass evacuation . . . was a tragic error," he said. "I cannot escape the conclusion that racial prejudice was its basic ingredient. . . . I think that it is clear—perhaps it was always clear—that the mass evacuation order issued by General DeWitt was never justified" (Daniels, 337).

Japanese Americans made the experience personal. "I am the wife of Albert Kurihara who cannot be here today due to a stroke he suffered last week," Mary Kurihara explained to the commission in 1981. "My husband is now in the hospital, but he still really wanted to testify. Albert has asked me to deliver his testimony." Kurihara was born in Hawai'i and was sent to Santa Anita assembly center and Poston concentration camp during the war. "I remember having to stay in the dirty horse stables at Santa Anita," Kurihara wrote. "I remember thinking, 'Am I a human being? Why are we being treated like this?' Santa Anita stunk like hell." From Poston, he was released to do "hard seasonal labor" harvesting sugar beets, "work which no one else wanted to do," and even after camp, "I was treated like an enemy by other Americans. They were hostile, and I had a very hard time finding any job. . . . This was the treatment they gave to an American citizen!" he exclaimed. "I think back about my younger brother, Dan, who was in the 442nd Regiment. In combat to defend his American native land, Dan suffered a bullet wound that damaged one-fourth of his head and caused him to lose an eye. . . . Every time I think about Dan . . . , it makes me so angry. Sometimes I want to tell this government to go to hell. This government can never repay all the people who suffered. But, this should not be an excuse for token apologies. I hope this country will never forget what happened," Kurihara concluded, "and do what it can to make sure that future generations will never forget" (Okihiro and Myers, 244).

The CWRIC issued its report, *Personal Justice Denied,* in December 1982. In it, the commission concluded: "The promulgation of Executive Order 9066 was not justified by military necessity, and the decisions which followed from it— detention, ending detention and ending exclusion—were not driven by analysis of military conditions. The broad historical causes which shaped these decisions were race prejudice, war hysteria and a failure of political leadership. Widespread ignorance of Japanese Americans contributed to a policy conceived in haste and executed in an atmosphere of fear and anger at Japan. A grave injustice was done to American citizens and resident aliens of Japanese ancestry who, without individual review or any probative evidence against them, were excluded, removed and detained by the United States during World War II" (*Personal Justice,* 1982, 18).

In June 1983, the CWRIC published its recommendations, which included a joint resolution of Congress signed by the president recognizing "that a grave injustice was done and offers the apologies of the nation for the acts of exclusion, removal and detention" (*Personal Justice,* 1983, 8). The commission also recommended presidential pardons for wartime convictions, Congressional restitution of lost positions, status, and entitlements, and reparations of $20,000 to each survivor of the exclusion orders and funds for the "general welfare" of the Japanese American community. Those findings and recommendations led to the Civil Liberties Act of 1988, and the achievement of redress and reparations for Japanese Americans.

Gary Y. Okihiro

References

Daniels, Roger. *Asian America: Chinese and Japanese in the United States since 1850.* Seattle: University of Washington Press, 1988.

Okihiro, Gary Y. and Joan Myers. *Whispered Silences: Japanese Americans and World War II.* Seattle: University of Washington Press, 1996.

Personal Justice Denied. Report of the Commission on Wartime Relocation and Internment of Civilians. Washington, D.C.: U.S. Government Printing Office, 1982.

Personal Justice Denied. Report of the Commission on Wartime Relocation and Internment of Civilians. Part Two. Recommendations. Washington, D.C.: U.S. Government Printing Office, 1983.

CONCENTRATION CAMPS

The term "concentration camp" was originally used during the late 19th century in what is now modern-day South Africa. From 1889 to 1902, Britain fought the Afrikaner (Dutch descendants) population of the region with the goal of retaining new resource-rich territories and expanding their imperial might on the African continent. As part of a scorched earth policy, the British military created camps to house both African and Afrikaner noncombatants, mainly women and children, among whom up to 45,000 died in captivity. The idea of the concentration camp is perhaps most often associated with the German Nazi regime's systematic detention and mass extermination of European Jews and others between 1939 and 1945. Those concentration camps were really death camps. The term concentration camp, thus, refers to the forcible confinement of a group of people not for any civil offenses they committed but simply because of their race, ethnicity, religion, and so forth. The United States has not been immune to the development and utilization of concentration camps within its borders.

On February 19, 1942, President Franklin Delano Roosevelt signed Executive Order 9066 that enabled the forcible removal and detention of all Japanese Americans residing on the West Coast of the continental United States on the basis of race. In fact, in 1936, President Roosevelt called for "concentration camps" for Japanese Americans. The president used the term correctly. Between 1942 and 1945, approximately 120,000 Japanese Americans were removed from their homes, taken to local "assembly" or "reception" centers and later confined in various "relocation" centers across the United States. In the wake of Pearl Harbor, and under the shadow of decades-long anti-Asian sentiment in North America, President Roosevelt and Lieutenant General John DeWitt took action to neutralize the supposed threats that first and second generation Japanese Americans posed to the U.S. domestic front. Across the board, Japanese Americans were considered "aliens" and "enemies," despite the fact that two-thirds were citizens and had pledged loyalty to the United States. In particular, Roosevelt and DeWitt argued that "military necessity" dictated that "relocation" and detention was prudent in order to forestall any possibility of espionage or further attack on the continental United States. However, this defensive rationale was supported by widespread racist beliefs in the basic inferiority and moral corruption of Japanese Americans, and there was no evidence of Japanese American disloyalty.

The U.S. government's design and implementation of the concentration camp system grew out of past federal efforts to relocate and segregate ethnic and racial minorities across the country. The civilian director of the War Relocation Authority (WRA), Dillon Myer, worked as director for the Bureau of Indian Affairs (BIA) after the war. Some relocation centers were located on or near BIA land. The forcible removal of American Indians, their confinement to reservations, and the BIA's "termination" policy under Myer are examples of federal acts of relocation, segregation, and assimilation. In addition, the democratic governing strategies and disciplinary security systems developed under the WRA would be used for decades to come, including in the establishment of detention camps for civil rights activists during the Cold War, and the present-day creation of detention centers supporting America's War on Terror, such as the numerous prisons for immigrants in the United States and the center at Guantanamo Bay.

The beauty of the mountains contrasts with the bleak barracks at Manzanar concentration camp. (Library of Congress)

WRA concentration camps were located across the country in Arizona, Arkansas, California, Colorado, Idaho, Utah, and Wyoming. Along with those large-scale facilities, which ranged from a minimum of 7,500 acres to over 20,000 acres of land each, the national system also included a number of transitional centers that housed thousands of recently apprehended Japanese Americans in the process of permanent placement. These "assembly centers" were often located in reclaimed horse race tracks, fairgrounds, migrant workers' camps, and other large facilities and spanned the entire West Coast, including Puyallup in Washington, Portland in Oregon, Mayer in Arizona, as well as a number in California, namely Fresno, Marysville, Merced, Pinedale, Pomona, Sacramento, Salinas, Santa Anita, Stockton, Tanforan, Tulare, and Turlock.

Life in the concentration camps was dangerous, laborious, and generally dehumanizing. Although evacuees lost hundreds of millions of dollars worth of property during the war, their loss of homes and livelihood was little punishment compared to the extreme sense of alienation, psychological trauma, and dislocation that characterized the experience of confinement. Traveling to concentration camps in unknown geographic locations, many evacuees feared for their life, making direct comparisons between the horrors they had heard of across the Atlantic and their own experiences. Upon arrival at the camps, the majority of which were in rugged, isolated landscapes, detainees were fingerprinted, medically examined, asked to swear loyalty to the United States, and accept the terms of forced labor at low wages. Individuals were housed in primitive accommodations in flimsy and uninsulated barracks made of tar-paper, pinewood, and celotex that offered little to no shelter from the harsh weather conditions and provided absolutely no privacy. High winds, dust, fire, and infectious disease were constant threats to the sustainability and quality of life of Japanese Americans in the camps. Communication and news from the outside world were limited and subject to search and surveillance. Initially fresh food and water were also hard to come by, but as internees began to forge community and organize democratic leadership these concerns would lessen.

Despite serious hardship and life-threatening conditions, Japanese Americans initiated systematic and well-organized efforts to maintain a "normal" life under a state of exception. This increased level of Japanese American participation in the daily life and upkeep of the concentration camps might be partly due to the more laissez-faire attitude of civilian bureaucrats who managed the day-to-day operations of the camps. Yet these improvements should be most duly credited to the perseverance and dedication of the Japanese Americans themselves, particularly those who organized crucial institutions in spite of the disciplinary and persecutory framework of confinement. Japanese Americans created hospitals, fire patrols, building crews, schools, theaters, farms and husbandry organizations, and other social groups that made camp life bearable. In one ironically poignant episode at Poston concentration camp in Arizona, residents slaughtered their own turkeys and decorated the barracks with hand-made cherry-blossom ornaments to celebrate Thanksgiving, all under the shadow of barbed wire and military guard posts.

The culture of the camps thus incorporated a paradoxical conformity to American patriotism and wartime ideology that existed in stark tension with the continuous presence of communal struggle and harrowing acts of self-determination. Faced with the foreclosure of those unalienable rights that are sanctified under the U.S. Constitution, many organized peaceful and sometimes actively defiant protest. Collective actions ranged from covert and habitual everyday activities to overt acts of civil disobedience. Many camps witnessed labor strikes and slow-downs. Generally, internees continued to observe cultural rituals and customs essential to Japanese American life when the WRA tried to assimilate Japanese Americans into majority, mainstream culture. And most dramatically, a number of Japanese American men resisted military conscription, refusing to take on this duty when so egregiously being denied those basic rights due to all other American citizens who were drafted to serve. Perhaps the most enduring legacy of the history of America's concentration camps remains the Japanese Americans' palpable spirit of collectivism, which fueled widespread efforts of social and cultural resistance within the camps and later movements for redress.

Jenny M. James

References

Daniels, Roger. *Concentration Camps: North America: Japanese in the United States and Canada during World War II.* Malabar, Florida: Robert E. Krieger, 1981.

Dickerson, James L. *Inside America's Concentration Camps: Two Centuries of Internment and Torture.* Chicago: Lawrence Hill Books, 2010.

Girdner, Audrie and Anne Loftis. *The Great Betrayal: The Evacuation of the Japanese-Americans during World War II.* London: Macmillan, 1969.

Saunders, Christopher. "South African War." In *Oxford Encyclopedia of the Modern World.* Edited by Peter N. Stearns. Oxford: Oxford University Press, 2008.

D

D'AQUINO, IVA TOGURI (1916–2006)

Born in Los Angeles on July 4, 1916, Iva Toguri was the daughter of Japanese American migrants, Jun and Fumi Toguri. Jun Toguri had migrated to the United States in 1899, and Toguri's mother, Fumi, arrived in 1913. Toguri was reared a Methodist, and she joined the Girl Scout as a child. She attended school in Mexico and San Diego before returning to her family in Los Angeles. After high school, Toguri attended the University of California, Los Angeles, and graduated with a degree in zoology.

Toguri was caught in Japan at the outbreak of World War II. She had left the United States for Japan in June 1941 about six months before the war to tend to an ill aunt. Toguri did not have a passport but a certificate of identification, which al lowed her to stay for six months in Japan. While caring for her aunt, Toguri visited the U.S. consulate in Tokyo to submit a passport application, which was rejected for lack of documentation. She was thus denied passage to the United States in October 1941, and on the first repatriation ship that left shortly after Pearl Harbor. She tried again about a year later in September 1942 but was unable to pay the passage after having been hospitalized for malnutrition. Consequently, Toguri, like many other Japanese Americans, spent the duration of the war in Japan.

The Japanese Security Police harassed Toguri because she was an American. Friends and family members urged her to become a Japanese citizen but she refused. She was classified as an "enemy alien," and was denied a war ration card. To sustain herself, Toguri worked as a part-time typist for the Overseas Bureau of NHK (Japan Broadcasting Corporation) in August 1943. A few months later, because of her skills in English language, the Japanese government ordered her to broadcast on Radio Tokyo like other Allied prisoners of war. Some of them assured Toguri she could actually help the U.S. war effort by comforting U.S. troops with American music and softening Japan's propaganda. While working for the Domei News Agency, Toguri met Filipe J. D'Aquino, a Japanese and Portuguese biracial citizen of Portugal, and they were married in April 1945. Toguri converted to Catholicism but declined her husband's Portuguese citizenship.

Toguri was one of 14 English-speaking radio announcers at Radio Tokyo, yet she alone was accused and tried for treason. She was, according to her accusers, Tokyo Rose, a name invented by U.S. soldiers for the alluring woman whose voice on the radio seduced them. In fact, Toguri hosted about 340 shows of *The Zero Hour* under the name "Ann" for announcer and later, "Orphan Annie" for the comic strip or a reference to orphans, the name given to troops separated from their units in battle. Toguri performed comedy sketches and introduced musical

San Francisco attorney Wayne Collins worked diligently to preserve Japanese American civil liberties. Here he assists Iva Toguri D'Aquino. (AP Photo)

recordings. For her 20-minute broadcasts, Toguri earned 150 yen or about seven dollars a month. She used some of her earnings to buy and smuggle in food to Allied prisoners of war.

After Japan's surrender and during the U.S. Occupation of that country, Toguri was entrapped by an offer of $2,000, the equivalent of a year's wage in Occupied Japan, to sell her story as "Tokyo Rose." In October 1945, the U.S. military promptly arrested her for trying to demoralize U.S. troops during the war. After spending a year in jail, she was released because the Federal Bureau of Investigation (FBI) and military investigators found no evidence to sustain the charge. Still, a prominent journalist, Walter Winchell, a member of the racist Native Sons of the Golden West, pressured the U.S. State Department to charge Toguri for treason. In Japan, the United States rearrested Toguri and imprisoned her in August 1948, and the following month sent her to San Francisco to stand trial in the United States.

The trial, begun in July 1949, was, at the time, the longest and costliest in U.S. history. San Francisco attorney Wayne Collins served on the team that defended Toguri, and she and her witnesses claimed her broadcasts aided the U.S. cause. In September 1949, despite an exhaustive five-year FBI investigation, which decided the evidence failed to warrant a prosecution, the San Francisco grand jury found Toguri guilty of speaking "into the microphone concerning the loss of [U.S.] ships" (Hirose, 149). For that, she was convicted of treason, had her citizenship revoked, fined $10,000, and sentenced to a 10-year term in prison. Collins, her attorney, remarked that the verdict was guilt "without evidence."

Toguri spent over six years in the Federal Reformatory for Women in West Virginia, was released in January 1956, and moved to Chicago where her father had begun a Japanese import business after his release from Gila River concentration camp in Arizona. The government continued to pursue Toguri when in April 1956 the Immigration and Naturalization Service tried to deport her to Japan. She, with the help of attorney Collins, fought the order successfully. She worked quietly in

Chicago to 1975 when Clifford Uyeda and the Japanese American Citizens League lobbied for a presidential pardon for her. The campaign succeeded in 1977 when President Gerald Ford pardoned her and thereby restored her U.S. citizenship. Investigations had found some of her key accusers had lied under oath when they testified and the FBI and the army pressured them into offering perjured testimony. In 2006, the World War II Veterans Committee awarded Toguri its annual Edward J. Herlihy Citizenship Award, citing "her indomitable spirit, love of country, and the example of courage she has given her fellow Americans."

Gary Y. Okihiro

Reference

Hirose, Stacey. "Iva Ikuko Toguri d'Aquino." In *Encyclopedia of Japanese American History*, pp. 148–50. Edited by Brian Niiya. New York: Facts On File, 2001.

DAY OF REMEMBRANCE

For decades after World War II, Americans worked hard to forget the painful memories of Japanese American internment. Thanks to a group of dedicated Japanese Americans, this systematic erasure of that history was challenged in 1978. In November 1978, the first Day of Remembrance was held at the Puyallup Fairgrounds, the site of what was formerly known as Camp Harmony in Washington State. On Thanksgiving weekend, more than 2,000 participants reenacted the evacuation of hundreds of Japanese American citizens residing in the Seattle-Tacoma metropolitan area over three decades before. Paying tribute to the suffering and persecution Japanese Americans endured during the war, the event raised awareness of this difficult history and created a renewed sense of solidarity among members of the Japanese American community.

Extending its scope beyond nonviolent protest or demonstration, the first Day of Remembrance featured collective activities that mixed historical reenactment, street theater, and political assembly. Its dramatic character was in part due to the professional background of its founders, Chinese American playwright Frank Chin and sansei actor, journalist, and activist Frank Abe. Chin and Abe spearheaded the campaign, approaching the Seattle Evacuation Redress Committee with a proposal to recreate the scenes and conditions of Japanese American removal during the war. Various generations, genders, and ethnicities came together to perform this collective ritual. Upon their arrival at gathering places around the Seattle area, participants were given manila name tags similar to those internees were required to wear during the war. Former evacuees wrote their own identification numbers on these cards. Then participants, led by military escort, processed in buses and cars to the recreated Camp Harmony on the Puyallup Fairgrounds. Upon their admittance through a symbolic barbed-wire fence, men and women congregated to listen to speakers and entertainers who bore witness to everyday life in the camps. There were readings of personal memoirs written of the camps, political calls for redress by local leaders, historical accounts of the events that led up to the creation of America's concentration camps, and personal oral histories of camp survivors.

This event received extensive local and national media attention; local television stations, the Associated Press, the *Pacific Citizen,* and other news outlets covered the event. The first Day of Remembrance did much to increase the visibility and efficacy of the national redress and reparations movement, which in the late 1970s was just beginning to make headway. It encouraged Seattle mayor Charles Royer to sign a resolution in support of the cause, as well as initiating Governor Dixie Lee Ray to call for an official Day of Remembrance in Washington State. Perhaps most importantly, however, was the effect the events had in revitalizing a sense of ethnic solidarity and group cohesion within the Japanese American community. More than any other event, the public collective nature of the day's events inspired crucial efforts at intergeneration dialogue among family members, who had for decades kept these experiences silent.

Since 1978, the Day of Remembrance activities have grown nationwide. The day is officially observed on February 19, the date President Franklin Roosevelt signed into law Executive Order 9066 that authorized the exclusion and concentration of Japanese Americans during the war. Each year, commemorative events are held across the country, in Japanese American neighborhood centers, at churches, on college campuses, at museums, and in the nation's capital. Activities include, but are not limited to, candlelight ceremonies, film screenings, poetry readings, political rallies, and art exhibits. Throughout the 1980s and 1990s, these memorials were paired with various reunions that took place at such concentration camps as Manzanar, Tule Lake, and others. These outings were organized in part to bring together former camp internees as a community and renew long lost friendships. By creating an opportunity for collective memory, personal reflection, and public education, these events work to ensure that this terrible history never will be repeated.

Jenny M. James

References

Maki, Mitchell T., Harry H.L. Kitano, and S. Megan Berthold. *Achieving the Impossible Dream: How Japanese Americans Obtained Redress.* Urbana: University of Illinois Press, 1999.

Murray, Alice Yang. *Historical Memories of the Japanese American Internment and the Struggle for Redress.* Stanford, CA: Stanford University Press, 2008.

Shimabukuro, Robert Sadamu. *Born in Seattle: The Campaign for Japanese American Redress.* Seattle: University of Washington Press, 2001.

Takezawa, Yasuko I. *Breaking the Silence: Redress and Japanese American Ethnicity.* Ithaca, NY: Cornell University Press, 1995.

DENATIONALIZATION ACT

In July 1944, the U.S. Congress passed the Denationalization Act (Public Law 405), which allowed individuals of Japanese descent to voluntarily renounce their U.S. citizenship. This unprecedented act emerged out of a historic moment of heightened conflict and instability in the concentration camps, particularly at Tule Lake, which was by then a segregation center. By 1943, internees who had been deemed disloyal to the U.S. government, indicating "their desire to follow the Japanese way of life," were transferred to this large camp in northern California. The number of Japanese Americans officially segregated from the ostensibly loyal and patriotic American internees amounted to at least 12,000, including another 4,000 family members of the "disloyal." These individuals were barred from seeking relocation out of the camps and faced more stringent rules and disciplinary procedures than other internees.

The government's segregation of seemingly "enemy aliens" from mainstream camp life inspired a militancy and resistance in the camps. In particular, the resegregation movement emerged as an outlet for many Japanese Americans who felt understandably betrayed and angered by the injustices that they faced during the war. At Tule Lake, two major resegregant organizations grew out of this feeling of communal resentment: the Sokoku Kenkyu Seinen Dana (Young Men's Association for the Study of the Motherland) and the Sokuji Kikoku Hoshi Dan (Society for Immediate Return to Serve the Motherland).

These organizations were ideologically diverse and drew upon pro-Japanese propaganda that prophesized an inevitable victory against the United States. Members of these groups inspired other camp inmates to reclaim their Japanese heritage, instituted Japanese style schools, and organized nationalist exercises in support of the Japanese government. While these resistant strategies were in truth mainly nonviolent, the camps were not immune to conflict or even combat, as was seen in the November 1943 Tule Lake uprising that was spurred by the death of an internee leading to martial law or military control of the camp.

Seeking to neutralize the growing resistance within the camps and perhaps even get rid of undesirable aliens, Attorney General Francis Biddle and other high-ranking officials of President Franklin Roosevelt's administration sought to create a legal pathway for individuals to renounce their U.S. citizenship. Once individuals officially gave up their citizenship, they could be classified as "illegal aliens" and therefore blocked from reintegrating into American society after internment. Ironically, the Denationalization Act, originally known as the Allen bill, was passed in lieu of more punitive measures that would have immediately nullified the citizenship rights of "disloyals" or even tried them for treason. The act, instead, put the onus on the internees themselves to decide their own fate and renounce their U.S. citizenship. By rescinding their legal allegiance to the United States, many individuals were faced with the risk of becoming stateless, depending on the outcome of the war.

While on the surface the Denationalization Act was meant to give individuals the freedom to repatriate to Japan and rescind ties with the United States if they so chose, it actually created a backdoor opportunity for the government to better police militant or resistant Japanese Americans. The U.S. government was surprised by the great number of renunciants, many of whom had not voiced anti-American sentiment or had not been officially members of "pro-Japan" organizations prior to their application. Over 70 percent of the issei in Tule Lake renounced their U.S. citizenship and in all of the camps a total of 3,186 individuals applied for denationalization. John Burling, a special assistant to the attorney general, held hearings at Tule Lake to rule on each application and after three months of proceedings in 1945, the majority of applications were accepted. Ironically, to renounce one's affiliation with the United States allowed many to stay in the camps, remain part of a community, and avoid the hostility of the American citizenry outside the camps' fences.

By the spring of 1945, some renunciants began to regret their decision and sought to withdraw their application. Some renunciants had made the decision to give up their citizenship in anger, fear, or for want of any viable path toward legal redress for the grievances they were forced to endure. Faced with the reality of deportation, and the pressing fact that the United States was posed to win the war, many renunciants now began the difficult and seemingly impossible fight to reclaim their rights as U.S. citizens. By the war's end, some 6,200 Japanese Americans were deported to Japan, and of that total between 1,800 and 2,000 were renunciants.

Thankfully, in 1946, attorney Wayne Collins and other lawyers for the American Civil Liberties Union took up the fight to restore their citizenship. In November of that year, Collins filed lawsuits against the U.S. Justice Department and successfully delayed deportation. He argued that the renunciants had acted under duress and coercion produced by the extraordinary circumstances of their own illegal internment. In the end, it was not until 1959 that these cases were resolved. Out of 3,186 requests for the reversal of renunciation, 2,780 were accepted. Although often overlooked within the history of internment, the Denationalization Act and renunciation hearings are an important reminder of the anxieties over citizenship and national belonging that were foundational to the development of the dehumanizing policy of internment and exclusion.

Jenny M. James

References

Girdner, Audrie and Anne Loftis. *The Great Betrayal: The Evacuation of the Japanese-Americans during World War II.* London: Macmillan, 1969.

Ngai, Mae M. *Impossible Subjects: Illegal Aliens and the Making of Modern America.* Princeton: Princeton University Press, 2004.

Robinson, Greg. *A Tragedy of Democracy: Japanese Confinement in North America.* New York: Columbia University Press, 2010.

DEWITT, JOHN L. (1880-1962)

John DeWitt, who rose to the rank of lieutenant general, was born on January 9, 1880, in Fort Sidney, Nebraska. Reared on army posts, DeWitt left Princeton University during his sophomore year for a career in the military. He joined the U.S. Army as second lieutenant during the Spanish-American War, and remained in the army for nearly 50 years, serving in both World Wars I and II.

Before World War I, DeWitt spent three tours of duty in the Philippines. From 1914 to 1917, he worked in the office of quartermaster general in Washington,

D.C. During World War I, he served as director of supply and transportation for the First Army Corps in France. At the end of the war, he was awarded the Distinguished Service Medal, and as a colonel served in the Army's War Plans Division as its assistant chief of staff. In 1930, DeWitt was appointed to quartermaster general, and in 1937 he served as the commandant of the Army War College. Two years later in 1939, DeWitt was promoted to commander of the Fourth Army at the Presidio of San Francisco, and assumed control over the Western Defense Command.

During the 1920s, as acting assistant chief of staff in the War Plans Division, DeWitt worked on a plan called the "Defense of Oahu" concerning the Hawaiian Islands. In that document, which anticipated war with Japan, DeWitt recommended actions for defending the island against its Japanese American civilian population. He proposed the declaration of martial law, suspension of civil liberties under military rule, registration of all enemy aliens, internment of those considered to pose a threat to security, and restrictions on labor, movement, and public information. Military necessity, DeWitt argued, would justify those extraordinary measures because "the establishment of complete military control over the Hawaiian Islands, including its people, supplies, material, etc., is highly desirable." Martial law, DeWitt contended, would secure the islands and enable the military to control and direct labor for the benefit of the war effort (Okihiro, 124).

After Japan's attack on Pearl Harbor on December 7, 1941, DeWitt wrote to the War Department that to defend the Pacific Coast, the area of his command, the army needed to establish broad civil control, antisabotage and counterespionage measures, and the removal of all persons of Japanese ancestry. "Military necessity" justified those measures, DeWitt maintained, because of the surprise attack at Pearl Harbor. His recommendations for the West Coast at the start of the U.S. entry into World War II bore a remarkable likeness to the plans he developed for the defense of the island of Oahu in the early 1920s.

DeWitt observed that intelligence reports showed the existence of hundreds of Japanese American organizations in California, Washington, Oregon, and Arizona that allegedly were actively engaged in advancing Japanese war aims. DeWitt pointed to the thousands of American-born Japanese who had gone to Japan to receive their education and thus became, presumably, pro-Japan. Their loyalties, DeWitt believed, were suspect.

A key figure in DeWitt's decision making was Karl Bendetsen who was sent from the army's provost marshall's office in Washington, D.C. to advise DeWitt on matters concerning aliens and Japanese Americans specifically. Although DeWitt distrusted the loyalty of Japanese Americans, he wavered in his position concerning actions to contain them. Thus, in January 1942, DeWitt declared: "I have little confidence that the enemy aliens are law-abiding or loyal in any sense of the word. Some of them yes; many, no. Particularly the Japanese. I have no confidence in their loyalty whatsoever" (Daniels, 45–46). At the same time, he hesitated about the need for a mass, forcible removal of all Japanese Americans from his command. Instead, in January 1942, DeWitt was thinking of evicting Japanese Americans only from areas surrounding a few strategic installations. Bendetsen and the provost marshal's office pushed for a mass removal from the entire Western Defense Command, and by February 1942, Bendetsen had converted DeWitt to his view.

On February 19, 1942, President Franklin Roosevelt issued Executive Order 9066, which authorized the army under DeWitt to prescribe military areas for the protection of vital installations against sabotage and espionage, and remove "any and all persons" from those zones. "Military necessity" prompted EO 9066, the president wrote, and he authorized the military to provide "transportation, food, shelter, and other accommodations as may be necessary . . . until other arrangements are made." DeWitt proceeded to implement the order.

The commander issued Proclamation 1 on March 2, 1942, dividing Washington, Oregon, California, and Arizona into two military areas, 1 and 2. Military Area 1 was further divided into a "prohibited zone," essentially a strip along the Pacific coastline and Mexican border, and a larger "restricted zone" adjacent to it. In addition, he named 98 strategic installations as prohibited zones to German, Italian, and Japanese aliens and "any person of Japanese ancestry." Japanese Americans were prohibited as an entire group. Military Area 2 contained no such prohibitions or zones.

DeWitt issued other proclamations establishing an 8 P.M. to 6 A.M. military curfew throughout Military Area 1 for all enemy aliens and all persons of Japanese ancestry. Another proclamation regulated the movement of the targeted people within Military Area 1, and yet another forbade Japanese Americans from leaving Military Area 1 where most of them lived. On March 24, 1942, DeWitt issued the first of his Civilian Exclusion Orders that began the forced removal of all Japanese Americans from the West Coast. Those actions began with Japanese Americans on Bainbridge Island near Seattle, and they worked their way southward to encompass the entire Japanese American population on the West Coast.

DeWitt put Bendetsen in charge of the operation, making him the head of the Wartime Civil Control Administration (WCCA), which was set up on March 11, 1942, to handle the army's forced evictions. "Instructions to All Japanese Living on Bainbridge Island" appeared on posts and in public areas, directing the island's Japanese Americans to settle their affairs and prepare for a departure from their homes. The instructions told them to pack bedding, clothing, eating plates and utensils, and toilet articles for each family member, but they could only take what they could carry. All the rest, the family's possessions of a lifetime had to be sold or stored entirely at the risk of the owner. The 54 Japanese American families on Bainbridge Island had just six days to get ready.

The army loaded the exiled Japanese Americans onto trains, and transported them to an assembly center at Puyallup Fairgrounds in Washington State. There, they were joined by others as the WCCA forcibly evicted Japanese Americans from their homes. The process was repeated 107 times from Washington to California based upon Bendetsen and his staff's systematic division of the West Coast into 108 areas for Japanese American exclusion, each area containing about a thousand people. By June 5, 1942, the army succeeded in removing all Japanese Americans from Military Areas 1 and 2.

DeWitt served as the head of the Western Defense Command until September 10, 1943, when he was relieved of his command. He was awarded a second Distinguished Service Medal for his service, and was assigned to head the Army and Navy Staff College in Washington, D.C. DeWitt retired in June 1947, and on June 20, 1962, at the age of 82, he died of a heart attack in Washington, D.C., and was buried in Arlington National Cemetery.

Carrie M. Montgomery

References

Daniels, Roger. *Concentration Camps: North America: Japanese in the United States and Canada during World War II*. Malabar, FL: Robert E. Krieger, 1981.

Okihiro, Gary Y. *Cane Fires: The Anti-Japanese Movement in Hawaii, 1865–1945*. Philadelphia: Temple University Press, 1991.

E

EISENHOWER, MILTON S. (1899–1985)

Younger brother of U.S. president Dwight D. Eisenhower and first director of the War Relocation Authority (WRA), which administered the Japanese American concentration camps, Milton Eisenhower was born in Abilene, Kansas, on September 15, 1899. He was the youngest of seven children who were all sons. Eisenhower attended public schools and in 1923, he graduated with a bachelor's degree in journalism from Kansas State University. He taught journalism until 1925, and went on to serve as U.S. vice counsel to Scotland. From 1928 to 1941, he was the information director for the Department of Agriculture under Secretary William M. Jardine. Although trained as a journalist with no military experience, President Franklin Roosevelt appointed Eisenhower director of the WRA in March 1942.

After the attack on Pearl Harbor, President Roosevelt signed Executive Order 9066 on February 19, 1942, authorizing the military to remove and provide for anyone under the powers of "military necessity." Later, the president issued an executive order that established the WRA, and named Eisenhower as its first director. Per the order, Eisenhower's responsibility was to "set up a War Relocation Authority to move the Japanese Americans off the Pacific Coast" (Eisenhower, 95).

At the time, Eisenhower knew very little about the problem of Japanese Americans on the West Coast. He was aware of rumors about a possible invasion by Japan of the Pacific Coast, and had heard about the hearings held to discuss a program of "national defense migration." Despite his ignorance of the situation, he was in charge of the government agency responsible for planning and implementing the mass removal and detention of some 120,000 Japanese Americans.

Eisenhower quickly concluded that the forcible, mass eviction of Japanese Americans was unwarranted and extreme. However, he "spent little time pondering the moral implications of the President's decision," Eisenhower later wrote (Eisenhower, 97), explaining, "it was clear to me that the question was not whether to evacuate the Japanese Americans (since that process was already under way) but rather how to carry out their relocation to the interior" (Eisenhower, 112). The WRA director was determined to carry out his duty as effectively and humanely as possible.

Eisenhower described his first three months as WRA director a nightmare. He had to staff the WRA. He looked at the Department of Agriculture where he had previously worked and the Department of Interior's Indian Service for models for his agency. Eisenhower attended numerous meetings, and traveled back

Milton Eisenhower (1899–1985) was the first director of the War Relocation Authority. He reportedly told his successor he could not sleep because of the troubling nature of the job. (AP Photo/George R. Skadding)

and forth from Washington to San Francisco, leaving him with little time to sleep. He also seemed bothered by the unsavory nature of the entire program, according to a story told by his successor, Dillon S. Myer.

Eisenhower struggled with the necessity of a complete, forcible removal of Japanese Americans, an alternative offered by government officials after the failure of a voluntary "evacuation." Eisenhower had hoped instead for an exclusion policy in which "only men were evacuated [and] the women and children remain in their homes" (Eisenhower, 116). Regardless of his personal opinion, Eisenhower, felt pressed for time, noting "the longer the WRA took to develop a relocation center, the longer the evacuees would be kept in the assembly centers along the coast" (Eisenhower, 119). He knew that the assembly centers were "makeshift quarters of tar paper shacks thrown up at racetracks and fairgrounds. There was virtually no privacy, conditions were primitive, with overcrowding and minimal facilities" (Eisenhower, 119).

By June 5, 1942, Eisenhower secured 10 sites for the WRA's concentration camps. These were on government property, and were able to hold at least 5,000 people, and as was required by "military necessity," they were located away from strategic installations. The WRA director explained: "we called the relocation camps 'evacuation centers.' Never did we think of them as concentration camps" (Eisenhower, 122).

While he disagreed with the forced, mass removal, Eisenhower was proud of some of his initiatives. He met with a group of Japanese Americans and established an advisory council to represent those affected by the evictions. He noted that this was the wisest thing he did as WRA director. To ensure that Japanese American students complete their college education, he asked the American Friends Service Committee's Clarence Pickett to recruit leading university educators to form the National Japanese Student Relocation Council. The council relocated nisei students from the camps to college campuses. Eisenhower also tried to protect Japanese American assets by having the Federal Reserve Bank in California guarantee the property and savings of those affected by the camps. That agreement failed to stop the millions of dollars lost by Japanese Americans during the war.

Of the wartime experience, Eisenhower wrote: "thousands of American citizens of Japanese ancestry were stripped of their rights and freedoms and treated almost like enemy prisoners of war. Many lost their homes, their business, their savings . . . [it] was a bad dream come to pass." Eisenhower believed that the mass removal might have been avoided. In his memoir, he asked, "How could such a tragedy have occurred in a democratic society that prides itself on individual rights and freedoms? How could responsible leaders make such a fateful decision?" He conceded that the forcible, mass removal and detention was an "inhumane event" (Eisenhower, 125).

In mid-July 1942, Eisenhower left the directorship of the WRA to serve as associate director for the Office of War Information, a post he held from 1942 to 1943. Dillon S. Myer assumed the role as WRA director. In a memorandum to the president, Eisenhower noted that the future of the WRA program "will doubtless be governed largely by the temper of the American public opinion," and, he added, the American people will hopefully "grow toward a better appreciation of the essential Americanism of a great majority of the evacuees" (Eisenhower, 123). Finally, Eisenhower recommended that Congress enact "a special program for the evacuees to help them find their place in American life after the war" (Eisenhower, 124).

After 19 years in the government, Eisenhower left the nation's capital to devote most of his time to education. On July 1, 1943, at the age of 43, Eisenhower became the president of Kansas State University, the institution where he had spent his years as an undergraduate. Eisenhower went on to serve as president of Pennsylvania State University (1950–1956) and Johns Hopkins University (1956–1967 and 1971–1972).

Eisenhower is remembered today as a government official and educator. He advised eight U.S. presidents, and worked as a high-level official for Presidents Calvin Coolidge, Herbert Hoover, and Franklin Roosevelt. He chaired five presidential commissions including the Commission on the Cause and Prevention of Crime during the start of the 1960s urban riots. He also served as a special ambassador to Latin America. Thirty-two U.S. and five foreign universities awarded Eisenhower 37 honorary degrees.

On May 2, 1985, Milton Eisenhower died in Baltimore, Maryland, from cancer.

Carrie M. Montgomery

Reference

Eisenhower, Milton S. *The President Is Calling.* Garden City, NY: Doubleday, 1974.

ENDO, MITSUYE (1920–2006)

A nisei, Mitsuye Endo successfully pursued *Ex parte Mitsuye Endo* 323 U.S. 283 (1944), a *writ of habeas corpus* (a lawsuit asking the court to examine whether the government has a right to detain someone or not), demanding her release from first, Tule Lake concentration camp and, then Topaz concentration camp. She challenged the government's right to detain citizens who the government already had determined to be loyal. Unlike the other better-known court cases surrounding the World War II experience of Japanese Americans where criminal charges were filed against the plaintiff for refusing to go to the camps, Endo filed the lawsuit after arriving at Tule Lake to try to leave the camp. The court also ruled differently in her case; the U.S. Supreme Court in 1945 ordered her unconditional release, and concluded that the government could not hold, intern, or jail a citizen that the government itself deems is loyal to the United States.

One of four children, Endo was born and raised in Sacramento, California, attending both elementary and high school there. Endo was a typist at the California Department of Motor Vehicles, because as Endo noted in an oral history, "there was so much discrimination against the Japanese Americans, the only position we could get was with the state, unless we worked for a Japanese firm" (Tateishi, 60).

In early 1942, state employees of Japanese ancestry, including 22-year-old Endo, were dismissed from their jobs; the state specifically cited the employees' ancestry as the reason for their dismissals. In response, along with her colleagues who also worked for the state and were already members of the Japanese American Citizens League (JACL), she joined the JACL. Through the members' efforts, they decided to hire James Purcell, an attorney from San Francisco, to represent them. At that time, Purcell was interested in finding U.S. citizens of Japanese ancestry who worked for the government to challenge the legality of dismissing government employees based on their ancestry.

When President Franklin Roosevelt signed Executive Order 9066 in February 1942, Endo was forcibly removed to the Walarga Assembly Center near Sacramento for a month (not Tanforan Assembly Center in San Bruno, contrary to popular belief), and then taken to Tule Lake concentration camp. While at Tule Lake, Purcell's representatives approached Endo and other detainees about filing a case to test whether it was constitutional to detain loyal citizens. The representatives found her to be a suitable candidate for such a lawsuit: her brother was drafted into the U.S. Army and her parents had remained in the United States since migrating, which, the representatives determined, demonstrated Endo's loyalty to the United States. Originally, Endo was reluctant to file the lawsuit. She recalled, "I was very young and I was very shy . . . when they [the representatives] came and asked me about it, I said, well, can't you have someone else do it first." Only until after the representatives argued that "it's for the good of everybody," she agreed even though she never met Purcell. Her petition was filed in July 1942 (Tateishi, 61).

On February 19, 1943, on the anniversary of EO 9066, Endo and her attorney applied for clearance from the government to leave Tule Lake. By the time her application was approved, she had already been moved to the Topaz camp. While the government approved of her leaving, acknowledging that the government was not holding her on a charge or even a suspicion of disloyalty, the government set conditions on her release. The government limited her employment and relocation options; the government refused to allow Endo to return to the West Coast, where she was originally from. Furthermore, if Endo had agreed to leave Topaz, she would have to agree to drop the lawsuit because she no longer could pursue a lawsuit about her detention if she were no longer detained. Even though she "was anxious to have my case settled, because most of my friends had already gone out, been relocated, and I was anxious to get out too," Endo remained at the camp until she was given freedom without conditions (Tateishi, 61).

In July 1943, the U.S. District Court, Northern District of California, denied Endo's petition, and the Court of Appeals for the Ninth Circuit affirmed that denial a month later. The case then went on to the U.S. Supreme Court. Though *Ex parte Endo* had been unanimously decided by the Supreme Court, agreeing that she was a loyal citizen and "Mitsuye Endo is entitled to an unconditional release by the War Relocation Authority" on October 16, 1944, the chief justice waited until December 18 to announce the court's decision in *Ex parte Endo* and in *Korematsu v. U.S.* simultaneously. The day before, on December 17, the army had already announced that loyal Japanese Americans would be allowed to return to the West Coast by January 2, 1945. Nevertheless, the Supreme Court stated clearly that the government could not detain a loyal citizen; however, the court failed to address the constitutionality of whether the government could detain anyone based on their ancestry.

After spending three years in Topaz, Endo relocated to Chicago in June 1945. Living in the Chicago suburbs for the rest of her life, she worked as an executive secretary, married Kenneth Tsutsumi, and reared three children. Upon reflecting on her experience, she expressed surprise that her case made it to the Supreme Court, "I thought it might have been thrown out of court because of all the bad sentiment toward us. . . . I'm awed by it. I never believed it, that I would be the one. . . . Do I have any regrets at all about the test case? No, not now, because of the way it turned out" (Tateishi, 61). According to her daughter, while Endo told stories of living in barracks under the supervision of armed guards, she did not talk about her case, unless asked. Endo was a very private person, "a person who has not wanted to draw attention to herself," Bill Yoshino, the Midwest director of the JACL, noted in 2004 when it honored Endo at a benefit celebrating the sixtieth anniversary of the JACL Chicago chapter.

Endo passed away at the age of 85 on April 14, 2006, in Willowbrook, Illinois.

Belle Yan

References

Daniels, Roger. "The Japanese American Cases, 1942–2004: A Social History." *Law and Contemporary Problems* 68(2) (2005): 159–71. Accessed February 11, 2012. http://www.jstor.org/stable/27592097

Ex Parte Mitsuye Endo, 323 U.S. 283 (1944) http://laws.findlaw.com/us/323/283.html

Noel, Josh. "Mitsuye Tsutsumi." *Chicago Tribune,* April 25, 2006. Accessed February 11, 2012. http://articles.chicagotribune.com/2006–04–25/news/0604250259_1_supreme-court-japanese-american-population-japanese-american-citizens-league

O'Hara, Delia. "A Wartime Story of a Brave American." *Chicago Sun-Times,* December 9, 2004. Accessed February 11, 2012. http://www.lexisnexis.com.ezproxy.cul.columbia.edu/hottopics/lnacademic

Tateishi, John. "Mitsuye Endo—Topaz." In *And Justice for All: An Oral History of the Japanese American Detention Camps,* 60–61. Seattle: University of Washington Press, 1984.

EVACUATION

"Evacuation" is used incorrectly to refer to the forced eviction of some 120,000 Japanese Americans from their homes during World War II. The term, "evacuation," connotes an emergency removal for the safety of those leaving an area of danger for a place of safety. Also, it usually involves people willing to leave an area in their self-interest. Instead, the forcible eviction was justified by "military necessity," which was not because Japanese Americans were endangered but because the government and military considered Japanese Americans to be a potential source of danger to the national security. Moreover, Japanese Americans were placed in concentration camps not for their safety; after all, barbed wire fences were not erected to keep intruders out but to keep Japanese Americans in and armed sentries had orders to shoot not outsiders but Japanese Americans seeking to leave the camp's confines.

Under the powers granted it by President Franklin Roosevelt's Executive Order 9066, the military issued proclamations, the first dated March 2, 1941, which divided the states of Washington, Oregon, California, and Arizona into two military areas. Military Area No. 1 was subdivided into a "prohibited zone," the West Coast and a strip of land along the Mexican border, and a larger "restricted zone" surrounding the prohibited zone. In addition, the proclamation designated 98 other prohibited zones, namely military installations, power plants, and other places of strategic interest. The two zones applied to Japanese, German, and Italian aliens and "any person of Japanese Ancestry," and an accompanying press release explained the eventual exclusion of all Japanese Americans from Military Area No. 1 and all prohibited zones.

The first "evacuation" was directed by the Navy at Japanese Americans living on Terminal Island in the port of Los Angeles. Five days before EO 9066, Navy secretary Frank Knox served eviction notices to mainly fishermen and cannery workers, giving them a month to vacate their homes. Adjacent was Long Beach Naval Station, the secretary noted, and fishermen knew the coastal waters and had shortwave radios, making them prime suspects in the Navy's view. Many of the men had already been taken in Federal Bureau of Investigation (FBI) sweeps in the days following Pearl Harbor, and now the remnants had to settle their affairs and leave. Then suddenly, on February 25, the Navy posted notices, informing Japanese Americans they had two days to leave their homes. "Near-panic swept the community," wrote Bill Hosokawa, "particularly those where the family head was in custody. Word spread quickly and human vultures in the guise of used-furniture dealers descended on the island. They drove up and down the streets in trucks offering $5 for a nearly new washing machine, $10 for refrigerators." A nisei

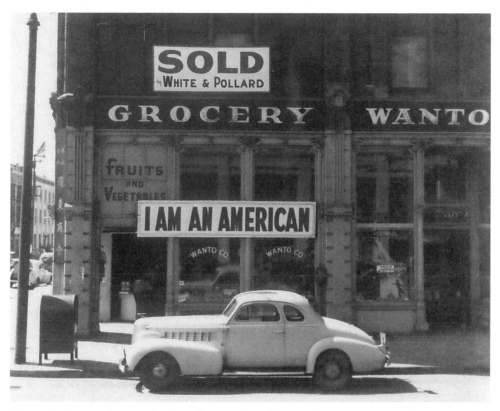

Evacuation is a euphemism for forced, unwarranted removal. Here, a Japanese American store-owner in Oakland, California protests the unconstitutional "evacuation." (National Archives)

volunteer who helped the islanders pack recalled: "The women cried awful. . . . Some of them smashed their stuff, broke it up, right before the buyers' eyes because they offered such ridiculous prices" (Okihiro, 60).

"The volunteers with trucks worked all night," wrote Virginia Swanson, a Baptist missionary on the island. "The people had to go, ready or not. Some had to be pulled forcibly from their homes. They were afraid they were going to be handed over to a firing squad. Why should they have believed me," she asked, "telling them to get into trucks with strangers?" At the Forsyth School, one of the reception centers prepared by white and Japanese Americans, Esther Rhoads was among the volunteers. "All afternoon trucks and Japanese kept coming," she described the scene in a letter to a friend. "They were tired and dazed as a result of the sudden exodus. . . . We have old men over seventy—retired fishermen whom the FBI considered ineffective, and we have little children—one baby a year old . . . practically no men between thirty-five and sixty-five, as they all are interned. . . . Where are these people to go?" she asked poignantly. "There are many Japanese with young leaders able to face pioneer life, but those who have come to our hostels represent a group too old or too young to stand the rigors of beginning all over again" (Okihiro, 61). And Terminal Island was just a dress rehearsal for the mass eviction and confinement program that would touch so many lives.

The Japanese American "evacuation" of World War II had precedents in U.S. history. An example was President Andrew Jackson's particular hatred of American Indians that resulted in their expulsion from the South during the 1830s when thousands of Choctaws, Creeks, Chickasaws, and Cherokees walked and died along the Trail of Tears to the Great American Desert to settle on land deemed unfit for human habitation. Other native peoples, the Unangan or Aleuts in Alaska, were, in the words of a government commission, "relocated to abandoned facilities in southeastern Alaska and exposed to a bitter climate and epidemics of disease without adequate protection or medical care" when Japan launched an attack on the Aleutian and Pribilof islands in the summer of 1942. There, "they fell victim to an extraordinarily high death rate, losing many of the elders who sustained their culture." While the government held the Aleuts under detention in southeastern Alaska, its military pillaged and ransacked their homes in the islands. Those forced removals, the commission concluded, along with the slow and inconsiderate resettlement thereafter, sadly followed the historical pattern of "official indifference which so many Native American groups have experienced . . . " (Okihiro, 61–62).

On March 24, 1942, the army issued a Civilian Exclusion Order that became the model for all other exclusion orders that effected the complete removal of Japanese Americans from the West Coast. The target of this experiment was the several hundred Japanese Americans who farmed on Bainbridge Island in Puget Sound, near Seattle and at the approach to Bremerton Naval Yard. Soldiers dressed in battle fatigues tacked up the notices, "Instructions to All Persons of Japanese Ancestry," on the island's utility poles, at the post office, and at the ferry landing. The Bainbridge Japanese Americans, mostly berry and truck farmers, had six days to close their farms, settle their affairs, and pack their possessions.

Bill Hosokawa described the "raw, overcast day" of March 30. "Although the Japanese had been given less than a week in which to settle their affairs and pack," he wrote, "they began to gather at the assembly point long before the designated hour; each of the fifty-four families carrying only the meager items authorized by the Army—bedding, linens, toilet articles, extra clothing, enamel plates and eating utensils. All else, the possessions collected over a lifetime, had to be stored with friends, delivered to a government warehouse, sold or abandoned. Farms developed over decades were leased or simply left to be overgrown by weeds." Armed soldiers directed the people onto a ferryboat, from which they viewed, some for the last time, their island home. In Seattle, a train took the islanders to California. "What impressed me most was their silence," wrote Thomas Bodine of the Bainbridge islanders as they boarded the train. "No one said anything. No one did anything" (Okihiro, 65). The train creaked out of the station and headed south for Manzanar assembly center and later, concentration camp.

Gary Y. Okihiro

Reference

Okihiro, Gary Y. "An American Story." In *Impounded: Dorothea Lange and the Censored Images of Japanese American Internment,* edited by Linda Gordon and Gary Y. Okihiro, 47–84. New York: Norton, 2006.

EXECUTIVE ORDER 9066

In the wake of the Japanese bombing of Pearl Harbor on December 7, 1941, the United States witnessed a rising tide of anti–Japanese American sentiment, most prevalently in the western states. In California and elsewhere, long-held prejudices and racism against Asian Americans were amplified by wartime propaganda. This persistent culture of discrimination, led by the president and federal government, quickly devolved into a consensus for the immediate, forced removal of all Japanese Americans from the West Coast. By early 1942, mayors of all the major urban areas supported mass removal as well as an ad-hoc committee of western senators and congressmen who lobbied heavily for the federal government to act on the supposed dire threats posed by the presence of Japanese Americans in the region.

While the Justice Department headed by Attorney General Francis Biddle was against the removal of Japanese American citizens, the War Department, under the leadership of Secretary of War Henry Stimson, his assistant, John McCloy, and the commander of the Western Defense Command, Lieutenant General John DeWitt, and the Navy under secretary Frank Knox made a case for presidential powers to authorize the "evacuation" and "relocation" of Japanese Americans and other "alien enemies" from what became the Western Theater of Operations.

Despite the few, weak voices of dissent within his cabinet, President Franklin D. Roosevelt signed into law Executive Order 9066 (EO 9066) on February 19, 1942. The order empowered the War Department to designate military areas in which "any or all persons may be excluded, and with respect to which, the right of any persons to enter, remain in, or leave shall be subject to whatever restrictions" imposed by the military.

The extraordinary range of powers the order granted to the War Department fell under the president's war powers, and was depicted as a pragmatic response to threats to the nation's security and a matter of military necessity. EO 9066 never specifically called for the exclusion of Japanese Americans, but it was well understood from the conversations and debates that led up to its signing that Japanese Americans were the main targets of this order. By contrast, German and Italian Americans remained virtually unscathed by the military's exclusion policies, even though they were implicitly invoked in the order's open-ended language and were seen by General DeWitt to be a comparable fifth column threat. In hindsight, the general expediency of the order also demonstrated a certain amount of recklessness on the part of Roosevelt, who failed to follow the usual channels of military decision-making, including seeking counsel from General George C. Marshall and the joint chiefs of staff who believed selective, not mass, detention was sufficient for the national security.

Escorted by armed soldiers, Japanese Americans board buses for Tanforan Assembly Center, April 29, 1942. (National Archives)

President Roosevelt's decision to authorize EO 9066 remains a point of historic controversy, and his personal motivations remain unclear until this day. Records show that he did seek out advice from those who had spoken out against "evacuation" and general anti-Japanese American sentiments. In early January, Roosevelt met with writer Louis Adamic, who encouraged the president to show restraint in the face of escalating wartime hysteria. Eleanor Roosevelt publicly spoke out in support of Japanese Americans who were facing persecution in the months following Pearl Harbor. Attorney General Biddle remained opposed to the evacuation of nisei, and was sure to have shared his thoughts with the president. And yet, throughout his political career and presidency, Roosevelt maintained what some might call a narrowly conservative, if not intolerant, stance on questions of ethnic equality, racial discrimination, and immigration. According to historians, Roosevelt believed that Japanese Americans were still Japanese at core and he regarded them as potentially dangerous and disloyal on racial grounds. In fact, as early as 1936, Roosevelt had recommended "concentration camps" for Japanese Americans, aliens and citizens alike.

During his presidency, Roosevelt's general position vis-à-vis racial and ethnic minorities, such as Japanese Americans and European Jews, was characteristic of an unfortunate and perhaps immoral feeling of indifference. Roosevelt refused to intervene in the Nazi Holocaust, and faced with the realities of Japanese American suffering and their loss of what the constitution considers to be basic and inalienable rights, he failed to offer any form of apology or reparations for their unfair treatment and financial losses during the war. It was only after Roosevelt's death, that President Harry Truman admitted any wrongdoing and made a case for Congress to compensate Japanese Americans for their losses incurred during the war, however meager and ineffective this early legislation may have been.

The deleterious effects of Roosevelt's EO 9066 continue to resonate for the Japanese American community and other ethnic groups deemed "alien enemies," as has been seen in the post-9/11 incarceration of enemy combatants without representation at Guantanamo Bay Detention Center and at other sites of exclusion within the United States and across the globe. Made under extraordinary circumstances, and with little foresight, the signing of Executive Order 9066 set a dangerous precedent for the extensive power that the executive branch of the U.S. government could exert during wartime and beyond.

Jenny M. James

References

Girdner, Audrie and Anne Loftis. *The Great Betrayal: The Evacuation of the Japanese-Americans during World War II*. London: Macmillan, 1969.

Robinson, Greg. *By Order of the President: FDR and the Internment of Japanese Americans*. Cambridge, MA: Harvard University Press, 2001.

FAIR PLAY COMMITTEE (HEART MOUNTAIN)

Hawai'i-born Kiyoshi Okamoto began in November 1943 the Fair Play Committee of One at Heart Mountain concentration camp. Okamoto was educated in Los Angeles, and he became a construction engineer. At the Heart Mountain camp, Okamoto was disturbed by "un-American practices" such as the loyalty questionnaire and nisei service in the military. Additionally, white War Relocation Authority (WRA) officials treated Japanese Americans with disdain and discriminated against them, and the WRA curtailed freedom of speech and provided substandard living and working conditions. More fundamentally, Okamoto saw the concentration camps as an un-American practice.

As the Fair Play Committee of One, Okamoto agitated for a clarification of the legal status of nisei and their rights as citizens in open forums. Over time, he attracted a number of members, and they formed the Heart Mountain Fair Play Committee (FPC). The committee gained renewed prominence when on January 20, 1944, Secretary of War Henry Stimson announced nisei would become subject to the draft because of the exemplary service of nisei volunteers in the army. This new policy represented another change in the government's classification of nisei men since Pearl Harbor from "enemy alien" and hence unacceptable for military service to volunteers, to draftees. To make matters worse, the change came on the heels of the WRA's loyalty questionnaire, which had asked if Japanese Americans were willing to serve in the U.S. military. The questionnaire stirred a storm of suspicion among Japanese Americans in the concentration camps, and those fears appeared to be confirmed by Stimson's announcement. A few, especially members of the Japanese American Citizens League (JACL), praised the government's change of heart as a way for nisei to demonstrate their loyalty on the battlefield. Most others, like members of the FPC, saw the government's action as another assault on Japanese American citizenship and rights. Having been removed and confined in concentration camps, they said, Japanese Americans were now being forced to serve to defend phantom freedoms denied them.

"We, the members of the FPC, are not afraid to go to war—we are not afraid to risk our lives for our country," the committee explained in a mimeographed bulletin to the Heart Mountain camp. "We would gladly sacrifice our lives to protect and uphold the principles and ideals of our country as set forth in the Constitution and the Bill of Rights, for on its inviolability depends the freedom, liberty, justice, and protection of all people including Japanese-American and all other minority groups" (Emi, 43). But Japanese Americans, without any charges against them or evidence of wrongdoing, have had their constitutional rights stripped away and were being forced to defend those lost liberties in racially segregated units. Is that the American way? they asked. "No!" Accordingly, the bulletin promised, FPC members will resist the draft until their rights as U.S. citizens are restored.

In March 1944, 12 nisei refused to board the bus to undergo selective service physical examinations, and by the end of the month, 54 of the 315 nisei young men ordered for selective service physicals failed to comply. The FPC called for a general strike. The WRA charged Okamoto with disloyalty, and quickly arrested him and shipped him off to Tule Lake concentration camp, which was a camp for "disloyals." Isamu Horino, another FPC leader, was charged with disloyalty and also sent to Tule Lake. A third FPC leader, Paul Nakadate, was subjected to a lengthy interrogation to ascertain his loyalty.

James Omura, editor of the *Rocky Shimpo,* a Japanese American newspaper based in Denver, praised the FPC's stand. Heart Mountain's camp director wrote to the WRA head, complaining that Omura's editorials bordered on "sedition," and asked for an investigation of the paper. In April 1944, federal agents seized Omura's records and correspondence, and the Alien Property Custodian, the manager of the paper's assets because it was formerly owned by noncitizen issei, and fired Omura and his staff.

On May 10, 1944, a federal grand jury in Cheyenne, Wyoming, indicted the 63 draft resisters. Their trial took place the following month in the largest trial for draft resistance in U.S. history. Federal district judge T. Blake Kennedy found them all guilty and sentenced them to three years in prison. "If they are truly loyal American citizens," Kennedy lectured, "they should . . . embrace the opportunity to discharge the duties [of citizenship] by offering themselves in the cause of our National Defense" (Daniels, 127).

The FPC leaders, seven of them, and editor James Omura were charged with unlawful conspiracy to counsel, aid, and abet draft violations. Their trial was held on October 23, 1944, in federal district court in Cheyenne, and Judge Eugene Rice sentenced the seven leaders to a four-year term at Leavenworth Federal Penitentiary. Omura won acquittal. On appeal more than a year later, the court agreed the judge's instructions to the jury were improper, and the seven FPC leaders were released from prison. Still, draft resistance continued at Heart Mountain concentration camp, and 22 more men were indicted and convicted of draft resistance.

The original 63 served just over two years of their three-year sentence, and on Christmas eve, 1947, President Harry Truman granted a presidential pardon to all nisei draft resisters. As Judge Louis Goodman stated in dismissing the indictments against 27 draft resisters from Tule Lake concentration camp, "it is shocking to the conscience that an American citizen be confined on the ground of disloyalty and then, while so under duress and restraint, be compelled to serve in the armed forces or be prosecuted for not yielding to such compulsion" (Emi, 47).

Gary Y. Okihiro

References

Daniels, Roger. *Concentration Camps: North America: Japanese in the United States and Canada during World War II.* Malabar, Florida: Robert E. Krieger, 1981.

Emi, Frank. "Draft Resistance at the Heart Mountain Concentration Camp and the Fair Play Committee." In *Frontiers of Asian American Studies: Writing, Research, and Commentary.* Edited by Gail M. Nomura et al., 71–77. Pullman: Washington State University Press, 1989.

FEDERAL BUREAU OF INVESTIGATION (FBI)

Begun as the Bureau of Investigation (BOI) in 1908, it was placed within the federal government's Department of Justice as the nation's investigative arm against criminal activity, including on American Indian reservations, and as its internal intelligence agency. The BOI became the Federal Bureau of Investigation (FBI) in 1935. For much of its history, from 1924 to 1972, the agency fell under the directorship of J. Edgar Hoover. During that tenure, the BOI and then FBI engaged in crime fighting but also in surveillance against espionage, especially during the Cold War, and the civil rights movement. Domestic surveillance or the counterintelligence program, called COINTELPRO, was used to spy on civil rights leaders like Martin Luther King, Jr. and black power movement leaders like Malcolm X.

The BOI began investigating Hawai'i's Japanese American community when workers struck against the sugar planters for higher wages and better conditions. In 1920, J. Edgar Hoover, then a special assistant to the U.S. attorney general, proposed a formal intelligence-gathering network involving the BOI, military intelligence, and the Hawaiian sugar planters' secret agents. As a result, a BOI agent, A. A. Hopkins, sent from the West Coast office cooperated with military intelligence during the 1920s, investigating the "Japanese problem," which involved domestic labor strife and an international conspiracy to foment a race war against white supremacy, according to the BOI and military intelligence. In 1922, the BOI's Hopkins compiled perhaps the first list of Japanese American names under the title "Japanese Espionage—Hawaii." The 157 on his list included 40 merchants and storekeepers, 31 Buddhist priests, 24 Japanese-language school principals and teachers, 19 laborers, 10 Christian ministers, and 4 professionals. Although labeled "espionage," the list clearly identified leaders of Hawai'i's Japanese American community and not spies. After all, the BOI believed, "He [the Japanese] does not become an American, save in very rare instances, always remaining a Japanese" (Okihiro, 127).

During the 1930s, military intelligence expanded its web to Japan's activities in Central and South America, and the BOI and then FBI intensified its investigations of Japanese Americans in the United States. An August 1934 State Department report charged that Japan maintained agents in every large city in the United States, and those agents, passing as ordinary workers and civilians, will rise up, when war is declared, to commit sabotage, rendering the West Coast defenseless. In 1939, President Franklin Roosevelt assigned domestic surveillance to the FBI against espionage, sabotage, and subversive activities, and military intelligence directed their efforts against threats to Army and Navy installations and their civilian workforce.

By June 1940, the FBI's J. Edgar Hoover could identify German, Italian, and communist leaders scheduled for internment during a national emergency, but confessed military intelligence knew more about Japanese Americans than his agency. The FBI's office in Hawai'i opened only in August 1939, and its agents relied upon military intelligence for much of its information on the islands' Japanese Americans. By September 1940, however, relying upon informants, one of the FBI's agents discovered that although the issei might have strong feelings toward Japan, Japanese Americans were "not organized for purposes of sabotage or subversive activity . . ." (Okihiro, 180). Moreover, the agent reported, the United States need not fear an uprising from Japanese Americans or the influence of Buddhist priests and Japanese-language schoolteachers. Those fears were groundless and exaggerated, his informants told him. With agents on each of the major islands, the FBI compiled information, and attached little significance to allegations of espionage and sabotage among Japanese Americans.

Military intelligence agreed with the FBI's assessment of the situation. They believed although a large majority probably held "pro-Japan" sentiments, Japanese Americans failed to pose a security threat in the event of a war with Japan. If their leaders, including Buddhist and Shinto priests, language-school teachers, and businessmen, were interned, "there need be no fear of the reaction of the local Japanese population in the event of war with Japan," an FBI memorandum stated (Okihiro, 182). Both the FBI and military urged a counterpropaganda campaign to secure the hearts and minds of the nisei to ensure their loyalty to the United States. In that way, the second generation would serve as a buffer against the first, and guarantee economic stability in the territory.

The FBI's director and West Coast offices shared that same mindset when the Bureau created the "ABC" list of "enemy aliens" destined for internment in the event of war. Those grouped under "A" were considered dangerous and required intense scrutiny, those under "B" were classed as potentially dangerous, and under "C," peripherally dangerous and involved mainly in propaganda activities. By early 1941, there were more than 2,000 Japanese Americans on the "ABC" list, together with German and Italian Americans. As was the case in Hawai'i, those included on the "ABC" list were Buddhist and Shinto priests, Japanese-language school principals and teachers, and businessmen. Hoover and his FBI maintained, even after Pearl Harbor, the internment of "enemy aliens" was sufficient to secure the nation from the danger of internal subversion but politicians, especially President Franklin Roosevelt, overrode that assessment in favor of the mass removal and confinement of Japanese Americans on the West Coast under the guise of "military necessity."

Gary Y. Okihiro

Reference

Okihiro, Gary Y. *Cane Fires: The Anti-Japanese Movement in Hawaii, 1865–1945.* Philadelphia: Temple University Press, 1991.

442ND REGIMENTAL COMBAT TEAM

With the successful precedents of Japanese Americans working as the Varsity Victory Volunteers in Hawai'i and serving in the Military Intelligence Service (MIS) and 100th Infantry Battalion, the U.S. government considered, especially in light of manpower shortages, the formation of another Japanese American unit. The army's chief of staff approved the plan on January 1, 1943, and four weeks later the War Department called for 1,500 volunteers from Hawai'i and 3,000 from the continent. Instead, nearly 10,000 answered the call in Hawai'i, and of that number, 2,686 men were selected. By contrast on the continent, only 1,138 qualified men volunteered from the concentration camps after about a month of recruiting. Their numbers increased in January 1944 when the government applied the draft to nisei.

The 442nd Regimental Combat Team was activated in February 1943. Most of its officers were white, while the foot soldiers, Japanese American. Beginning in May 1943, they trained at Fort Shelby, Mississippi, where the barracks leaked, sand and dust got into food and bedding, and the rains and mud made the roads impassable. Japanese Americans designed their regiment's patch, showing a silver arm and hand holding a torch against a field of blue. The design symbolized the freedom and liberty denied them but for which they fought. Over 18,000 Japanese American soldiers wore that patch.

Members of the 442nd Regimental Combat Team, mostly Japanese Americans, rescued the "Lost Battalion" in the Vosges mountains. The 442nd was among the most decimated, most decorated units of World War II. (Center for Military History)

In June 1943, the 100th Infantry Battalion returned to Fort Shelby after training in Louisiana. There the men of the two units met, and rivalry between them led to friction and name calling such as "buddhaheads" for Japanese Americans from Hawai'i and "kotonks" for those from the continent. Those from the continent thought those from the islands behaved very Japanese or like "buddhas," and the latter retaliated with "kotonk" or the sound made by a tiny brain that rattled when shaken. In August, the 100th Battalion shipped out of Camp Shelby for duty overseas.

While the 100th fought bloody battles in Italy, the 442nd trained and sent over 500 replacements for the devastating losses suffered by the 100th. By March 1944, they were ready. Transport ships made the 28-day journey to Italy, arriving in May 1944, and in June the 442nd joined forces with the 100th, which, during the first few months of fighting, had suffered immense casualties. Together, the 442nd moved up the Italian peninsula engaging the enemy in town after town.

A nisei soldier described his battle strategy. "You work as a team . . . those guys from the islands taught me something I never saw on the Mainland . . . you really have a buddy system. When you get into trouble you don't leave your buddy, ever, and he won't leave you, and this is a tremendous thing. You make it or you don't make it, together." In that way, he said, "You're never alone, and you know that. It keeps you going" (Tanaka, 62).

Perhaps the best-known action engaged by the men of the 442nd was the mission to rescue the "Lost Battalion." Deep in the Vosge forest in France was the battered 3rd Battalion of the 141st Regiment, 36th Division. They were trapped and hemmed in by German troops in October 1944. Other units had tried to reach the 3rd Battalion but were beaten back. The assignment was given to the 442nd to reach the "Lost Battalion." The 442nd had been through weeks of difficult fighting leading to the liberation of the town of Bruyeres. They had just two days rest when they received their orders to move into the dense forest where fighting was fierce and combat, hand-to-hand. "From the very first day until we reached them, it seemed like an eternity," a soldier recalled. "It couldn't have been more than a week. We lost officers and men right and left every day. We lost so many men you couldn't count." The Germans laid down a terrible artillery barrage, cutting off supplies and reinforcements. With the 100th guarding a flank, the 442nd advanced. "There was no thought of turning back," a soldier recalled. "Never. We didn't think about turning back. No one even mentioned it. We just kept plowing forward to reach the 'Lost Battalion,' period" (Tanaka, 92–93). Finally, they reached the "Lost Battalion," having suffered over 800 casualties in less than a week to rescue 211 men.

A Japanese American Army chaplain described an incident exemplary of the war's brutality and humanity. The brother of a dead soldier asked him to assist in the burial of his brother who had been killed that day. There were thousands of bodies, the chaplain remembered, and after a search they found the nisei soldier's body. There were German prisoners of war (POWs) standing nearby, and several asked if the men needed a hand carrying the body of the fallen Japanese American. They refused because "well, I'm ashamed to say it," admitted the chaplain, "we hated the Germans so much—to think that a German who had killed this boy . . . was going to touch his body again." At graveside, the chaplain said The Lord's Prayer, and the Germans knelt and recited it in German. After the service was over, the chaplain asked a sergeant what he thought about the Germans reciting The Lord's Prayer. "He said, 'You know, Chaplain, I was going to stand up, go over and push his face in . . . to think that he would say a prayer over the body of one he might have helped to kill.'" But then he realized that there was no Japanese father in the prayer's "our father," no American father, no German father. "Our father," the nisei soldier realized, meant "'the Germans were our brothers and we were fighting each other and killing each other. You know, Chaplain, for a minute there, I was ashamed that we, as brothers, were killing each other'" (Tanaka, 103).

A group from the 442nd was among the first Allied troops to release prisoners from the Dachau concentration camp in Germany. Ichiro Imamura described how a scout shot off the chain to the camp, and upon entering they realized the bodies sprawled on the snow-covered ground were alive because they were moving slowly. "Many of them were Jews," Imamura wrote in his diary. "They were wearing black and white striped prison suits and round caps. A few had shredded blanket rags draped over their shoulders. . . . The prisoners shuffled to their feet after the gates were opened. They shuffled weakly out of the compound. They were like skeletons—all skin and bones. . . . They were starving" (Tanaka, 117). The men moved on after several days near Dachau.

The men of the 442nd were among the most decorated and decimated of the war. Mary Matsuda, the sister of slain Sergeant Kazuo Matsuda, reminded her listeners of the debt they owed to those who had made the supreme sacrifice. "We have won the war against fascism abroad," she said, "but that is not our whole duty. We must sacrifice selfishness for the larger interest of society and courageously live the principles of tolerance and fair play in our daily lives in contact with our neighbors" (Tanaka, 168). Democracy demanded adherence to those ideals.

Gary Y. Okihiro

Reference

Tanaka, Chester. *Go For Broke: A Pictorial History of the Japanese American 100th Infantry Battalion and the 442nd Regimental Combat Team.* Richmond, CA: Go For Broke, 1982.

G

GERMAN AMERICANS

With war declared on December 7, 1941, German American aliens, like Italian and Japanese American aliens, became "enemy aliens." As such, under a presidential proclamation, any enemy alien 14 years old or over was liable to apprehension, restraint, and removal. Habeas corpus and the Fourteenth Amendment's equal protection clause failed to extend to enemy aliens, U.S. courts had ruled. The threat of invasion made them liable to summary arrest and detention.

The Federal Bureau of Investigation (FBI) apprehended enemy aliens identified as dangerous, allegedly, to the nation's security. For Italian and Japanese Americans, those targeted for internment were men who had served in their country's military, newspaper publishers and editors, radio broadcasters, and language schoolteachers. In the first few weeks of the war, the FBI picked up some 1,260 German Americans. Like the other enemy aliens, German American aliens were subject to the military's curfews and prohibited zones along the West Coast, and those apprehended were placed in internment camps run by the Justice Department's Immigration and Naturalization Service (INS).

Eddie Friedman, born to Jewish parents in Hamburg, Germany in 1892, immigrated with his wife to San Francisco in 1931. In Germany, Friedman was an attorney and judge, but in the United States, he sold and delivered home baked Viennese cookies and pastries and worked as an elevator operator in San Francisco's office buildings. In September 1940, Friedman and his wife registered under the Alien Registration Act, and on December 8, 1941, FBI agents broke into their home and ransacked the place looking for evidence, and then took him in. As he signed the proclamations to take in German and Italian American enemy aliens, President Franklin Roosevelt remarked, according to his attorney general, "I don't care so much about Italians. They are a lot of opera singers. But the Germans are different; they may be dangerous" (Christgau, 54).

Wolfgang Thomas was born, like Friedman, in Hamburg, Germany, in 1904. He was a businessman, married a German American, and immigrated and settled with her and their two small children in Seattle, Washington. He worked for an import firm, and applied for U.S. citizenship but was told he had to wait three years. On December 8, 1941, the Seattle FBI office received word from Washington, D.C. to apprehend Thomas as a dangerous enemy alien. They entered his home, searched the place, seizing films, letters, and books, and escorted Thomas to their car. The agents explained to Thomas's wife they were taking him to the Seattle INS office, and that was it.

Eddie Friedman was driven to FBI headquarters, and turned over to the INS. At the temporary detention station, he encountered other German and Italian and Japanese American aliens. All the men were handcuffed, and the German and Italian Americans were assigned beds along the outer perimeter and Japanese Americans, the inner beds. On December 17, 1941, the German American aliens were told they were heading for Bismarck, North Dakota, and they were placed on board a train. The passenger train had barred, blacked-out windows, and guards with machine guns faced the men. In Portland, the train picked up 22 more enemy aliens, including Wolfgang Thomas. They reached Bismarck on December 20, 1941, and were loaded onto army trucks and taken to Fort Lincoln where they met 292 captured German seamen taken from ships in U.S. ports. German Americans numbered 118.

Friedman developed fence sickness, he told his fellow internees, being cooped up behind barbed wire. He wrote to Edward Ennis, director of the Alien Enemy Control Unit, and to Eleanor Roosevelt, the president's wife. He was merely "selling cookies and pastries," he wrote to Roosevelt, when he was apprehended. "As you are in a position to help people in distress more than anybody else in the country, I would like to ask if it would be possible to bring about an early release" (Christgau, 61).

In February 1942, news spread through the camp that a Japanese American internee, Jinosuke Higashi, had committed suicide after his comrades had given him a farewell party. On March 25, 1942, Wolfgang Thomas received word that he was ordered for internment following his Alien Enemy Hearing Board appearance. The board considered him potentially dangerous. Three days later, Eddie Friedman was paroled but not back to San Francisco, which was a restricted zone for enemy aliens. He had to live outside the prohibited zone and have sponsors. He could not meet those conditions, but on April 24, 1942, Friedman finally received word he could return to his home in San Francisco because restrictions had been lifted. Four days later, Friedman climbed the steps to his apartment, opened the door, and announced to his waiting wife, "It's me. Hello . . . I'm home" (Christgau, 81).

Wolfgang Thomas received word of his release on May 28, 1943. He left Fort Lincoln on June 5, and two days later he was home. "It is a wonderful feeling," he wrote to the officer in charge of Fort Lincoln, "to be home with my family again" (Christgau, 85).

Gary Y. Okihiro

Reference

Christgau, John. *"Enemies": World War II Alien Internment.* Ames: Iowa State University Press, 1985.

H

HIRABAYASHI, GORDON K. (1918–2012)

Born in Seattle to issei parents who had converted to Christianity in Japan while learning English, Gordon Hirabayashi grew up in a rural farm community outside of Seattle during the 1920s and 1930s. His mother and father, Hirabayashi would recall years later, provided him with ideal examples of dedication to beliefs, conduct in accordance with those principles, and protest in the face of injustices. "If my father was the quiet and solid foundation with his unostentatious dedication to the oneness of belief and practice," Hirabayashi remembered, "my mother was the fire, providing warmth and sometimes intense heat. She was an activist, outgoing, articulate, feisty" (Hirabayashi, 9).

Hirabayashi graduated from Auburn High School (Auburn, Washington), and in 1937 entered the University of Washington. While a student at the university, Hirabayashi participated in Christian youth activities and became a religious pacifist. He joined the Quakers, and applied for and received conscientious objector status before Pearl Harbor.

Sometime in early 1942, Hirabayashi decided he needed to bear witness against the mass removal and confinement of Japanese Americans. He turned himself in to the Federal Bureau of Investigation (FBI) after purposefully disregarding the army's curfew orders and refusing to report for "evacuation." A court convicted him of violating the curfew and exclusion orders, and sentenced him to a prison term of 90 days. Bail was set at $5,000 if Hirabayashi agreed to join his fellow Japanese Americans at the Puyallup Assembly Center. Instead, based on his principles, Hirabayashi chose to remain in the King County jail.

On appeal, the U.S. Supreme Court heard the *Hirabayashi* case in May 1943, and rendered a decision the following month in favor of the government. Chief Justice Harlan Stone contended the case did not involve a citizen's civil liberties or constitutional protections against racial prejudice but the government's ability to wage war successfully. The court essentially held the military was exempt from judicial review during times of national emergencies.

Although he joined the unanimous vote against Hirabayashi, Supreme Court Justice Frank Murphy wrote a stinging rebuke. "The broad provisions of the Bill of Rights . . . are not suspended by the mere existence of a state of war. . . . Distinctions based on color and ancestry are utterly inconsistent with our traditions and ideals." Murphy's observation, however, failed to sway the justices. In reference to Japanese Americans held in U.S. concentration camps, Justice Murphy observed: "It bears a melancholy resemblance to the treatment accorded to members of the Jewish race in Germany . . ." (Daniels, 276).

Gordon Hirabayashi (1918–2012) challenged the constitutionality of the military's treatment of Japanese Americans. Here, on November 7, 1999, he helps dedicate the camp, renamed in his honor, in which he was imprisoned just outside Tucson, Arizona. (AP/Wide World Photo)

In addition to his jail time for violating the curfew and exclusion orders, Hirabayashi spent a year in federal prison, along with other conscientious objectors, for refusing induction into the U.S. military.

After the war, Hirabayashi earned a doctorate in sociology from the University of Washington. He taught in Lebanon and Egypt, and in 1959 accepted at position at the University of Alberta in Canada where he remained until his retirement in 1983.

Based on new evidence that the government had lied to the U.S. Supreme Court in his 1943 case, Hirabayashi joined the *coram nobis* campaign of the 1980s to reverse his World War II conviction and those of Fred Korematsu and Minoru Yasui. Hirabayashi wrote of that opportunity, "I fully expected that as a citizen the constitution would protect me. Surprisingly, even though I lost, I did not abandon my beliefs and values. Accordingly, when the discovery of government misconduct in my case during the war was revealed 40 years later, giving me the opportunity to petition for a re-hearing, I did not hesitate for a moment" (Hirabayashi, 5).

In 1986, a court of appeals ruled the government had seriously prejudiced its case by suppressing evidence, and vacated Hirabayashi's conviction of violating the "evacuation" order but let stand his violation of the military curfew. After an appeal of that decision, the court reversed both of Hirabayashi's convictions. But because the government chose not to appeal those lower court rulings before the U.S. Supreme Court, a reversal of Hirabayashi's wartime conviction was not achieved.

In 1999, an area of the Coronado National Forest in Arizona was renamed the Gordon Hirabayashi Recreation Site, and after Hirabayashi's death in 2012, President Barack Obama awarded him the Presidential Medal of Freedom, the nation's highest honor for civilians, for his principled stand against the mass removal and detention of Japanese Americans. Jeanne Sakata wrote a play, *Dawn's Light: The Journey of Gordon Hirabayashi,* which premiered in Los Angeles in 2007. Based on Hirabayashi's wartime ordeals, the play followed a solitary man's fight against his country's betrayal of its constitutional ideals and promises.

Perhaps summing up his life's achievements, Hirabayashi told a gathering of Quakers in Canada, "For myself, I have appreciated the confrontations and the opportunities for personal growth especially the challenge to seek the inner light. Frequently as I looked across the murky waters towards an unknown future, the only realistic position available was the idealistic one" (Hirabayashi, 21).

Gary Y. Okihiro

References

Daniels, Roger. *Asian America: Chinese and Japanese in the United States since 1850.* Seattle: University of Washington Press, 1988.
Hirabayashi, Gordon. *Good Times, Bad Times: Idealism Is Realism.* Canadian Quaker Pamphlet, No. 22. Argenta, BC: Argenta Friends Press, 1985.

HOHRI, WILLIAM MINORU (1927–2010)

A political activist and advocate for Japanese American redress, William Minoru Hohri was born on March 13, 1927, in San Francisco, California. His father was a Christian minister who led a small congregation consisting mainly of Japanese Americans. On the night of the attack on Pearl Harbor, the Federal Bureau of Investigation (FBI) apprehended him and sent him to a Department of Justice internment camp in Montana. The family never learned of the charges, and there was no trial. In April 1942, the rest of the Hohri family was sent to the War Relocation Authority's Manzanar concentration camp in southern California.

Manzanar, located in a remote high desert area, was, according to Hohri, strategically placed there by the federal government to neutralize the alleged threat Japanese Americans posed to the nation's security. "In other words," as Hohri put it, "Manzanar's geography insured that we couldn't exercise our ingrained 'Jap' sneakiness against power lines, aircraft factories, naval bases, shipyards, and such. . . . We were guilty by reason of racial perversity, but in the natural prison of Manzanar, we were harmless" (Hohri 1988, 15).

The desert conditions produced high winds and dust storms that blew dirt and sand into the unfinished barracks. The camp was still under construction when Hohri and his family arrived and the barracks lacked windows, potable tap water, and a sewage system. The facilities improved later, but Hohri truly felt they were wards of the federal government. They were given military clothes left over from World War I, forbidden to speak Japanese in public meetings, and given menial jobs for which they were paid less than 10 cents an hour because they were considered "evacuees," not prisoners of war whose wages were subject to the Geneva Convention's minimum wage standards. "We were prisoners. Not prisoners of war," explained Hohri, "for we were not from the enemy nation. We felt more like criminals" (Hohri 1988, 19).

According to Hohri, one of the more demoralizing aspects of the camp was the poor education he and his peers received. Hohri was 15 when he was detained and was most affected by the boredom of life in the camps and lack of proper schooling, which was frustrating and led to later difficulties in college for many of the young people who had received their schooling in the camps. However, while at the University of Chicago, Hohri was able to take remedial classes that allowed him to catch up on material that he had never learned.

After graduating in June 1944, Hohri, like many of his classmates, left Manzanar "because camp was just destroying us psychologically—our morale" (Hohri 1998). He began working and supported his siblings by sending them money. In March 1945, Hohri tried to reenter the camp in order to talk to his parents and advise his father about future job prospects. However, he was not allowed in and the guards demanded a permit, which was not necessary as the exclusion order had been lifted in January 1945 and Japanese Americans were legally allowed to travel freely. When Hohri argued with the guards, they put him in jail and issued an individual exclusion order just for him, requiring him to leave the state of California by midnight. Of that experience, Hohri said in an interview, "And the thing about (laughs) experiences like that is, if you're running a government, don't do that to people because those kinds of people come back to haunt you. And I think that's what happened as far as the Redress Movement goes" (Hohri 1998).

True to his word, after the war, Hohri became a big proponent of the redress and reparations movement. Hohri sued the U.S. government, believing it was important for Japanese Americans to win the lawsuit in order to recover their rights and dignity. He rejected euphemisms such as "relocation" and insisted on the use of terms such as "exclusion" and "detention" to highlight the unconstitutionality of the actions of the U.S. government. In May 1979, he helped form the National Council for Japanese American Redress (NCJAR) to obtain monetary compensation for the losses suffered by Japanese Americans during World War II. Hohri was the lead plaintiff in a 1983 class action lawsuit against the U.S. government. The lawsuit sought a total of $27 billion in damages to be paid to 125,000 surviving detainees for 22 causes of action. NCJAR, however, lost the suit and on appeal, the U.S. Supreme Court let the judgment stand. Despite the defeat, Hohri's efforts, together with the other actions of the redress and reparations movement, led to the 1988 Civil Liberties Act that was signed by President Ronald Reagan. The act issued an apology to Japanese Americans, and through the act, a sum of $20,000 was paid to surviving detainees.

For Hohri, his lawsuit was an important step in enumerating and making public the unconstitutional actions of the U.S. government. He later stressed this point in an interview: "So it [the lawsuit] set a standard. The statement of injuries is very important, because the legislation doesn't do that. [It] doesn't define injuries. It doesn't state what they are. My own feeling is that if you had to state the injuries the legislation would have never passed, because Congress does not like to put the government in the position of having to admit to error" (Hohri 1998).

William Hohri wrote three books, one of which detailed the redress and reparations movement, *Repairing America: An Account of the Movement for Japanese-American Redress* (1988). He died on November 12, 2010, in Los Angeles.

Jasmine Little

References

Hohri, William. Interview by Darcie Iki and Mitchell Maki. Discover Nikkei. Los Angeles: Japanese American National Museum, June 12, 1998.

Hohri, William Minoru. *Repairing America: An Account of the Movement for Japanese-American Redress*. Pullman: Washington State University Press, 1988.

Martin, Douglas. "William Hohri dies at 83; Sought Money for Internees." *New York Times*, November 24, 2010.

Woo, Elaine. "William Hohri, 83; Led Battle for Redress after Being Interned at Manzanar." *Los Angeles Times*, November 21, 2010.

HOOD RIVER INCIDENT

The history of Japanese Americans during World War II usually calls forth vivid images of barbed wire, tarpaper barracks, and observation guard towers. Yet, the reach of anti-Japanese American sentiment and racial hostility extended far beyond the concentration camps into small town America. The Hood River incident of 1945 is a prime example of the everyday prejudice and racist beliefs that contributed to the government's systematic removal and detention of the Japanese American community. Although Dillon Myer, the War Relocation Authority's director, had famously promised that incidents of violence against Japanese Americans would be the exception rather than the rule during the war, acts of discrimination and aggression were not unusual, especially on the West Coast.

In early 1945, the small community of Hood River, Oregon, became the site of a national scandal that dramatized the rise of racial prejudice and wartime hatreds. In January of that year, leaders of the local American Legion Post removed the names of 16 Japanese American veterans from the local honor roll. Their rationale was a collective doubt in these veterans' allegiance to the United States, and possible dual citizenship with Japan—a fallacious belief that seemed ludicrous considering some of these men had lost their lives fighting on behalf of the United States. Veterans who were removed included a serviceman who had shown bravery in combat on the European Front and was awarded a Bronze Star for his efforts. Most notably, the group included Frank Hachiya who served in military intelligence and died in the Philippines on January 3, 1945, after showing great courage. Hachiya's bravery was recognized with the military's posthumous awarding of the Distinguished Service Cross; the media coverage of his death increased pressure on the legion to reverse their initial decision. As the *New York Times* wrote in an editorial, "Perhaps Private Hachiya never knew that the Legion post had dishonored him back home. Perhaps some day what is left of him may be brought back to this country for reburial among the honored dead."

The news of the egregious activities in Hood River spread across the nation. *Life Magazine* ran a lengthy article covering the event; *Collier's* deemed the incident a product of "blind hatred." John Haynes Holmes, a founder of the National Association for the Advancement of Colored People and the American Civil Liberties Union, compared the Hood River erasure to Nazi Germany, stating: "When Hitler came to power he shocked the world by removing names of Jewish soldiers from the war memorials of Germany." After receiving such negative publicity, the national commander of the American Legion, Edward Scheiberling, ordered the Hood River Post to replace the names on March 12, 1945, six weeks after their initial removal.

The symbolic act of the desecration of the honor roll was paired with reports of discrimination against local Japanese Americans who had remained in Washington and Oregon to maintain agricultural operations during the war. Some Washington-based farmers, for example, found it difficult to sell their produce in the area due to an increasingly insular and uncomfortable racial climate. In the first couple months of 1945, a local organization named the Oregon Property Owners Protective Association held a rally to call for deportation and enforcement of 19th-century alien land laws against Japanese Americans. Membership in this association was made up of legionnaires who had voted for the removal of the names. The legion had been a vehicle of anti-Japanese sentiment and xenophobic lobbying since earlier in the century. Around this same time in 1945, the legion had published advertisements in the local Hood River newspaper publicly warning Japanese Americans to avoid returning to their homes upon release from the camps.

Despite these local accounts of discrimination and exclusion of Japanese Americans in the Pacific Northwest, some members of the community sought to counteract their fellow citizens' racist actions. In Hood River, some individuals came together to advocate for and aid those Japanese American residents who decided to return to their homes and reclaim their property. A nation-wide boycott of apples grown in the region attempted to put counterpressure on the area's more conservative groups. Yet, these efforts did not fully assuage the damage done by the townspeople's racist activities. Not surprisingly, fewer than half of the town's former Japanese American residents returned to the river valley after the war.

Jenny M. James

References

Girdner, Audrie and Anne Loftis. *The Great Betrayal: The Evacuation of the Japanese-Americans during World War II*. London: Macmillan, 1969.

Okihiro, Gary. *Columbia Guide to Asian American History*. New York: Columbia University Press, 2001.

"Private Hachiya, American." *New York Times,* February 17, 1945.

Tamura, Linda. *The Hood River Issei: An Oral History of Japanese Settlers in Oregon's Hood River Valley*. Urbana: University of Illinois Press, 1993.

HOSOKAWA, WILLIAM (1915–2007)

Born in Seattle on January 30, 1915, to Japanese migrants, William "Bill" Kumpai Hosokawa was a journalist and author. He attended the University of Washington School of Journalism where an advisor told him he would never get a job at a newspaper because he was Japanese. His advisor's words proved to be true and, with no other options after graduation, he moved to Singapore in 1938 with his new wife Alice Miyake to start an English-language newspaper.

Hosokawa returned to the United States in 1941, a few weeks before the Japanese attack on Pearl Harbor. With Japanese American leaders being rounded up by the Federal Bureau of Investigation (FBI), James Sakamoto, publisher of the *Japanese American Courier* and member of the Japanese American Citizens League (JACL), suggested creating an Emergency Defense Council to serve as a liaison between the Japanese American community and the U.S. government. Hosokawa became the council's executive secretary. In that role, Hosokawa wrote a report to emphasize Japanese American patriotism and assimilation for the Tolan Committee hearing, a Congressional investigation held in early 1942. Reflecting on the hearings, Hosokawa wrote, "In Seattle, the strategy we adopted was to point out that Japanese Americans were loyal citizens and upstanding, productive members of the community who posed no security risk" (Hosokawa, 1998, 30). However, his efforts did not change anti-Japanese opinions. Instead, when the government began the forced removal and confinement of Japanese Americans in 1942, the council cooperated with the government's program and endorsed the military plans for eviction.

Hosokawa soon became one of the victims of EO 9066 when he was forcibly removed with his wife and young son Michael on May 15, 1942, and sent to Camp Harmony in Puyallup, Washington. Describing the journey to Puyallup, Hosokawa wrote, "The caravan, escorted by military vehicles, made its way into the fairgrounds through a gate in a high barbed wire fence. In an instant we were transformed from free American citizens to prisoners in our own country" (Hosokawa, 1998, 34). This "assembly center" was located an hour outside of Seattle on state fairgrounds that had been converted, like many other fairgrounds, into a holding camp while permanent facilities were being built. Hosokawa described his accommodations as a mere shed unfurnished except for a steel cot and a single light. To address the issues that arose in the camp, Sakamoto with Hosokawa as his assistant agreed to help the camp administrators.

During this time, Hosokawa began writing a weekly column called "From the Frying Pan" in the *Pacific Citizen,* the newspaper of the JACL. In his column, Hosokawa discussed the discrimination facing Japanese Americans. However, he continued to support the U.S. government's war efforts and asserted Japanese American patriotism and the importance of cooperation with the government. On July 2, 1942, Hosokawa, still detained, opened his column with: "A hundred thousand Americans of Japanese blood and their parents are living unobtrusively behind barbed wire today as their part toward American victory in a fight to the finish against the Axis" (Hosokawa, 1978, 6).

Sakamoto and Hosokawa stressed cooperation and loyalty and believed that Japanese Americans should make the best out of the situation. However, conflict arose when a group argued that the JACL was a tool of the U.S. government and the camp administration was undemocratic. The failure to fight EO 9066 was denounced as a failure of the JACL to fulfill their duties to the Japanese American community. Nevertheless, the majority of Japanese Americans voted to retain the JACL and assembly center administration. Hosokawa, who had been erroneously linked with the upstart group, was marked as a subversive. Because of that error, when the Puyallup detainees were moved to the permanent Minidoka concentration camp in Idaho in August 1942, Hosokawa and his family were separated and confined at Heart Mountain concentration camp in Wyoming.

While at Heart Mountain, Hosokawa helped found the camp newspaper *The Heart Mountain Sentinel* with Vaughn Mechau, head of the Reports Department for the War Relocation Authority (WRA). Hosokawa created a popular newspaper that dealt with topics of Japanese American interest such as the activities of the WRA, Congressional decisions, and national news. Of achieving a middle ground between criticizing government activities yet maintaining a relationship with the WRA, Hosokawa wrote, "It [*The Heart Mountain Sentinel*] had to give voice to its readers' anger, supporting their demands for justice and providing articulate leadership, but it also had to be cautious about fueling the anger of citizens unjustly imprisoned" (Hosokawa, 1998, 52).

As the course of the war changed, the WRA began to encourage internees to find jobs in nearby Midwestern cities. Hosokawa was offered a job as a copyeditor at *The Des Moines Register*. In October 1943, nearly a year and a half after being forcibly removed and confined, Hosokawa and his family were allowed to leave Heart Mountain to start a new life in Des Moines, Iowa. After three years there, Hosokawa pursued a position as copyeditor at the *Denver Post*. With Alice, Mike, and new daughter Susan, Hosokawa moved to Denver to start work at the paper in the summer of 1946, beginning a 38-year career with the *Denver Post*.

Hosokawa would go on to publish 10 books, including *Nisei: The Quiet Americans,* intended to create an "understanding and appreciation of the Japanese American minority" (Hosokawa, 1969, x). In 1990, Hosokawa was awarded an honorary doctorate from the University of Denver, and he received a lifetime achievement award from the Asian American Journalists Association in 2003. Hosokawa died on November 9, 2007, at the age of 92.

Jasmine Little

References

Broom, Jack. "Newsman Bill Hosokawa defeated bias, his own anger." *The Seattle Times,* November 14, 2007. http://seattletimes.nwsource.com/html/localnews/2004012907_hosokawaobit14m.html.

Gallo, Bill. "Champion of Japanese Culture—and Dignity." *Rocky Mountain News*, February 15, 2008. http://m.rockymountainnews.com/news/2008/feb/15/champion-of-japanese-culture—-and-dignity/.

Haislip, Anna. "Tribute to Hosokawa's Humility." *Denver Post,* February 17, 2007. http://www.denverpost.com/news/ci_8284582.

Hosokawa, Bill. *Nisei: The Quiet Americans.* New York: William Morrow, 1969.

Hosokawa, Bill. *Out of the Frying Pan: Reflections of a Japanese American.* Boulder: University Press of Colorado, 1998.

Hosokawa, Bill. *Thirty-Five Years in the Frying Pan.* New York: McGraw-Hill, 1978.

Temple, John. "Temple: Dreams, Dignity fill Hosokawa's tale." *Rocky Mountain News,* February 10, 2007. http://m.rockymountainnews.com/news/2007/feb/10/btempleb-dreams-dignity-fill-hosokawas-tale/

ICKES, HAROLD L. (1874–1952)

Harold L. (Leclair) Ickes served as U.S. secretary of the interior from 1933 to 1946 under Presidents Franklin Roosevelt and Harry Truman. During his time in the Roosevelt cabinet, Ickes also served as director of the Public Works Administration (PWA). In 1944, the War Relocation Authority (WRA) that administered the government's concentration camps for Japanese Americans fell under Ickes's Interior Department. Despite his administrative responsibility as custodian of those camps, Ickes was a fierce constitutionalist and a fiery orator, and was often the lone, oppositional voice advocating for the rights of Japanese Americans during World War II.

Ickes was well aware his pro–Japanese American rights stance rendered him an outsider in the White House as well as a minority in public opinion. He summed up his convictions at a San Francisco press club meeting, reportedly stating to a hostile audience: "I am a Constitution man, fair weather or foul. Right now we're having foul weather" (Girdner and Loftis, 405).

After President Roosevelt issued Executive Order 9066 that authorized the removal and confinement of all persons of Japanese ancestry in the Western Defense Command, the question of where to put the some 120,000 displaced people was of immediate concern. Ickes urged that the camps set up for them be geared toward positive programs. He made it clear. "If it is to be a program merely of keeping them under guard in concentration camps, we are not interested" (Daniels, 88).

Ickes knew the outcome was far from positive. As he explained in an April 1943 letter to the president: ". . . [T]he situation in at least some of the Japanese internment camps is bad and is becoming worse rapidly . . . Even the minimum plans that had been formulated and announced for them have been disregarded in large measure, or, at least, have not been carried out. The result has been the gradual turning of thousands of well-meaning and loyal Japanese into angry prisoners" (Daniels, 149). As he explained, "the abnormal and restrictive environment" of the camps intensified Japanese American "resentment and accentuated frictions," resulting in violence and protest in the camps (Weglyn, 302, fn. 29).

As the WRA became increasingly subject to harsh criticism, Ickes rose to its defense, despite having branded the agency's so-called relocation centers "fancy-named concentration camps." He likened the WRA's critics to a "lynch party," and he promised under his watch the WRA would not be "stampeded into undemocratic, bestial, inhuman action" by the "vindictive, bloodthirsty onslaughts of professional race-mongers" (Weglyn, 218).

As early as June 1944, Ickes wrote the president urging him to revoke the orders excluding Japanese Americans from the West Coast because "there is no substantial justification for continuation of the ban from the standpoint of military security" (Weglyn, 219). Military necessity was the justification for EO 9066. The president chose to postpone that decision until after the 1944 election, but resettlement, though not en masse release of Japanese Americans, had already begun. Ickes, who maintained a farm in Olney, Maryland, hired several Japanese Americans to work there once they had been cleared to leave the concentration camps.

Hot tempered and quick tongued, Ickes reprimanded conservative governors Walter Edge of New Jersey and John Bricker of Ohio together with the liberal mayor of New York City, Fiorello La Guardia, when they protested Japanese American resettlement in areas under their respective jurisdictions. In response to the officials' public statements against Japanese American resettlement, Ickes sarcastically observed, "this is a strange fife and drum corps to be playing the discordant anthem of racial discrimination" (Girdner and Loftis, 352).

Ickes favored Japanese American reintegration into American life, and he opposed the repatriation of so-called disloyal Japanese Americans to Japan. While confined in the camps, Japanese Americans were permitted to renounce their U.S. citizenship, which was an extraordinary action on the part of the government. Rarely was renunciation allowed, especially during times of war and stress. On November 1, 1945, Ickes wrote to Attorney General Tom Clark on that matter. "I believe it would be unjust in the extreme to treat all renunciants as a class, without individual differentiation," he cautioned. "I think that deportation of renunciants could in many cases be called seriously into question on the grounds of legality, justice, and plain decency" (Weglyn, 257). Moreover, Ickes supported the idea of compensation from the government for losses sustained by interned Japanese Americans.

Harold Ickes, although an outspoken advocate for the fair and just treatment of Japanese Americans during and after the war, harbored complicated beliefs about the concentration camps, struggling like many others to balance individual civil liberties against the needs of national security. Yet he was, more than others with similar authority, steadfast in his defense of the Constitution and the civil rights of Japanese Americans.

Kia S. Walton

References

Daniels, Roger. *Concentration Camps: North America: Japanese in the United States and Canada during World War II*. Malabar, FL: Robert E. Krieger, 1981.

Girdner, Audrie and Anne Loftis. *The Great Betrayal: The Evacuation of Japanese-Americans during World War II*. New York: Macmillan, 1972.

Weglyn, Michi. *Years of Infamy: The Untold Story of America's Concentration Camps*. New York: William Morrow, 1976.

INTERNAL SECURITY ACT

The Internal Security Act of 1950, passed in the midst of the Cold War and just after the outbreak of the Korean War, consisted of two parts: Title I or the Subversive Activities Control Act and Title II, the Emergency Detention Act. Both Titles I and II became known as the McCarran Act after Senator Pat McCarran, a cosponsor. The U.S. Supreme Court declared unconstitutional Title I's requirement that Communists register with the government, and that portion was repealed in 1968. But Title I's restrictions on organizations labeled communist, and all of Title II remained the law of the land.

Ironically, liberal politicians introduced Title II, hoping to derail the passage of Title I. McCarran called Title II a program for "establishing concentration camps into which people might be put without benefit of trial, but merely by executive fiat . . . simply by an assumption, mind you, that an individual might be thinking about engaging in espionage or sabotage" (Okamura, 73). Congress, however, passed both Titles I and II. President Harry Truman vetoed the legislation, scoring it as "a long step toward totalitarianism" and as putting the government into "the thought-control business," but Congress overrode his veto.

Under Title II, the Justice Department prepared six internment camps, despite its head, Attorney General J. Howard McGrath's characterization of the act as "a symbol of the national hysteria over Communism." The camps included the War Relocation Authority's concentration camp at Tule Lake, which had just been vacated in 1946. The Internal Security Act and Justice Department camps faded away with the end of the Korean War and a decline in anticommunist fervor. In 1957, Congress stopped providing funds to maintain the six detention centers, and the Internal Security Act might have become a relic of the Cold War except for the social movements of the 1960s.

Massive protests against the U.S. war in Southeast Asia, the African American–led civil rights movement, student protests and youthful rebellion, and urban unrest sparked renewed interest among Cold War warriors in protecting the nation from the threat of internal subversion. Civil liberties activists knew about the detention program, and the Citizens Committee for Constitutional Liberties asked journalist Charles Allen, Jr. to write an exposé of the camps in their attempt to get the Internal Security Act repealed. Allen's 60-page pamphlet, *Concentration Camps, U.S.A.*, was published in 1966, and it described the FBI's Operation Dragnet, a secret program of mass arrests of "potential spies and saboteurs" within a few hours, and the Justice Department's internment facilities.

African Americans Stokely Carmichael, H. Rap Brown, and Martin Luther King, Jr. expressed fears of concentration camps for civil rights dissidents in their speeches, and shortly after King's assassination, Attorney General Ramsey Clark appeared on national television to deny the existence of Department of Justice concentration camps. He was asked if he supported repeal of Title II, Clark was evasive: "I believe there are more important things to work on, for example, passage of a fair housing law" (Okamura, 75).

On May 6, 1968, the House Un-American Activities Committee released a report on guerrilla warfare advocates in the United States, and the committee's chairman, Edwin Willis, associated the communist with the African American threat. "There can be no question about the fact that there are mixed communist and black nationalist elements in this country which are planning and organizing guerrilla-type operations against the United States," he said. These elements have declared war on the United States, Willis maintained, and as such have lost their civil liberties and should be interned in concentration camps under the Internal Security Act of 1950. Despite Attorney General Clark's rejection of chairman Willis's opinion, the national press featured articles on "America's Concentration Camps."

The Asian American Political Alliance (AAPA), formed about this time in Berkeley, California, of students and community members, distributed a leaflet entitled "Concentration Camps, USA," which summarized the dangers of Title II. AAPA members joined in rallies sponsored by the Black Panther Party in nearby Oakland where they warned against Title II's concentration camps, and AAPA began a petition drive, calling on Congress to repeal Title II.

After the American Civil Liberties Union refused to join in this Title II repeal campaign, Raymond Okamura brought the matter to the Japanese American Citizens League (JACL) for its endorsement. He and others formed a small group within the JACL in the belief that Japanese Americans, victims of World War II's concentration camps, should lead the campaign for repeal in solidarity with African Americans and other peoples of color who might be the victims of Title II. Throughout the summer of 1968, the group worked to get the JACL to commit to this effort. Most of the JACL leaders opposed the repeal campaign, but the activists won their case at the JACL national convention in August 1968, and Okamura was appointed cochair of the repeal committee.

JACL members, AAPA students, and volunteers set out to educate the American people about the Japanese American concentration camps and the dangers of Title II. JACL chapters petitioned members of Congress, and AAPA students began letter-writing campaigns. In Congress, a bill to repeal Title II was introduced on September 19, 1968, and the Law Center for Constitutional Rights filed suit on November 18, 1968, to have Title II declared unconstitutional. In the spring of the following year, deputy attorney general Richard Kleindienst added fuel to the fire when *Atlantic* magazine quoted him as saying: "If people demonstrated in a manner to interfere with others, they should be rounded up and put in a detention camp" (Okamura, 85).

By 1971, the nation's mood had turned from the threat of internal subversion to the interests of civil liberties. Politicians led the repeal effort, and Congress easily passed the Title II repeal bill. President Richard Nixon signed it into law on September 25, 1971, ending another legacy of the World War II concentration camps.

Gary Y. Okihiro

Reference

Okamura, Raymond. "Background and History of the Repeal Campaign." *Amerasia Journal* 2:2 (1974): 73–94.

ISHIGO, ESTELLE (1899–1990)

Known for documenting the hardships and everyday life in the internment camps through her art, Estelle Ishigo was a white American woman born in Oakland, California, in 1899. She grew up unwanted by her wealthy parents. A nurse reared her until she was 12 when she was turned over to a series of strangers and relatives, one of whom sexually abused her. After this difficult childhood, Ishigo graduated from high school and spent much of her young adulthood "roaming the streets alone, looking for adventure" (Okazaki). While studying at the Otis Art Institute in Los Angeles she met her future husband, a San Francisco–born nisei (second generation Japanese American) named Arthur Shigeharu Ishigo (1902–1957). She described her feelings for the young, aspiring actor as love at first sight. The two defied the antimiscegenation laws that governed California and most of the United States by fleeing to Mexico to marry in 1928. Upon returning to the United States, she found a job as a teacher at the Hollywood Art Center, but on December 7, 1941, Ishigo was fired because she was married to a Japanese American.

After President Franklin Roosevelt's Executive Order 9066, the husband and wife were forced to pack up all their belongings and move to the Pomona Assembly Center. Here, Ishigo began to draw and paint her experiences of life under confinement. From Pomona, Arthur was sent to Heart Mountain concentration camp in a remote area of Wyoming. Of all the concentration camps, Heart Mountain was the farthest north and thus experienced the most brutal winters. Ishigo realized she could not possibly be separated from her husband, the love of her life, and so she decided to go to Heart Mountain with him. In the concentration camp she obtained a job in the documentary section of the Reports Division. She was paid $19 per month and as an employee of the War Relocation Authority (WRA) her artwork was government property. When she was released from Heart Mountain, a U.S. archivist seized her artwork, but she managed to smuggle out many of her drawings and watercolors packed between her clothes and Arthur's when they returned to Los Angeles.

In the camp her work focused on the lives of women and children in particular. The harsh weather conditions made routine activities such as gathering coal or walking home from school near-deadly situations because the extreme cold and dust storms attacked the lungs of the women and schoolchildren. She viewed her role in the camps as producing a document to the atrocities committed at Heart Mountain. She stated that she "hoarded and kept every note and sketch . . . because I wanted to cry out to all those beyond that desolate horizon, look what you've done. Why? It makes no sense at all" (Okazaki). She used watercolor, charcoal, and pencil sketches in particular as her favorite mediums. However, she disliked the effects of the watercolor and complained that it made everything look "too clean and untroubled" (Ishigo Papers). She enjoyed the intensity and bleakness offered by the charcoal and pencil sketches, although she is most remembered for her watercolors that spoke to the heterogeneity of camp life.

Despite the dire circumstances of life at Heart Mountain, much of the time was spent trying to accomplish daily and routine activities for survival such as washing clothes, which was extremely difficult in the cold desert environment. Ishigo took scenes of these daily activities as a springboard for her art and subtly showed the realities of the camp. Along with depictions of the difficult chores, she painted scenes of overcrowded rooms and latrines that the women and children were forced to use during their stay. At the same time, Ishigo's watercolors portray a feeling of normalcy as she also documented camp activities such as baseball games and Memorial Day services.

Working at Heart Mountain caused Ishigo to identify strongly with the Japanese American experience. She later wrote, "Strange as it may sound, in this desperate and lonely place, I felt accepted for the first time in my life. The government had declared me a Japanese and now I no longer saw myself as white. I was a Japanese American. My fellow Heart Mountain residents took me in as one of their own" (Okazaki). Despite that assertion, critics say that Ishigo's artwork appear like a social critic with an eye of an outsider. In fact, her whiteness may have allowed her to imagine herself in a place other than within the fences of the concentration camp.

After three-and-a-half years at Heart Mountain, Ishigo and her husband were released to Los Angeles where they worked in fish canneries. Ishigo lived in seclusion after her husband passed away in 1957. However, the California Historical Society asked her to show her painting in their *Months of Waiting* exhibit on the concentration camp experience. Shortly after, in 1972, her book *Lone Heart Mountain,* which she wrote and sketched while confined was discovered by the Hollywood Chapter of the Japanese American Citizens League (JACL) and published. In the pages of her memoir she wrote of the psychic power that the mountain, Heart Mountain, held over her and all those at the camp: "Imprisoned at the foot of the mountain, towering in its silence over the barren waste, we searched its gaunt face for the mystery of our destiny" (Ishigo, 1972, 32).

Shortly before her death, Steven Okazaki, a Japanese American documentary filmmaker, released the short film *Days of Waiting* (1990), which chronicled Ishigo's life and work within the camps. The filmmaker discovered the artist in her senior years living in destitution, but the poignant short film struck a chord with audiences and critics for the portrayal of a wife dedicated to her husband and an artist devoted to documenting life at Heart Mountain. The film won the Academy Award for Best Documentary Short Subject and the George Peabody Award.

Estelle Ishigo died in 1990 in Los Angeles.

Kassandra M. Lee

References

Dusselier, Jane. "Embodied Identity? The Life and Art of Estelle Ishigo." *Feminist Studies* 32:3 (2006): 534–46.

Ishigo, Estelle. "The Estelle Ishigo Papers, 1941–1957." Collection 2010. Department of Special Collections. Charles E. Young Library. University of California, Los Angeles.
Ishigo, Estelle. *Lone Heart Mountain*. Los Angeles: Anderson, Richia, and Simon, 1972.
Okazaki, Steven. *Days of Waiting*. Mouchette Films, 1990.

ISSEI

Issei is a Japanese term used to describe the first generation of migrants from Japan most of whom left Japan between 1868 and 1924. During this period approximately 275,000 migrants arrived in the United States and settled mostly in Hawai'i and on the West Coast. Japanese migration to the United States can be roughly divided into two waves: those who came between 1885 and 1907, and those who arrived between 1908 and 1924. Prior to this a small number of Japanese had arrived in the United States. For example, on May 17, 1868, the *Scioto* carried the first group of Japanese American laborers to Hawai'i, and on May 27, 1869, a small number of Japanese arrived in San Francisco on the *S.S. China* as political refugees. Comprised of mostly men, and one or two women, the political refugees came with the hope of establishing a successful farming colony. However, the land proved inhospitable to the plants that they brought, and the colony soon fizzled out. Through the 1880s, Japanese migration to the United States comprised mainly of small isolated communities of work-study students. In 1880, the census reported the total Japanese American population as 148.

The history of the issei in Hawai'i is different. The 1868 group of Japanese migrant laborers, including two women and one child, were brought to Hawai'i to supplement and displace Chinese workers on sugar plantations whose contracts were running out and who preferred self employment. The Japanese, as contract laborers, were bound to 36 months of work. However, the experience of the first migrant laborers went badly, and the Japanese government was skeptical about authorizing more labor contracts. After 1868, they refused to grant further requests for Japanese migrant laborers.

By the late 19th century, three significant events led to a dramatic change in the pattern of Japanese migration. First, Congress passed the 1882 Chinese Exclusion Act; second, Hawai'i's need for cheap laborers to work the sugar plantations grew; and third, economic shifts in Japan brought on rapid industrialization and militarization. Those factors led to a revision of Japan's prior position on migration and opened the door for the first large-scale wave of migration of Japanese contract laborers. The exclusion of Chinese workers in 1882 heightened the need for another source of cheap labor, which the Japanese supplied. U.S. employers recruited Japanese workers for the express purpose of replenishing the labor force on farms, railroads, mines, and other businesses. Between 1885 and 1894, over 30,000 issei arrived in Hawai'i as contract laborers, and many of those, because of West Coast labor recruiters and the prospect of earning more wages, left the sugar plantations for opportunities on the continent.

Unlike European immigrants, Asian and Japanese American workers had to navigate racist laws and practices, in large part, because they were classified as

Issei, first-generation Japanese Americans, and their children, the nisei or second generation, at a garden club meeting in Oregon, July 1924. (Underwood Archives)

"aliens ineligible to citizenship" as specified by the Naturalization Act (1790), which limited naturalization to "free white persons." Restrictive statutes like the California Alien Land Law (1913) were written as such, preventing "aliens ineligible to citizenship" from owning land. Subsequent acts in California systematically excluded issei from owning, leasing, and sharecropping land, thus limiting their upward mobility in agriculture.

Because they were recruited as migrant laborers like the Chinese before them, Japanese American migrants were overwhelmingly men. Women were a mere 9 percent of Hawai'i's Japanese in 1890, and they increased to 22 percent in 1900, 31 percent in 1910, and 41 percent in 1920. Women constituted only 4 percent of the U.S. continental Japanese Americans in 1900, but they rose to 13 percent in 1910 and 35 percent in 1920. Most of that increase was due to the migration of so-called "picture brides," who escaped the restrictions of the Gentlemen's Agreement. Despite the employers' desire that Japanese Americans work for a period and return to Japan after the completion of their contracts, Japanese Americans formed roots in Hawai'i and on the West Coast. The infusion of women was one indication of that desire to form permanent communities in the United States.

Women, through their labor and reproductive powers, led to the growth in communities and families. Importantly, their children, the nisei, were U.S. citizens by birth as guaranteed by the Fourteenth Amendment of the Constitution. The second generation added stability to a formerly migrant population, and they, when of age, could claim the rights of citizenship such as land ownership. Yet in the years before World War II, the issei still faced large-scale racism and labor discrimination as they were forced into the lowest rung of labor with exploitative and low-paying jobs.

In 1924, the Asian Exclusion Act brought Japanese migration to a screeching halt and therewith any change in the numbers of issei. Importantly, during the years leading up to World War II the issei were the primary targets of investigations and anti-Japanese racist sentiments. Civilian and military intelligence saw the issei as essentially Japanese and hence "pro-Japan," a characterization especially critical during World War II when Japan became the enemy. In addition, the United States saw the issei as detrimental to its efforts to "Americanize" the nisei. So although useful as laborers, according to the government and employers, the issei comprised "aliens" and thus constituted a potentially threatening presence within the United States.

Autumn Womack

ITALIAN AMERICANS

In May 1942, the Joint Fact-Finding Committee on Un-American Activities in California, also called the Tenney Committee, held hearings in San Francisco to investigate allegations of Fascist activities and influence. The city and state, the committee held, had to be secured from the wartime threat of disloyalty, and enemy aliens, including Italian and German Americans, had to prove their loyalty to the United States. After Pearl Harbor, Italian American noncitizens, some 600,000 of them, were classified as "enemy aliens," and they had to register and carry pink booklets identifying them as such, and were required to turn in contraband such as shortwave radios. Some of their homes were raided and searched, and they were subjected to the military curfews along the West Coast. The some 10,000 Italian American aliens living in the prohibited zones of California were forced to move, and finally, nearly 300 Italian Americans were abruptly taken away from their homes and families and confined in internment camps.

In 1939 at the start of the war in Europe, President Franklin Roosevelt secretly ordered the Federal Bureau of Investigation (FBI) and military intelligence to create a list of "potentially dangerous" persons in the event of war. The outcome was the Custodial Detention List. In addition, the FBI placed wiretaps on persons suspected of subversive activities, and in June 1941, the United States closed Italian and German consulates and repatriated their diplomatic staff. Those preparations were operationalized on December 7, 1941.

During the first few weeks of the war, the FBI detained nearly 300 Italian Americans. All of them were summarily removed, and were not charged with any crimes. They were simply apprehended under emergency procedures. For Italian Americans, most had been placed by the FBI on the Custodial Detention List, which included members of allegedly pro-Fascist organizations like the Federation of Italian War Veterans, an organization of World War I veterans, editors and writers of Italian-language newspapers and broadcasters on Italian-language radio, and Italian-language school teachers. The dubious charge of disloyalty for many of those on the Custodial Detention List was admitted by an August 1942 Justice Department document, citing a "lack of evidence of any subversive activities" on the part of the Italian World War I veterans who had fought on the Allied side against Germany.

Filippo Molinari, an employee of *L'Italia*, San Francisco's Italian-language newspaper, remembered the night of December 7, 1941. "I was the first one arrested in San Jose the night of the attack on Pearl Harbor," he wrote years later. "At 11 P.M. three policemen came to the front door and two at the back. They told me that, by order of President Roosevelt, I must go with them. They didn't even give me time to go to my room and put on my shoes. I was wearing slippers. They took me to prison . . . . and finally to Missoula, Montana, on the train, over the snow, still with slippers on my feet, the temperature at seventeen below and no coat or heavy clothes!" (Scherini, 13).

FBI agents apprehended Carmelo Ilacqua at his San Francisco home in December 1941. They took him to an Immigration and Naturalization Service facility, after searching his home. His family knew nothing of his whereabouts except a phone message that he was leaving for "parts unknown." Ilacqua left behind his wife and six-year-old daughter. Under armed guards and with other Italian and Japanese Americans, Ilacqua traveled by train to Fort Missoula. There, Ilacqua appeared before an Enemy Alien Hearing Board, comprised of two army officers and two citizens to prove his loyalty to the United States. The initial decision went against Ilacqua, but he petitioned for a second hearing, which was favorable. The board, without much evidence, was "thoroughly impressed with the alien's loyalty to the U.S. and his truthfulness when he stated he 'believed Italy would be better off if the Allies won the war as he had always been opposed to the Axis.' He stated he fought against the Germans once and would fight them again, and the board's conclusion was that 'this man is very loyal to the U.S.'" (Scherini, 15). Ilacqua was released in September 1943.

Italian fishermen along the California coast where they controlled about 80 percent of the fishing fleet were forcibly removed from waters designated by the military as a prohibited zone for enemy aliens. The Coast Guard confiscated their boats, and although the Coast Guard paid monthly compensation to the boat owners, the fishermen lost their livelihoods and homes. Some of the evicted Italian Americans moved in with family members outside the exclusion zone, and others moved into migrant labor camps, which were poorly furnished. Eighty-nine-year-old Placido Abono had to be carried out of his Bay Area home on a stretcher, and Celestina Loero was forced to leave her home of 50 years despite having two sons and two grandsons serving in the U.S. armed forces. Sixty-five-year-old Martini Battistessa threw himself in front of a passenger train in Richmond, California; 57-year-old Giuseppe Mecheli, a fisherman, cut his throat with a butcher knife; 65-year-old Stefano Terranova leaped to his death from a building; and 62-year-old Giovanni Sanguenetti of Stockton hanged himself. For all of those Italian Americans, life was no longer possible. Terranova, ordered to leave his home, wrote a note before his suicide: "I believe myself to be good, but find myself deceived . . ." (Fox, 2). After five months, the exclusion order was lifted, and Italian American aliens were allowed to go back home.

No Italian American filed suit for redress against the U.S. government for losses sustained during the war. Unlike Japanese Americans, Italian Americans as individuals or groups have not sought an apology from the government, and by contrast many believe, like most Japanese Americans before the redress and reparations movement, the experience was a shameful episode better forgotten. The Commission on Wartime Relocation and Internment of Civilians considered German Americans and the testimony of one Italian American but made no recommendations for those groups. In 1992, the Sons of Italy's Social Justice Commission wrote to President George Bush, requesting an apology for the wrong committed against Italian Americans during World War II. The government's response was the forced removal and internment applied to so few German and Italian Americans that no redress was necessary.

Gary Y. Okihiro

References

Fox, Stephen. *The Unknown Internment: An Oral History of the Relocation of Italian Americans during World War II.* Boston: Twayne, 1990.

Scherini, Rose D. "When Italian Americans Were 'Enemy Aliens'." In *Una Storia Segreta: The Secret History of Italian American Evacuation and Internment during World War II.* Edited by Lawrence DiStasi, 10–31. Berkeley: Heyday Books, 2001.

JAPANESE AMERICAN CITIZENS LEAGUE

A successor organization to the American Loyalty League formed in 1923, the Japanese American Citizens League (JACL) began in 1930 to promote the rights of Japanese American citizens by stressing assimilation and Americanization. As its creed declares, "I am proud that I am an American citizen of Japanese ancestry, for my very background makes me appreciate more fully the wonderful advantages of this nation."

Like other Asian American groups, Japanese Americans faced racism expressed in peoples' attitudes and behaviors and codified in laws and statutes that discriminated against them. To counter those institutionalized forms of racism such as school segregation, alien land laws, and restrictive immigration acts, Asian Americans formed various organizations to defend them in courts and in the political arena. Issei or first generation Japanese Americans formed the Japanese Association to promote their interests, and they urged their children, the nisei, to establish the American Loyalty League and the JACL.

Leaders of the JACL drew from the educated, middle class, and their politics were conservative and accordingly drew criticism from liberals and Japanese Americans of the working class. Civil rights, JACL leaders believed, were earned from 100 percent Americanism and patriotism, and thus any taint of attachment to Japan was harmful to the status of Japanese Americans in the United States. In their lobbying efforts, for instance, the JACL emphasized loyalty and patriotism to gain citizenship for World War I Japanese American veterans. Also in the 1930s, JACL lobbyists won repeal of the Cable Act, which revoked the citizenship of anyone married to an "alien ineligible to citizenship" or Asian migrant.

World War II tested the JACL leadership on that very point of loyalty and patriotism. How could they explain the government's actions against Japanese Americans as an entire group? many in the Japanese American community asked. Government agencies pressured the JACL and nisei to cooperate with their forced removal and detention, and tried to recruit informants, which the JACL endorsed, to spy on their parents and others for any "pro-Japan" sentiments. By doing that, the government maintained, Japanese Americans were performing their duty as citizens and demonstrating their loyalty to the United States. JACL leaders defended the government's program of mass removal, and argued that Japanese Americans could prove their loyalty by going quietly into the concentration camps.

Of course, those contentions drew fire from many in the Japanese American community who believed the mass removal and detention derived from racism and violated their constitutional rights. JACL leaders became the targets for threats and beatings in the camps, such as Fred Tayama in Manzanar concentration camp. Tayama and other JACL leaders had to be removed from the camp for their personal safety. Indicative of the unpopularity of the JACL position on the concentration camps, membership dropped to a low of about 1,700 members. Even its wartime president admitted membership in the JACL was "a thing to be shunned" (Kitayama, 220).

After the war, the JACL recovered some of its diminished standing in the Japanese American community by lobbying successfully for the Japanese American Claims Act (1948) that enabled financial redress for a few and the McCarran-Walter Act (1952) that allowed issei naturalization and citizenship. With the civil rights movement led by African Americans and the coming of age of the sansei or third generation, the JACL moved toward a greater emphasis on civil liberties for all and away from assimilation and Americanization. An important move was the JACL's alliance with the National Association for the Advancement of Colored People (NAACP) in the California state supreme court case, *Méndez v. Westminster* (1946–47), involving the segregation of Mexican American children in the public schools. The JACL and NAACP contended in their support of Méndez's challenge that racial discrimination violated the Fourteenth Amendment of the Constitution's equal protection clause.

At its 1970 national convention, Edison Uno proposed that the JACL begin a movement for redress and reparations. A year later, Uno joined in the JACL's successful campaign to repeal Title II of the Internal Security Act (1950), which directed the Justice Department to establish concentration camps for persons suspected of engaging in "or probably will conspire with others to engage in, acts of espionage or sabotage." After Uno's untimely death, Clifford Uyeda chaired the JACL national committee on redress, and at the JACL national convention in 1978, the committee proposed a plan for redress or monetary compensation for the wartime losses and Uyeda was elected JACL national president.

John Tateishi headed the JACL's redress committee, and the JACL supported the establishment of a commission to investigate whether the U.S. government had committed a wrong against Japanese Americans during World War II. The Commission on Wartime Relocation and Internment of Civilians began its work in 1980 and filed its report three years later. The Civil Liberties Act (1988), which provided redress and reparations to Japanese Americans, was a consequence of the commission's report and recommendations.

The JACL maintains its headquarters in San Francisco, and publishes its newspaper, the *Pacific Citizen*. The JACL creed, written by Mike Masaoka in 1940, declares: "Because I believe in America, and I trust she believes in me, and because I have received innumerable benefits from her, I pledge myself to do honor to her at all times and in all places, to support her Constitution; to obey her laws; to respect her flag; to defend her against all enemies, foreign or domestic; to actively assume my duties and obligations as a citizen, cheerfully and without reservation whatsoever, in the hope that I may become a better American in a greater America."

Gary Y. Okihiro

Reference

Kitayama, Glen. "Japanese American Citizens League." In *Encyclopedia of Japanese American History.* Edited by Brian Niiya, 219–20. New York: Facts On File, 2001.

JAPANESE AMERICAN CLAIMS ACT

Passed in 1948, the Japanese American Claims Act enabled Japanese Americans to lodge claims against "damage to or loss of real or personal property" as a result of "the evacuation of the Japanese people from the West Coast." The Act was a victory for the Japanese American Citizens League (JACL), which had lobbied successfully for its passage.

However, the Act failed to establish that the mass removal and detention of Japanese Americans was an injustice or even an impropriety. Instead, the government merely conceded, in the words of a Senate report, "The Government did move these people, bodily, resulting losses were great, and the principles of justice and responsible government require that there should be compensation for such losses" (Daniels, 296).

A House of Representatives committee added, "the loss was inflicted by a voluntary act of the Government without precedent in the history of this country. Not to redress these loyal Americans in some measure for the wrongs inflicted upon them would provide ample material for attacks by the followers of foreign ideologies on the American way of life, and to redress them would be simple justice" (Daniels, 297).

Japanese American losses, the government agreed, involved hurried sales of personal items to meet "evacuation" deadlines, vandalism to and theft of property and buildings, and the complications of having to manage business affairs while being excluded from certain zones and confined in concentration camps.

Despite the Act, Congress allocated just $38 million to compensate all claims, and claims were limited to a few categories and required proof that were too often missing because of papers lost or destroyed during the forced removal. Moreover, the Act did not cover inflation and the rise in land values, anticipated profits and losses, and interest gains. In all, Japanese Americans filed some 23,000 claims, totaling $131 million in damages under the 1948 act. The Justice Department, in charge of handling those claims, processed them agonizingly slow, trying to ensure that the government was not "cheated" by its victims.

During 1950, Justice processed only 210 claims, and awarded compensation to a mere 73 people. Understandably, claimants settled for less. For instance, a 92-year-old issei agreed to accept $2,500 for his $75,000 claim because he believed he would not live long enough to see any of his compensation. In another case, the government cut an award in half because the Japanese American claimant was married to a white woman and in Washington state property was held jointly. Despite that interpretation, the white woman had accompanied her husband and their small children into a concentration camp, and was still denied compensation for her part of the losses.

Redress, thus, was partial. An estimate put the total Japanese American loss in 1945 dollars at $203 to $251 million. The 23,000 claims under the 1948 act, accordingly, were modest, not accounting for all of the losses suffered by over 120,000 Japanese Americans or for their lost opportunities because of confinement during the boom years of World War II. Because of those shortcomings and the injustices of the concentration camps, Japanese Americans launched a redress and reparations movement after the last claim under the 1948 act was settled in 1965. The movement resulted in the Civil Liberties Act (1988).

Gary Y. Okihiro

Reference

Daniels, Roger. *Asian America: Chinese and Japanese in the United States since 1850*. Seattle: University of Washington Press, 1988.

JAPANESE AMERICAN EVACUATION AND RESETTLEMENT STUDY

The Japanese American Evacuation and Resettlement Study (JERS) was a research project headed by Dorothy Thomas, a professor of rural sociology at the University of California, Berkeley. JERS was one of the three studies by social scientists on the forced removal and confinement of Japanese Americans during World War II. The first was a project of the War Relocation Authority (WRA) of community analysts, mainly anthropologists and sociologists, who provided data and information to the WRA for a more efficient administering of the camps. The second study was the Bureau of Sociological Research led by Alexander Leighton, involving a group of social scientists under the sponsorship of the Office of Indian Affairs at the Poston concentration camp in Arizona. JERS, according to Thomas, was a study of enforced mass migration in which the usual factors of push–pull that impelled and attracted immigrants were inoperable. Thomas, a social demographer, was interested in the phenomenon of migration and its effects.

Public policy would be a practical outcome of JERS, Thomas predicted, for postwar Europe and its problems of displaced populations and demographic imbalances. JERS anthropologists, Thomas explained, would study cultural conflict between Japanese and American norms and the process of assimilation among issei, nisei, and kibei—social psychologists would examine the effects of social disorganization and collective adjustment, economists the impact of the mass removal on California agriculture, and political scientists the roles of government, pressure groups, and the press, and the constitutional issues involved.

Supported by foundations and the University of California, JERS received the endorsement of WRA director Milton Eisenhower and a promise of full cooperation with JERS researchers. Thomas recruited University of California students, both nisei and white, to staff JERS. Many of them went on to serve distinguished careers, and all of them contributed in varying degrees to the research project. Japanese Americans Tamotsu Shibutani and S. Frank Miyamoto, in particular, became influential scholars, and James Sakoda, Charles Kikuchi, Tamie Tsuchiyama, and

Haruo Najima made substantial contributions to the study of the concentration camps. Whites such as Morton Grodzins and Rosalie Hankey, who joined JERS in 1943, wrote landmark books on the camps, and Virginia Galbraith, Robert Billigmeier, and Robert Spencer provided additional research on this study. Thomas dispatched the student researchers to the various camps to work as participant observers. Additionally, JERS researchers studied the resettlement of Japanese Americans outside the camps, particularly in Chicago where a JERS office opened in the spring of 1943.

The politics and ethics of research loomed large over the JERS project because its researchers attempted to delve into the private lives of Japanese Americans while depending upon their keepers, the WRA, to permit that interaction. WRA directors and researchers, in the hope of running more efficient, trouble-free camps, pressed JERS researchers for information. Thomas agreed to provide only summaries of significant findings and to direct JERS field researchers to cooperate with the WRA periodically and informally. With that agreement, JERS researchers ran the risk of being accused of serving as WRA informants or *inu* (dogs) in Japanese and of being beaten by the internees. Also, the reliability of JERS data was suspect when Japanese Americans, the subjects, assumed a breach in confidentiality.

In the end, the JERS project published three books: Dorothy S. Thomas and Richard S. Nishimoto, *The Spoilage* (1946); Dorothy S. Thomas, *The Salvage* (1952); and Jacobus tenBroek et al., *Prejudice, War and the Constitution* (1954). JERS also launched careers and other, related books like Morton Grodzins, *Americans Betrayed* (1949) and Rosalie H. Wax, *Doing Fieldwork* (1971). More importantly, the JERS collection of materials on the concentration camps remains a highly significant and equally problematic body of information on the Japanese American wartime experience, and JERS publications shaped and continue to influence historical interpretations of the camps. Some of those major themes include the causes for the mass removal and detention, Japanese American behaviors inside the camps, and the importance of the concentration camps for U.S. democracy.

Gary Y. Okihiro

JAPANESE LATIN AMERICANS

Japanese migrated to Mexico and several Latin American countries during the late 19th and early 20th centuries. As in the United States, they were recruited for their labor, mainly agricultural work. With the start of World War II, military necessity was the U.S. justification for exerting its influence over the entire Western Hemisphere, which it saw as an American sphere of interest since the 19th-century under the Monroe Doctrine. To secure the hemisphere, the United States pressured the governments of Mexico and countries in the Caribbean and Central and Latin America to send their Japanese, Germans, and Italians to the United States for use as hostages in exchange for U.S. prisoners of war held by Japan and the Axis powers.

In that program, approximately 3,000 Japanese, Germans, and Italians were forcibly deported to the United States. Over two-thirds or roughly 2,300 were Japanese, and over 80 percent of them were from Peru. They included consular and diplomatic officials of Axis countries but also, for Japanese Latin Americans, small businessmen, teachers, tailors, and barbers. About half were family members, called voluntary internees, of the targeted men. Peru was active in this program because its government saw it as a convenient way to rid itself of undesirable Japanese Peruvians. In exchange, the United States supplied arms to the Peruvian military. By early 1942, Peru deported about 1,000 Japanese, 300 Germans, and 30 Italians; Bolivia, Colombia, and Ecuador evicted some 850 Germans, Japanese, and Italians, and 184 were evicted from Panama and Costa Rica.

The roots of that program reached back to before the entry of the United States into World War II. In 1939, with the outbreak of war in Europe, the United States stationed FBI agents in U.S. embassies throughout Latin America to compile information on Axis nationals and sympathizers. After Pearl Harbor in early 1942, the United States led in the formation of the Emergency Advisory Committee for Political Defense, comprised of the United States, Argentina, Brazil, Chile, Mexico, Uruguay, and Venezuela. The committee, to secure the hemisphere, urged the passage of restrictions against subversion and the internment of Axis nationals. As a result, during the war, 16 Latin American countries interned at least 8,500 Axis nationals, and 12 Caribbean and Central and Latin American nations, including Bolivia, Colombia, Costa Rica, the Dominican Republic, Ecuador, El Salvador,

Japanese Latin Americans en route to internment camps in the U.S. (AP Photo/National Japanese American Historical Society)

Guatemala, Haiti, Honduras, Nicaragua, Panama, and Peru, shipped their Axis nationals to the United States.

Once in the United States, the State Department held the internees in camps run by the Justice Department's Immigration and Naturalization Service (INS). When the U.S. government arranged for their expulsion, it provided no visas for Japanese from Mexico, Central America, the Caribbean, and Latin America. Thus, they arrived on U.S. soil as undocumented or illegal immigrants. In most cases, the INS confiscated their passports, and as illegal aliens they were subject to deportation proceedings and repatriation. Moreover, as enemy aliens, Japanese internees were classified as dangerous or believed to be dangerous. Although framed within the legal system, the U.S. government's program operated outside the law.

By July 1942, the United States had deported approximately 1,100 Japanese to Japan and 500 Germans to Germany in exchange for American prisoners of war. The following year, in September 1943, over 1,300 Japanese originally from Costa Rica, Cuba, Ecuador, El Salvador, Guatemala, Mexico, Nicaragua, Panama, and Peru left New York for Japan. Nearly 40 percent were from Peru. From January to October 1944, Peru deported an additional 700 Japanese men, women, and children, and 70 Germans to the United States, and Bolivia, Costa Rica, and Ecuador contributed over 130 enemy aliens to the United States. total. By then, the United States had stopped shipments to Japan and Germany, and the INS internment camps grew overcrowded.

In the summer of 1945, with the war winding down, President Harry Truman issued a proclamation authorizing the deportation of enemy aliens considered to be dangerous to the public peace and safety. Some Latin American countries, fearing the United States would return the enemy aliens to them, wanted them expelled from the hemisphere. After the war, in December 1945, the United States sent to devastated Japan about 800 Peruvian Japanese. Deportation hearings were slow, some former internees challenged their removal from the United States, and others asked to return to their former homes in Latin America. During the first half of 1946, at least 130 Peruvian Japanese went to Japan, from May to October 1946 about 100 Japanese returned to Peru, and during 1945–46, nearly 600 Germans returned to Latin America. Some 300 Japanese Peruvians remained in the United States, and they were finally granted legal residence status in 1954.

Despite suffering forcible removal and detention at the hands of the U.S. government like Japanese Americans, most Japanese Latin Americans were not included in the redress and reparations extended to Japanese Americans in the Civil Liberties Act of 1988. They, like Japanese Americans, experienced the trauma of dislocation, separation of families, and considerable economic losses. Most never returned to their countries, homes, and livelihoods that had occupied decades of their productive years.

Seiichi Higashide was born in Hokkaido, Japan, in 1909, migrated to Peru in 1931, was a shopkeeper in Ica, Peru, and in 1942 was seized by police and forcibly deported to the United States where he was interned at the INS camp in Crystal City, Texas. Higashide urged Congress to include Japanese Latin Americans in the redress bill, declaring, "It is imperative that the U.S. proceed to complete the repair by extending redress to all the Latin American deportees whose rights, wealth, homes and reputation were taken away. It is my fervent prayer and request of this my third and final motherland" (Higashide, 246). Higashide passed away in 1997 in the United States.

Gary Y. Okihiro

Reference

Higashide, Seiichi. *Adios to Tears: The Memoirs of a Japanese-Peruvian Internee in U.S. Concentration Camps*. Seattle: University of Washington Press, 1993, 2000.

KIBEI

Nisei or Japanese Americans born in the United States who grew up and were educated in Japan were called kibei. Perhaps 15 to 20 percent of the nisei were kibei, numbering more than 11,000. There were various reasons for the practice of issei parents sending their children, generally males, to Japan. Some were sent to learn the language and culture; others accompanied their parents' return to Japan, and later, chose to return to the United States, which was the land of their birth.

During World War II, the kibei became a particular source of anxiety among some in the U.S. government because of their education in Japan and not in the United States. In that way, they believed, the kibei were more Japanese than U.S.-educated nisei and were, accordingly, less loyal to the United States. Although the assumption was unproven, the kibei as a collective group encountered greater suspicion as potential security threats and as "troublemakers." At the same time, because of their Japanese-language fluency, the kibei were much sought after by the U.S. Army for their Military Intelligence Service Language School and value in army units as translators and interrogators.

Ty Sasaki was born in Oakland, California in November 1924. He was the oldest in a family of eight brothers and two sisters. In 1934, Sasaki's mother took him and three of his brothers to Japan to live with their grandfather. That move might have been spurred by economic necessity, his parents not having the means to take care of or feed the children. In Japan, Sasaki felt alienated as an American, and his grandfather was a poor caregiver, drinking using most of the money his parents sent from the United States for the children's upkeep. Sasaki, the eldest, cared for his younger brothers while trying to cope in school.

Sasaki passed junior high school, and earned admission to a five-year high school program. Because Japan was at war the entire time Sasaki lived there, his schooling included heavy doses of military training such as drills with wooden guns and military camping expeditions. After nearly six years of schooling in Japan, Sasaki and his brothers returned to California. "It got so bad that [I] couldn't take it any more," he said. The immediate problem was his grandfather's failings, and the brother had "to run away from grandpa" with money supplied by their parents. Sasaki, 16 years old at the time, returned to Los Angeles in July 1941 with war on the near horizon (Takahashi, 76).

Sasaki found it difficult to readjust to conditions in the United States. At home, he was a stranger to his parents and other siblings. It took them years to develop intimacy as a family. At school, Sasaki knew only Japanese so he had to relearn English. Then the war broke out between the country of his birth and Japan. He encountered racism like all other Japanese Americans, but Sasaki felt discrimination from other nisei who treated him as an outsider, racism from whites as an "enemy alien," and suspicion from the concentration camp administrators as a "troublemaker."

Kibei, given their multiple problems, formed support groups like the Kibei Citizens Council of San Francisco. They held conferences in which they discussed Americanization programs and their role as kibei citizens within Japanese American communities and the U.S. nation. But the war intervened, and the kibei were cast as a "pro-Japan" faction. As Sasaki explained it, "I got no country now. Even my own country, come back from Japan, come to my own country, come home, and then we're treated like this. So, why belong to America? They don't treat us as loyal" (Takahashi, 79).

Harry Ueno, a kibei, organized the Manzanar Mess Hall Workers' Union after hearing complaints about the poor quality and meager quantity of food and charges of theft from the camp supplies. Sugar and meat especially were in short supply; "they just disappeared altogether," Ueno remembered. Things improved after Japanese Americans agitated, and Ueno organized workers into a union. His intention was justice in an unjust camp situation, which Ueno described as "hatred, discrimination, and everything like that . . . we felt every day, and in the camp, the way they treated the people was the same." He was not a "troublemaker" or a "pro-Japan" agitator, Ueno explained. "Many people misunderstand the Kibei image. When the war started, many of them volunteered to join the Army and also many volunteered to teach in the Army language schools, and many joined in the military intelligence unit. . . . They participated and were a big part in the United States war effort" (Embrey et al., 36, 89, 95). Kibei, too, were patriots.

Gary Y. Okihiro

References

Embrey, Sue Kunitomi, Arthur A. Hansen, and Betty Kulberg Mitson (Eds.). *Manzanar Martyr: An Interview with Harry Y. Ueno*. Fullerton: Oral History Program, California State University, 1986.

Takahashi, Jere. *Nisei/Sansei: Shifting Japanese American Identities and Politics*. Philadelphia: Temple University Press, 1997.

KIKUCHI, CHARLES (1917–1988)

Writer, researcher, and social worker, Charles Kikuchi was born in the San Francisco Bay area. His father belonged to Japan's merchant class, but as a 13-year-old ran away from home and left for sea as a cabin boy. After nine years of sailing in 1900, he landed in California where he worked as a migrant laborer in the fields and orchards of the state. With a friend, he joined the U.S. Navy, became a fisherman, and worked in a lumber camp. In 1913, he returned to Japan to marry, and returned with his bride to San Francisco's East Bay. There they settled, opened a barbershop, and had eight children. Charles Kikuchi, born in 1917, was the couple's second child and first son.

Growing up among other migrant families, Kikuchi's neighbors were Italians, Portuguese, Filipinos, and Mexicans. His family was relatively well off, although his father frequently lost his earnings drinking and gambling. Kikuchi went to public school knowing little English, so his teacher called on his parents to discuss with them the child's language problem. Without comprehending what the teacher said, Kikuchi's father blamed him for being stupid and beat him, kicking Kikuchi across the floor. Not only was his child a failure, Kikuchi's father shouted, he disgraced the family and Japanese race and was unfit to be his son.

To escape his father's fury, Kikuchi's mother put him in an orphanage. "I do not recall much about the place," Kikuchi wrote because he was just seven years old at the time. Yet he remembered: "We youngsters worked in the fields in the daytime and slept in the yard under the stars, waking up mornings under blankets heavy with dew. But not long after I got there one of the children died in the solitary-confinement room of what appeared to be mistreatment and lack of food and water" (Adamic, 193). The authorities closed the orphanage because it was a front to exploit children's labor.

Kikuchi was institutionalized again in a place for orphans, delinquents, and castoffs, consisting of African Americans, American Indians, an Egyptian, and several Mexicans. From that home, he attended school, and in 1934 graduated from high school. He moved to San Francisco to work and support himself in college, but he encountered anti-Asian racism that prevented him from getting a haircut, rent a room, or secure a job. He finally found a job as a "houseboy" for a white family, and entered San Francisco State College in the fall of 1935. After graduating in 1939, Kikuchi enrolled in the social welfare program at the University of California, Berkeley, on the eve of Pearl Harbor.

In the weeks following Japan's attack, Kikuchi managed to secure a job as a researcher for the Japanese American Evacuation and Resettlement Study (JERS) headed by University of California social demographer, Dorothy Swaine Thomas. JERS was one of the three major research projects on Japanese Americans during the war, and Kikuchi's collection of 64 nisei life histories remains one of the most important documents of the JERS project and of the wartime experience. Broadly, those thousands of pages of life histories examine how racism affected the lives of the second generation, the process of nisei identity formation, and nisei perspectives on U.S. democracy.

Thomas was impressed with Kikuchi's reports from Gila River concentration camp, and she commissioned him to record nisei life histories in Chicago in March 1943. Those Japanese Americans had left the camps for relocation in Chicago, and JERS followed them to study their reintegration into American society. The work was important as a document of the wartime Japanese American experience, but it also served to stabilize Kikuchi in his struggle over identity. As he recalled decades later, "It never occurred to me that the wartime experience and my activity with JERS were a therapeutic contribution to my process of becoming an emotionally balanced Nisei, capable to coping with occasional, overt racism and the wider social problems of American society" (Kikuchi, 180).

In addition to his life histories, Kikuchi kept a diary starting with the day Japan attacked Pearl Harbor. Thomas urged him to continue that practice during his confinement at Tanforan assembly center and Gila River concentration camp. She told him his diary would be a valuable contribution to the JERS project. Paid $12.50 a week by JERS, Kikuchi continued his diary in Chicago and the postwar period. His diary, Kikuchi explained, helped him sort out his confusion about being Japanese American and the stresses associated with that, and it was useful in evaluating his research techniques while collecting the life histories. A portion of his diary was published as *The Kikuchi Diary: Chronicles from an American Concentration Camp* (1973).

While at Tanforan, Kikuchi received his master's degree is social work from the University of California, which sent the diploma to him addressed to "Horse Stable #10." Because of his degree, the camp administrators at Gila appointed Kikuchi to head its social welfare department. In organizing the department, Kikuchi's efforts to train nisei women was met with resistance from Japanese American men who resented women's advancement over men. That experience, Kikuchi noted, alerted him to patriarchy within the Japanese American community, and why nisei women, despite their achievements in education, chose to engage in social activities rather than aspire to professional careers. In addition, Kikuchi wrote, those insights led him to include more nisei women in his Chicago life histories even when men outnumbered women by more than 10 to 1.

After completing his research for JERS, Kikuchi joined the military. He married a world-renowned dancer and had two children while working as a clinical social worker for the Veterans Administration in New York City for 23 years. Upon retirement in 1973, he traveled around the world and participated in social causes for peace and justice. During an International March for Peace in the Soviet Union (Russia), Kikuchi wrote to his friend that he was asking questions of both Russians and Americans about the status of racial minorities in their countries. Walking from Odessa to Kiev, Kikuchi fell ill, returned home to the United States, and passed away on September 25, 1988.

Gary Y. Okihiro

References

Adamic, Louis. *From Many Lands*. New York: Harper & Brothers, 1939.
Kikuchi, Charles. "Through the JERS Looking Glass: A Personal View From Within." In *Views from Within: The Japanese American Evacuation and Resettlement Study*. Edited by Yuji Ichioka. Los Angeles: UCLA Asian American Studies Center, 1989.

KOREMATSU, FRED (1919–2005)

Korematsu's issei parents migrated to California in 1905. Their third of four sons, Fred Korematsu, was born in Oakland, California, in 1919. Korematsu worked at his family's San Leandro flower nursery, and attended public schools, graduating from Oakland's Castlemont High School in 1938. He went on to attend Los Angeles City College but dropped out after only three months because of financial reasons.

In June 1941, Korematsu tried to join the Navy but was rejected. He trained to become a welder and joined the Boiler Makers Union, which expelled its Japanese

American members after Japan's attack on Pearl Harbor. Similarly, his supervisor at the shipyard where he worked fired him when he discovered Korematsu was a Japanese American. When Lieutenant General John DeWitt, head of the Western Defense Command, issued an order prohibiting Japanese Americans from leaving Military Area 1 in March 1942, Korematsu underwent plastic surgery to alter his eyes and nose, changed his name to "Clyde Sarah," and claimed to be of Spanish and Hawaiian descent.

In May 1942, DeWitt ordered all Japanese Americans to leave their homes. Korematsu refused to obey that order, and went into hiding in the Oakland area. On May 30, police arrested and held him in the Alameida county jail in Oakland. During police questioning, Korematsu explained he tried to disguise his "race" because he and his Italian girlfriend, Ida Boitano, had planned to flee California for Arizona to get married and "so that I would not be subjected to ostracism . . ." (Irons, 1983, 95). Meanwhile, his parents and brothers had been forcibly evicted from their home and were being held at the Tanforan assembly center south of San Francisco.

Ernest Besig, director of American Civil Liberties Union (ACLU) in northern California, asked Korematsu, who had been transferred to the San Francisco county jail, if he was willing to use his situation and case to test the legality of the mass, forcible removal and detention of Japanese Americans. When Korematsu agreed, Besig assigned San Francisco attorney Wayne Collins to defend him. The national ACLU voted against sponsoring Korematsu's case, and directed Besig to refrain from pursuing the legal challenge to President Roosevelt's Executive Order 9066, which authorized the military to remove Japanese Americans from the West Coast. Besig chose to ignore the national board's instruction, and continued with the case.

For Korematsu, before Besig's approach, he had discussed with his older brother, Hiroshi, the pending military exclusion order and their response to it. Hiroshi Korematsu was chair of the

Fred Korematsu challenged the military's exclusion orders for Japanese Americans. His unsuccessful constitutional challenge was heard by the U.S. Supreme Court in 1944. (Chris Stewart/San Francisco Chronicle/Corbis)

San Francisco YMCA's committee on alien resettlement, and he wrote to government officials his concern over the care of dispossessed aliens in Department of Justice internment camps. But when the military's exclusion orders were given, Hiroshi Korematsu chose to obey the order while his younger brother, Fred, chose to defy it.

Moreover, as FBI investigators found, Fred Korematsu "stated that he believed that the statute under which he is imprisoned was wrong . . . and that he intended to fight the case even before being approached by the Civil Liberties Union" (Irons, 1983, 98). Korematsu was transferred from prison to the Tanforan assembly center where he rejoined his family members to await his trial. At Tanforan, Hiroshi organized a meeting to discuss Fred's upcoming trial. Some said he should drop the challenge because it would bring more trouble onto Japanese Americans. Others told Fred to proceed as he chose. "So I decided to go ahead and see the thing through," Korematsu determined. As he explained to Besig, assembly centers were "definitely an imprisonment under armed guard with orders shoot to kill. In order to be imprisoned, these people should have been given a fair trial in order that they may defend their loyalty at court in a democratic way, but they were placed in imprisonment without any fair trial!" (Irons, 1983, 99). In his decision to submit his case to the court, Korematsu intended to fight for the civil rights of Japanese Americans as a whole.

Three weeks after his arrest on June 20, 1942, Korematsu's attorneys, led by Collins, charged the president, Congress, and military with having engaged in unconstitutional actions against Korematsu and, in effect, Japanese Americans, by seeking to deny them a hearing or other due process protections. The judge was Martin Welsh, a veteran of California's state courts and a member of the white supremacist Native Sons of the Golden West. Welsh, however, left for vacation, and Korematsu's case fell to federal judge Adolphus St. Sure for trial.

St. Sure found Korematsu guilty of violating the military order, and sentenced him to a five-year probationary term. But the judge refused to impose the sentence, so military policemen grabbed Korematsu, who had been released by the court after posting bail, and refused to permit Korematsu to walk out of the court and onto the street. The startled judge bowed to the military, and allowed them to forcibly take Korematsu to Army headquarters at the Presidio and then to Tanforan assembly center.

Korematsu's attorney Collins filed an appeal with the Circuit Court of Appeals in October 1942, and his case ended at the U.S. Supreme Court in May 1943. The court sent the case back to the Court of Appeals for a decision on the legality of the military's exclusion order. The Court of Appeals upheld Korematsu's conviction, and the case returned to the Supreme Court for a final judgment. The nine members of the court met in October 1944 to discuss and decide on the *Korematsu* case. After much debate, the Supreme Court rendered a majority decision on *Korematsu* on December 18, 1944. The majority held that in wartime, citizenship carries heavier burdens than in peace, and because of "real military dangers," the government was justified in excluding Korematsu. The Constitution, the majority declared, does not forbid the military measures taken to secure the nation against a perceived danger. Three justices dissented.

After his released from Topaz concentration camp, Korematsu moved to Salt Lake City, Utah, where he found work repairing water tanks. Paid only half of what his white coworkers received, Korematsu protested and was told the police would arrest him as a Japanese American troublemaker. Korematsu quit the job. He moved to Detroit, Michigan, worked as a draftsman, married Kathryn Pearson in October 1946, and had a daughter and a son.

In the 1980s, a constitutional scholar, Peter Irons, discovered that government lawyers had lied to the Supreme Court in the Japanese American wartime cases, including *Korematsu*. That finding allowed for a writ of error *coram nobis* appeal of those cases because they were decided upon erroneous and misleading evidence. On November 10, 1983, U.S. district court judge Marilyn Hall Patel heard one of Korematsu's *coram nobis* attorneys, Dale Minami, tell the court: "We are here today to seek a measure of the justice denied to Fred Korematsu and the Japanese American community forty years ago." Korematsu testified: "I still remember forty years ago when I was handcuffed and arrested as a criminal here in San Francisco." He went on to explain, "As long as my record stands in federal court, any American citizen can be held in prison or concentration camps without a trial or a hearing," and added, "I would like to see the government admit that they were wrong and do something about it so this will never happen again to any American citizen of any race, creed or color" (Irons, 1989, 25–26).

Patel reminded her listeners that the legal precedent set by the Supreme Court decisions that affirmed the constitutionality of the government's treatment of Japanese Americans "stands as a constant caution that in times of war or declared military necessity our institutions must be vigilant in protecting constitutional guarantees." With that warning, Patel granted the petition for a writ of *coram nobis,* which had asked that Korematsu's conviction be vacated. The government failed to carry the appeal to the Supreme Court so the matter was not resolved by the only court that could repeal its decisions.

Korematsu was vindicated in 1988 when Congress enacted the Civil Liberties Act, which issued an apology for the exclusion and detention of Japanese Americans during World War II, and provided $20,000 to each survivor of the camps. On August 10, 1988, President Ronald Reagan signed the legislation into law. Ten years later, President Bill Clinton awarded Korematsu the nation's highest civilian honor, the Presidential Medal of Freedom. Korematsu continued his fight against perceived injustices like the racial profiling of Muslims and South and West Asians following the tragedy of September 11, 2001, including the detention of alleged "terrorists" at the U.S. naval station at Guantanamo Bay, Cuba. The Japanese American experience, Korematsu explained, should offer a lesson against denials of civil and human rights.

Fred Korematsu died on March 30, 2005, and was buried at the Mountain View Cemetery in his hometown of Oakland.

Gary Y. Okihiro

References

Irons, Peter. *Justice at War.* New York: Oxford University Press, 1983.
Irons, Peter. *Justice Delayed: The Record of the Japanese American Internment Cases.* Middletown, CT: Wesleyan University Press, 1989.

KURIHARA, JOSEPH YOSHISUKE (1895–1965)

A war veteran and dissident nisei leader, Joseph Yoshisuke Kurihara was born in 1895 on the island of Kaua'i. His parents were among the tens of thousands of Japanese who came to the islands of Hawai'i beginning in the 19th century, most of them recruited to work on the islands' sugarcane plantations. Kurihara began his formal education when he was eight years old, at a public grammar school in Honolulu. In 1915, he boarded a steamship for San Francisco, hoping to study medicine at St. Ignatius College (now the University of San Francisco). Upon his arrival in California, Kurihara joined the St. Francis Xavier Japanese Catholic Mission, a community that strongly supported his educational plans but made him aware that he needed a high school diploma in order to enter college. Mission members therefore encouraged him to attend the preparatory school St. Ignatius (located next to, and associated with, the college of the same name).

At St. Ignatius, Kurihara focused on history and elocution—important subjects in preparatory schools across the country, as well as topics that greatly influenced his later life. The 21-year-old Kurihara entered St. Ignatius's annual elocution contest during his second year at the school. He chose to memorize and deliver "Rienzi's Address to the Romans," a piece by English author Mary Russell Mitford that exemplified the ideas of justice and civil rights that Kurihara learned in his history courses. In this "Address," Rienzi—a character based on the 14th-century Italian politician Cola di Rienzi, who led a successful revolt against Rome's nobility and later introduced several governmental reforms—calls on the people to rebel in the name of freedom. In the middle of World War II, Kurihara drew extensively upon the knowledge of rhetoric, ethics, and history that he gained from his experiences at St. Ignatius 25 years earlier. It was during World War I, however, that he served in uniform for the first time.

Eager to fight for the United States (perhaps because of his idolization of Rienzi and similar leaders), Kurihara headed to his local military registration board on June 5, 1917. Rather than waiting to be drafted, he enlisted in the U.S. Army and was soon deployed to France, where he experienced the horrors of war firsthand. Two decades later, he wrote:

> Let those who agitate for war fight it out. Let them carry that heavy pack and hike to the front for days and nights without a decent meal. Let them drink the muddy water, and let them go without a bath, so the cooties can flourish on their filth! [. . .] Let them live under bombardment with death staring them in the face, and see if they ever will ask for another war! ("I Was in the War")

Of course, soon after Kurihara voiced this diatribe, the United States was at war again, and he found himself imprisoned by the country for which he so recently had put his life on the line.

Failing to acknowledge his patriotism as a war veteran, the U.S. government—via President Franklin Roosevelt's signing of Executive Order 9066 on February 19, 1942—impounded Kurihara (and over 120,000 other Japanese Americans) at Manzanar, a concentration camp in California's desert region, plagued by extreme temperatures and brutal dust storms. Within months, Kurihara became famous inside Manzanar's fences. On July 28, he spoke out against the prevailing ideology among the camp's most intellectual detainees, who argued that nisei (who, unlike their issei parents, were U.S. citizens) would be best positioned to fight discrimination and educate citizens for leadership. Before the order to leave his home and work, Kurihara explained, he was "100 percent American," but the minute Executive Order 9066 went into effect he swore "severance of [his] allegiance to the United States, and became 100 percent pro-Japanese. [. . .] If any one, any nisei, thinks he's an American I dare him to try to walk out of this prison. This is no place for us. It's a white man's country" (Speeches). A number of listeners agreed with Kurihara's convictions, and so he became a major voice in the camp.

On December 5, 1942, six masked men entered the Manzanar residence of nisei Fred Tayama and bludgeoned him with clubs. Many in the camp detested Tayama, a former restaurant owner who exploited his workers and who, at a Utah meeting of the Japanese American Citizens League, called himself a representative of Japanese Americans everywhere. Tayama accused Harry Ueno, a popular chief cook at one of Manzanar's mess halls who organized and headed the camp's Kitchen Workers Union, of having been of one his assailants. Ueno's subsequent arrest and exile to a jail in the nearby town of Independence triggered great protest: claiming that Ueno was wrongfully incarcerated, Kurihara and others marched to Manzanar's administration building and loudly demanded his release.

Standing, microphone in hand, atop an oil tank, the 47-year-old Kurihara delivered one of his most famous and controversial speeches: "Why permit that sneak [Tayama] to pollute the air we breathe?" he asked a crowd of 2,000. "Let's kill him and feed him to the roving coyotes! [. . .] If the Administration refuses to listen to our demand, let us proceed with him and exterminate all other informers in this camp" ("Murder"). While the administration responded by returning Ueno to Manzanar, he still was confined to a jail on the camp's grounds, and protests continued. Soon, the military police came to break up the impassioned crowd; soldiers fired tear gas grenades and gunned down two young Japanese American men. Kurihara was jailed in the nearby town of Bishop, then transferred three times—to Moab, Utah, to Leupp, Arizona, and finally to Tule Lake, California. At Tule Lake, Kurihara became a key informant for Rosalie Hankey, a researcher for the Japanese American Evacuation and Resettlement Study, which collected a large number of photographs, letters, and journals of evacuees and government officials alike.

Two months after the war ended, Kurihara boarded the first ship bound for Japan, where he had never been before, and remained there the rest of his life, not once returning to the United States that rejected and disillusioned him. He died of a stroke in 1965, yet his strong, dissident voice remains in our memory.

Daniel Valella

References

Kurihara, Joseph Y. "I Was in the War." *Kashu Maininchi,* May 19, 1940.
Kurihara, Joseph Y. "Murder in Camp Manzanar." Unpublished typescript, 2–3, [April 16, 1943], Japanese American Evacuation and Relocation Records, O8.10, 67/14c, Bancroft Library, University of California, Berkeley.
Kurihara, Joseph Y. [Speeches]. Unpublished typescript, 1–2, [Nov. 1945], Japanese American Evacuation and Relocation Records, O8.10, 67/14c, Bancroft Library, University of California, Berkeley.
Tamura, Eileen H. "Value Messages Collide with Reality: Joseph Kurihara and the Power of Informal Education." *History of Education Quarterly* 50:1 (2010): 1–33.
Unrau, Harlan D. *The Evacuation and Relocation of Persons of Japanese Ancestry during World War II: A Historical Study of the Manzanar War Relocation Center*. U.S. Dept. of the Interior, National Park Service, 1996.

KUROKI, BEN (1917-)

Ben Kuroki was a nisei technical sergeant in the U.S. Army Air Force who served during World War II. He and his brother were among the few Japanese Americans to serve in the Air Force, and Kuroki is notable for being allowed to fly in combat missions over Japan. Rumor had it Air Force recruiters thought "Kuroki" was a Polish name. Still, Kuroki and his brother faced racism and discrimination while serving in the uniform of their country.

Ben Kuroki was born on May 16, 1917, in Hershey, Nebraska. He was one of 10 children of issei farmer parents. After the attack on Pearl Harbor, Kuroki's father insisted that his sons enlist in the army. Kuroki and his brother Fred first tried to enlist at the Grand Island recruiting center but were rejected for being Japanese. They eventually enlisted two months later at North Platte.

The Kuroki brothers faced discrimination from the beginning during their time at a training camp in Texas where white soldiers taunted them with jeers. They felt isolated from the rest of the soldiers. During basic training, Kuroki recalled, "There was so much prejudice among the recruits there, that I wondered if it would always be like that; if I would ever be able to overcome it. Even now I would rather go through my bombing missions again than face that kind of prejudice. . . . Because of this discrimination we were the loneliest two soldiers in the Army" (Kuroki, 5).

After completing basic training, the army sent Kuroki to clerical school in Colorado, and then to Louisiana to await permanent assignment. He was the last to be assigned, and spent his time peeling potatoes while his fellow soldiers were given permanent assignments and left for final training. Because of Army discrimination against Japanese Americans, Kuroki was unlikely to be a bomber pilot. He was told that his best hope was to fly in a bomber crew as an enlisted soldier or as a gunner. Kuroki was finally assigned to the 409th Bomb Squadron of the 93rd Bomb Group. However, a few days before his scheduled departure, Kuroki's commanding officer told him he had been transferred to another outfit and would not be leaving. After speaking with the officer, Kuroki was later reassigned to the outfit and left for Ft. Myers, Florida, a few days later. Again, before the outfit was preparing to leave Ft. Myers to go overseas, Kuroki was transferred out of the squadron only to be later transferred back after he insisted.

In August 1942, Kuroki was deployed to England as a top turret gunner in a Consolidated B-24 Liberator. The 93rd Group was assigned to the Eighth Air Force, and flew its first missions over German-occupied France. In June 1943, Kuroki was included in a detachment of the 93rd Bombardment Group sent to North Africa to take part in Operation Tidal Wave, a mission to attack the Ploesti oil fields in Romania. Kuroki was a gunner in one of the B-24s that participated in an August 1, 1943, mission. After the completion of this mission, the detachment supported the Allied landings in Italy in September 1943, and finally returned to its main base in England where it operated until Germany's defeat in May 1945.

Kuroki felt uneasy bombing civilians during those missions over Germany, but, he declared: ". . . we were in no position to be sentimental about it. The people knew they were in danger, and they could have gotten out of it. Besides, we weren't fighting against individual people, but against ideas. It was Hitlerism or democracy, and we couldn't afford to let it be Hitlerism" (Kuroki, 8).

After the Ploesti raid, Kuroki completed his required 25 missions, but volunteered to participate in five more. Kuroki stayed overseas for an extra three months, and returned home in 1943. He received two Distinguished Flying Crosses, one for the mission over Ploesti, and the Air Medal with four Oak Leaf Clusters.

In 1944, in the midst of the draft resistance movement at Heart Mountain concentration camp, the government used Kuroki, the war hero, to smear the resisters as "un-American" and to bolster its Army recruitment effort among nisei in the camps. The Army Air Force, with the cooperation of the War Relocation Authority, dispatched Kuroki to Heart Mountain and two other concentration camps to give speeches to nisei about patriotism and the need to serve in the military. Of the Japanese American draft resisters, Kuroki told the press, "These men are fascists in my estimation and no good to any country. They have torn down [what] all the rest of us have tried to do. I hope that these members of the Fair Play Committee [organization of nisei draft resisters] won't form the opinion of America concerning all Japanese Americans" (Daniels, 128).

After his time in the United States, Kuroki requested to fly missions over Japan and was initially rejected. However, Secretary of War Henry Stimson reviewed his request and Kuroki was allowed to join the Twentieth Air Force where he served in the 21st Bomber Command. He flew 28 missions over Japan, and apparently was the only Japanese American allowed to participate in air combat missions in the Pacific theater.

Nicknamed "Most Honored Son," Kuroki was eventually liked by his fellow crewmen. Kuroki's time in the Air Force left him with a feeling of camaraderie with his fellow soldiers, but he was still uneasy about racism in the United States once he returned. After the war, Kuroki enrolled at the University of Nebraska, Lincoln, where he studied journalism. He worked for newspapers in the United States, and retired in 1984 as an editor at the *Star Free Press* in Ventura, California.

In August 2005, Kuroki received the Distinguished Service Medal. On receiving the award Kuroki said, "I feel that it gives credence to the word 'democracy,' and it's Americanism at its very best. I feel that more so than any personal glory it gives to me" (Yenne, 141). Kuroki was the subject of the PBS documentary, *Most Honorable Son: Ben Kuroki's Amazing War Story* (2007).

Jasmine Little

References

Daniels, Roger. *Concentration Camps: North America: Japanese in the United States and Canada during World War II*. Malabar, FL: Robert E. Krieger, 1981.

Kuroki, Ben. *Ben Kuroki's Story*. Salt Lake City: Japanese American Citizens League, 1944.

Martin, Ralph G. *Boy from Nebraska: The Story of Ben Kuroki*. New York: Harper & Brothers, 1946.

Sterner, Douglas. *Go For Broke: The Nisei Warriors of World War II Who Conquered Germany, Japan, and American Bigotry*. Clearfield, UT: American Legacy Historical Press, 2008.

Yenne, Bill. "They Also Served." *Rising Sons: The Japanese American GIs Who Fought for the United States in World War II*. New York: St. Martin's Press, 2007.

L

LOYALTY QUESTIONNAIRE

In February 1943, the War Relocation Authority (WRA) administered a questionnaire to determine the "loyalty" of Japanese Americans in the concentration camps. The questionnaire, required of all Japanese Americans over 17 years of age, would help establish, the WRA held, those who could be trusted for release to work, attend college, or serve in the military outside the camps and identify the "disloyals" or "troublemakers" inside the camps. The WRA called their instrument the Application for Leave Clearance.

The heart of the questionnaire was Questions 27 and 28. The former asked: "Are you willing to serve in the armed forces of the United States on combat duty, wherever ordered?" Question 28 asked: "Will you swear unqualified allegiance to the United States of America and faithfully defend the United States from any or all attack by foreign or domestic forces, and foreswear any form of allegiance or obedience to the Japanese emperor, to any other foreign government, power or organization?" Both questions were complicated and troubling, and they triggered what became known as "the registration crisis."

Women could not serve in the U.S. military on combat duty, a convention at the time for all American women even those who volunteered in military auxiliaries. Issei or first-generation Japanese Americans could not by U.S. law become citizens; they thus remained citizens of Japan. If they foreswore that allegiance, they would become stateless and no nation would look after their interests. During the war, the Spanish government represented Japan's citizens in the United States. Even the WRA realized its error in the wording of Question 28 for the issei, so they changed the wording to "Will you swear to abide by the laws of the United States," but by then the damage had been done.

The WRA questionnaire, accordingly, caused a crisis in the camps and among families, dividing people and generations. The questionnaire was a trap, many camp residents believed, to render issei stateless and thus subject them to repatriation to Japan and to trick nisei into admitting, by foreswearing loyalty to Japan, to disloyalty to the United States. By swearing allegiance to the United States, would that abrogate one's civil rights and the ability to contest or challenge the concentration camps? some asked. These answered Questions 27 and 28 conditionally, "Yes, if my rights as a citizen are restored" or "No, not unless the government recognizes my right to live anywhere in the United States" (Daniels, 262). Many answered "No-No" in protest against their forced removal and confinement, and some answered "Yes-Yes" because their parents wanted to remain in the United States. In sum, the questions' answers failed to achieve the WRA's purposes for them.

Nearly 75,000 of the 78,000 Japanese Americans in the camp filled out the questionnaire, and of that number, about 6,700 answered "No" to Question 28, and they were promptly classified as "disloyal." Even the approximately 2,000 who qualified their answers to that question the WRA classed as "disloyal." Because so many, more than one-third, of Tule Lake's Japanese Americans refused to answer the questionnaire, the WRA selected Tule Lake as the concentration camp for disloyals. The WRA designated Tule Lake a segregation center, and removed those who answered "Yes-Yes" to other camps, and relocated all those who answered "No-No" to Tule Lake. The WRA's presumption, thus, was Tule Lake's more than 18,000 Japanese Americans were "disloyal" and "troublemakers" and they were the enemies of the United States. The facts were not that simple.

About a third of Tule Lake's segregants came from other concentration camps, another third comprised their families, and a final third, presegregation Tule Lake residents. Many of those simply refused to move out of Tule Lake or out of the concentration camps. As two nisei brothers explained, "We'd like to sit in Tule Lake for a while. We don't want to relocate. The discrimination is too bad. I see letters from people on the outside. There are fellows in Chicago who want to came back [to camp] but are not allowed in" (Daniels, 264).

A young nisei mother expressed her disillusionment with the United States that found expression in her answers to the loyalty questionnaire. "I have American citizenship," she wrote. "It's no good, so what's the use? . . . I feel that we're not wanted in this country any longer. Before the evacuation I had thought we were Americans, but our features are against us. . . . I found out about being American. It's too late for me, but at least [in Japan] I can bring up my children so that they won't have to face the same kind of trouble I've experienced" (Daniels, 264).

Gary Y. Okihiro

Reference

Daniels, Roger. *Asian America: Chinese and Japanese in the United States since 1850*. Seattle: University of Washington Press, 1988.

MAGIC INTERCEPTS

In September 1940, U.S. intelligence managed to break Japanese codes used in Japan's encoded transmissions to its consular offices in the United States. Those intercepts, codenamed MAGIC in 1941, enabled U.S. officials, including the president, to listen in on secret Japanese diplomatic and military messages both before and after the Pearl Harbor attack. The MAGIC intercepts were valuable in helping President Franklin Roosevelt and his military strategists in the conduct of the war with Japan and, through Japan's diplomatic communications, with Germany.

The Japanese government relied on an encrypting system called RED by U.S. intelligence during the 1930s, and its successor called PURPLE, again, by U.S. intelligence beginning in 1939. To send messages, a clerk typed the text with an electric typewriter that conveyed the signal to a machine cipher called by the Japanese, the machine, which enciphered the text and transmitted it. The machine was the premier encrypting device of the 14 separate crypt systems used by the Japanese foreign ministry to communicate with its embassies abroad. The MAGIC complex encompassed all of those 14 systems.

When PURPLE made its appearance in March 1939, a special team was assembled from the army's Signal Intelligence Service (SIS) to break into the new system. The Japanese made an error by using the same message in both the RED and PURPLE systems for a time during the transition from RED to PURPLE, and that mistake gave the army team an entry into the replacement system having already deciphered the RED system. Still, the team required 18 months of exhausting labor to break the PURPLE system and build an analog machine, which duplicated Japan's the machine, to decipher intercepted Japanese transmissions. That success meant all messages in the network of the Japanese foreign ministry, called MAGIC, could be read, and that remained the case throughout the war.

No historian, having examined the MAGIC evidence and documents relevant to the decision to forcibly remove and confine some 120,000 Japanese Americans, believes that the MAGIC intercepts support the government's claim of "military necessity." A few nonhistorians have maintained that MAGIC shows the United States had cause for alarm over Japanese American espionage and sabotage. In fact, the MAGIC transmissions implicate Japan's consular offices with collecting information and having been instructed to advance Japan's interests among Japanese and African Americans. Those efforts were fleeting and ineffectual, and failed to generate action from sympathy or agreement. As all of the U.S. government's

U.S. intelligence analysts at work at army headquarters in Arlington, Virginia, 1944. The two Purple code machines deciphered Japanese government and military messages. (AP/ Wide World Photo)

agencies concluded, not a single Japanese (or African) American was ever convicted of having served Japan in espionage or sabotage during World War II. In fact, the general charged with the Western Defense Command and with executing EO 9066 could point to no evidence in support of his exclusion orders other than "racial affinities" and "the Japanese race is an enemy race . . ." Japanese Americans, in his view, were potential enemies, and the very fact that "no sabotage has taken place to date [1942] is a disturbing and confirming indication that such action will be taken" (CWRIC, 6).

The MAGIC intercepts were immensely helpful in the U.S. conduct of the war, both in Europe and the Pacific, but they bear little relevance to nor help explain the Japanese American experience during World War II.

Gary Y. Okihiro

Reference

Personal Justice Denied. Commission on Wartime Relocation and Internment of Civilians (CWRIC). Washington, D.C.: U.S. Government Printing Office, 1982.

MANZANAR PILGRIMAGE

The Manzanar Pilgrimage held in December 1969 was the first pilgrimage to a U.S. concentration camp. Its purposes were to commemorate the experience of Japanese Americans during World War II and mobilize the community to ensure that injustices like the camps would never again victimize any group of Americans. Sponsored by the Organization of Southland Asian American Organizations, a coalition of activists working on issues of civil rights and education, the Manzanar Pilgrimage had more modest immediate intentions—to clean and restore the camp's cemetery in honor of the dead. As one of the organizers, Sue Kunitomi Embrey, recalled, "My mother was a very staunch Buddhist and she would always say, 'Those poor people that are buried over there in Manzanar in the hot sun—they must be so dry. Be sure to take some water [as offerings]. She always thought it was important to go back and remember the people who had died." In addition to remembering the dead, the pilgrimage highlighted the ongoing campaign to repeal Title II of the Internal Security Act. Passed in 1950 during the Cold War over President Harry Truman's veto, Title II authorized the government to apprehend and detain anyone suspected of engaging in espionage or sabotage.

Many Japanese Americans believe the nation must never forget the injustices of World War II. Here, they memorialize that history at the Manzanar National Historic Landmark, California on April 27, 2002. (Associated Press)

Shortly after that first pilgrimage, activists formed the Manzanar Committee with Warren Furutani and Sue Kunitomi Embrey served as cochairs. Embrey was confined in Manzanar during the war, and her memories of the camp haunted her. Decades later she would recall the Manzanar riot: "the crunching of several hundred booted feet on the gravel road brings goose bumps to my arms even today. Since 1969 [the first pilgrimage], I have walked through the former campsite ruins countless times without fear. Yet, I cannot explain the one time when I walked from the car and stopped by the entrance along the barbed-wire fence. A sudden vision of a crowd, MPs with machine guns, fallen men in a pool of crimson. It was gone as suddenly as it had appeared. It was a scene I had not witnessed when it happened. But it brought on a fleeting faintness" (Embrey, xvii).

About 150 people participated in the first pilgrimage. On the 38th annual Manzanar Pilgrimage held in 2007, approximately 1,100 people attended, and since the tragic attacks of September 11, 2001, and the onset of the U.S. "war on terror," South and West Asian, Muslim, and Arab Americans have joined the pilgrimage. They, like Japanese Americans during World War II, were casualties of war inflicted upon them by their own government. The Manzanar Pilgrimage begins in Los Angeles and winds its way to Manzanar, and to the north the biennial Tule Lake Pilgrimage, which began in 1974, serves a similar purpose for those living in the Bay Area.

The pilgrimages have served to shape a sense of community, having shared a history, and they have helped to mobilize other social movements such as the Title II campaign that culminated with repeal in 1971, and the movement for redress and reparations that ended with passage of the Civil Liberties Act of 1988.

Gary Y. Okihiro

Reference

Embrey, Sue Kunitomi. "Introduction." In *Manzanar Martyr: An Interview with Harry Y. Ueno.* Edited by Sue Kunitomi Embrey, Arthur A. Hansen, and Betty Kulberg Mitson. xv–xviii. Fullerton, CA: Oral History Program, California State University, 1986.

MANZANAR RIOT

The Manzanar riot of December 1942 was one of several significant acts of open resistance in the War Relocation Authority (WRA) concentration camps. On December 5, Fred Tayama, a well-known leader of the Japanese American Citizens League (JACL), was beaten, and a suspect, Harry Ueno, was arrested for that assault and was removed from the camp and confined in the jail at the nearby town of Independence. The next day at a mass meeting attended by over 2,000 Japanese Americans, the people drew up demands for presentation to the camp director by a negotiating committee of five men. These included Ueno's unconditional release and an investigation into general camp conditions by the Spanish consul (during the war, Spain represented the interests of citizens of Japan).

When the negotiating committee, joined by about a thousand people, marched to the administration building to present their petition, military police armed with rifles, machine guns, and tear gas blocked their progress. They, however, allowed the five men through, and the camp director promised Ueno's return if the crowd dispersed, which they did, but they reassembled later that evening to demand again Ueno's immediate release.

From Harry Ueno's perspective, two jeeps filled with military police came to his barrack to arrest him the night of December 5. He had no idea about what he was charged with or why he was being arrested. He knew, nonetheless, that the authorities held him in contempt. When he asked that his family be notified about where he was, Ueno said, Ned Campbell, the WRA camp's assistant director, shot back at him "with hatred in his face": "Nobody is going to know where you are going to. I won't let anybody know where you are. And you are going to stay there for a long time" (Embrey, Hansen, Mitson, 54).

After a night in the Independence jail, much to Ueno's surprise, the police returned him to Manzanar. Looking out the window of his camp prison cell, Ueno saw military police putting on their gas masks. People outside were singing the Japanese Navy marching song perhaps to keep warm, and they did not threaten the soldiers. According to Ueno, "No Nihonjins [Japanese] I could see carried any sticks or weapons or anything. The crowd were all kinds—women, young people, Nisei, Kibei, all of them." Unprovoked, the soldiers simply began lobbing tear gas into the crowd. Because of the wind, the "smoke just covered the whole area; people were running away. I couldn't see the movement because my view was from in front of the police station. But the campsite was all filled up with people beyond the administration building." A sergeant in charge exhorted his men, "Remember Pearl Harbor" and "Hold Your Ground,'" Ueno recalled. He repeated that several times as if to stiffen the resolve of the troops. "I could see some of the young MPs kind of shaking, scared because the crowd [was] so big there." Before the gas cleared, the soldiers started shooting (Tateishi, 199, 200; Embrey, Hansen, Mitson, 56).

There was confusion among the troops and their commanders, according to Ueno who was inside the police station and overheard them. No one seemed to know who ordered the shooting, but it was clear that a young Japanese American, James Ito, was killed and another, Katsuji Kanagawa, was mortally wounded. Nine others lay wounded on the street. Most were shot in the back, indicating they were running away from the soldiers. At the hospital, the dead and injured arrived and were placed on stretchers in the corridors. The army tried to coerce the attending physicians and nurses to falsify their records to indicate that the bullets entered from the front to justify the military's action of firing into a confrontational mob, according to a hospital staff member. Dr. James Goto, the chief medical officer and surgeon, refused, and the next day he was dismissed and relocated to another concentration camp (Tateishi, 237).

Throughout the night bells tolled, and people held meetings while soldiers patrolled the camp. More suspected informers were beaten that night and their families threatened. The next morning, on December 7, the military took over the camp and arrested the negotiating committee members and other leaders of the resistance. Despite that show of force, a new committee confronted the military commanding officer to demand Ueno's release, and they, too, were arrested. The WRA sent them to isolation centers at Moab, Utah and Leupp, Arizona. Suspected collaborators, called *inu* (dog) in Japanese, and their families were likewise removed from Manzanar for their protection.

Block managers distributed black armbands to wear while mourning for the two dead and in solidarity with the resistance movement. Between two-thirds and three-fourths of the camp population wore those armbands, showing the extent of the discontent. Camp observers described Manzanar as shaken for weeks, and long conferences and meetings between the camp director and Japanese Americans followed in an uneasy though subdued camp.

Gary Y. Okihiro

References

Embrey, Sue Kunitomi, Arthur A. Hansen, and Betty Kulberg Mitson (Eds.). *Manzanar Martyr: An Interview with Harry Y. Ueno.* Fullerton: California State University, Oral History Program, 1986.
Tateishi, John. *And Justice for All: An Oral History of the Japanese American Detention Camps.* New York: Random House, 1984.

MARTIAL LAW

As the smoke still rose over the devastated Pacific Fleet in Pearl Harbor, at 3:30 P.M. on December 7, 1941, Hawai'i's governor Joseph Poindexter turned over the territory's government to the military and thereby surrendered civil liberties and a democratic form of government. Lieutenant General Walter Short following the governor's proclamation affirmed, "I have this day assumed the position of military governor of Hawaii, and have taken charge of the government . . ." (Anthony, 5). Short then informed President Franklin Roosevelt of that declaration of martial law in Hawai'i and suspension of the writ of habeas corpus of which the president approved. The writ of habeas corpus is one of the fundamental rights of citizenship in which persons must be informed of the charges against them and given the right to a trial before a judge or jury.

Martial law meant the military governor alone controlled the legislative, executive, and judicial functions of the government. He issued general orders that regulated conduct, and his military police and courts enforced his regulations. The military controlled all aspects of peoples' daily lives, including their livelihoods, leisure time, and even their movement. The military regulated the prices and sale of food, gasoline, liquor, firearms, instituted press censorship, decreed curfews and blackouts, froze wages and employment, and controlled the hours of work, collection of garbage, speed limits, parking, bowling alleys, the water supply and its chlorination, and restaurants, bars, and places of amusement. In short, the military ruled over all aspects of life in the islands.

When he turned over the reigns of government to the military on December 7, Hawai'i's governor was under the impression that the duration of martial law would be brief, only for the duration of the emergency set off by Japan's attack on Pearl Harbor, perhaps a few days or weeks. Clearly, by the Battle of Midway in June 4–5, 1942, in which its Navy was destroyed, Japan no longer posed a danger to Hawai'i, and thus the emergency was past. But Lieutenant General Delos Emmons, who replaced Short as military governor, refused to relinquish his powers and extended martial law to October 24, 1944, when it ended with a proclamation from President Roosevelt.

On February 24, 1944, Duncan, a civilian worker at Pearl Harbor, got into a quarrel with two marine sentries stationed at the gate. He was arrested, taken into custody, and was convicted of assault and battery against military personnel by a provost court. He was sentenced to six months in the Honolulu county jail. Duncan appealed to the U.S. district court in Hawai'i for a writ of habeas corpus, claiming his trial under military rule was unconstitutional. Further, by 1944, Duncan contended, there was no "military necessity" for martial law in Hawai'i, nor was it imperative to try a civilian before a military court. Duncan's petition was served on the sheriff of the City and County of Honolulu, Duke Kahanamoku, and thus the case is known as *Duncan v. Kahanamoku*. The case was one of two heard by the U.S. Supreme Court, challenging martial law in Hawai'i.

The Supreme Court heard and decided *Duncan v. Kahanamoku* after end of martial law effective October 24, 1944. In a divided opinion rendered in 1946, the court declared that the Constitution and especially the Bill of Rights apply in the Territory of Hawai'i as well as elsewhere in the United States, and the military commander is not exempt from U.S. law but is subject to it even under martial law. The lawfulness of military rule must be decided on the basis of its necessity for the public safety. *Duncan v. Kahanamoku* (1946) effectively closed the chapter on Hawai'i under martial law, an extraordinary measure in U.S. history, and more broadly it affirmed the principles of democracy and the application of the U.S. Constitution even during times of war.

It did not, however, end the debate over who instituted martial law in the territory. The army tried to wash its hands of responsibility for what can only be seen as an antidemocratic act, while the governor who surrendered his powers to the military might have had his legacy in mind when he blamed the military. On March 25, 1946, the secretary of war submitted for insertion in the *Congressional Record* his defense of the military's actions: "The Army did not in any sense oust or overthrow the civil government of the Territory," the secretary claimed. "The civil authorities of the Territory continued for the most part to function as before, their authority supported and assured by martial law." From his perspective, Governor Poindexter recalled December 7 when General Short requested of him a declaration of martial law and suspension of the writ of habeas corpus: "During the conference I put this question to Gen. Short: 'As commanding general, charged with the defense of these islands, do you consider it absolutely essential to the defense of these islands that martial law be declared and the privilege of the writ of habeas corpus be suspended?' He answered emphatically: 'I do.' I then told him that I was reluctant to do as he requested, that I was a civilian unversed in military matters but he was a soldier charged with the duty of safeguarding Hawaii from the enemy, and that I must yield to his judgment as to what measures should be taken in discharging this duty" (Anthony, 8, 97).

In reality, the military had long planned for martial law in the islands. Army and Navy intelligence since at least World War I, when Japan was an ally of the United States, investigated Japanese Americans in Hawai'i. For the military, the "Japanese problem" involved their numbers, Buddhist temples and Japanese-language schools, and their labor militancy especially after the 1920 strike of Filipino and Japanese American sugar plantation workers on the island of O'ahu. The strike, they believed, was orchestrated by Japan as part of its campaign for global dominance against white supremacy. In Hawai'i, the military strategists held that Japan connived to control the economic and political life of the territory under the cover of democracy and civil liberties. Military rule was the only sure way to combat that peaceful invasion and subversion.

The Summerall report of 1922 summarized the military's concerns over the islands' "Japanese problem." A year earlier, the army's War Plans Division (WPD) considered the defense of Hawai'i in a document drawn up in 1921 and revised in 1923 called the Orange War Plan (Japan was assigned the color orange). The plan proposed the declaration of martial law, internment of enemy aliens and civilians deemed security risks, and restrictions on labor, movement, and the press and public information. John DeWitt, the acting chief of staff in the WPD who detailed the Orange War Plan, was a colonel at the time. He would later become the general in charge of the U.S. West Coast, and the commander responsible for implementing President Roosevelt's EO 9066. DeWitt argued for the Orange War Plan's martial law or "the establishment of complete military control over the Hawaiian Islands, including its people, supplies, material, etc." on the grounds of "military necessity" (Okihiro, 124).

Martial law, accordingly, governed Hawai'i for most of the war years not because of Pearl Harbor but because of military strategies laid during the 1920s.

Gary Y. Okihiro

References

Anthony, J. Garner. *Hawaii under Army Rule*. Honolulu: University Press of Hawaii, 1955, 1975.

Okihiro, Gary Y. *Cane Fires: The Anti-Japanese Movement in Hawaii, 1865–1945*. Philadelphia: Temple University Press, 1991.

MASAOKA, MIKE (1915–1991)

Born in Fresno, California, but reared in Salt Lake City, Utah, Mike Masaoka was an unusual nisei. He grew up away from Japanese American communities, his father died when he was nine years old, he converted to Mormonism, and he legally changed his name from Masaru to Mike. In high school, he was a champion debater, went on to the University of Utah where he graduated in 1937 majoring in economics and political science, and secured a job as a speech instructor at the University of Utah. Unlike many nisei, Masaoka grew up among whites, and he was comfortable in their company. Some Japanese Americans considered him "cocky, aggressive, bursting with enthusiasm and ideas" (Takahashi, 87).

In the summer of 1941, with the prospect of war with Japan looming, Saburo Kido, president of the Japanese American Citizens League (JACL), a nisei rights organization, decided to hire a fulltime staffer to advocate for Japanese Americans among white Americans. The person had to be outgoing, fearless, and polished. Masaoka seemed ideal for the position. He was also well-connected politically. Kido hired Masaoka as the JACL's national secretary and field executive in August 1941.

Masaoka immediately established a two-point program for the JACL to enhance the organization's ongoing loyalty campaign. First, Masaoka set out to build the JACL into a national organization, and second, he steered the JACL toward claiming equal rights for all Japanese Americans. Masaoka believed that repeated demonstrations of Japanese American loyalty, indeed, of super patriotism earned them those rights. To promote those twin goals, Masaoka coined the phrase for his JACL campaign, "Better Americans in a Greater America."

The slogan comes from the JACL creed composed by Masaoka in 1940. It begins with: "I am proud that I am an American citizen of Japanese ancestry, for my very background makes me appreciate more fully the wonderful advantages of this nation. I believe in her institutions, ideals and traditions; I glory in her heritage; I boast of her history; I trust in her future. She has granted me liberties and opportunities such as no individual enjoys in this world today." The creed goes on to exhort, "Although some individuals may discriminate against me, I shall never become bitter or lose faith, for I know that such persons are not representative of the majority of the American people." As a result, the creed concludes, "I pledge myself to do honor to her at all times and all places; to support her constitution; to obey her laws; to respect her flag; to defend her against all enemies, foreign and domestic; to actively assume my duties and obligations as a citizen, cheerfully and without any reservations whatsoever, in the hope that I may become a better American in a greater America" (Daniels, 1971, 24–25).

After Pearl Harbor, the federal government chose to work with the JACL to seek its cooperation with its program of forced removal and confinement and to serve as an intermediary between the military and Japanese American community. On February 19, 1942, President Franklin Roosevelt issued Executive Order 9066, authorizing the military to remove and provide for Japanese Americans. The JACL met the following month, and decided to cooperate with the military's efforts as a sign of patriotism to prove their loyalty to the United States. The JACL called that agreement "constructive cooperation."

Earlier, in hearings conducted by a Congressional committee, JACL leaders had expressed their willingness to cooperate with the government. In February 1942, Masaoka testified before the committee: "With any policy of evacuation definitely arising from reasons of military necessity and national safety, we are in complete agreement. . . . If, in the judgment of military and federal authorities, evacuation of Japanese residents from the West Coast is a primary step toward assuring the safety of this Nation, we will have no hesitation in complying with the necessities implicit in that judgment" (Daniels, 1988, 219).

Despite advocating constructive cooperation, Masaoka and other JACL leaders held the action was simply a temporary suspension of their claim for equal protection under the law. The circumstances dictated that practical decision. It was not an admission of disloyalty, nor was it a confession of guilt. As Masaoka put it, cooperation with the government was designed to advance the "greatest good for the greatest number." Individual claims to rights had to be deferred for the good of all Japanese Americans.

Still, the JACL leadership was surprised when few Japanese Americans opposed their policy of cooperation. Few resisted the eviction and confinement orders. "Both [JACL president] Kido and I were quite·surprised and pleased that there was practically no public outcry or challenge against the decision to cooperate with the Army," Masaoka reflected after the war. "We believed that such total compliance indicated the general agreement of the evacuees that cooperation was indeed proper under those tumultuous and threatening conditions" (Daniels, 1988, 221). But the JACL leaders also knew, in light of the army's legal and military muscle, Japanese Americans had no realistic alternative to cooperation.

Contrarily, the JACL opposed Japanese Americans who challenged the army's exclusion orders. The JACL slogan, "the greatest good for the greatest number," Masaoka wrote in April 1942, prevented the organization from endorsing legal contests such as the case brought by Minoru Yasui who had violated the military's curfew orders to test the constitutionality of the army's instructions. He derided the "self-styled martyrs" who were willing to face jail sentences for violating the army's orders simply for the publicity. "Good Americans," the JACL leaders stated, "do what our government tells us." In line with Christian belief, Masaoka wrote: "Because our sacrifice is greater, let us trust that our rewards in that greater American will be that much the greater" (Daniels, 1988, 222, 223).

Masaoka, besides advising Japanese Americans to "do what our government tells us" and ridiculing those who challenged the government's actions, with other JACL leaders urged the nisei to inform on other Japanese Americans, including their parents, when suspecting any "anti-American" or "pro-Japan" sympathies. Masaoka advised the War Relocation Authority (WRA) in running the concentration camps, urging the WRA to pursue a policy of Japanese American assimilation, and he was among those who advocated military service for the nisei to prove their loyalty to the United States. After the war, while lobbying for Japanese American rights, Masaoka used that military service to justify those claims that for others were a birthright. Military service, he testified, showed a faith in the "ultimate triumph of fair play and justice in the American way . . ." (Takahashi, 127).

As JACL lobbyist in Washington, D.C., Masaoka played a part in the passage of the Japanese American Evacuation Claims Act (1948), which brought some relief for the economic losses sustained during the war, and the McCarran-Walter Immigration and Naturalization Act (1952), which granted naturalization to issei. After leaving the JACL's employment, Masaoka continued to lobby in the nation's capital, representing Japanese businesses, he published an autobiography, and after suffering ill health and several heart attacks, Mike Masaoka died on June 26, 1991.

Gary Y. Okihiro

References

Daniels, Roger. *Asian America: Chinese and Japanese in the United States since 1850.* Seattle: University of Washington Press, 1988.
Daniels, Roger. *Concentration Camps: North America: Japanese in the United States and Canada during World War II.* Malabar, FL: Robert E. Krieger, 1971.
Takahashi, Jere. *Nisei/Sansei: Shifting Japanese American Identities and Politics.* Philadelphia: Temple University Press, 1997.

MCCARRAN-WALTER ACT

In 1952, the Congress passed over President Harry Truman's veto the Immigration and Naturalization Act, also known as the McCarran-Walter Act after its sponsors, Senator Pat McCarran and Representative Francis Walter. McCarran saw the act in Cold War terms, to defend the nation and Western civilization from contamination and destruction by alien forces. Immigration policy, he believed, was a matter of national security to combat the threat of communism. McCarran was a devout Catholic and an ardent anticommunist.

The McCarran-Walter Act replaced the 1917 Immigration Act, and it remains the nation's foundational immigration law. It is notable in preserving the national origins quota of the 1924 Johnson-Reed Act that established racist quotas favoring Northern Europeans and discriminating against Southern and Eastern Europeans and especially Africans and Asians. Denying the charge of racism, the McCarran-Walter sponsors claimed to favor "similarity of cultural background," which corresponded with Northern Europeans and Western civilization. Meanwhile, Africans and Asians were constrained by quotas that limited their admission into the United States to about 100 per country each year.

Despite its racist core, the act extended naturalization to Japanese and Korean Americans, a right denied them since the 1790 Naturalization Act, which limited naturalization to "free white persons." Earlier, during the 1940s and 1950s, other Asian groups were given the right to naturalize—the Chinese, Filipinos, and South Asians. The McCarran-Walter Act, thereby, eliminated race as a requirement for citizenship through naturalization. At the same time, it created an Asia Pacific Triangle, which imposed annual quotas of 100 of people from and originally from that triangle. In those ways, the McCarran-Walter Act finally removed race as a qualification for U.S. citizenship while preserving immigration restrictions for Asians to prevent them from entering the United States in large numbers.

The McCarran-Walter Act introduced preferences that shaped the nature of immigration, including a preference for applicants with the education and skills for occupations considered to be in short supply in the United States, and family reunification preferences for the spouses, children, and parents of permanent resident aliens. Those preferences, reinforced by the 1965 Immigration Act, would prove highly influential in shaping the demography of Asians in the United States.

Finally, indicative of the McCarran-Walter Act's Cold War concern over communism and internal security, the act featured deportation provisions for aliens considered by the U.S. government detrimental to the public interest, and the denaturalization and loss of U.S. citizenship if engaged in subversive activities, involved with organizations against the national interest, or even refusing to testify about those activities and organizations.

For Japanese Americans specifically, the McCarran-Walter Act ended their classification as "aliens ineligible to citizenship," which had prevented their entry into citizenship and therewith, rights. The alien land laws, for instance, which limited issei economic mobility was based on that legal category of "aliens ineligible to citizenship." Moreover, as aliens and "enemy aliens" during World War II, Japanese Americans were more easily denied their rights as permanent residents and, in the case of the nisei, citizens. That denial facilitated martial law and selective detention of Japanese Americans in Hawai'i, and the mass removal and detention of Japanese Americans on the West Coast.

Gary Y. Okihiro

MCCLOY, JOHN J. (1895–1989)

Born in Philadelphia, John J. McCloy was a lawyer and banker. As assistant secretary of war during World War II, McCloy played a prominent role in the mass removal and detention of Japanese Americans as well as the defense of those actions years later. He participated in installing the program of exclusion, calling it the best way to solve the West Coast's "enemy alien" problem. The army's plan to create prohibited zones for enemy aliens, McCloy said, around airplane plants and military installations might "exclude everyone—whites, yellows, blacks, greens—from that area and then license back into the area those whom we felt there was no danger to be expected. . . ." That action can be defended, he assured the military, "we can cover the legal situation . . . in spite of the constitution . . . " In that way, "You may, by that process, eliminate all the Japs [alien and citizen] but you might conceivably permit some to come back whom you are quite certain are free from any suspicion" (Daniels, 1981, 46).

Again, in a February 1, 1942, meeting with the attorney general and other Justice and War Department officials, McCloy, a lawyer and in response to the nation's top legal officer, repeated his opinion of the Constitution. Attorney General Francis Biddle called this meeting to inform his War Department colleagues that his Justice Department opposed the mass removal of Japanese Americans from the West Coast despite the army's claim, as put by Allen Gullion, the provost marshal general, of the "military necessity to move citizens, Jap citizens." After Biddle restated his opposition, McCloy replied: "You are putting a Wall Street lawyer in a helluva box, but if it is a question of the safety of the country

[and] the Constitution. . . . Why the Constitution is just a scrap of paper to me" (Daniels, 1981, 55–56).

By early February 1942, the military had persuaded McCloy of the necessity of a mass removal of Japanese Americans from the West Coast. McCloy had previously believed the establishment of prohibited zones around strategic sites was sufficient for the national security but the army convinced him otherwise. On February 11, 1942, McCloy's chief, Secretary of War Henry L. Stimson, placed a call to the White House to talk with President Franklin Roosevelt. After that, McCloy called Army headquarters in San Francisco. McCloy reported, "we talked to the President and the President, in substance, says go ahead and do anything you think necessary . . . if it involves citizens, we will take care of them too. He says there will probably be some repercussions, but it has got to be dictated by military necessity, but as he puts it, 'Be as reasonable as you can'" (Daniels, 1981, 65). Eight days later, President Roosevelt signed Executive Order 9066 (EO 9066), which authorized the military to "do anything you think necessary" justified by "military necessity."

The man in charge of the operation, Lieutenant General John DeWitt, head of the Western Defense Command, acknowledged the centrality of McCloy in his plans for implementing EO 9066. As soon as he received word of the president's decision, DeWitt and his staff worked on what he called "the plan that Mr. Mc-Cloy wanted me to submit" (Daniels, 1981, 65). Although General Mark Clark, the army's chief of staff in Washington, D.C., opposed mass removal and confinement on the basis that it was impractical, expensive, and required too much military manpower, DeWitt's Western Defense Command proceeded with the preparations supported by the politicians and lawyers in the War Department, McCloy, and Stimson.

McCloy was also a central figure in the change of administration policy from disallowing nisei service in the military to allowing them to serve voluntarily and then by subjecting them to the draft. In May 1942, McCloy wrote, "it might be well to use our American citizen Japanese soldiers in an area where they could be employed against the Germans. I believe that we could count on these soldiers to give a good account of themselves" (Daniels, 1981, 145). That summer, the army recruited men from the concentration camps for its Military Intelligence Service Language School, and in January 1943 the government announced the formation of a segregated combat unit of Japanese Americans. McCloy was a staunch advocate of putting nisei in army uniforms and thereby earn the rights of citizenship. Similarly, McCloy favored the relocation of nisei students from the concentration camps to college campuses, and encouraged Clarence Pickett, executive secretary of the American Friends Service Committee, to take up that work of student relocation.

After the war, McCloy testified before Congress in support of the Japanese American Claims Act (1948), which failed to consider the constitutional issues involved in the mass removal and detention but offered compensation for economic losses sustained as a result. But he defended the government's action before the Commission on Wartime Relocation and Internment of Civilians in

November 1981. He urged the commission to conclude, "under the circumstances prevailing at the time and with the exigencies of wartime security, the action of the President of the United States and the United States Government in regard to our then Japanese population was reasonably undertaken and thoughtfully and humanely conducted" (Daniels, 1988, 337–38).

Gary Y. Okihiro

References

Daniels, Roger. *Asian America: Chinese and Japanese in the United States since 1850*. Seattle: University of Washington Press, 1988.
Daniels, Roger. *Concentration Camps: North America: Japanese in the United States and Canada during World War II*. Malabar, FL: Robert E. Krieger, 1981.

MILITARY INTELLIGENCE SERVICE LANGUAGE SCHOOL

The army's Japanese Language School opened in November 1941 with 45 Japanese Americans and 15 non-Japanese. Army intelligence needed Japanese-language experts to translate documents and broadcasts and interrogate Japanese prisoners-of-war. Because of the military exclusion orders, the Japanese Language School, which operated in San Francisco within the exclusion zone, had to move in May 1942 to Camp Savage, Minnesota, outside the Western Defense Command. At Camp Savage, the school was enlarged and given the name, Military Intelligence Service Language School (MISLS), and placed under the army's Military Intelligence Division.

As the number of instructors and students grew to nearly 200, the course of study also enlarged from Japanese language to Japanese history, geography, and the specialized language of the military. When the facilities became too small, in 1944, the school moved to Fort Snelling about five miles away. After Japan's surrender on September 2, 1945, the school reached its peak with 1,836 students in October 1945, and by then MISLS had graduated some 6,000, mainly Japanese Americans but also Chinese, Korean, and white Americans. President Harry Truman called them "our human secret weapons," and their existence remained a classified secret until 1973. The MISLS soldiers were vital to U.S. strategists in the Pacific war, and their service on the frontlines saved American and Japanese lives at the risk of their own, being targets for U.S. and Japanese snipers. Nisei soldiers were commonly mistaken for the enemy by U.S. soldiers, and some had to have white bodyguards to protect them.

Kazuhiko Yamada, the only MISLS soldier attached to 3,000 U.S. marines fighting on New Britain Island, confessed that his main worry was being shot by his fellow American troops. Perhaps he knew of the case of Sergeant Frank Hachiya who parachuted behind enemy lines in the battle to retake the Philippines, and was later killed by an American soldier who mistook him for an infiltrating Japanese soldier. Before his death, Hachiya delivered a set of tactical maps used by the Japanese Army. The identity confusion could also save enemy lives. MISLS Kenny Yasui impersonated a Japanese officer, and ordered a group of Japanese soldiers to surrender in the battle for Burma.

Translator Minoru Hara volunteered from Poston concentration camp, and went to the MISLS at Camp Savage, thereby going from the 135-degree heat of the Arizona desert to the minus 42-degree bitter cold of Minnesota. He trained from November 1942 to July 1943 in Japanese language and translation, and from July to August 1943, he underwent basic training in Mississippi. In January 1944, Hara and a team of translators shipped out to San Francisco where they stayed on Angel Island, and the next month sailed for the combat zone in the South Pacific. In May 1944, Hara interviewed the first of several hundred Japanese prisoners-of-war who were mere skin-and-bones from starvation. The nisei soldiers made and fed them rice balls, which the Japanese soldiers thankfully gulped.

Meanwhile captured documents began pouring in, and the men worked to translate them. At one point, Hara recalled, so many U.S. soldiers crowded around him and the others that they could not read the documents. One of them refused to move back so Hara yelled at him, "Get your ass back!" and the soldier said, "Okay, okay" (Ichinokuchi, 65). When Hara looked up, he saw the sheepish grin of his commander, General Charles Hurdis. Later, a Japanese prisoner asked him who the man he yelled at was, having noticed the two stars on his lapel. When Hara told him, the Japanese soldier was amazed, saying he would have been shot had he said that to his commanding officer. In the battle, one of the nisei translators was killed by enemy fire. "Losing Terry Mizutari the previous night," Hara wrote, "all of us were a bit shaken and jittery" (Ichinokuchi, 68).

In subsequent battles, Hara remembered interrogating captured Korean and Taiwanese forced laborers who were conscripted to build airfields and fortifications for the Japanese Army. They, along with the captured Japanese soldiers, Hara noted, were just as human as the Americans. Many Japanese uttered the word mother with their last breath. His parents, Hara wrote, often dreamed of Japan, knowing they could never become U.S. citizens. They did everything they could to advance Japan's cause. How would they feel, he mused, if a Japanese soldier killed him? At the same time, the nisei soldiers enjoyed listening to Japanese music on captured records, which U.S. soldiers resented.

Even after the war ended, the MISLS men proved invaluable in the Allied Occupation of Japan. Major General Charles Willoughby, military intelligence chief for General Douglas MacArthur's command, summed up the achievements of the MISLS soldiers: "The Nisei saved a million lives and shortened the war by two years" (Ichinokuchi, 79). Most of the MISLS men were volunteers, and many were kibei, a group suspected of disloyalty in the wartime concentration camps. Like other nisei soldiers, the MISLS men fought two wars, one against the enemy abroad and the other, against racism at home.

Gary Y. Okihiro

Reference

Ichinokuchi, Tad. *John Aiso and the M.I.S.: Japanese-American Soldiers in the Military Intelligence Service, World War II*. Los Angeles: MIS Club of Southern California, 1988.

MILITARY NECESSITY

The doctrine of "military necessity" in the Japanese American concentration camp experience derives from the U.S. president's executive powers, which entrusts him with defending the nation from all threats, domestic and foreign. Both martial law in Hawai'i and the mass removal and confinement of Japanese Americans along the West Coast were justified on those grounds of "military necessity." President Franklin Roosevelt's Executive Order 9066, which authorized the mass removal and detention, justifies the order as necessary for "the successful prosecution of the war." And according to Assistant Secretary of War John McCloy, who conveyed the news to the army's Western Defense Command on February 11, 1942, the president, he said, will authorize the military to take all measures to ensure the nation's security "but it has to be dictated by military necessity . . ." (Daniels, 65).

The decision to deploy military necessity as the justification for martial law in Hawai'i was an easy one. As the territory's governor recalled of a December 7, 1941, meeting with the military commander who had asked him to declare martial law and suspend the writ of habeas corpus that day: "During the conference I put this question to Gen. Short: 'As commanding general, charged with the defense of these islands, do you consider it absolutely essential to the defense of these islands that martial law be declared and the privilege of the writ of habeas corpus be suspended?' He answered emphatically: 'I do.' I then told him that I was reluctant to do as he requested, that I was a civilian unversed in military matters but he was a soldier charged with the duty of safeguarding Hawaii from the enemy, and that I must yield to his judgment as to what measures should be taken in discharging this duty" (Anthony, 8). With that, the governor surrendered civilian democracy for military rule. Thereupon the military governor informed President Roosevelt who agreed with the transfer of powers.

The justification of military necessity for the continent was thornier. All of the president's men were not in agreement. While West Coast politicians agitated for the removal of Japanese Americans in January 1942, a government intelligence agency reported to Washington, D.C., "word of mouth discussions [continue] with a surprisingly large number of people expressing themselves as in favor of sending all Japanese to concentration camps" (Daniels, 62). In the midst of those discussions on January 30, 1942, President Roosevelt met with his cabinet to discuss the situation. The military was concerned about "dangerous Japanese" in Hawai'i, members heard, and several, particularly Navy Secretary Frank Knox, expressed their unhappiness that more was not being done in Hawai'i to contain the Japanese menace. At an earlier December 19, 1941, meeting, the cabinet had agreed to intern all Japanese aliens in Hawai'i on an isolated island away from military installations.

Racism—not "military necessity"—prompted the "ouster" of Japanese Americans. Oakland, California, February 1942. (Library of Congress)

On February 1, 1942, Attorney General Francis Biddle informed the military and War Department during a meeting in his office that he opposed the removal of "American citizens of the Japanese race." An incredulous provost marshal, the army's chief legal officer, replied: "Well, listen, Mr. Biddle, do you mean to tell me if the Army, the men on the ground, determine it is a military necessity to move citizens, Jap citizens, that you won't help us?" In answer, Biddle repeated his decision to oppose the plan. At that point, John McCloy addressed Biddle: "You are putting a Wall Street lawyer in a helluva box, but if it is a question of the safety of the country [and] the Constitution. . . . Why the Constitution is just a scrap of paper to me" (Daniels, 55–56). Biddle, the nation's chief legal officer, had cited the Constitution and its protections as applicable to Japanese Americans.

After the meeting, the military suspected Biddle and his Justice Department were simply trying to put the army in a bad light. The legal concerns aside, an army officer reported, "we insist that we could also say that while all whites could remain, Japs can't, if we think there is military necessity for that." General John DeWitt, Army commander on the West Coast, added: "they are trying to cover themselves and lull the populace into a false sense of security" (Daniels, 56). Still, the War Department and Army headquarters in Washington, D.C. directed DeWitt not to say anything public about the military's plans for Japanese Americans until a policy was decided upon.

The politicians were not under the same directive. On February 4, 1942, California governor Culbert Olson took to the radio airwaves to warn citizens, "it is known that there are Japanese residents of California who have sought to aid the Japanese enemy by way of communicating information, or have shown indications of preparation for fifth column activities," thereby stoking public fears. Olson's accusation was patently false, but he went on to announce general plans "for the movement and placement of the entire adult Japanese population in California at productive and useful employment within the borders of our state, and under such surveillance and protection . . . as shall be deemed necessary" (Daniels, 60).

The army seemed particularly receptive to West Coast politicians who urged the removal, confinement, and deployment of Japanese Americans in their states. As the provost marshal argued, "If our production for war is seriously delayed by sabotage in the West Coastal states, we very possibly shall lose the war. . . . From reliable reports from military and other sources, the danger of Japanese inspired sabotage is great . . ." (Daniels, 64). The military's strategy, he wrote, should not be influenced by the need for Japanese American labor, humanitarianism, or fear of retaliation from Japan.

The president's EO 9066, justified on the basis of "military necessity," affirmed that position taken by most in the military command. Some, including Brigadier General Mark Clark of the Army's General Headquarters, disagreed with mass removal and confinement because of the drain on military personnel required to move, house, and guard the concentration camps for Japanese Americans. But the military did not make the public policy, which politicians in the executive branch of government shaped. Even Attorney General Biddle conceded on February 12, 1942, in correspondence to Secretary of War Henry Stimson, in reference only to issei or non-citizens, "I have no doubt that the Army can legally, at any time, evacuate all persons in a specified territory if such action is deemed essential from a military point of view . . ." (Daniels, 69). "Military necessity," thus, provided the cover and justification for a policy largely drawn up by the War Department and ultimately, the president.

Gary Y. Okihiro

References

Anthony, J. Garner. *Hawaii under Army Rule.* Honolulu: University Press of Hawaii, 1955, 1975.

Daniels, Roger. *Concentration Camps: North America: Japanese in the United States and Canada during World War II.* Malabar, FL: Robert E. Krieger, 1981.

MUNSON REPORT

In October 1941, with war with Japan appearing inevitable, Special Representative of the United States, Curtis B. Munson, was sent to the West Coast and Hawai'i to compile a report on the "loyalty" of individuals of Japanese descent. Munson's assignment was part of over a decade's worth of surveillance and spying by the U.S. government that included efforts by Army Intelligence, Navy Intelligence, and the Commerce, Justice, and State Departments. Ultimately, the report stressed the loyalty of an overwhelming number of Japanese Americans, and stated that even the "disloyal" would pose little danger to the national security because they hoped to avoid concentration camps or mob action. But Munson was also horrified at the potential for subversion among Japanese Americans.

Munson carried out his investigations in October and the first few weeks of November 1941; he covered the three naval districts that included California, Washington, and Oregon as well as Hawai'i. Munson indentified four divisions among Japanese Americans: the issei or first-generation Japanese Americans; nisei or second-generation Japanese Americans born and educated in the United States; the kibei, a subgroup of nisei who were educated in Japan; and the sansei or third-generation Japanese Americans. Munson's report focused primarily on the issei and nisei, and he found that those generational groups retained strong cultural ties to Japan *and* the United States. Importantly, Munson found that Japanese ancestry did not automatically translate into anti-American sentiment as was maintained by most anti-Japanese forces. Further, the report documented that there was no "Japanese problem" in terms of national security. Munson pointed to the number of nisei who joined the U.S. Army as evidence of their loyalty and commitment to the United States. Munson went on to predict that in the event of war between Japan and the United States, there was no evidence to suggest that Japanese Americans would rebel against the United States. Instead, they would support the U.S. war effort, he believed. Further, the report claimed, the threat posed by Japanese Americans to the national security was so low that those "disloyal" individuals could be easily identified from the "loyal" majority. Significantly, Munson's findings were in keeping with the reports of the Federal Bureau of Investigation (FBI) and Naval and Army intelligence that gathered and catalogued information on the "loyalty" of Japanese Americans on the West Coast and in Hawai'i.

At the same time, Munson found that "dams, bridges, harbors, power stations etc., are wholly unguarded. The harbor of San Pedro [Los Angeles port] could be razed by fire completely by four men with hand grenades and a little study in one night. Dams could be blown and half of lower California could actually die of thirst. . . . One railway bridge at the exit from the mountains in some cases could tie up three or four main railroads." So despite the large number of "loyal" Japanese Americans, Munson believed, "there are still Japanese in the United States who will tie dynamite around their waist and make a human bomb out of themselves" (Daniels, 28).

In early November 1941, the 25-page, secret Munson Report arrived on President Franklin Roosevelt's desk. The president was so disturbed by the report he immediately sent a memorandum to Secretary of War Henry Stimson, calling his attention to the investigator's concern over sabotage. In December 1941 before the Pearl Harbor attack, Army Intelligence drafted a reply, which was never sent in the confusion set off by the war. In it, the army's response correctly maintained, "widespread sabotage by Japanese is not expected . . . identification of dangerous Japanese on the West Coast is reasonably complete" (Daniels, 28).

Following December 7, 1941, and the hurried round up of both aliens and citizens in Hawai'i and on the West Coast, Munson submitted a second set of recommendations to the president. Munson suggested the government authorities should make a public statement encouraging an attitude of tolerance toward Japanese Americans and their integration into the nation's war effort. Such a statement, Munson contended, would both secure the loyalty of the Japanese American community and diffuse the fanatic, anti-Japanese sentiment that was sweeping over the United States. More particularly, Munson suggested that agencies like the Red Cross and Civilian Defense should incorporate the nisei into their war efforts, that defense industries should hire nisei workers, and that the United States should boost nisei as community leaders. The strategy was to split the generations between issei and nisei, which was generally followed by governmental agencies in their dealings with Japanese Americans during the war. In the end, Munson's suggestions were largely ignored, and Japanese Americans, issei and nisei alike in Hawai'i and the West Coast, were stripped of their civil liberties and placed in internment and concentration camps.

Autumn Womack

Reference

Daniels, Roger.*Concentration Camps: North America: Japanese in the United States and Canada during World War II*. Malabar, FL: Robert E. Krieger, 1981.

MYER, DILLON S. (1891–1982)

Dillon Myer succeeded Milton Eisenhower as director of the War Relocation Authority (WRA) and served from 1942 to 1946. Born in Licking County, Ohio, on September 4, 1891, Myer was one of four children. He spent his childhood days on a farm, and attended the college of agriculture at Ohio State University. After he received his bachelor of science degree in 1914, he took his first job as an agronomy instructor at the University of Kentucky. After two years, he moved to take jobs as an agricultural agent in different cities and as district supervisor of an agricultural extension service. In 1926, he graduated with a master's degree in education from Columbia University. Between 1933 and 1942, Myer held several government related jobs, working within the Agricultural Adjustment Administration and Soil Conservation Service until he accepted the position as WRA director in 1942.

At the helm of the WRA, Myer managed the 10 concentration camps that held Japanese Americans who had been forced from their homes after Japan's attack on Pearl Harbor. In his book, *Uprooted Americans: The Japanese Americans and the*

War Relocation Authority during World War II (1971), Myer explained the transfer of power from Eisenhower, the WRA's first director, to him. On June 13, 1942, Myer and his wife entertained Eisenhower and his wife and others at their home in Falls Church, Virginia. During the evening, Eisenhower asked Myer if he would consider becoming the WRA's director. A few days later they met again to discuss the offer. "I asked Milton [Eisenhower] if he really thought that I should take the job, [and] he replied, 'Yes, if you can do the job and sleep at night.' He said he had been unable to do so. I was sure that I could sleep, and so agreed to accept the position . . ." (Myer, 3). Apparently, Myer's conscience was not as tender as Eisenhower's.

Myer believed that "evacuation" was within the constitutional power of the national government. On July 7, 1943, in testimony before the subcommittee of the House Committee on Un-American Activities, Myer explained that the "danger of invasion of [the West] Coast by Japan and the possibility that an unknown and unrecognizable minority [Japanese Americans] might have a greater allegiance to Japan than to the United States, called for a process that protected national and military security." He added that the need for speed created the "unfortunate necessity" of removing the entire group instead of treating them as individuals by trying to separate the "disloyals" from the "loyals" (Myer, 1943).

Myer conceded there were many indications showing Americanism among Japanese Americans, but it was impossible, he claimed, to conduct adequate investigations or grant hearings for them. Two-thirds of the Japanese Americans were U.S. citizens and as such were entitled to the Constitution's protection, and 72 percent never visited Japan. Although he was not sympathetic to the forcible eviction of Japanese Americans from their West Coast homes, Myer reasoned he was merely doing his job. At the same time, Myer admitted he had "little previous knowledge of Japanese American people" (Myer, 29).

The WRA, Myer recalled, had to tend to three main tasks. Foremost was caring for the some 120,000 people, ranging from newborn infants to the elderly, in the 10 concentration camps. Second was the longer-range program of resettling the confined Japanese Americans into "normal" communities in the American interior. And third was a public relations campaign to quiet the criticisms emerging from the press about the WRA and its treatment of Japanese Americans, which many saw as too lenient.

Myer described the Japanese Americans as "dazed, confused, and frustrated" (Myer, 31), and he recognized the bleak state of the concentration camps. The army built the barracks, he wrote, of wood and tarpaper, and there were no cooking or plumbing facilities in the barracks. Surrounding the camp was a barbed wire fence with watchtowers and guards. The camps were deliberately located in "out-of-the-way places, largely desert or wastelands," and they were "desolate and forbidding . . ." The 10 concentration camps, he admitted, were "abnormal cities" with populations numbering 7,000 to 20,000 each (Myer, 32).

Like all cities, the concentration camps had to have a way to feed the people, house them, ensure internal security, and provide employment, medical care, education, and religious and recreational facilities. There were problems, Myer wrote, mainly because of the rough conditions in the camps. Confinement led to apathy and bitterness, he observed, and the crowded conditions, lack of privacy, and lack of freedom added to unhappiness among Japanese Americans. Families grew apart, and conflicts arose between the camp administrators and Japanese Americans. Those erupted into mass protest at Poston concentration camp in November 1942, and a riot at Manzanar concentration camp two weeks later.

The next major problem faced by the WRA was the registration crisis in the fall of 1943. Local draft boards had classified nisei men as ineligible for military service, and in September 1942, the government classified them as aliens. But the army announced the formation of a segregated Japanese American combat team in January 1943, and President Roosevelt agreed that the army could benefit from the use of nisei soldiers. The following month, the WRA decided to administer a "loyalty questionnaire" under the misleading title, "Application for Leave Clearance." Questions 27 and 28 on that instrument asked: are you willing to serve in the U.S. armed forces, and will you swear unqualified allegiance to the U.S. and foreswear loyalty to the Japanese emperor.

The questionnaire and questions 27 and 28 in particular caused a huge uproar in the concentration camps. Many Japanese Americans felt insulted by the questionnaire because they had been placed into the camps by a government that had doubted their loyalty in the first place. In addition, U.S. law prevented issei from acquiring U.S. citizenship, and now the United States asked them to foreswear allegiance to the only nation, which considered them its citizens. Would girls, women, and the elderly answer "yes" to serving in the U.S. military when the general U.S. population was immune from that service? And finally, minors and children were likely to follow the lead and advice of their parents. Despite those complicating factors, the WRA ruled that those who signed "no" to Question 28 were disloyal.

The registration crisis resulted in mass protests, and of the nearly 75,000 who filled out the questionnaires, about 6,700 answered "no" to Question 28. An additional 2,000 qualified their answers, and the WRA classed them as "disloyals." The WRA moved those "disloyals" into one camp, Tule Lake concentration camp, and treated those Japanese Americans with particular severity.

In April 1944, Myer proposed a plan for closing the concentration camps. The steps involved revoking the military exclusion order, which kept Japanese Americans outside the Western Defense Command, and developing an orderly plan to liquidate the WRA's holdings and camps. In December 1944, the War Department revoked the exclusion order, and the U.S. Supreme Court held, in the case of *Mitsuye Endo,* the government could not hold loyal Japanese Americans. Justice William O. Douglas, writing for a unanimous court, blamed the WRA for detaining a loyal U.S. citizen against her will. Justice Douglas, of course, erred because the entire U.S. government, including the president, Congress, and Supreme Court, participated in the mass removal and confinement of Japanese Americans.

Throughout 1945, Japanese Americans began leaving the camps, and by July 1945 the WRA announced that all of the 10 concentration camps, except Tule

Lake, would be closed. Jerome concentration camp in Arkansas had closed earlier in June 1944. Tule Lake was the last to close in March 1946, and what remained was the liquidation of WRA property. The WRA closed its regional offices in 1946, and in June 1946 the WRA ceased to operate.

Myer's work as keeper of concentration camps did not end with the WRA's closing. On May 8, 1946, President Harry Truman awarded Myer the nation's medal of merit. In the words of Interior Secretary Harold Ickes, "By his scrupulous adherence to democratic concepts in his administration of the War Relocation Authority, Dillon Myer has established a precedent for equitable treatment of dislocated minorities. In doing so, he salvaged for American democracy a minority group . . . and at the same time he saved the United States from jeopardizing its standing as a democracy in the eyes of other nations" (Drinnon, 163). The next year, President Truman offered to Myer the post of commissioner of the Bureau of Indian Affairs.

As head of the bureau, Myer supervised about 450,000 Native Americans organized into several hundred tribes and bands. The bureau maintained a staff of about 12,000, including teachers and others who operated 93 boarding schools and medical personnel in 62 hospitals in 17 states and Alaska. Myer instituted a policy of "termination" to assimilate Native Americans by eroding their sovereignty and disregarding treaty obligations. The bureau closed hospitals on reservations, roads fell into disrepair, and infant mortality and incidents of tuberculosis rose. Myer was forced out of his bureau position in 1953.

Dillon Myer died in Silver Springs, Maryland, of cardiac arrest on October 21, 1982, at the age of 91.

Carrie M. Montgomery

References

Drinnon, Richard. *Keeper of Concentration Camps: Dillon S. Myer and American Racism.* Berkeley: University of California Press, 1987.

Myer, Dillon S. Constitutional Principles Involved in the Relocation Program, Statement by Dillon S. Myer before a subcommittee of the House Committee on Un-American Activities, July 7, 1943.

Myer, Dillon S. *Uprooted Americans: The Japanese Americans and the War Relocation Authority during World War II.* Tucson: University of Arizona Press, 1971.

NATIONAL JAPANESE STUDENT
RELOCATION COUNCIL

In March 1942, about a month after President Franklin Roosevelt's Executive Order 9066, a group of educators expressed their concern over the impending, mass removal of Japanese Americans from the West Coast. The presidents of institutions with substantial numbers of nisei students, like Lee Paul Sieg of the University of Washington, Robert Gordon Sproul of the University of California, Berkeley, and Remsen Bird of Occidental College, met with faculty, students, and church groups to discuss ways to allow the approximately 2,500 nisei students affected by the military's exclusion orders to continue their education.

The first conference to discuss nisei student relocation was held on March 21, 1942, at the YMCA of the University of California, Berkeley. Members agreed to coordinate their student relocation efforts, establish a central office for a Student Relocation Committee with funds supplied by the YMCA and YWCA, and appoint Joseph Conard, a Berkeley graduate student at the time, to act as the committee's executive secretary. The group urged the military to exempt college students from the wholesale removal, and when that appeal failed, members worked to have nisei students transfer to campuses east of the exclusion zone.

In presenting the case for the committee, Berkeley's Sproul stressed the importance of the nisei students as future leaders of the Japanese American community, and noted that government sponsorship of their education, including scholarships, was an "insurance on the future welfare of the American Nation" (Okihiro, 31). Sproul's argument would ultimately prove persuasive with influential government officials and foundation and church heads who bankrolled much of the student relocation effort.

The discussion among educators spread from the West Coast to the Midwest and East Coast. The University of Minnesota's president wrote to 17 of his fellow presidents, asking their advice on hiring refugee Germans and "our willingness to accept as graduate students, Americans of Japanese extraction who may be forced to leave the restricted areas on the west coast. Have you considered the matter at all?" he queried (Okihiro, 31). The University of Illinois, its president replied, will not admit Japanese Americans because they brought problems and responsibilities such as the public's perception that Japanese Americans were being given special privileges. Several institutions, nonetheless, such as the University of Kansas, University of Colorado, and Grinnell College in Iowa expressed their willingness to admit nisei students.

W. C. Coffey, president of the University of Minnesota, on the suggestion of his counterpart at the University of Wisconsin, wrote to the War Relocation Authority's director, Milton Eisenhower, in the belief that student relocation should be a matter of national policy. A federal program, Coffey wrote, with Army approval would insulate institutions from public criticism for enrolling Japanese American students. Moreover, Coffey and others argued, a systematic, coordinated effort was needed. By the end of April 1942, Eisenhower was ready to appoint an advisory committee, and on May 5, 1942, he asked Clarence Pickett, executive secretary of the American Friends Service Committee in Philadelphia, to consider a national program for the relocation of nisei students. The American Friends Service Committee was already involved in the program on the West Coast.

Student relocation was complicated, Eisenhower knew, and he wanted a partnership between the WRA and the private sector. Japanese American exclusion was based on the fiction of "military necessity" so their presence outside the camps had to conform to that dictate. Thus, prospective students had to be cleared as loyal to the United States and posing no security risk. Schools had to be away from major urban centers, military installations, vital industries, and transportation systems, and they could not be engaged in classified research. Finally, the population around the institution had to be receptive to Japanese Americans in their community. Those prerequisites involved the WRA, FBI, and placement field offices to handle the flow from concentration camp to campus.

Pickett invited representatives from the YMCA and YWCA, the American Friends Service Committee, governmental agencies, and the Japanese American Citizens League (JACL) to meet in Chicago on May 29, 1942. There, the 46 members drew up qualifications for student applicants. Prospective students had to be certified as loyal citizens and serve as outstanding representatives of the Japanese people. Thus, academic and personality ratings were equally important in their selection because they needed to spread "better attitudes toward the Japanese race" (Okihiro, 38). The nisei students were to be goodwill ambassadors for an entire people.

The meeting also concluded that a work of equal importance was the public relations campaign to develop attitudes favorable toward Japanese Americans. In that, the members outlined, faculty, students, administrators, ministers, business leaders, and military veterans were key figures in the outreach program. Finally, the Chicago meeting established the National Student Relocation Council headed by Robbins Barstow, president of Hartford Seminary, to oversee the entire program. During the summer of 1942, the council began the work on the criteria for student selection and the administrative mechanism to implement the project.

By October 1, 1942, the council's West Coast office had received 2,321 applications from nisei who hoped to attend college that fall, and by December the military had cleared 344 institutions, which had 1,800 openings. Because clearance was slow, there were insufficient numbers of students qualified for those openings. In addition, two-thirds of those openings were for women, and two-thirds of the applicants were men. Volunteers, mainly whites, performed most of the work of recruiting and advising students, rating their applications, corresponding with government agencies and colleges, and arranging for student travel and accommodations. The task was monumental, and the generosity and kindness extended by those volunteers to the nisei students were heartfelt and much appreciated.

The students faced enormous pressures. They were away from family and friends who languished in concentration camps. They had to perform well academically, and they had to behave as exemplary citizens not only of their country of birth but also of their cultural community. Kiyo Sato, a student at Hillsdale College in Michigan in March 1943, reflected upon her situation to her sponsors. "I realize the responsibility I have," Sato wrote. "Most of the people here in Hillsdale have not seen a Japanese face before and also many of them have not heard of evacuation. . . . I don't know how I can ever thank you for this opportunity," she acknowledged. "I hope to prove worthy of such a chance" (Okihiro, 72).

In March 1943, the council changed its name to the National Japanese American Student Relocation Council, and moved its headquarters from the West Coast to Philadelphia. By May 1946, the council had on file the names of 3,613 students at 680 institutions. The council closed its doors on June 30, 1946. The students in the council's files represented only about 6 percent of the total population of nisei. Even after their selection, comprising an elite group, those students faced limited options, constrained to those institutions that were willing to accept Japanese Americans and by their budgets. Those factors no doubt affected nisei life choices and careers after graduation.

Still, most were exceedingly grateful for the opportunity to leave the concentration camps and continue their education. One of those was Tadao Sunohara who studied at the University of Utah. In gratitude, Sunohara gave to his alma mater a five-foot-high bronze statue. The gift, unveiled in 1991, is a replica of the Peace Child of Hiroshima, depicting Sadako Sasaki, a 12-year-old girl who died of leukemia a decade after the atomic bomb exploded on her city. Shortly after being diagnosed with cancer, Sasaki began folding gold paper cranes because a friend told her if she completed 1,000 cranes, a symbol of hope, she would not die. Sasaki made 600 cranes before succumbing to leukemia. In tribute, her classmates folded the remaining 400, and the 1,000 paper cranes were buried with her. The statue shows the child lifting a paper crane toward the sky.

In presenting the statue to his wartime school, Sunohara said his gift was in part a repayment of a debt owed to the University of Utah for its understanding and compassion in admitting Japanese Americans. But it was also a gift of hope, like the uplifted hands of the Peace Child, that war would nevermore disfigure the lives of humankind.

Gary Y. Okihiro

References

Austin, Allan W. *From Concentration Camp to Campus: Japanese American Students and World War II*. Urbana: University of Illinois Press, 2004.

Okihiro, Gary Y. *Storied Lives: Japanese American Students and World War II*. Seattle: University of Washington Press, 1999.

NI'IHAU INCIDENT

On December 7, 1941, following the Pearl Harbor attack, Japanese pilot Shigenori Nishikaichi, unable to make it back to his aircraft carrier, crash landed on Ni'ihau Island. Born on April 21, 1920, in Hashihama, Japan, the Naval Airman 1st Class was the second son of Ryōtaro and Fusako Nishikaichi. The pilot served in China, returned to Japan and attended naval flying school, and visited his parents for the last time in September 1941. Before embarking on his secret mission that led to war with the United States, Nishikaichi wrote to his parents: "What was my purpose in going through hard work to train my skill? It was for this day. People may have had doubt about me; God alone knew my ambition. I have no regrets" (Beekman, 17).

Nishikaichi participated in the second wave of the attack on O'ahu's military installations. He flew his fighter in formation to protect the bombers and torpedo planes from fighter attack. But without defenders, the fighters strafed targets on the ground, including parked planes, hangars, and buildings at the U.S. Naval Air Station at Kaneohe and nearby Bellows Field. Later, Nishikaichi engaged American fighters that were able to take off. He shot one down, but his aircraft took on six hits, one bullet narrowly missing his knee and another, puncturing his gas tank. With gas escaping, his engine stalled and started up again. His speed diminished, Nishikaichi fell behind his retreating comrades who had finished their mission and were returning to the carrier force.

Nishikaichi left O'ahu and headed north for his home base, passing Kaua'i and then spotting Ni'ihau just beyond. The distance took about 30 minutes, and with his fuel low and leaking he decided to crash-land on Ni'ihau, which Japanese maps showed, incorrectly, as uninhabited. Nishikaichi could clearly see a village, ranch houses, and pastures. He decided to crash-land in a pasture, and the impact broke loose his harness and knocked him unconscious. Howard Kaleohano watched the plane circle and then crash. He rushed to the plane and pulled out the dazed pilot, taking away his papers and pistol in the process. Kaleohano knew nothing of the Pearl Harbor attack.

Ni'ihau was owned by a single family since 1864. Originally populated by Hawaiians and ruled by ali'i or chiefs, Ni'ihau like neighboring Kaua'i was among the first islands of the Hawaiian chain settled by Polynesians. They were the last to submit to Kamehameha in 1810 after he threatened an invasion, and became a part of the Hawaiian kingdom. Elizabeth Sinclair bought Ni'ihau and parts of Kaua'i from the kingdom in 1864, and her grandson, Aubrey Robinson, closed Ni'ihau to visitors since 1915. The Robinson family controlled the island as its private domain when the Japanese pilot landed.

Kaleohano and his wife hosted and fed Nishikaichi, and summoned Ishimatsu Shintani, an issei Japanese worker for the Robinson family, to translate. When Shintani learned who the pilot was, he paled and left quickly, so Kaleohano called for the other Japanese on the island, Yoshio Harada, to translate for him. Harada was a nisei born on Kaua'i, and was married to another, nisei, Umeno (Irene). They moved to Ni'ihau in 1939. Both spoke Japanese fluently but learned it from their parents and the language school. From the pilot they discovered that Japan had attacked Pearl Harbor.

For several days, the people of Ni'ihau held Nishikaichi, not knowing what to do with him. Meanwhile, the pilot plotted his escape. He managed to wound Ben Kanahele who with the help of his wife, Ella, subdued and killed Nishikaichi. Harada who witnessed the struggle turned a gun on himself and committed suicide. After stabbing Nishikaichi with his hunting knife, Ben Kanahele explained his reaction, "I was so mad!" he said (Beekman, 83).

When the U.S. Army finally arrived on Ni'ihau, they transported Kanahele to the hospital on Kaua'i to treat his wounds, and took Umeno Harada and Ishimatsu Shintani as prisoners for allegedly conspiring with the Japanese pilot. They were put in the Waimea jail on Kaua'i where Army guards kept them under surveillance 24 hours a day. They shackled and interrogated Harada, and searched her clothing. She refused to cooperate, and went on a hunger strike. The military transferred Harada to the internment camp on Sand Island, O'ahu, and then to Honouliuli. Not a U.S. citizen, Shintani was interned on the continent.

Meanwhile, when Shigenori Nishikaichi failed to return to his carrier, Japan notified his parents that he had died a hero in the Pearl Harbor attack, and the Navy promoted him posthumously to special duty ensign. Only after the war did the story of his landing and death on Ni'ihau become known. Back in Nishikaichi's hometown, the people erected a granite cenotaph in his honor. "It is honorable for [a] flower and warrior to fall," its inscription read. "Having expended every effort, he achieved the greatest honor of all by dying a soldier's death in battle, destroying both himself and his beloved plane. . . . His meritorious deed will live forever" (Beekman, 96).

Umeno Harada, after 33 months of internment, returned to Kaua'i where she was born. Many shunned her, and some hated her. She was penniless, and worked long hours for her relatives in their dressmaking shop sewing to earn a living and support her three children. There were days when she and her children considered suicide. She kept a photograph of her husband on her family, Buddhist altar. When she was able in December 1945, Harada had the remains of her husband and the Japanese pilot brought to Kaua'i for cremation and burial. The army confiscated the ashes of Nishikaichi, and shipped them to Japan.

In August 1945, the army presented Ben Kanahele with two citations for the role he played in Ni'ihau incident. Kanahele, "though unarmed," a citation read, "courageously attacked the armed and desperate Japanese enemy and, though three times wounded by pistol fire at close range, succeeded in disarming and killing his opponent" (Beekman, 103). Howard Kaleohano, the first to take the pilot into custody, was awarded the Medal of Freedom in May 1946.

Gary Y. Okihiro

Reference

Beekman, Allan. *The Niihau Incident.* Honolulu: Heritage Press of Pacific, 1982.

NISEI

Nisei is a Japanese term used to describe the second generation of children born in the United States of Japanese migrant parents. Nisei were born as early as the

1890s, but it was not until the interwar years that the nisei would emerge as a distinct generation who would struggle to carve out an identity that could negotiate their relationship to their migrant parents and their U.S. citizenship.

The nisei population began to grow at a steady rate between 1908 and 1924. According to U.S. Census figures, in 1910 the number of nisei was documented at 4,502, but by 1920 this number had swelled to nearly 30,000. The shifts in population patterns were due to the 1908 Gentleman's Agreement, a pledge that prohibited the migration of Japanese male laborers (issei or first generation) into the United States. However, until 1924, wives, children, and parents were allowed to join their family members in the United States.

Born with U.S. citizenship, the second generation of Japanese Americans was often viewed especially by scholars as the cultural, political, and social bridge between Japan and the United States. Commonly, they attended both Japanese- and English-speaking schools, whites expected them to be well versed in American holidays and excel as model American citizens, while issei parents tried to instill in them Japanese cultural traditions. In addition, the age gap between parents (issei) and children (nisei) meant that the regular issues of adolescence were magnified by the added cultural differences including education, language, age, and customs.

But more than the age gap or the pressure placed on the nisei to be a cultural bridge, the experience of the second generation of Japanese Americans is unique because of the economic and racial politics that punctuated their lives, including

Each concentration camp was surrounded by barbed wire, and, in the distance, guard towers manned by armed soldiers. (AP/Wide World Photo)

the two world wars, the Great Depression, high racial tensions, and exclusionary immigration acts. Although the role of the nisei in the history of Japanese American internment during World War II is often privileged in contrast to their parents, the ways in which this generation addressed cultural, political, and economic realties before World War II is of equal importance to their historical narrative.

During the interwar years, education, religion, and print culture were three sites that were particularly important to the formation of nisei identity and to the history of this second generation in the United States. Because of their status as citizens who routinely faced discrimination and racism, cultural, educational, and religious institutions are particularly important for understanding how this generation negotiated their place within the United States. Education was held as one of the most valuable ways that the nisei could secure the citizenship rights denied to their parents, succeed economically, and assert themselves as Americans. Within American public schools, the push for Americanization and assimilation was particularly strong and contributed to the stereotype of nisei being *overly* Americanized. However, even with advanced education, often including college, Japanese Americans found that racist sentiments ran deep. Even with degrees from colleges and universities like the University of California, Berkeley, they were excluded from the professional workforce and, without access to labor unions, nisei were often relegated to menial labor within their own communities. Further, many members of this generation graduated from high school and college at the height of the Great Depression, and as such faced even more difficulty finding employment.

A nisei wrote in 1937, "I am a fruitstand worker. It is not a very attractive nor distinguished occupation   I would much rather it were doctor or lawyer . . . but my aspiration of developing into such [was] frustrated long ago. . . . I am only what I am, a professional carrot washer" (Daniels, 23). Of course, that frustration was due to racism that limited that nisei's upward mobility, which was a central feature of their "Americanization." White leaders like the University of Hawaii president advised the nisei, "Do not count on education to do too much for you, do not take it too seriously. Do not expect a college degree, an A.B. or a Ph.D. to get you ahead unduly in this world" (Okihiro, 144). Instead, he counseled, nisei should be content to accept work in agriculture as laborers.

Faced with the reality that their race and ethnic identity would always trump their legal status as citizens, the nisei began developing cultural organizations meant to both affirm citizenship rights and strengthen community identity. The most famous of these organizations was the Japanese American Citizens League (JACL). "I am proud that I am an American citizen of Japanese ancestry, for my very background makes me appreciate more fully the wonderful advantages of this nation," the JACL creed, written in 1940 on the eve of World War II, began. "I believe in her institutions, ideals and traditions; I glory in her heritage; I boast of her history; I trust in her future" (Daniels, 24).

Like the JACL, the press was a useful mode for building and enunciating nisei identity. Churches and religious institutions, both Christian and Buddhist, were often segregated spaces in which nisei could discuss and develop their identity as Japanese Americans. Unlike the public schools, which inaugurated nisei into

American culture, religious institutions provided an avenue for developing strong cultural and racial ties with the Japanese American community.

In spite of their status as citizens, the nisei were targeted as threats to national security during World War II and were included in the massive round up and internment of Japanese Americans in U.S. concentration camps.

Autumn Womack

References

Daniels, Roger. *Concentration Camps: North America: Japanese in the United States and Canada during World War II*. Malabar, FL: Robert E. Krieger, 1981.

Hosokawa, Bill. *Nisei: The Quiet Americans*. Boulder: University Press of Colorado, 1969.

Okihiro, Gary Y. *Cane Fires: The Anti-Japanese Movement in Hawaii, 1865–1945*. Philadelphia: Temple University Press, 1991.

Yoo, David K. *Growing Up Nisei: Race Generation, and Culture among Japanese Americans of California, 1924–49*. Urbana: University of Illinois Press, 2000.

NISEI STUDENT RELOCATION COMMEMORATIVE FUND

The Nisei Student Relocation Commemorative Fund began in 1976 with a group of nisei in New England brought together by Nobu Hibino of Portland, Connecticut. Hibino graduated from Lowell High School in San Francisco, and attended the University of California, Berkeley. World War II and the mass removal and confinement interrupted her education just short of her degree in the second semester of her senior year. Hibino and her family were held at Tanforan assembly center and then at Topaz concentration camp. In the summer of 1943, the National Japanese American Student Relocation Council (NJASRC) hired Hibino to work in its main office in Philadelphia. Through the NJASRC, Hibino was able to complete her education at Boston University and received her degree from the University of California, Berkeley.

After attending a conference on nisei retirement held in San Francisco by the Japanese American Citizens League (JACL), Hibino decided to organize a similar gathering for nisei in New England. She searched through telephone directories for Japanese American names, and a few months after the San Francisco conference held a New England Nisei Retirement Conference at Boston University. Twenty-four nisei attended, including Lafayette Noda who, like Hibino, was a former employee of the NJASRC during the war. The group decided to meet periodically for picnics and Japanese New Year's celebrations, and they called themselves the New England Nisei. In the course of their socializing, they realized that many of them shared the experience of completing and attending college during the war under the auspices of the NJASRC. That recognition led to the idea of establishing a scholarship fund to combat racism by promoting student access to higher education.

Lafayette Noda was a student at the University of California, Los Angeles, when the war halted his education. He was confined at Heart Mountain and later, at

Amache concentration camp. Noda gained admittance to Swarthmore College in Pennsylvania in 1944 to complete his degree, and while there he volunteered with the NJASRC, although he received no assistance from them. Still, Noda's involvement with the NJASRC prompted him to actively support the proposal for a student scholarship fund.

The New England Nisei, after months of planning, launched the Nisei Student Relocation Commemorative Fund (NSRCF) in 1980. The fund, the nisei believed, emerged from their Japanese value of ongaeshi or reciprocity and the repayment of a debt. It was an expression of gratitude for the help provided them during World War II by assisting students who, like them, were casualties of war. The Nisei Student Fund's purpose is expressed in its slogan, "Extending Helping Hands Once Offered to Us." Appropriately, in June 1982, the fund's first recipient of a monetary award was the American Friends Service Committee in Philadelphia, the body that helped organize the NJASRC.

Thereafter, the Nisei Student Fund decided to give scholarships to poor and underprivileged Asian American and Pacific Islander students "to aid and uplift" them. They focused on Southeast Asian Americans who were refugees of war, like Japanese Americans during World War II. With scholarships, the Nisei Student Fund encourages Southeast Asian American high school students to continue their education. Nobu Hibino explained, "It's the same because we were forced to leave our homes. They were forced to leave for political reasons" (Ito, 144). However, Japanese Americans were U.S. citizens and most were fluent in English, while Southeast Asians were refugees and many of them faced cultural and linguistic barriers. But both student groups experienced the trauma of war, and shared a hope to improve their lives through education.

A recipient of the Nisei Student Fund's scholarship, Seng Suy, exemplified those convergences. Suy, from Philadelphia, won the scholarship in 1990. Suy described his life in Cambodia where he was forced to labor and starvation was a daily concern. In the United States, poverty continued to haunt Suy and his family. As he described it, "All my life I grew up knowing only poverty. I want to see life beyond poverty. The only way I can beat poverty is through a good education" (Ito, 146).

For Cambodian American Leark Vath, a 1993 award recipient who attended the University of California, San Diego, the Nisei Student Fund's scholarship enabled him to continue into college. A graduate of Modesto High School in California, Vath testified: "The award really inspired me to go to college and gave me a new found sense for humanity because since I came to the U.S., I had always thought of this country as nothing but a bunch of greedy people. I know this society is solely based on money, but not I know there are people out there that really care for people like me" (Ito, 147).

Since 1983, the Nisei Student Fund has awarded more than $588,800 to 608 students, and its endowment has grown to $1.1 million. Scholarships in 2012 are now limited to high school students with at least one parent who was born in Cambodia, Laos, or Vietnam.

Gary Y. Okihiro

References

Ito, Leslie A. "Nisei Student Relocation Commemorative Fund." In *Storied Lives: Japanese American Students and World War II*. Edited by Gary Y. Okihiro, 140–51. Seattle: University of Washington Press, 1999.

Nisei Student Relocation Commemorative Fund. http://www.nsrcfund.org.

O

OBATA, CHIURA (1885–1975)

Born in Sendai, Japan, in 1885, Obata learned to paint at an early age. He migrated to San Francisco in 1903, having convinced his father "the greater the view, the greater the art; the wider the travel, the broader the knowledge" (Hill, 3). Here, Obata worked as a "schoolboy" performing domestic work to support himself while studying English. He also worked as an illustrator for Japanese-language publications. During the 1906 San Francisco earthquake, Obata made numerous sketches and paintings depicting the devastation.

Obata met and later married Haruko Kohashi, an educated woman from Fukuoka, Japan. She had migrated to San Francisco in 1910 at the age of 17, and lived in a boardinghouse owned by her aunt. Kohashi studied English and sewing, and planned to return to Japan to teach dressmaking. Instead, in 1912, she married Obata. They had four children, and reared them in San Francisco.

Haruko assisted her husband with his brushes and paint, and, an artist in her own right, she was one of the first teachers of Japanese flower arrangement (ikebana) in San Francisco. "Papa [Obata] used to complain about the other things I did," Haruko recalled, "but he never complained about the time I took to teach ikebana because it was teaching Japanese art to Americans, and he thought that was a good thing" (Hill, 4).

With anti-Japanese feeling running high, whites attacked Obata on the streets of San Francisco, and spat on him. Once, he rose to defend himself against eight men who attacked him. Instead, the police arrested him for the street brawl. At the same time among the city's elite, "Japonism" or Japanese design and decorative art became fashionable. Obata won several commissions to paint murals for large department stores during the 1920s, and in 1924, he designed the sets for the San Francisco Opera's production of *Madame Butterfly*.

Obata lived and worked in San Francisco Japantown, and there he enjoyed the company of Japanese American artists such as Matsusaburo Hibi. He took trips to Yosemite and the Sierra Mountains, and they provided him with, in Obata's words, "the greatest harvest for my whole life and future in painting" (Hill, 5). Obata joined other artists in forming the East West Art Society, and in 1922 the society held its first painting exhibition at the San Francisco Museum of Art.

Obata was a professor of art at the University of California, Berkeley, from 1932 to 1954. Faculty invited him to teach a summer class in 1932, and students responded so enthusiastically that the art department hired him as a lecturer and two years later promoted him to assistant professor. "I always teach my students beauty," Obata stated. "No one should pass through four years of college without . . . [a] knowledge of beauty and the eyes with which to see it" (Hill, 7). Like his students, Obata saw his art as a work in progress. "I am not a finished artist," he declared emphatically. "I am studying until I die" (Hill, 8).

World War II and the mass detention of Japanese Americans interrupted his university teaching career. After a hurried displacement from their home, Obata and his family arrived in Tanforan assembly center. His wife, Haruko, recalled their introduction to Tanforan, which was a horse racetrack. "When we arrived at Tanforan it was raining; it was so sad and depressing. They gave us a horse stable the size of our dining room with a divided door where the horse put his head out—that was our sleeping quarters. There were two beds made of wood, bunk beds, and another bed on the opposite wall. . . . There was nothing else, nothing. That one time I cried so much. That was the only time I cried; it was awful" (Hill, 27, 29).

While in Tanforan and Topaz concentration camps, Obata continued his art. Three days after his arrival at the assembly center, Obata offered to start an art school for the Tanforan adult education program. He believed artistic creativity would lift the spirit of the people. Using his university connections, Obata obtained art materials for the classes. His former students, including Masao Yabuki and Miné Okubo, served as art teachers, and together they urged artistic documentation of the camp to leave a record for future generations. Okubo would later publish her book of drawings of the camp experience, *Citizen 13660* (1946).

During the 1943 registration crisis during which the War Relocation Authority required all Japanese Americans to declare their "loyalty," some Japanese Americans in Topaz called Obata an *inu* or "pro-American" sympathizer, and one of them attacked him with an iron pipe in the bathhouse on April 4, 1943. After 19 days in the Topaz hospital, the camp administrators released Obata and his family to insure their safety. "Why I was attacked, I myself do not know," Obata wrote to a friend. Conditions in the camp, he speculated, "can cause even a person in a splendid state of mind to weaken to rumors, which are constantly present. . . . In any case, this abnormal state of life can contribute to such dreadful acts. I feel sorry for the attacker, who has not yet been identified, for his attempt to kill or hurt me will not better his life" (Hill, 93).

While Obata was recuperating in the Topaz hospital, a military guard shot and killed an elderly resident, Hatsuki Wakasa, while he was walking with his dog near the camp's barbed-wire fence on April 11, 1943. Obata recorded that killing in a drawing, one of the last images he would paint of Topaz. The drawing shows Wakasa bent over from the bullet, his fingers extended, falling headfirst to the ground.

Obata and his family moved to Salt Lake City, then Chicago, and resettled in St. Louis where they lived until 1945 when they returned to California. Obata resumed his position at the University of California, Berkeley. Obata taught for nine more years, and retired in 1954.

For 15 years, Obata led tours to Japan in the spring and autumn to introduce Americans to Japanese arts, gardens, and architecture. "The purpose of the trip," Obata explained, "is to achieve better understanding. I'm doing this in the hope that the two countries can talk fully, and if there is something like war, they can find some way to find agreement, and won't do that kind of unnecessary thing if they can communicate on a better level" (Hill, 110). In 1965, Obata received the Emperor's Medal for his contributions toward promoting understanding between Japan and the United States. Eleven years later, Haruko received the Emperor's Medal for her lifelong work teaching flower arrangement (ikebana). They were the first husband and wife in the United States to be so honored.

Obata died in 1975 at the age of 90.

Gary Y. Okihiro

Reference

Hill, Kimi Kodani. *Chiura Obata's Topaz Moon: Art of the Internment.* Berkeley, CA: Heyday Books, 2000.

OKADA, JOHN (1923–1971)

A writer and librarian, John Okada was born in 1923 in Seattle, Washington, where he lived the first 19 years of his life. Such stability did not last long for Okada, however. In the middle of his sophomore year at the University of Washington, he and his family (along with most of Seattle's Japanese American community) were forcibly evicted and held in a nearby "assembly center" at the Puyallup Fairgrounds, before being put on a train to the Minidoka concentration camp in Idaho.

Okada saw his time in Minidoka as both a harrowing experience and a rude interruption of his studies, so he made sure to be among the first group of nisei to obtain clearance to leave the camp to attend college outside its barbed-wire fences. He enrolled for a year at Scottsbluff Junior College in Nebraska, after which he enlisted in the U.S. armed forces. At Minnesota's Camp Savage, Okada trained with the Military Intelligence Service to be a Japanese/English translator, and he then took basic training at Camp Blanding—near Jacksonville, Florida—before being assigned to the "Flying 8 Ball," the nickname for the 8th Army Air Forces Radio Squadron Mobile, in Guam. Okada quickly earned the rank of sergeant, volunteering to fly dangerous missions in B-24 aircrafts and to translate radio messages that he intercepted from the Japanese militia who controlled the islands below. After the surrender of Japan, effectively ending World War II, on August 15, 1945, Okada completed his final five months of active military service in the position of interpreter for the U.S. Occupation Forces.

Okada returned to the University of Washington in 1946 to earn his bachelor's degree in English and to write and stage dramatic productions as part of a campus playhouse. He continued his studies at the postgraduate level, receiving his master's degree in English from Teachers College at Columbia University in New York City. It was in Manhattan that he met Dorothy Arakawa, whom he married on June 24, 1950, in Seattle. The couple soon had a daughter and a son, and Okada returned to the University of Washington yet again for a second BA, this time in library science. He held a brief stint as an assistant in the business reference section of the Seattle Public Library, where he continued to read widely, before moving his family to Michigan and taking a similar but better-paying position at the Detroit Public Library. Stability still failed to kick in for Okada, who quickly changed jobs once more, serving as a technical writer for Chrysler Missile Operations in Sterling Township. Most importantly, though, Okada used his time in Detroit to compose the manuscript for *No-No Boy*, his only novel, published in Japan in 1957 by Charles E. Tuttle Company.

Okada got his idea for the book from a personal acquaintance named Hajime "Jim" Akutsu, who also had been interned in Minidoka during World War II. In 1943, Akutsu had answered "no" and "no" (thus, he was a "no-no boy," like the novel's protagonist, Ichiro Yamada) to questions 27 and 28 of the infamous "loyalty questionnaire" administered to male internees at the concentration camps that year. The questions read:

> 27. Are you willing to serve in the armed forces of the United States on combat duty wherever ordered?
> 28. Will you swear unqualified allegiance to the United States of America and faithfully defend the United States from any or all attack by foreign or domestic forces, and forswear any form of allegiance or obedience to the Japanese emperor, to any other foreign government, power or organization?

Believing those questions to be offensive and blasphemous, if answered in the affirmative, Akutsu refused to say "yes" to either one and was convicted as a draft resister and imprisoned for two years as a result. Okada spent several days interviewing Akutsu to learn more about his life, and *No-No Boy* soon took shape. Not only does it look at crucial questions for Japanese Americans during and after World War II; it addresses issues of importance to all Americans, as it traces the lineage of many racist structures and practices that divide white from Asian, Asian from black, and black from white in U.S. society.

When the novel was first released, it was almost entirely ignored. Charles Tuttle, its publisher, claimed that even the Japanese American community rejected the book. Several scholars have suggested that the timing of *No-No Boy* was as bad as could be (it was too soon), since a number of Japanese Americans either wanted to strike the awful internment years from their memories or to keep these thoughts to themselves. Either way, a published novel retelling the experience of the camps was not something many people looked forward to reading in 1957.

In the 1970s, though, *No-No Boy* was rediscovered by a group of Asian American writers who found its theme of dueling identities (Japanese/American) particularly well explored. The book is widely considered the first Asian American novel, and dramatist Ken Narasaki adapted it into a stage play (keeping the original title) in 2009. The play had its world premiere on March 26, 2010, at the Miles Memorial Playhouse in Santa Monica, California.

Unfortunately, the popularity of *No-No Boy* and the recognition of Okada as one of the greatest Asian American fiction writers came after his death, of a heart attack, in 1971. At the time, the virtually unknown Okada was living in southern

California, where he worked as a technical writer for Hughes Aircraft and as publications manager for Analog Technology (an aerospace contractor), both while in the process of composing another novel about the issei. After several unsuccessful attempts to get this second literary project recognized, Okada's wife burned the entirety of the near-complete manuscript, leaving no trace of the creative process behind it.

Okada's legacy lives on in various forms. *No-No Boy* is now on reading lists in hundreds of high schools and universities in the United States, literary scholars continue to demonstrate the importance of the writer and his work, and Stanford University constructed an undergraduate residence hall—"a focal point for students to explore the Asian American experience"—in Okada's name in 1979.

Daniel Valella

References

Abe, Frank. *In Search of No-No Boy.* Seattle: Washington Civil Liberties Public Education Program, 2007

Cheung, King-Kok. "John Okada." In *The Heath Anthology of American Literature.* Edited by Paul Lauter. Stamford, CT: Cengage Learning, 2009.

Okada, John. *No-No Boy.* Seattle: University of Washington Press, 1980.

"Okada." http://www.stanford.edu/group/themed/ethnicandfocus/okada.html

OKAMOTO, KIYOSHI (1888–1963)

Kiyoshi Okamoto, founder of the Heart Mountain Fair Play Committee, was born in Hawai'i sometime in 1888 or 1889. Okamoto spent two years at the University of Hawai'i studying chemistry and engineering. He later worked as a sugar mill superintendent and a soil engineer until he moved to San Pedro, California, to introduce papaya. After the stock market crash of 1929, he taught at a public high school in Los Angeles to 1942 when he and all Japanese Americans along the West Coast were forcibly removed from their homes and placed in concentration camps. Often described as a loner, Okamoto never married and therefore had no children.

In 1942, at the age of 55, Okamoto arrived at Heart Mountain concentration camp where he is credited being the first nisei to call for redress for Japanese Americans, bringing attention to the exclusion and detention of World War II. Okamoto sent letters and petitions protesting the deprivation of Japanese American civil liberties to Guy Robertson, Heart Mountain camp director, and President Franklin Roosevelt. Okamoto fought against corruption in the camp, inadequate wages, and deprivation of property, and for due process of law.

In 1943, Okamoto began to protest against the Selective Training and Service Act of 1940, which the government ignored to exclude and then altered to include nisei men. Previously, the U.S. government classified Japanese Americans IV-C or "enemy aliens" unfit to serve in the military. Identifying himself as the Fair Play Committee of One, Okamoto encouraged nisei to resist the draft as long as they were deprived of their civil liberties, handing out antidraft flyers. He attended several meetings at Heart Mountain in which he demonstrated an impressive knowledge of constitutional law. Later, on January 26, 1944, with Frank Emi and Paul Nakadate, two well-known nisei, and 300 members, they launched the Fair Play Committee (FPC).

The FPC had one primary goal: to oppose the military draft as long as the nisei were denied their constitutional and civil rights. In his essay, "Loyalty Is a Covenant," Okamoto explained that the U.S government violated the fundamentals of democracy when it forced 120,000 people into concentration camps without due process of law. Highlighting constitutional rights, Okamoto declared: "The cornerstones of these Instruments of our Government are Justice, Liberty, Security, Freedom, and the protection of Humane Rights. These are flagrantly violated in the various procedures of our evacuation, deportation and detention" (Okamoto, Early 1944).

Okamoto and the FPC garnered strong support with growing members and favorable newspaper articles. Okamoto made connections with the editor of the Japanese American newspaper *Rocky Shimpo,* James Omura, who published articles and editorials on behalf of the FPC. While not a member of the FPC, Omura supported it, explaining in a letter to Okamoto that his support was based on principles alone. According to Omura, his hope in "giving publicity to the movement in Heart Mountain" was to "assist somewhat in decreasing and. . . eliminating this situation" (Omura, April 10, 1944). Furthermore, in a newspaper article, "Let Us Not Be Rash," Omura argued that the "Nisei are well within their rights to petition the government for redress of grievances" and that they "should at all times stand firm on [their] God given rights" (Omura, February 28, 1944).

Okamoto and the FPC continued to fight for their civil liberties, arguing that the nisei had a moral right to demand "judicial and orderly procedures in molding of our destines" (Okamoto, February 25, 1944). He encouraged nisei to protest the draft by avoiding to report for their physical examinations. For his activities, Okamoto gained the attention of the War Relocation Authority (WRA) and Heart Mountain administrators as an agitator and troublemaker.

That reputation led to his removal to Tule Lake concentration camp when it became a segregation center for "troublemakers" and "dissidents." Heart Mountain director Guy Roberston argued that Okamoto's removal was necessary to break the back of draft resistance, and he called Okamoto a "crackpot with a strong loyalty to Japan," although Okamoto had never visited Japan (Muller, 81). Still, removed from Heart Mountain, Okamoto continued to protest the draft and encouraged the FPC not to lose courage. He exhorted the draft resisters, "You are making the fight for yourselves, your children, the other Minorities of this Nation and the Constitution and the Bill of Rights. It is a holy fight" (Okamoto, May 7, 1944).

In Heart Mountain concentration camp, 63 men refused to report for their physical induction examinations. As a result, the government arrested all of them, and sentenced them to three years in prison. Concerned with the growing impact of the FPC, the government arrested the seven leaders, including Okamoto and James Omura. While Omura, a newspaper editor, was acquitted citing freedom of speech, the seven leaders of FPC were found guilty of violating the Selective

Training and Service Act of 1940, and all were sentenced to four years in Leavenworth Federal Penitentiary.

In 1946, after the end of the war, Okamoto and the six other FPC leaders had their sentences overturned on appeal. The following year, President Harry Truman pardoned the Japanese Americans who resisted the draft during World War II, including the members of the FPC, restoring their rights as citizens. After prison, Okamoto continued to seek redress for the concentration camps.

Okamoto was last seen heading into the wilderness in California. Like his date of birth, Okamoto's date of death is uncertain, although he is believed to have died around 1963.

Carrie M. Montgomery

References

Muller, Eric L. *American Inquisition: The Hunt for Japanese American Disloyalty in World War II.* Chapel Hill: University of North Carolina Press, 2007.

Okamoto, Kiyoshi. Letter to Fair Play Committee. May 7, 1944. http://www.resisters.com/docs.htm.

Okamoto, Kiyoshi. "Loyalty Is a Covenant." Early 1944. http://www.resisters.com/docs.htm.

Okamoto, Kiyoshi. "We Should Know." February 25, 1944. http://www.resisters.com/docs.htm.

Omura, James. Letter to Kiyoshi Okamoto. April 10, 1944. http://www.resisters.com/docs.htm.

Omura, James. "Let Us Not Be Rash." *Rocky Shimpo,* February 28, 1944. http://www.resisters.com/docs.htm.

OKUBO, MINÉ (1912–2001)

Born in 1912 to Japanese migrant parents in Riverside, California, Miné Okubo was a nisei (second-generation Japanese American) who would later become a prominent figure in the movement for redress and reparations for Japanese Americans who were forcibly evicted and confined during World War II.

Expressing an early and promising interest in art, Okubo followed her passion into higher education, attending Riverside Junior College (now Riverside City College) and transferring to the University of California, Berkeley, where she completed her bachelor's degree in 1935 and graduated the following year with a master's degree in fine arts.

Through an art fellowship, Okubo traveled to and throughout Europe over the course of 18 months between 1938 and 1939. However, with rising national tensions in Europe, Okubo made plans to return to California. Upon receiving an alarming letter informing her that her mother was seriously ill, Okubo made for home immediately. Soon after her return to California, sadly, Okubo's mother passed away.

The loss of her mother was not the only major event in Okubo's young life. On December 7, 1941, Okubo listened to the radio announce the news, "Pearl Harbor bombed by the Japanese!" Stunned as much as any American, Okubo began to think about the repercussions that would follow for Japanese Americans in particular.

On April 24, 1942, Civilian Exclusion Order No. 19 was issued in Berkeley, California. Many were surprised that the exclusion orders affected the nisei and issei (first-generation Japanese American) indiscriminately. For Okubo and many others, it heightened the reality that the exclusions were blatantly anti-Japanese on the basis of race, not as military risks as the government claimed.

Okubo was interned at Tanforan Assembly Center in San Bruno, California, and later in the Central Utah Topaz concentration camp from 1942 to 1944. Within those two places, Okubo sketched the realities of camp life for Japanese Americans. Reflecting, she writes, "[t]ime mellows the harsh and the grim. I remember the ridiculous, the insane, and the humorous incidents and aspects of camp life. I was an American citizen, and because of the injustices and contradictions nothing made much sense, making things comical in spite of the misery" (Okubo, ix). Okubo drew nearly 2,000 sketches of daily life for the detained Japanese Americans.

For Okubo, it was "[t]he humor and the pathos of the scenes [that made her] decide to keep a record of camp life in sketches and drawings" (Okubo, 53). She recalls, "[t]here was a lack of privacy everywhere. The incomplete partitions in the stalls and barracks made a single symphony of yours and your neighbors' loves, hates, and joys. One had to get used to snores, baby-crying, family troubles, and even to the jitterbugs" (Okubo, 66).

Free people, both at home and abroad, failed to appreciate the indignities endured by confined Japanese Americans. Some wrote letters to her exclaiming, "how lucky [she] was to be free and safe at home" (Okubo, 61). In reality, Okubo and tens of thousands of other confined Japanese Americans slept on mattresses made of hay in abandoned horse stalls, scrambled for food every night in overcrowded mess halls, battled fierce winds with dilapidated housing, and were always within the range of the potent stench of human waste. Japanese Americans were, ironically, "close to freedom, and yet far from it" (Okubo, 81).

Okubo writes in Citizen 13660, "A feeling of uncertainty hung over the camp; we were worried about the future. Plans were made and remade as we tried to decide what to do. Some were ready to risk anything to get away. Others feared to leave the protection of the camp" (Okubo, 139).

During her confinement, Okubo was scouted by Fortune magazine to work as an illustrator on their Japan issue and was released to work in New York City on the April 1944 issue. Two years later, in 1946, Okubo published her first book, Citizen 13660.

Of her original 2,000 sketches, 206 were compiled as the telling illustrations in Okubo's highly pictorial recounting of her experiences in the camps where she was first assigned the number 13660, after which her book, Citizen 13660, was named. She notes,"[i]n the camps, first at Tanforan and then at Topaz in Utah, I had the opportunity to study the human race from the cradle to the grave, and to see what happens to people when reduced to one status and one condition" (Okubo, ix).

Citizen 13660 served both as memory to the abuses suffered by Japanese Americans during World War II and as a highly effective political tool in the efforts for redress and reparations that were organized by primarily Japanese Americans. Although well received, the book fell out of favor because, as Okubo recalls, "[t]he war was forgotten in the fifties. People throughout the country were rebuilding their lives" (Okubo, x). It was in the 1970s that *Citizen 13660* made its way back onto the political stage. Okubo explains, "[f]or the third generation Sansei . . . the seriousness of the evacuation had at first been difficult to comprehend. . . . By the 1970s, however, they were growing up and many were in college. When they understood what had happened to their parents and grandparents during World War II, they were incensed" (Okubo, x).

Because of that groundswell of interest, *Citizen 13660* was reprinted in 1973 and was again educating the U.S. public about the existence and experience of the concentration camps. Miné Okubo "believed that some form of reparation and an apology were due to all those who were evacuated and interned," and was one of many who testified in 1981 before the Congressional Commission on Wartime Relocation and Internment of Civilians (Okubo, xi). While every testimony played its part, Okubo offered powerful documentation when she gave a copy of *Citizen 13660* to the commission.

During and after the time of *Citizen 13660*'s reprinting Okubo remained an important figure within the Japanese American community. Okubo appeared on the televised program *The Nisei: The Pride and the Shame,* a CBS News special with Walter Cronkite in 1965; she was chosen as one of the top 12 women pioneers in *A History of California (1800–present)* in 1987; and she received the Lifetime Achievement Award from the Women's Caucus for Art of the College Art Association in 1991.

Okubo lived the remainder of her life in New York City in Greenwich Village. On February 10, 2001, at the age of 88, Miné Okubo passed away.

Kia S. Walton

References

Hanstad, Chelsie et al. "Mine Okubo." *Voices from the Gaps.* University of Minnesota, 2004. http://voices.cla.umn.edu/artistpages/okuboMine.php.
Miné Okubo Collection. Riverside City College. http://library.rcc.edu/riverside/okubo/.
Okubo, Miné. *Citizen 13660.* Seattle: University of Washington Press, 1983.
Robinson, Greg and Elena Tajima Creef (Eds.). *Miné Okubo: Following Her Own Road.* Seattle: University of Washington Press, 2009.

OMURA, JAMES (1912–1994)

Nisei journalist James Matsumoto Omura was born on November 27, 1912, on Bainbridge Island, Washington. When he was young, his mother became quite ill and had to place herself in the care of her sister, who lived in Nagasaki, Japan. Omura's three youngest siblings moved in with their grandmother, while Omura and his two other brothers decided to remain on Bainbridge Island. Omura left home at the age of 13 to work as a salmon canner in Ketchikan, Alaska, and Anacortes, Washington, before moving to Pocatello, Idaho, where he continued his formal education and started on his path to becoming a journalist.

Omura was named editor of his school newspaper in 1928. Three years later, he returned to Bainbridge Island, where he became the first nisei to be honored as a delegate in journalism to the State of Washington Student Leaders' Conference. In 1932, Omura graduated from Seattle's Broadway High School and was recruited by the University of Washington but (in the heart of the Great Depression) could not afford to attend. Nonetheless, he quickly began his career as a journalist, serving briefly as the editor of the Los Angeles–based *New Japanese American News* before moving to San Francisco, where he was the editor of the *New World Daily* from 1934 to 1936. An editorial that the *Daily* published on nisei leadership garnered Omura harsh criticism from members of the Japanese American Citizens League (JACL), who claimed that the piece defamed one of the group's leaders. Omura resigned from his editorship in January 1936 over disagreements with the paper's publisher.

Disenchanted by his first professional experiences in journalism, Omura went four years without writing any articles, choosing instead to work as a flower farmer. He returned to the newspaper business in 1940, first publishing a column in the *Japanese American News* and then working with a brand-new nisei magazine called *Current Life,* which sought to win upward mobility for U.S.-born Japanese Americans. On February 23, 1942, the U.S. Congress called Omura to testify before its Tolan Committee, whose purpose was to evaluate the merit of President Franklin Roosevelt's decision to remove Japanese Americans and others of foreign origin from their homes on the West Coast. In his testimony, Omura voiced his strong disagreement with the president's policy and with the JACL's support of it. While Omura expected many nisei to protest alongside him, very few did so.

To avoid forced evacuation, Omura drove from his California residence to Denver, where an office for *Current Life* would soon be transformed into an Evacuee Placement Bureau, which assisted many Japanese Americans who hastily left their Pacific Coast homes for Colorado. Omura filed three racial discrimination cases through the War Manpower Commission, whose task was to balance the country's labor needs of agriculture, industry, and the armed forces. Indeed, the number of nisei doing domestic and offshore military work increased significantly after Omura's filings. With the help of the Washington, D.C.–based law firm Callender, Callender & Wallace, Omura also came close to suing for reparations on behalf of those forcibly removed and confined, though not enough Japanese Americans expressed interest in the lawsuit for it to come to fruition.

In January 1944, Omura took on two major positions: director of public relations for the Japanese Publishing Company, and English editor for the company's Denver-based bilingual (Japanese/English) newspaper, *Rokk Nippon* (soon to become *Rocky Shimpo*). In this paper, one month later, Omura published his most famous and controversial piece of writing—a column titled "Let Us Not Be Rash," in which he argued that interned Japanese Americans would have clear justifications for choosing to resist the draft. "The Nisei are well within their rights to petition the government for a redress of grievances," Omura wrote. "The Constitution gives us certain inalienable and civil rights. The government should restore a large part of those rights before asking us to contribute our lives to the welfare of the nation." Unlike Omura's previous efforts, "Let Us Not Be Rash" saw at least some praise and allied action from Japanese Americans. Of course, the column was not without its detractors. Less than two months after the *Rocky Shimpo* published Omura's piece, the Office of Alien Property Custodian Leo Crowley (whom President Roosevelt appointed to prevent trading with the enemy) informed the newspaper's publisher that the federal government would shut down the publication unless Omura were promptly fired. To ensure that the *Rocky Shimpo* would survive, Omura resigned.

The grand jurors of the State of Wyoming indicted Omura, as well as seven leaders of the Heart Mountain concentration camp's Fair Play Committee, on charges of "aiding and abetting violation of the Selective Service Act of 1940." Omura was acquitted on the basis of the First Amendment, specifically its right of freedom of the press, though the other seven defendants were convicted and served 18 months at Leavenworth Federal Penitentiary before seeing their conviction overturned. Although he was found not guilty, Omura lost the respect of the Japanese American community at large and could not find employment as a journalist anywhere. As a result, he embarked on a career in landscape contracting, which proved quite successful.

More than four decades after World War II came to a close, Omura finally received positive recognition for his journalism and activism. His 1983 treatise on cultural heritage was a major part of the Bainbridge Island Historical Exhibit that toured the United States from 1988 to 1990. Omura also received the Asian American Journalists Association's Lifetime Achievement Award in 1989. Five years later, the National Coalition for Redress/Reparation honored him with its Fighting Spirit Award. Several historians have written recently of his importance, while filmmaker Frank Abe (whose nisei father, an internee during World War II, subscribed to the *Rocky Shimpo* to read Omura's editorials) released a PBS documentary in 2001 about the internment experience, titled *Conscience and the Constitution,* which prominently features Omura's life.

Omura died in Denver on June 20, 1994. He was survived by a wife and two children.

Daniel Valella

References

Abe, Frank, dir. *Conscience and the Constitution.* Monarch Films, 2001.

Fugita, Steve. "James Matsumoto Omura." In *Distinguished Asian Americans.* Edited by Hyung-Chan Kim. Westport, CT: Greenwood Press, 1999.

Hansen, Arthur A. "Peculiar Odyssey: Newsman Jimmie Omura's Removal from and Re-generation within Nikkei Society, History, and Memory." *Nikkei in the Pacific Northwest: Japanese Americans and Japanese Canadians in the Twentieth Century.* Edited by Louis Fiset and Gail Nomura, 278–30. Seattle: University of Washington Press, 2005.

Nelson, Douglas W. *Heart Mountain: The History of an American Concentration Camp*. Madison: State Historical Society of Wisconsin, 1976.

Omura, James. "Let Us Not Be Rash." *Rocky Shimpo*, February 28, 1944.

100TH INFANTRY BATTALION

The 100th Infantry Battalion was a segregated U.S. Army unit of mainly Japanese American men who served during World War II. Hawai'i's Territorial National Guard eagerly recruited all men except Japanese Americans who nonetheless volunteered and formed Company D of the Guard's 1st Regiment during World War I. Those men failed to see combat duty, and again during the interwar period the Guard preferred not enlisting Japanese Americans. Still, about 40 Japanese Americans were in the National Guard in October 1940 when it was federalized and divided into two regiments, the 298th and 299th Infantry. Their numbers increased with the draft, and by December 1941, there were 1,500 nisei recruits serving in integrated units of the 298th and 299th.

On the day of Japan's attack on Pearl Harbor, a nisei soldier recalled, the men of the 298th and 299th lined up for roll call and were issued rifles, ammunition, and bayonets. They dug trenches and served on guard details against the possibility of an enemy landing and attack. But three days later, on December 10, 1941,

Mainly but not solely comprised of Japanese American soldiers from Hawai`i, the 100th Infantry Battalion set an example for the later, larger 442nd Regimental Combat Team. (Center for Military History)

Japanese American soldiers had their firearms taken away, and they were ordered to remain inside their barracks. Military guards armed with machine guns ringed their quarters for two days and, then, without explanation their firearms were returned and they resumed their duties. Apparently someone distrusted the Japanese American soldiers.

Over the next six months, the men of the 298th strung barbed wire, patrolled beaches, and manned machine gun emplacements as the military decided the fate of the nisei soldier. Doubts about Japanese American loyalty prompted the army to expel the 317 nisei volunteers serving in the Territorial Guard in January 1942, leading some nisei to organize the Varsity Victory Volunteers, a labor battalion. Even the Japanese Americans in the 298th and 299th were under suspicion, and on February 1, 1942, the War Department proposed to discharge or transfer all of them. The army, however, faced a manpower shortage in the islands so it kept the men despite fearing an armed uprising. In mid-May, the army's commander in Hawai'i suggested creating a segregated unit of Japanese Americans from the 298th and 299th and have them removed from the islands. The army's chief of staff in Washington, D.C. approved the plan, and on May 28, 1942, authorized the formation of the proposed battalion.

Without notice or fanfare, nisei soldiers from the 298th and 299th were ordered to report of Schofield Barracks on the island of O'ahu where they were housed in tents some distance from the other troops. Their rifles were taken away, and their camp was surrounded by barbed wire. On June 5, they were designated the Hawaiian Provisional Battalion, and were taken to Honolulu's Pier 31. In the early afternoon, they were placed in the hold of the *Maui,* and that evening set sail with 1,432 men on board. "Before we had any chance to bid goodbye to our loved ones," one of the men, Spark Matsunaga, recalled, "we found ourselves on board a troopship sailing for God-knew-where. Speculation was rife that we were headed for a concentration camp" (Okihiro, 251).

On their arrival in Oakland, California, the Hawaiian Provisional Battalion became the 100th Infantry Battalion. The men emerged from the *Maui's* hold in the dark of night, and were loaded onto trains that took them to Camp McCoy, Wisconsin, where they trained to fight for democracy while in another part of Camp McCoy, Japanese American leaders were confined behind barbed wire. In fact, the men suspected they were headed for a concentration camp because their train had window blinds to prevent them from knowing their destination, and when the train finally stopped, some of the men peered out and saw the barbed wire and guard towers of a concentration camp. That was where the leaders were being confined.

In the hold of the *Maui* and during the five-day train ride, the nisei soldiers gambled in card and dice games. Thousands of dollars switched hands. Their attitude was, given their uncertain fate, they were living on borrowed time and had nothing to lose. The expression in Hawaiian pidgin, spoken by the men, was go for broke or go for it all. That phrase, "Go For Broke," became the motto of the 100th Infantry Battalion, arising from the men's predicament as soldiers in the U.S. Army, having little choice and even less to lose.

Spark Matsunaga described the men's attitude during their seven months at Camp McCoy, "We pictured ourselves as a battalion of forced laborers." Japanese Americans marched with wooden guns because they were not trusted, and they played the part of the enemy when they faced white troops in mock combat. In October 1942, 26 men were assigned to a secret project on Cat Island, Mississippi, where they wore heavy padding and face guards and hid in the bushes. Trainers sent their dogs to find those nisei because the army believed Japanese emitted a distinctive odor. The idea was to use trained dogs in the Pacific theater to locate Japanese snipers hiding in the tropical vegetation. Of course, the soldiers reported, even the dogs knew they were Americans, making no distinction between their trainers and their prey.

The men of the 100th Infantry Battalion served with great distinction in North Africa and Italy where they earned the name "the Purple Heart Battalion" at the Battle of Monte Cassino in early 1944. Monte Cassino was a mountain fortress, as its name suggests, which the Germans had secured with some of their best troops. Hitler was determined to halt the Allied advance up the Italian peninsula. So the fighting there was desperate. Over 40 days and against great odds, the men of the 100th struggled to climb the hill and in the process suffered immense casualties. Company A began the battle with more than 170 men, and when it ended, only 23 remained. After five months of fighting in Italy, the 100th was reduced from about 1,300 men to 521, the rest were killed, wounded, missing, or held as prisoners.

In June 1944, the 100th Infantry Battalion became the first battalion of the 442nd Regimental Combat Team comprised of Japanese Americans from Hawai'i and the continent.

Gary Y. Okihiro

Reference

Okihiro, Gary Y. *Cane Fires: The Anti-Japanese Movement in Hawaii, 1865–1945*. Philadelphia: Temple University Press, 1991.

P

PEARL HARBOR

Called Pu'uloa by the original inhabitants of O'ahu, the Hawaiians, the waters of that splendid bay named by foreigners Pearl Harbor became the main target of Japan's attack that began World War II for the United States. In 1873, the secretary of war sent two generals, ostensibly on vacation in Hawai'i, to survey the islands for their military value. The anticipation was war with a maritime nation, so the secretary wanted information on the islands' strategic value to the United States. The generals stayed in Hawai'i for two months, gathering information. Both stressed the value of Pearl Harbor as an excellent harbor for military and commercial purposes. In the years to come, those U.S. interests in Hawai'i, for military and commercial benefits, would influence U.S. policy over the fate of the islands.

In 1876, a price for reciprocity or the entry of Hawaiian sugar into the United States duty free was permission to use Pearl Harbor as a U.S. military base. The agreement boosted the previously slumping sugar industry, which grew about 2,000 percent during the years the Reciprocity Treaty was in effect. In 1887, the Hawaiian king gave Pearl Harbor to the United States for its exclusive use as a naval station. With U.S. military support in 1893, whites overthrew the Hawaiian kingdom and asked for U.S. annexation. When the United States refused, whites declared a Hawaiian Republic on July 4, 1894. Four years later, on July 7, 1898, President William McKinley, an ardent proponent of Manifest Destiny, signed a joint resolution of Congress and therewith annexed Hawai'i.

The Navy built Pearl Harbor into a citadel for its Pacific Fleet. Pearl Harbor was called the "Gibraltar of the Pacific." Situated mid-Pacific, the fleet was critical for U.S. global ambitions, which included the Western Hemisphere and the Pacific as American territories. Ships transported labor, raw materials, and goods produced in fields and factories, and the Navy ensured their safety as they plied the seas. Moreover, military strategists envisioned Hawai'i as an outpost, a buffer against attack from Asia, whether peaceful as in migration or an armed invasion. Pearl Harbor, thus, anchored the frontline, and the Hawaiian Islands were like an armed flotilla pointed toward Asia.

Japan was well aware of that strategy even though war planners in Tokyo believed an attack on Hawai'i would never succeed. Contrarily, Admiral Isoroku Yamamoto, commander in chief of Japan's Navy since 1939, decided an attack could succeed through airpower. In early spring of 1940, with diplomacy failing, Yamamoto developed the strategy of island hopping, taking islands, building airfields from which to launch bombing raids, and moving on to the next stretch of oceans and islands. With preparations complete, on November 25, 1941, the fleet, which included six aircraft carriers, embarked on a secret mission to a rendezvous point to the north of Japan. There, they set sail for Hawai'i without radio contact, without tracks left by oil spills or garbage, and without lights at night. They succeeded, and U.S. intelligence lost their scent.

But on December 6, through intercepts, the United States knew Japan was about to make a major move about eight hours before the attack on Pearl Harbor began. The warning, however, was delivered to the Hawaiian commander two hours after the first bombs fell on the U.S. Pacific Fleet. Within minutes, the Japanese attackers destroyed 152 of 230 U.S. planes, sank five of six battleships, and damaged about a dozen other ships. Approximately 2,500 Americans were killed in the surprise attack. The Pacific Fleet was saved from complete destruction because, by chance, its three aircraft carriers and their escort vessels were out at sea, and by 1944 four of the damaged battleships were recovered, repaired, and returned to sea.

"A date which will live in infamy," thundered President Roosevelt before a joint session of Congress, declaring war on the Empire of Japan and Axis Powers, and "Remember Pearl Harbor" became the slogan for this war. The U.S. military in Hawai'i had long prepared for that war with Japan, but Washington, D.C. anticipated internal subversion, not an external attack at the onset of war. Hawai'i's governor recalled Interior Secretary Harold Ickes telling him, "Washington felt there would never be an attack by Japan but had instructed the army and navy locally to be on guard against sabotage" (Okihiro, 208). Accordingly, the military's posture changed from "attack alert" to "sabotage alert," and the army stationed soldiers at harbor facilities, public utilities, and water pumping stations weeks before Pearl Harbor. The precautions, the governor observed, was "a sort of undeclared form of martial law" (Okihiro, 209).

The Pearl Harbor attack triggered martial law for Hawai'i, a defensive plan first proposed decades earlier, and it led to the apprehension of Japanese American leaders, both alien and citizen, and a number of German and Italian aliens. Friday night before the attack on Sunday, U.S. intelligence drew up a revised list of names for internment. A group representing Army intelligence, the FBI, and the civilian police decided on the fate of Japanese Americans placed on that list. If two of the three agreed, the person was interned. The group failed to investigate consular agents, language-school principals and teachers, and other community leaders because "they were aliens and they were prime and with very few exceptions they were picked up as a unit." Whether they were subversives was not the issue; they were interned because they were leaders. "So there were some things operating against the Japanese, to tell you the truth," the representative from the Honolulu police admitted (Okihiro, 209).

In addition to that acknowledgement, the U.S. government knew there was no evidence of espionage or sabotage on the part of Japanese Americans in Hawai'i. The army's Board of Inquiry into the Pearl Harbor disaster found "no single instance of sabotage . . . up to December 7," and "in no case was there any instance of misbehavior, despite a very exhaustive investigation being made constantly by the FBI, and by G-2 [Army intelligence], as well as by Naval Intelligence." Despite that, Navy secretary Frank Knox in January 1942 reported that Pearl Harbor was a result of "the most effective fifth column [subversive] work that's come out of this war, except in Norway" (Okihiro, 228), and the press published sensational stories of cane fields cut by Japanese American workers pointing the attack planes toward Pearl Harbor and shot down Japanese pilots wearing school rings from institutions in Hawai'i. All of those claims were false.

Gary Y. Okihiro

Reference

Okihiro, Gary Y. *Cane Fires: The Anti-Japanese Movement in Hawaii, 1865–1945.* Philadelphia: Temple University Press, 1991.

POSTON STRIKE

Following the beating of a kibei (nisei educated in Japan) in Poston concentration camp on November 14, 1942, the camp's security police rounded up about 50 Japanese Americans for questioning. They detained two suspects for further questioning, and kept them for several days in jail pending the arrival of the Federal Bureau of Investigation (FBI). Meanwhile, family and friends of those two agitated for their release, reflecting the general sentiment of the camp.

Delegations from the camp's residents met with camp administrators on November 17 and 18 to insist on the men's innocence and demand their release. Those proved fruitless, so on November 18, the delegates called for a mass meeting in front of the jail where the men were being held, attracting a crowd estimated at about 2,500. The protestors demanded the unconditional and immediate release of the two prisoners. The camp administrators urged patience and rejected the demand, leading to the resignation of Poston's Community Council, Issei Advisory Board (IAB), and block managers, all of the bodies for community self-rule.

That night, November 18, Japanese Americans elected a new body called the Emergency Committee of 72 and its working core, the Emergency Council of 12. Those new governing entities called for a general strike, except for essential services like the mess hall, hospital, schools, and fire department, to shut the camp down the next day. Hardliners among Poston's administrators favored calling in the military to crush the uprising, while others urged negotiation and compromise. Japanese Americans were likewise divided, and the strikers had to exert pressure, including threats and beatings, to maintain solidarity within the group.

As described by an eyewitness, "This was no ordinary strike. . . . It was a community upheaval. . . ." Blocks were organized, regular shifts of men, women, and children stood watch beside fires lit to keep the crowd warm. Flags designating each block were raised to show support for the strike. Pictures of *inu* or informers were posted, and speakers denounced informers and expressed repeatedly their grievances. "Community sentiment had crystallized in the demonstration, and for the first time since evacuation there was a sense of striking back at oppressors" (Spicer et al., 133).

On November 23 and 24, negotiations to end the strike were carried out, and in those meetings it became clear that the camp residents chaffed against rules that stifled their independence. The two men held in jail simply provided an opening for a discussion of broader and deeper issues troubling Poston's residents. The strikers wanted the ability to settle disputes among Japanese Americans, greater autonomy in hiring and firing workers, and more responsibility in managing the camp's administrative and economic structures. This time, Poston's administrators granted recognition to the Emergency Committee, and released one of the prisoners but held the other for a trial to be held inside the camp. Those responses satisfied the strike leaders, and the crisis subsided.

The Poston strike followed a history of Japanese American resistance in the camp. Broadly, Japanese Americans believed the U.S. government held them against their will and without justification, and it was thus responsible for housing, feeding, and clothing them in the War Relocation Army (WRA) concentration camps. They accordingly refused to perform labor that failed to benefit them directly. The *Poston Official Information Bulletin* editorialized, "Let Us Cooperate," noting many construction projects were being delayed due to a lack of workers. It argued, "whatever is constructed, planted, or built here is for our benefit," and went on to express cooperation as a Japanese virtue, reminding readers that Japanese were never lazy and urged, "never in this history of America has a person of Japanese descent ever been on relief. Let us not spoil our fine record at Poston by breaking this splendid precedent" (Okihiro, 27).

Following WRA policy, Poston's administration limited voting and office holding and to nisei or U.S. citizens against Japanese Americans who preferred the elders, the issei, over their children. On June 5, 1942, the WRA's director, Dillon Myer, issued a directive barring issei or noncitizens from voting and holding office. Just over two weeks later on June 23, Poston's City Planning Board recommended that no distinction be made between citizens and noncitizens in voting and office holding, and proposed three branches of government in the camp. Poston's administrators, accordingly, dissolved the Planning Board three days after it defied the WRA director's instructions and sponsored an election. The camp's residents thereby lost interest in so-called self-government. As a WRA study found, "It is incorrect to assume that the residents were either entirely in favor of or vitally interested in the establishment of local government. The exclusion of Issei from office engendered some opposition. The vast majority of residents, however, remained disinterested spectators" (Okihiro, 28).

In the WRA-sponsored election, the nisei chose and served on the Community Council, which had little support. In fact, many in the camp called it a "child council" and its members, "stooges" or *inu* (dogs). The council operated that summer but in September 1942, in defiance of WRA policy, Poston's Japanese Americans formed the Issei Advisory Board (IAB), consisting of an issei representative for each block. During the Poston strike, 20 former IAB members were elected to the Emergency Committee of 72, and the Emergency Executive Council of 12 excluded nisei members except for a kibei, showing the community's preference for issei leaders.

After successfully negotiating the end of the strike, the Emergency Committee transformed itself into a new City Planning Board, consisting of one issei and one nisei elected from each block. The board developed plans, like the old board, for community government. The Poston strike thereby achieved its goal of a more democratic form of Japanese American self-rule within the constraints of the concentration camp. There would be no preference for U.S. citizen over noncitizen, the board decided, and issei and nisei alike could participate in voting and holding office.

Gary Y. Okihiro

References

Okihiro, Gary Y. "Japanese Resistance in America's Concentration Camps: A Reevaluation." *Amerasia Journal* 2 (Fall 1973).
Spicer, Edward H., Asael T. Hansen, Katherine Luomala, and Marvin K. Opler. *Impounded People: Japanese-Americans in the Relocation Centers.* Tucson: University of Arizona Press, 1969.

PUBLIC LAW 503

President Franklin Roosevelt's Executive Order 9066 authorized the military to remove and provide for "all persons" for the successful prosecution of the war. It also authorized the military to declare areas from which anyone could be excluded. To enforce EO 9066, the president's men knew, required Congressional action, a law to specify the crime of violating a military order and its punishment. Those were the purposes for Public Law 503 passed on March 19, 1942, and signed by the president two days later.

Ordinarily, the Justice Department was in charge of drafting such legislation for the Congress. Attorney General Francis Biddle, however, opposed EO 9066 and expressed his distaste for the administration's plan of mass removal and detention for Japanese Americans. Biddle advised Roosevelt that his EO 9066 could be enforced through his general war powers and did not require legislation. The military was furious, believing Biddle was simply passing the buck to the War Department. Karl Bendetsen, chief of the aliens division of the provost marshal general's office in the War Department, was particularly annoyed with what he considered to be a sign of weakness. The Justice Department, Bendetsen told a State Department official, "should remember that the Army's job is to kill Japanese not to save Japanese" (Irons, 65).

Bendetsen, accordingly, drafted the bill to submit to Congress, and gave it to John McCloy, the assistant secretary of war, three days after Roosevelt's EO 9066. Violation of the military exclusion order, Bendetsen's draft stated, was a felony with penalties of a $5,000 fine and a maximum prison term of five years. The exclusion order applied to aliens and citizens alike. The draft insisted on making that crime a felony and not a misdemeanor. "You can shoot a man to enforce a felony,"

Bendetsen quoted General John DeWitt who led the military's exclusion effort on the West Coast (Irons, 65). Instead, McCloy reduced the violation to a misdemeanor and a maximum jail sentence of a year.

An agreeable Senate took on Bendetsen's bill on March 13, spending an hour listening to a single witness from the army. The Senate Military Affairs Committee passed it unanimously, and sent it to the full Senate for a vote. The House was even quicker, holding a 30-minute hearing on March 17 before passing it on to the full House for a vote. During the House debate on March 19, only one spoke against the bill, Representative E. A. Michener from Michigan. Michener suggested the law would interfere in the rights of citizens, and the bill, thus, should be debated and carefully considered. Instead, a mere 10 minutes were devoted to the bill, and it passed by voice vote. The Senate took longer to allow Senator Robert Reynolds of North Carolina to denounce Japanese Americans as fifth-column agents and saboteurs in the Pearl Harbor disaster. All of those charges were refuted by the government's investigations. The Senate passed the bill 30 seconds after debate ended, also on March 19.

Public Law 503 provided for the enforcement of EO 9066, and it was the basis upon which the government's prosecution of Japanese Americans such as Minoru Yasui, Gordon Hirabayashi, and Fred Korematsu rested. And properly but ironically, upon signing Public Law 503, Roosevelt put the onus upon the Justice Department, the federal government's law-enforcement agency, to enforce its provisions through criminal prosecutions.

Gary Y. Okihiro

Reference

Irons, Peter. *Justice at War.* New York: Oxford University Press, 1983.

R

REDRESS AND REPARATIONS

The history of the Japanese American movement for redress poses a number of complex political and philosophical questions. How can present generations bear responsibility and make amends for the sins of their forefathers? How can one adequately measure individual and/or communal suffering in monetary terms? How can the payment of reparations be successfully administered to all who were incarcerated or personally affected by historical trauma? What counts as sufficient apology for the systematic destruction of individual liberties and human rights? For decades following World War II, community organizers, activists, lawyers, and politicians pursued various paths to attain justice. While their beliefs often diverged, and their efforts to address these questions took disparate forms, the Japanese American community eventually achieved its common goal to attain restitution for the crimes committed against them during World War II.

On August 10, 1988, President Ronald Reagan signed into law HR 442, otherwise known as the American Civil Liberties Act. This unprecedented legislation offered an official apology for the physical, emotional, and financial injuries that Japanese Americans incurred during the war and pledged to pay $20,000 to every survivor of the concentration camps. The act publicly recognized the illegality and immorality of the government's system of exclusion and incarceration, admitting to the grave injustice "done to both citizens and permanent residents of Japanese ancestry." In turn, and perhaps more surprisingly, the act confessed to the fact that these wartime crimes were motivated "largely by racial prejudice, wartime hysteria, and a failure of political leadership." In addition to offering restitution, the act created a fund to support educational endeavors to ensure that these injustices would never be repeated. Two years after the act was passed, Japanese Americans began to receive checks of restitution accompanied by a letter from President George Bush acknowledging their losses and paying homage to those painful memories that can never fully heal. Unfortunately, for most issei who had already passed away, this apology came much too late.

The first national call for redress came in 1970 when activist Edison Uno introduced a resolution at the national convention of the Japanese American Citizens League (JACL). Founded in 1929, the JACL had during World War II served as an official governmental liaison with inmates, held desirable positions in the concentration camps, and fueled Japanese American efforts at resettlement and integration after the war. Their early pro-American conservatism, however, gave way in the 1960s to direct criticism of the government's actions. With Uno's leadership, the JACL began surveying the community and holding public forums in which members could share their views about seeking redress. The overwhelming response was in support of pursuing some movement, particularly in terms of monetary compensation. By 1976, the JACL had acquired essential allies, including the first Japanese American U.S. congressman formerly held prisoner in the camps, Norman Mineta from California. Thanks to Mineta's political savvy, that same year the JACL created a national committee specifically focused on the issue. By the fall they had unanimously adopted a resolution calling for financial reparations. While the JACL did much to increase visibility and popularity for the cause, organizers soon realized that their movement would eventually have to find a more powerful stage to air their concerns: the nation's capital.

In 1979, the JACL worked with key congressional leaders, including Congressman Mineta and Senators Daniel Inouye and Spark Matsunaga, to propose a presidential commission to study the federal government's wrongdoings during the war and publicly document the atrocities and hardships internees faced. After the bill was passed in Congress, President Jimmy Carter signed into law the Commission on Wartime Relocation and Internment of Civilians (CWRIC) in July 1980. Leaders in the JACL saw this as a key avenue to achieve firm factual grounding for their legislative goals for redress. Over the next three years, the commission oversaw research and investigative work to compile evidence of possible misdeeds. Its most important action, however, occurred between July and December 1981, in which the CWRIC held 11 official televised hearings in 10 cities throughout the United States. Over 750 witnesses delivered emotionally moving testimonies to their experiences in the camps, including Yuji Ichioka, who was six at the time of incarceration. Ichioka, like many, expressed his sense of relief in sharing his experiences: "to me, [the hearings are] a collective cartharsis . . . we're saying we're tired of deferring to white people, basically. We've shown too much respect, too much deference for too long." The commission's administration of these hearings provided an important venue for Japanese Americans to stand together as a united community. Their publicity also importantly raised awareness for the cause with the American people, a critical step toward successful federal legislation. On June 16, 1983, the commission released its findings in an influential report entitled *Personal Justice Denied*, which recommended that Congress appropriate monies to provide $20,000 to each victim of the concentration camps.

Between 1982 and 1988, legislators and lobbyists worked together to make good on the commission's recommendations. As the movement for national redress continued, a number of alternative redress movements developed concomitant to these mainstream congressional efforts. In California and Washington, former state employees of Japanese descent successfully lobbied for redress payments for unlawfully being terminated from employment during the war. A parallel movement also emerged to achieve redress in the federal court system. The National Council for Japanese American Redress, an organization often antagonistic to the more established JACL, administered a fund-raising campaign to actively pursue lawsuits against the federal government. Their goal was to move for a Supreme Court reversal of the orders of exclusion and sought $24 million in monetary damages. While the Supreme Court ruled unanimously against their suit in

June 1987, the research and evidence for the government's withholding of information during the war proved vital in the final push toward the passing of HR 442. After almost two decades of steady work, the Japanese American community witnessed the passage of the Civil Liberties Act. By this time, lobbyists and congressional leaders had created a capacious bipartisan coalition that included both Republican and Democratic leaders, and received allegiance from key non-Japanese American organizations such as the Veterans of Foreign Wars. On September 17, 1987, the House of Representatives passed HR 442 by a vote of 243 to 141. In April of the following year, the Senate approved their own version of the bill, to a margin of 69 to 27 votes. After President Reagan signed the act into law in 1988, the final hurdle came in the form of budget appropriation.

The diligence and dedication of countless individuals and community organizations undoubtedly were the primary ingredients for achieving national redress. Nevertheless, there were other sociohistorical factors that influenced the creation of a viable public policy of Japanese American reparation. Firstly, during the late 1980s there was a keen sense of urgency for the legislation to be complete due to the issei generation's increasing age; this could be the last chance the nation had to bear witness to their suffering. Secondly, the end of the century witnessed a global movement for human rights, in which numerous nations were pressured to enact political efforts of restitution, not only including the United States, but also Germany, South Africa, and Australia. Finally, by the mid-1980s there had arisen a substantial cultural archive of fiction, film, histories, and visual art that attested to the pain and horror of life in the camps. Thanks to the decades-long activism and political strategizing, the Japanese American community and the American public at large had begun to believe that the concentration of American citizens during World War II was not simply a misfortune, but an illegal system of racial persecution and demolishing of this community's inalienable rights.

Despite the apparent success of the Civil Liberties Act, many Japanese Americans still question the value and long-term effects of redress. In part, the legislative promise of the act fell short, where many of those touched by the system of internment were left out of the benefits of its administration. In the end, 82,219 of more than 120,000 internees received redress payments; only 28 refused their checks. The majority of these recipients had been forcibly excluded and confined in the camps. Many victims remain invisible to its promises—Japanese Americans who resided in Hawai'i during the war as well as a number of Japanese Latin Americans still are denied the reparation they rightly deserve. Although some might argue that the Civil Liberties Act brought legislative closure to Japanese Americans' confinement during World War II, for many who endured this dehumanizing system of racial persecution, the wounds can never be redeemed.

Jenny M. James

References

Hohri, William Minoru. *Repairing America: An Account of the Movement for Japanese-American Redress.* Pullman: Washington State University Press, 1988.

Maki, Mitchell T., Harry H.L. Kitano, and S. Megan Berthold. *Achieving the Impossible Dream: How Japanese Americans Obtained Redress.* Urbana: University of Illinois Press, 1999.

Murray, Alice Yang. *Historical Memories of the Japanese American Internment and the Struggle for Redress.* Stanford, CA: Stanford University Press, 2008.

Takezawa, Yasuko I. *Breaking the Silence: Redress and Japanese American Ethnicity.* Ithaca, NY: Cornell University Press, 1995.

RESETTLEMENT

A War Relocation Authority (WRA) term, also called relocation, used principally to describe the program to relocate Japanese Americans from the concentration camps to the outside. As the WRA director Dillon Myer described it, the resettlement program began as a plan to put Japanese Americans to work in as many as 50 agricultural camps throughout the U.S. West, and from there scatter them to jobs in both rural and urban centers where they could reestablish their lives. The plan failed when western governors refused to cooperate, but the idea of relocating Japanese Americans to specific sites and purposes continued to guide the WRA policy.

The first was the seasonal leave program. Because of labor shortages during the war and the need for agricultural production, the Wartime Civil Control Administration (WCCA) and WRA as early as April and May 1942 decided to permit Japanese Americans to leave the camps for seasonal, agricultural work. Employers paid for their transportation and agreed to wages at the prevailing rates, and the government, provided housing for the laborers. By the end of June, approximately 1,500 Japanese Americans worked in the fields of Idaho, Utah, and Montana, and around mid-October, some 10,000 harvested sugar beets and labored in agriculture.

Another WRA program involved student leaves to continue their education beyond the camps' high schools. With the WRA's encouragement, the American Friends Service Committee helped establish the National Student Relocation Council (NSRC) at a meeting in Chicago in May 1942. John Nason, president of Swarthmore College, was named chairman of the NSRC. The government cleared institutions to take Japanese American students, the WRA handled the leave papers from the camps, recruiters visited the camps and selected prospective students, and by November 1942, Nason reported, the NSRC placed some 330 students in 93 colleges and universities for the fall term.

In the case of both seasonal and student leaves, the government was concerned about possible security issues posed by Japanese Americans outside the concentration camps. Local sheriffs and police departments were held responsible for the seasonal workers, while schools could not be located near strategic sites nor could they be institutions working on defense research. Accordingly, many of the nisei students attended schools in isolated, rural areas and at small, liberal arts colleges rather than large, research institutions. As of May 1, 1946, the NSRC had in its records the names of 3,613 students at 680 institutions, and the council closed its doors on June 30, 1946.

The U.S. military offered a way out of the concentration camps. In November 1941, there were 3,188 Japanese Americans in the armed forces. Shortly after Pearl Harbor, the army discharged recently inducted Japanese Americans from active duty although some remained with their units. Nisei were ordered into labor battalions, and others were given menial assignments like work in the kitchens. On March 1942, the selective service refused to accept any Japanese American enlistees, and in September 1942 the Selective Service System classified Japanese Americans as IV-C or as aliens unacceptable for service. Prior to that order, some local draft boards classified Japanese Americans as IV-F or as ineligible for military service.

Meanwhile, because the army needed soldiers capable of understanding and translating Japanese-language documents, beginning in July 1942 the army recruited some 6,000 Japanese Americans from the WRA concentration camps to its Military Intelligence Service (MIS) language school at Camp Savage, Minnesota, and later, at nearby Fort Snelling. Those MIS graduates served in the Pacific theater, translating captured documents, monitoring radio broadcasts, and interrogating Japanese prisoners.

Japanese Americans from Hawai'i formed the 100th Infantry Battalion, and in January 1943, the army announced the formation of a special Japanese American combat unit, which became the 442nd Regimental Combat Team. Volunteers from the concentration camps joined the segregated combat team after having filled out several forms swearing to their loyalty to the United States. In January 1944, Japanese Americans became subject to the draft. In all, approximately 26,000 Japanese Americans served in the U.S. military during World War II, about half from the continent and most of those from the concentration camps.

A fourth and the largest WRA program was the indefinite leave and general relocation policy that removed Japanese Americans from the camp. Indefinite leaves were only granted when the applicant had a firm job offer, the person posed no security risk, the local community accepted Japanese Americans living among them, and applicants agreed to keep the WRA informed of their current address. To account for those relocated Japanese Americans, the WRA established area offices in cities like Chicago, Cleveland, Minneapolis, Des Moines, Milwaukee, and New York City. By July 1943, there were 42 field offices from Spokane to Boston. At first, those offices worked to ascertain the community's acceptance of Japanese Americans and through public relations created a favorable climate for them.

Employers, concerned citizens, and church members participated in this program of relocation. In the fall of 1942, the Federal Council of Churches of Christ in America supplied funds to develop a network of resettlement committees across the country. Local churches were the most active together with organizations like the YMCA and YWCA. Those committees, some called Fair Play Committees, reached out to neighborhoods to make them receptive to Japanese Americans, they contacted employers and secured jobs, and they helped with housing and schooling concerns. They tried to ease the transition from concentration camps into communities by serving as liaison and contact groups between Japanese Americans and mainly white Americans.

The demand for Japanese American labor was considerable; the Chicago area alone had 10,000 requests that went unfilled. Thousands who first left the camps via the seasonal leave system applied to make their leaves indefinite by remaining in the areas of their employment. In that way, by December 1943, there were 3,900 Japanese Americans in the Salt Lake City area and 3,000 in the Denver area, accounting for nearly 40 percent of the total nationwide. To speed up the process, the WRA administered the "Application for Leave Clearance" in February 1943 with its Questions 27 and 28 that led to mass protests. Still, clearance was cumbersome, requiring FBI background checks on each Japanese American. By the end of 1943, the FBI had completed over 77,000 cases, and by early 1944 about 2,000 remained.

The WRA gave to Japanese Americans released from the camps $25 per person, a $3 per diem while traveling, and bus or train fare. Church groups in Chicago, Cleveland, Cincinnati, and Des Moines operated hostels to house Japanese Americans temporarily and cheaply. Large-scale relocations of several thousand Japanese Americans involved companies like the Seabrook Farms in New Jersey and Becker Farms in Michigan. Other large recruiters of Japanese American workers were the International Harvester Company and Stevens Hotel in Chicago.

In 1944, some 18,000 Japanese Americans left the concentration camps for work outside the barbed-wire fence. The war and the work of the concentration camps were winding down, and the WRA declared the final phase of the relocation program in December 1944. On December 18, 1944, the Supreme Court ruled the government could no longer keep loyal citizens in detention against their will. A day before that unanimous decision, the army announced that effective January 2, 1945, the exclusion order would be lifted. Japanese Americans could return to the West Coast. About that time, approximately 80,000 Japanese Americans still remained in WRA concentration camps.

To relocate those to the West Coast, the WRA set up field offices in Los Angeles, San Francisco, and Seattle in early 1945, and about 25 district offices to manage the returning Japanese Americans. As the WRA camps closed, Japanese Americans resettled in places receptive to them. By 1946, when the WRA resettlement program ended, about 50,000 Japanese Americans lived in areas away from the West Coast, their former homes. Roughly 57,000 returned to the West Coast from whence they had been forcibly evicted. Some 5,600 of those came from resettlement sites in states such as Illinois, Colorado, and Utah. Before the war, California had the largest number of Japanese Americans on the continent. About half of those returned to the state by 1946. California's figures before and after the war coincided roughly with the pattern for the West Coast as a whole; about half returned, and these did not necessarily return to their former homes, farms, and towns. In fact, many relocated elsewhere away from former neighbors and friends and away from the stigma and shame of having been distrusted and victimized by their government.

Gary Y. Okihiro

ROOSEVELT, ELEANOR (1884–1962)

Eleanor Roosevelt, born Anna Eleanor Roosevelt (the Roosevelt surname was already in her family), married Franklin Delano Roosevelt in 1905. In 1932, Eleanor Roosevelt became the 34th First Lady of the United States. As First Lady, Roosevelt had to choose between supporting her husband, the president, and her own personal politics. During the World War II, the forced removal and confinement of some 120,000 Japanese Americans was an ethical question about which Eleanor Roosevelt proved to be publicly ambivalent.

After Pearl Harbor, many of the nation's leaders and much of the greater U.S. public supported the idea of removing all persons of Japanese ancestry from the Western Defense Command. Eleanor Roosevelt was staunchly opposed to that displacement on the primary basis of "race." Just prior to the U.S. declaration of war, with the permission of the Justice and State departments, First Lady Roosevelt issued a statement that vouched for the safety of Japanese Americans. It read: "I see absolutely no reason why anyone who has had a good record—that is, who has no criminal nor anti-American record—should have anxiety about his position. This is equally applicable to the Japanese who cannot become citizens but have lived here for thirty or forty years . . ." (Girdner and Loftis, 7).

First Lady Eleanor Roosevelt, with War Relocation Authority head Dillon Myer, visited the Gila River concentration camp in 1943. Privately, Mrs. Roosevelt condemned the camps, but publicly supported them. (National Archives)

After Japan's attack on Pearl Harbor, Eleanor Roosevelt quickly embarked on a tour of the West Coast by train with New York mayor, Fiorello LaGuardia. This was a strategic endeavor; in the wake of the surprise attack, the West Coast was brimming with hysteria at the thought of a Japanese invasion. The visit was an attempt to cleave the fast growing rift between the wider U.S. public and those who were being unfairly accused of being threats to national security, Japanese Americans. Eleanor Roosevelt took ample photographs with Japanese Americans, which were to be distributed by the Associated Press wire service. The campaign to quell the fear was effective in terms of publicity. On December 15, 1941, the *New York Times* published one of the tour photographs. One day later, Eleanor Roosevelt put words to the visual as she wrote in her "My Day" column: "This is perhaps the greatest test this country has ever met." She continued, warning the United States that if it failed to act fairly with its own citizens, "then we shall have removed from the world, the one real hope for the future on which all humanity must now rely" (Beasley et al., 278).

Though perhaps grandiose in her estimation of the United States, Eleanor Roosevelt's earnest appeal to the public may have held some sway with many readers. According to public opinion polls of the time, Eleanor was well-liked and respected across political parties, gender, and class. In 1993, the Siena Institute conducted a survey amongst historians and professors and Eleanor Roosevelt was rated the most influential woman of the 20th century. She was considered an unofficial diplomat and helped to secure allies for the United States. Yet, however popular the First Lady was and remains, her role as the president's wife afforded her no official governmental authority in affairs either foreign or domestic. As such, the extent of her social influence hardly reached the political grounds of the Japanese American concentration camps.

The forced eviction of Japanese Americans from their homes and relocation to internment camps would proceed without Eleanor Roosevelt's approval. On February 19, 1942, President Roosevelt issued Executive Order 9066, which ultimately allowed for the forced removal and confinement of Japanese Americans in military zones. Although widely considered a champion of civil rights, very quickly after EO 9066 was issued, Eleanor Roosevelt publicly changed her position on the matter of concentration camps. In a radio broadcast she stated, "It is obvious that many people who are friendly aliens have to suffer temporarily in order to insure the vital interests of this country while at war" (Beasley et al., 279). This uncharacteristic backtracking is telling of Eleanor Roosevelt's personal and political bind. For the sake of a unified front around which the United States could rally itself, Eleanor Roosevelt publicly supported the internment of Japanese Americans. Yet in correspondence with a personal friend, Roosevelt wrote that the U.S. concentration camps were "just one more reason for hating war—innocent people suffer for a few guilty ones" (Beasley et al., 280).

Despite her rhetoric, Eleanor Roosevelt acted to help minimize the damage to Japanese Americans. She tried to ensure that even in the dislocation families remained together by intervening with the War Relocation Authority. She helped to gain the early release of some internees, and had the bank accounts of released, "loyal" Japanese Americans made accessible to them after the banks had frozen their accounts. She appealed to the Justice Department to prevent Japanese American disenfranchisement and to investigate the claims of anti–Japanese American violence and employment discrimination. And she, in her "My Day" column, tried to present both the WRA and Japanese Americans positively.

In 1943, Eleanor Roosevelt, at the request of the president, visited the Gila River concentration camp in Arizona after he became concerned with the demonstrations occurring within the camps. In her public report, she chose to avoid the topic of the political climate of the camps and focused on the perceived highlights, like attempts on the part of internees to organize schools and the esthetic quality of intern-made and tended gardens. What she chose to share with the public was that families were under great distress in the camps. She later urged President Roosevelt to relax the ban on Japanese Americans in the Western Defense Command, and noted that Japanese Americans had not only been moved for their own safety, as the government had rationalized, but because they were also feared as competitors. The racism of the exclusion did not escape First Lady Roosevelt.

For the remainder of her husband's presidency and life, Eleanor Roosevelt continued to negotiate the line between galvanizing the United States for the war effort and advocating for the civil rights of those Americans who were victimized by the war. After President Roosevelt died, Eleanor Roosevelt resumed publicly aligning herself with those who opposed the U.S. concentration camps.

Kiu S. Walton

References

Beasley, Maurine H., Holly C. Shulman, and Henry R. Beasely (Eds.). *The Eleanor Roosevelt Encyclopedia.* Westport: Greenwood Press, 2001.

Girdner, Audrie and Anne Loftis. *The Great Betrayal: The Evacuation of Japanese-Americans during World War II.* New York: Macmillan, 1972.

Ng, Wendy. *Japanese Internment during World War II: A History and Reference Guide.* Westport, CT: Greenwood Press, 2002.

ROOSEVELT, FRANKLIN D. (1882–1945)

Franklin D. Roosevelt served as U.S. president from 1933 to 1945. His singular importance to Japanese Americans derives from his term during World War II when he signed Executive Order 9066, which authorized the military to remove and detain Japanese Americans. Signed on February 19, 1942, EO 9066 marks the start of the concentration camps, but its origins long predate that fateful day.

The United States anticipated war with Japan decades before that nation's attack on Pearl Harbor on December 7, 1941. At least as early as World War I, U.S. military planners were concerned with "the Japanese problem" in Hawai'i. Military and civilian intelligence investigated aliens, radicals, and communists who allegedly threatened the nation's security, and from 1917 to 1918 the army took a special interest in German "enemy aliens" both in Hawai'i and on the continent. But in the islands where Japanese Americans comprised a substantial percentage of the population and were the principal labor force for the territory's sugar plantations, the mainstay of the economy, "the Japanese problem" eclipsed all other security concerns.

By the time Roosevelt became president, U.S. intelligence agencies had already determined that Japanese Americans endangered the nation's security by their increase in numbers through high birthrates, the number of men of military age, the number of eligible voters, their racial and cultural attributes, and their dubious national loyalty. The Bureau of Investigation, forerunner of the FBI, prepared lists of Japanese Americans it considered dangerous to the domestic order, and the army in Hawai'i planned to declare martial law on the outset of war with Japan and therewith suspend civil liberties, enabling the unimpeded detention of Japanese American community leaders.

Soon after he assumed the presidency, Roosevelt received a report from military intelligence gauging the potential for internal subversion among Japanese Americans in Hawai'i. The memorandum described the possibility of a surprise attack by Japan involving a naval landing and an uprising among Japanese Americans. Military planners accordingly directed their strategies toward fending off an external invasion while neutralizing "hostile sympathizers" in the islands.

On August 10, 1936, Roosevelt expressed his concern over that scenario, and asked the military if it had any recommendations to make to meet that expected danger. "Has the local Joint Planning Committee (Hawaii) any recommendation to make?" he inquired. "One obvious thought occurs to me—that every Japanese citizen or non-citizen on the Island of Oahu who meets these Japanese ships or has any connection with their officers or men should be secretly but definitely identified and his or her name placed on a special list of those who would be the first to be placed in a concentration camp in the event of trouble" (Okihiro, 173–74).

The president's use of the term concentration camp is notable, along with his lumping of citizen with noncitizen. U.S. citizenship for Japanese Americans, according to Roosevelt, failed to confer the rights of citizens as guaranteed under the Constitution.

Two weeks later, the president persisted. He inquired of the military, "what arrangements and plans have been made relative to concentration camps in the Hawaiian Islands for dangerous or undesirable aliens or citizens in the event of national emergency" (Okihiro, 174). It appears Roosevelt's mind was set on his indiscriminate view of Japanese Americans as a collective group, whether aliens or citizens, and his anticipation of concentration camps for those "dangerous and undesirable aliens or citizens." In reply, the military reassured the president it had for years remained alert to the possibility of espionage and sabotage and had made preparations to contain the danger.

Historians have focused on Roosevelt in seeking out the causes for the mass removal and detention of Japanese Americans during World War II because his EO 9066 authorized the concentration camps. And while military, political, and economic interests pushed for Japanese American exclusion, in the end, it was the president who made the decision to sign the instrument that enabled the action.

Long before World War II, Roosevelt held racial prejudices against Japanese Americans, favoring their immigration exclusion and discriminatory legislation against them to preserve the "racial purity" of the white race. He believed they were unassimilable, and were thus culturally distinctive and even undesirable. And he was well aware of "the Japanese problem" that allegedly threatened the national security as presented by civilian and military planners. The civil liberties of that group of U.S. citizens were, accordingly, an abstraction that carried few political consequences for Roosevelt. In fact, he probably thought their removal and confinement would advance the U.S. war effort, which was his overriding concern when he signed EO 9066.

Despite the president's leading role in the wartime concentration camps, his executive order had to be interpreted and implemented by the military and then by the civilian agencies, the Wartime Civil Control Administration and War Relocation Authority, that carried out the president's order. Those, too, were key figures in the determining the nature of the Japanese American concentration camps.

Gary Y. Okihiro

References

Okihiro, Gary Y. *Cane Fires: The Anti-Japanese Movement in Hawaii, 1865–1945.* Philadelphia: Temple University Press, 1991.

Robinson, Greg. *By Order of the President: FDR and the Internment of Japanese Americans.* Cambridge, MA: Harvard University Press, 2001.

SANTA ANITA RIOT

There would be many other acts of resistance that followed but the Santa Anita riot, begun as a strike, was the first mass action by Japanese Americans while under confinement. Administrators at the Santa Anita assembly center employed citizen laborers to manufacture camouflage nets for the U.S. military. Japanese Americans worked 44-hour weeks in eight-hour shifts, and in the summer of 1942, some 800 of them produced 22,000 nets or about 250 large nets each day.

One day in June 1942, a net worker sat down, and refused to return to work. He said he was hungry and could not work. Soon others joined him, and by the day's end all 800 workers sat down and shut down production. The quantity and quality of food in the assembly center was an issue, but so were job conditions such as the dust from the netting material triggering allergic reactions and the dye fumes that irritated the eyes, nose, and lungs. Moreover, workers had to labor under the hot sun, often kneeling for eight hours on a concrete floor for which they were paid a meager $8. The strikers also charged the administration with using pressure tactics to force the nisei to "volunteer" for the net factory work by closing the high school, which many nisei attended and freezing all other jobs until the net laborers reached their quotas.

There were rumors about white administrators profiting from the assembly center's supplies, stealing them and selling them on the black market, and of a blacklist kept by the administration of nisei who refused to work at the net factory. A few workers returned to work the afternoon of the strike, and by the next day, when Santa Anita's administrators agreed to improve the food and allowed women to work four hours a day, the strike ended. But the strike prompted grievances to surface among the general assembly center population. Two days after the strike ended, Japanese Americans called a meeting to discuss conditions in Santa Anita, and the administration responded by apprehending six Japanese Americans who allegedly attended that meeting. Before long, 11 were taken in and held in a jail.

The southern California branch of the American Civil Liberties Union (ACLU) agreed to defend several of those charged with participating in the "illegal" meeting where Japanese, a forbidden language for meetings in the assembly center, was spoken. Two Japanese Americans, Ernest Wakayama and his wife, Toki, sought a writ of habeas corpus to test the grounds for their confinement. The ACLU's plan was to use the Wakayama case to challenge certain aspects of the government's program of forced removal and confinement. Later, the ACLU dropped the Wakayama case in favor of more promising actions that more directly challenged the constitutionality of EO 9066 and the army's program of mass evictions and confinement.

Meanwhile, the army eliminated Japanese American councils in all Wartime Civil Control Administration "assembly centers" and tightened the rules. In August 4, 1942, three days after having ended the councils, the army launched a search for contraband in the Santa Anita center that even the military head characterized as overbearing. The military police took electric hot plates used by parents to warm baby formulas and by family members to prepare food for their sick, and their high-handed intrusion into private spaces angered many Japanese Americans. Soon crowds formed, and a suspected informer was beaten. The army called in 200 troops in anticipation of a riot, and for three days held the center under martial rule.

Before the soldiers arrived, a crowd of hundreds of people marched toward the administration building cornering and driving away white administrators and assembly center police. "They were absolutely terrified," a Japanese American eyewitness remembered, because they were afraid the protestors would tear them "from limb to limb" (Girdner and Loftis, 192). But the army arrived, and they stood shoulder to shoulder with their helmets on and holding rifles with fixed bayonets. An elderly woman with a cane walked between that line of soldiers and the crowd, halting the troops' advance and breaking the tension. She prevented what could have been a bloody confrontation.

In the aftermath, several police officers resigned, and the army identified and removed 23 young nisei, 20 men and three women, for no apparent reason except to institute discipline among the center's Japanese Americans. A nisei wrote to her former teacher about the events of August 4 and the army's rule. "People have had to put up with so much here," she began, "most of which was unnecessary: the ban on Japanese literature; Japanese records; and the denial of free speech, assembly, press, freedom of religion . . . the search, and many other things" (Girdner and Loftis, 193–94). The Santa Anita riot, she knew, was essentially a protest against injustice.

Gary Y. Okihiro

Reference

Girdner, Audrie and Anne Loftis. *The Great Betrayal: The Evacuation of the Japanese-Americans during World War II*. London: Macmillan, 1969.

SEABROOK FARMS

In the fall of 1943, the War Relocation Authority (WRA) administered a compulsory "Application for Indefinite Leave Clearance," which was intended to streamline the process for the relocation of Japanese Americans from the concentration camps. For release, the WRA held and "military necessity" dictated, Japanese Americans had to first agree to remain loyal to the United States. Accordingly, on the questionnaire were Questions 27 and 28, the former asking if the respondent was willing to serve in the U.S. military, and the latter, if the respondent would foreswear loyalty to the Japanese emperor and pledge allegiance to the United States. Because of their ambiguity, the questions led to a great uproar in the concentration camps and to the establishment of Tule Lake as a camp for the "disloyals."

Nonetheless, those determined to be "loyal" were given an opportunity to leave the WRA camps to work in selected industries. Seabrook Farms in New Jersey was one of those work sites approved by the government. Charles Seabrook began Seabrook Farms around 1912 when he bought his father's farm and turned it into a farm with a greenhouse and canning and freezing capacities. After a downturn in the 1920s, the business thrived in the following decade because of new methods in quick freezing vegetables, which Seabrook pioneered. After a strike in 1934, which netted the workers higher wages, Seabrook abandoned the practice of hiring migrant laborers and instead employed settled residents. By 1939, Seabrook Farms was the largest farm in the state with over 6,000 cultivated acres of vegetables and more than 2,000 workers during the peak season.

In need of laborers during World War II, Seabrook began to recruit from the WRA concentration camps. Skilled agriculturalists and a captive population, Japanese Americans seemed an ideal source of labor. Offering free transportation and nothing to lose, Seabrook's representative dangled the prospect of employment to Japanese Americans in Jerome concentration camp in mid-April 1944. Already in Seabrook since January 1944 were about a dozen Japanese American men, all U.S. citizens, from Granada concentration camp. They had proven their value to their employers, and thus the recruitment for more. This time, the company wanted entire families.

Delegates from Jerome went to New Jersey to inspect the facilities, and they journeyed to Washington, D.C. where the WRA's director, Dillon Myer, assured them that the WRA approved and encouraged the move. Thus began the family relocation to Seabrook Farms, including issei and nisei families from Jerome and Rohwer concentration camps and the camps in Poston and Gila River, Granada, Topaz, Heart Mountain, and Manzanar. They worked 12-hour days for 35 to 50 cents an hour with a day off every two weeks. They lived in concrete blocks similar to the camp barracks, and had to take care of their own food and cooking. They were held under semiconfinement, and the company regulated much of their lives. By the end of 1946, there were over 2,500 Japanese Americans comprising some 500 families working for the Seabrook Farms Company.

The company prospered as the result of Japanese American labor. In 1949, Seabrook produced 65 million pounds of frozen and 10 million pounds of canned vegetables. Even after the war, Japanese Americans, like the 178 Japanese from Latin America from the Crystal City camp, continued to arrive in Seabrook seeking employment. But for the vast numbers of Seabrook's Japanese Americans, the company was merely a holding place between the concentration camps and freedom. Most left as soon as they could. By 1949, Japanese Americans numbered

Japanese Americans at work at Seabrook Farms, New Jersey, a halfway house to freedom. (Associated Press/Wide World Photo)

less than 1,200, and by 1954, their total dwindled to about 900. Those declines mirrored the company's shrinking fortunes throughout the 1950s as competitors with newer and quicker plants eclipsed Seabrook's capacities. Seabrook eventually closed, but a small Japanese American population remained.

Gary Y. Okihiro

SLOCUM, TOKUTARO (1895–1974)

Born in Japan, Tokutaro "Tokie" Nishimura migrated with his parents to the United States at the age of 10, and was among the few Japanese Americans in North Dakota. When his parents decided to move to Canada, Tokie asked to remain in North Dakota where Ansel Perry Slocum reared him. Tokie adopted his name and became Tokie Slocum, attended the University of Minnesota, and continued into Columbia University's law school. Slocum left law school to serve in the military during World War I, and for his heroism was awarded the rank of sergeant major, making him at the time the highest ranking Asian American in the U.S. Army.

Slocum returned to Columbia to complete his law studies, but in 1925 the U.S. Supreme Court rescinded the citizenship of Japanese American World War I veterans who had become naturalized under a 1918 law. The 1918 act opened naturalization to any alien veteran of World War I, and Slocum had gotten his U.S. citizenship under that provision. Now having lost his U.S. citizenship, a law degree meant nothing because most states required U.S. citizenship to be admitted to the bar. Slocum thus left law school, and campaigned to have the naturalization rights of issei veterans restored.

Slocum participated in the founding meeting of the Japanese American Citizens League (JACL) in 1930, and four years later served as a lobbyist for the organization. In 1935, Congress restored to issei veterans the right to naturalization and citizenship due to the efforts of Slocum and the JACL. After Pearl Harbor, Slocum and the JACL cooperated with the FBI in identifying "disloyal" Japanese Americans for apprehension, and at Manzanar concentration camp Slocum served on the camp police force. Many in the camp, accordingly, targeted him and other JACL leaders, like Fred Tayama, as informers or *inu* (dogs). As a result, after the Manzanar riot of December 1942, Slocum and other JACL leaders fled Manzanar for an abandoned Civilian Conservation Corps camp in nearby Death Valley to escape being beaten by irate Japanese Americans in Manzanar.

Slocum was also an anti-Fascist but unlike Karl G. Yoneda he saw the demise of fascism as a pro-American project. He believed he was an American patriot foremost. As a leader of the Anti-Axis Committee of Los Angeles, Slocum urged cooperation with the government's treatment of Japanese Americans. "We are facing this problem today because of the short-sightedness of the Japanese leaders in America up to this time," he wrote shortly after Pearl Harbor, blaming Japanese Americans and not white racism. "They thought only in terms of being Japanese. In order that we not repeat the mistake that our fathers made, we must break our ties with Japan. . . . We must not expect comfort or luxury in time of war. Cooperation with the federal government is essential" (Daniels, 209).

His friends described Slocum as a spellbinding orator who could sway audiences "when he spoke about loyalty to America." A JACL leader recalled of Slocum's speech at a JACL convention: "It was the first time that I heard such an eloquent, high-powered speech in English from a person of Japanese ancestry. Clarence Arai was fluent but Slocum was a firebrand orator. No better person could instill enthusiasm in the hearts of delegates. I was deeply impressed with his oratory despite the fact that I had been raised in an environment in Hawaii where there was constant talk of Americanism" (Hosokawa, 39).

Slocum was a rarity among Japanese Americans. He was an issei who was reared by and grew up among whites, he was a U.S. Army veteran of World War I and at the time the highest ranking Asian American officer, and through his status as a veteran, achieved his U.S. citizenship through an act for which he lobbied. Slocum was one of the few issei JACL members by virtue of his citizenship at a time when JACL membership among nisei was at a low point because of World War II and the organization's position on the concentration camps. Slocum's remarkable life, nonetheless, points to the diversity among the group called Japanese American.

Gary Y. Okihiro

References

Daniels, Roger. *Asian America: Chinese and Japanese in the United States since 1850.* Seattle: University of Washington Press, 1988.
Hosokawa, Bill. *JACL in Quest of Justice.* New York: William Morrow, 1982.

SOGA, YASUTARO (1873–1957)

An influential newspaper publisher in Hawai'i, Yasutaro Soga was born in Tokyo in 1873, and studied English law before switching to chemistry. He migrated to Hawai'i in 1896 to work on sugar plantations, which caused him to identify with the exploited workers. He began his career in journalism with the *Hawaii Shimpo* in 1899, and took over the *Yamato Shimbun* in 1905. Besides changing the editorial contents of the paper, Soga changed the *Yamato Shimbun*'s name to *Nippu Jiji* in 1906, and made it one of the territory's most influential Japanese-language dailies. In 1919, Soga introduced an English-language section to the *Nippu Jiji*, indicating the emergence of the nisei or second-generation Japanese Americans whose primary language was English.

Like Kinzaburo Makino, editor of the rival *Hawaii Hochi*, Soga was an active leader of various Japanese American causes, most notably the sugar plantation strike of 1909. In his paper, Soga published in 1908 a call by Motoyuki Negoro, a Honolulu attorney, to begin a campaign for higher wages, which became the Zokyu Kisei Kai or Higher Wages Association that spearheaded the 1909 strike. The strike involved some 7,000 workers on all of the major sugar plantations on the island of O'ahu, inflicting losses totaling an estimated $2 million to the planters. Soga and other strike leaders were arrested, imprisoned on conspiracy charges, and fined. Upon their release on July 4, 1910, a crowd of nearly 1,000 cheered the strike leaders, solidifying their position as leaders of Hawai'i's Japanese American community.

On December 7, 1941, Soga and other community leaders were apprehended and confined in concentration camps. His account of his ordeal, *My Life in Barbed Wire* (1948), later published as *Life Behind Barbed Wire: The World War II Internment Memoirs of a Hawai'i Issei* (2007), is a rich, primary account in English of Hawai'i's internment program. *My Life* begins with his arrest, his experiences at Honolulu's immigration station, and his observations of confinement at the Sand Island camp. Soga described the "bloodthirsty" conditions at the immigration station where one wrong move might have provoked his death. He noted that the men were forced to eat outdoors in the rain, and described how German and Italian prisoners ate first while the Japanese ate after them on their dirty mess kits cleaned only in a bucket of filthy water. "I couldn't stand that because even these prisoners looked down on us," Soga wrote (Okihiro, 214).

In the Sand Island camp, Soga observed that priests, editors, businessmen, and physicians performed unfamiliar manual labor and were, accordingly, exhausted by the work of putting up tents in which they slept. In the pouring rain, Soga noted, the men struggled to erect 20 tents, which they completed around nine o'clock at night. Then sweaty and soaked by the rain, the men went to bed on wet cots and in tents flooded with pools of water. Soga told of an internee who attempted suicide by slashing his wrist with a razor blade after repeated questionings by the FBI, and he testified to the breakdown of morale and social order. "We grew desolated more and more," Soga wrote. "Our joyless days continued day after day. In order to divert our feelings, smutty stories (sexual and obscene) were popular in every tent" (Okihiro, 216).

On December 14, 1941, Soga related, Ryoshin Okano, a priest, was found with a knife in his possession. Several guards quickly surrounded Okano and pointed their pistols at him, stripped him naked and searched him, and then turned to his work mates. Despite nightfall, Soga recounted, "we were gathered in the open space and we took off our clothes. We had to remain standing for a long time until they finished searching our clothes. Other guards searched our tents and took away our fountainpens and pencils. We were frozen to death in the cold, windy, and barren field" (Okihiro, 217).

On New Year's Eve 1941, Soga reported, the camp commander Carl F. Eifler called all the Japanese American internees together to make an example of George Genji Otani, one of their elected leaders. Eifler simply wanted to flex his authority over the internees. Eifler claimed Otani insulted one of his soldiers, and with a threatening look, told Otani in front of the others that he should have been promptly shot to death for his insolence. Instead, Eifler ordered guards to take Otani to an isolation cell at army headquarters, where he was confined for a week and given only water and hard crackers to eat.

Sand Island, Soga noted, was designed to break the spirit of the internees. These were the leaders of the Japanese American community, and were the voice, heart, and minds of the people. Breaking them, in effect, meant the subservience of all Japanese Americans in the islands. Their harsh treatment was designed to inspire fear among Hawai'i's Japanese Americans to coerce them into docility and productivity. And thus, the ever-present display of arms, the omnipresent guards, the frequent and unexpected roll calls, and punishment meted out for insolence and a host of other offenses testified to the fact that the internees had little control over their futures and their lives were inconsequential. "None of us could see a light in our future," Soga noted despondently (Okihiro, 223).

From Sand Island, Soga was taken along with over a thousand other Japanese Americans to internment camps on the U.S. continent. He described life in the War Department's Lordsburg camp and the Department of Justice Santa Fe camp in New Mexico. After nearly four years under confinement, on November 13, 1945, Soga was released and returned to Hawai'i where he resumed publishing in the *Hawaii Times,* the renamed successor of his *Nippu Jiji* managed by his son, Shigeo. Besides newspaper writing, Soga was a poet. He wrote there was nothing more sorrowful than war, because all of life's sadness is brought together in that single place and time.

Soga died on March 7, 1957, at the age of 83, and was buried at the historic, O'ahu Cemetery in Nu'uanu.

Gary Y. Okihiro

References

Okihiro, Gary Y. *Cane Fires: The Anti-Japanese Movement in Hawaii, 1865–1945.* Philadelphia: Temple University Press, 1991.
Soga, Yasutaro. *Life Behind Barbed Wire: The World War II Internment Memoirs of a Hawai'i Issei.* Translated by Kihei Hirai. Honolulu: University of Hawai'i Press, 2007.

SUMMERALL REPORT

In the aftermath of the 1920 strike of Filipino and Japanese American sugar plantation workers on the island of O'ahu, Major General Charles P. Summerall, commander of the army's Hawaiian Department, submitted an assessment of "the Japanese situation in relation to our military problem" to the federal Hawaiian Labor Commission investigating the strike. The 1923 federal commission alleged Hawai'i's Japanese Americans posed a national defense problem of a magnitude that "submerges all others into insignificance." Japanese Americans, the commission warned, were poised to "sweep everything American from the Islands" and install Japan's rule in Hawai'i (Okihiro, 95–97). The commission provided as evidence of that threat Summerall's report.

For years, the army's Hawaiian Department had kept track of what it called "the Japanese problem." Military intelligence, using Japanese, Chinese, and Korean American informants, collected statistical information on Japanese American organizations, tracked the activities of certain individuals, and met all steamships and checked their passenger lists. That data supplied the evidence for Summerall's report. The military concern included the Japanese American population and its growth, their concentration and areas of settlement, Japan's consul general and his agents, Japanese-language schools, Buddhism and Shintoism, the ethnic press, economic activities, the education of nisei in Japan, called kibei, and nisei voters and their voting patterns. Of particular concern was the loyalty of the second generation because they were coming of age during the 1920s.

The struggle for the hearts and minds of the nisei was a cornerstone of the Summerall report. Japanese-language schools, the report alleged, "had for its principal purpose the inculcating into the young Hawaiian born Japanese child the knowledge that he was a Japanese citizen and that the Yamato race was the greatest race on earth." That education made nisei children "almost as much Japanese as their parents were when they left Japan," and it produced a whole generation of military-age youth loyal to Japan. Even less American were nisei educated in Japan, the kibei, who were "at heart Japanese and can never be changed into material for American citizenship" (Okihiro, 120).

Americanization was also important in Summerall's report. Addressed was Christian minister Takie Okumura's Americanization campaign targeting nisei to stay on plantations and not pursue upward mobility and to assimilate into American life. The Boy Scouts movement was held up as praiseworthy in that process of nisei assimilation and loyalty. "Under the efficient guidance of some of the best members of the American community," the report praised, "the scout leaders are instilling into these boys the thought that they are Americans and that they must always conduct themselves as American boys are taught to do in the United States" (Okihiro, 119).

Examining the Japanese American vote, the report cited demographic trends to predict that by 1930, Japanese Americans would constitute 23 percent of all voters in Hawai'i, by 1940, 38 percent, and by 1950, 46 percent. Moreover, it charged, Japanese American voted as a bloc, increasing their political clout. In the general election of 1922, for instance, over 95 percent of nisei voted for the Democratic candidate in the Delegate to Congress race, rather than the Republican candidate who was the choice of the territory's white oligarchy. That voting pattern, the Summerall report noted, would favor Japanese over American interests.

The 1920 strike, the report claimed, opened a new area of concern for the military. Japanese Americans were vital to the islands' industries, and their rising militancy and unionization threatened to wrest control from whites. Japanese American upward mobility was termed an invasion and their acquisition of skills was potentially dangerous to the national security because "their expert and detailed knowledge if directed against the United States could do irreparable damage in a remarkably short time" (Okihiro, 120). Japanese Americans, the report stated, controlled the fishing industry, rice cultivation, and the taxi business. They dominated as barbers, blacksmiths, builders and contractors, plumbers, watchmakers, and confectioners, and as operators of drugstores, dry goods stores, fish markets, florist shops, restaurants, and theaters.

Japanese culture, the Summerall report maintained, promoted the "solidarity of the Japanese race," and cemented the relationship between issei parent and nisei child. Parental love, accordingly, was "one of the most serious drawbacks towards the Americanization of the Hawaiian born Japanese . . ." (Okihiro, 121). Respect and love for parents translated, in this report, to allegiance to the country of the parents, Japan. In that way, Japanese culture and the Japanese American family held dangers for the nation's defense.

The 47-page Summerall report, having weighed the evidence, concluded the nisei were "a military liability to the United States." It predicted that in an emergency, a majority of the nisei would remain neutral, depending on local conditions, while only a small number would be loyal to the United States. The report stated categorically that the nisei "can never be assimilated" but could be "Americanized," especially after "the present generation of alien parents has passed away" and "the strong Japanistic centers of influence in the Territory have been eliminated" (Okihiro, 122).

Gary Y. Okihiro

Reference

Okihiro, Gary Y. *Cane Fires: The Anti-Japanese Movement in Hawaii, 1865–1945.* Philadelphia: Temple University Press, 1991.

T

THOMAS, DOROTHY SWAINE (1899–1977)

Born in Baltimore, Maryland, Dorothy Swaine Thomas received her undergraduate degree from Columbia University in 1922, and her doctorate from the University of London remarkably two years later. She worked as a researcher for the Federal Reserve Bank and Yale University, and briefly taught at Columbia's Teachers College. In 1939–40, Thomas joined the renowned Carnegie Foundation–funded study of African Americans led by the Swedish economist and sociologist, Gunnar Myrdal, that eventuated in Myrdal's landmark study, *An American Dilemma* (1944). Thomas married W. I. Thomas, one of the founders of the Chicago School of Sociology, and in 1940 took a position as professor of sociology at the University of California, Berkeley.

Before her work on Japanese Americans during World War II, Thomas had no interest in Japanese Americans. Her research mainly involved the social aspect of the business cycle such as birth, death, marriage, divorce, crime, poverty, and so forth as statistical measures and consequences. She later turned to children and some of their social problems and programs directed at them. Just before the war, Thomas published a work on internal migration for the Social Science Research Council, and it was this study, along with another work on Swedish population movements, that framed her research on Japanese Americans.

Thomas organized the Japanese American Evacuation and Resettlement Study (JERS) in the spring of 1942 after receiving funding from the Rockefeller Foundation, Columbia Foundation, the Giannini Foundation, and the University of California. She also secured the cooperation of Milton Eisenhower, director of the War Relocation Authority (WRA), to open the concentration camps to her field researchers. JERS employed University of California faculty from anthropology, social welfare, economics, and political science in various capacities, and hired University of California graduate students as field researchers.

JERS, Thomas wrote, was principally a study of "enforced mass migration" in which the usual push–pull forces of immigration were inoperable. She, accordingly, conceived of the "evacuation" as an "unselective outmigration enforced upon the Japanese population." That phenomenon, she contended, had its counterpart in Europe where war forcibly displaced large numbers of people rendering them involuntary migrants, and the problems associated with their resettlement in areas other than their places of origin paralleled the resettlement of Japanese Americans away from their West Coast homes.

Faculty support of JERS soon dwindled due to wartime demands on their time, so Thomas had to take on sole leadership of the study for which she had little training or knowledge. Her fieldworkers, all graduate students, looked to her for direction and leadership, but complained she failed to convey to them what they were supposed to be studying and noted that the overall project lacked theoretical rigor and orientation. Meanwhile, events transpired so quickly Thomas and her researchers had little time to reflect on the work and its plan; they improvised and reacted to activities around them.

Both subjects of her study, government policies and Japanese American internees, Thomas wrote, presented problems for JERS. Numerous government agencies shaped camp regulations, and these changed over time and in place, each camp administering the rules differently. Even the policies, she decried, were "often conflicting in purpose and application" and thus "multiple lines of contact had to be established and maintained." The subjects of those government policies, Japanese American internees and their social adjustment and interaction, could not be studied in the usual way of surveys or questionnaires. They had to be interviewed and observed directly, leading to complications of trust between researchers and Japanese Americans, physical danger for the researchers, and questions over the validity of subject responses under extreme conditions of stress within the camps among an "insecure, increasingly resentful people" toward government imposed policies and the conditions of their detention (Thomas and Nishimoto, vi–vii).

Despite Thomas's lack of expertise on Japanese Americans and the concentration camps, her principal, coauthored work, *The Spoilage* (1946), and the JERS publications and archive set the intellectual framework for most of the studies that followed.

Gary Y. Okihiro

Reference
Thomas, Dorothy Swaine and Richard S. Nishimoto. *The Spoilage.* Berkeley: University of California Press, 1946.

TOLAN COMMITTEE
In late February 1942, the Select Committee of the House of Representatives began hearings on the West Coast on "national defense migration." The committee took testimony in San Francisco, Los Angeles, Portland, and Seattle. Democrat John Tolan of Oakland, California, served as the committee's chair, and hence the name, Tolan Committee. The subject, "national defense migration," featured prominently in the government's program of mass removal of Japanese Americans and some of the consequences of that action.

Numerous witnesses testified to the wisdom of that "migration," while a few were against it. Fifteen Japanese Americans gave testimony to the Tolan Committee. Of that total, all but two agreed with the government program of mass removal. The Japanese American Citizens League (JACL), presuming to speak for the community, asked for "no undue discrimination" against Japanese Americans in the conduct of the removals, but also deferred to the concerns of "military necessity and national safety." In San Francisco, JACL national secretary Mike Masaoka assured the committee: "If, in the judgment of military and federal authorities, evacuation of Japanese residents from the West Coast is a primary step toward assuring the safety of this Nation, we will have no hesitation in complying with the necessities implicit in that judgment" (Daniels, 219).

Another JACL leader, James Sakamoto, a past president of the organization, told the Tolan Committee in Seattle that Japanese Americans were so loyal that they "'turned in' [to the FBI] whom we thought should be checked into." Nisei were in fact advised to turn in even their parents if they exhibited any "pro-Japan" sympathies. Although Sakamoto believed mass removal was unnecessary, he, like Masaoka, agreed: "We will be only too happy to be evacuated if the Government orders us, because we feel that the basic loyalty at a time such as this is to obey the order of the Government to which we owe true allegiance" (Daniels, 220). Overall, the JACL advocated special surveillance for their parents, the issei, but the rights of citizenship for their generation.

The two Japanese Americans who opposed the government's program and the JACL's position were James Omura and Caryl Fumiko Okuma. Publisher of *Current Life,* a magazine directed at nisei, James Omura told the committee that the victimization of Japanese Americans on the basis of race will tarnish U.S. history and the nation would never again "stand high in the council chambers of justice and tolerance." The act would also serve as an indictment against "every racial minority in the United States." Japanese Americans deserve the right to be treated as individuals and not as a race, Omura argued. "Are we to be condemned merely on the basis of our racial origin?" he asked. Caryl Fumiko Okuma, managing editor of *Current Life,* added that Japanese Americans were being tried in the press, and "press propaganda," in her words, was precipitating a landslide "toward mass evacuation and it is picking up momentum" (*National Defense Migration,* 11230–33).

A notable non-Japanese who testified before the Tolan Committee was then California attorney general Earl Warren who would later become chief justice of the U.S. Supreme Court. Warren appeared before the committee in February 1942 with maps showing how Japanese farms abutted against major defense plants and were aligned under power lines pointing, seemingly, toward major aircraft factories. His maps, Warren contended, showed some Japanese plotted to spy on and undermine the security of installations critical for the national defense. The problem for law enforcement, Warren complained, was separating the citizen from the alien among the Japanese.

Madera, California mayor, John Gordon, submitted testimony alleging that Japanese, if left free, could inflict "terrific damage," and it was impossible for the police to distinguish the "dangerous" Japanese from the innocent. Accordingly, the only "safe procedure" was to "take up all Japanese and intern them." Unlike the "Japs," Gordon continued, Italians were "well assimilated, and we do not regard even the Italian aliens as alien in fact." Italians were loyal, and "we feel it is safe to let the Italians continue their normal life in this community." Likewise, all Germans, aliens and citizens alike were regarded as "national of this country." National defense migration, thus, should target only Japanese (*National Defense Migration,* 10995).

The committee's concerns were the effects of a mass removal when Japanese Americans were so vital to the agriculture of the West Coast. J. Murray Thompson, regional head of the agricultural adjustment administration, testified California's fresh vegetable production, which was 32 percent in value for the nation as a whole, was vital for the conduct of the war. In 1940, Japanese farms in California totaled 40 percent of the state's vegetable acreages. Those farms and Japanese "stoop" labor, thus, were critical for the food supply of the nation. But Filipino and Mexican labor, Thompson offered, could substitute for the loss of Japanese production, although that transition needed to be carefully planned and executed.

The Tolan Committee completed its work in March 1942. Although the decision to remove all Japanese Americans from the West Coast had already been made in Washington, D.C., the committee's hearings provided evidence in support of that government policy.

Gary Y. Okihiro

References

Daniels, Roger. *Asian America: Chinese and Japanese in the United States since 1850.* Seattle: University of Washington Press, 1988.

National Defense Migration. Hearings before the Select Committee Investigating National Defense Migration. House of Representatives, 77th Congress, 2nd Session. Washington, D.C.: Government Printing Office, 1942.

TULE LAKE RIOT

Tule Lake concentration camp was set up in northern California on Modoc Indian land in April 1942, and in the summer of 1943, the War Relocation Authority (WRA) converted Tule Lake into a maximum-security camp for "disloyals." The camp in the spring of 1944 held over 18,000 Japanese Americans behind a man-proof, six-foot high chain link fence topped with barbed wire spiked with guard towers at intervals along the perimeter manned by soldiers with machine guns. During the riot in 1943, an enhanced military presence with eight tanks occupied the camp.

The Tule Lake riot really began in 1942 with the forcible removal and detention of Japanese Americans, which was an unjust act that required redress. That was the essential charge of Japanese Americans throughout the war. But the immediate cause was the visit of the WRA's director, Dillon Myer, to the Tule Lake camp on November 1, 1943. Myer's visit prompted a Japanese American delegation to demand a meeting with him to outline their grievances, including racism among the WRA staff, inadequate food, and overcrowding. More fundamentally, a leader said, Japanese Americans asked that they "be treated humanely."

Some of the white, WRA administrators feared for their safety having seen a crowd of thousands of Japanese Americans pressing around the building in which Myer and the others met. The next day, November 2, those staff members visited

Tule Lake concentration camp was the place of segregation, a "riot," military rule, and a prison within a prison. (Time Life Pictures/Getty Images)

the head of the military police responsible for Tule Lake concentration camp, Lt. Col Verne Austin, and asked him to intervene and guarantee their safety. Austin commanded a battalion of about 1,200 soldiers. Antagonism rose between WRA administrators and their Japanese American charges, and after a minor scuffle between those elements, the camp's director called in the military.

Tanks rolled into the concentration camp on November 4, and the army declared military rule and its determination to stamp out the protest by removing troublemakers. Austin imposed a 6 A.M. to 7 P.M. curfew and arbitrarily arrested and detained Japanese Americans without charges or hearings. He disbanded a community group, the Daihyo Sha Kai, and apprehended its members, required identification badges to be worn by everyone 12 years and older, and mounted a comprehensive sweep of the entire camp to uncover and take into custody agitators and confiscate weapons. On November 26, three groups of about 150 men, each carrying full field equipment and a gas mask and all officers bearing side arms, clubs, and gas grenades, marched through the camp to carry out their commander's orders.

In late November, the army erected a stockade surrounded by barbed-wire fence and guard towers, building in effect, a prison within the concentration camp to segregate the apprehended men from the rest of the camp. And within the stockade, the army built a box called the "bull pen" in which to punish anyone it chose. The bunks in the stockade sat on bare ground, which was frozen in the winter, and being confined there was a life and death struggle. The men received no extra clothing or blankets despite temperatures that fell below freezing. Over 150 men were held in the stockade.

Beatings were common under martial law to punish and extract information. A former security officer recalled with delight the night of November 4 when the tanks rumbled into Tule Lake. He described the interrogation room where fists and baseball bats were preferred over conversation. "None of the three Japs were unconscious but all three were groggy from the blows they received, especially the one . . . hit with the baseball bat," the officer began. When one of them refused to do as ordered, he said, "I knocked my Jap down with my fist. He stayed down but was not unconscious. [Q] hit his Jap over the head with the baseball bat . . ." That night in all, 18 Japanese Americans were "severely beaten with baseball bats," according to a deposition, and some required "hospitalization for several months and the mentality of one was impaired permanently as the result of the beating he had received" (Drinnon, 142–43).

On January 1944, the army conducted an election to decide on the status of the Daihyo Sha Kai, which was an elected, representative body. The question put to Japanese Americans was whether to retain the Daihyo Sha Kai, most of whose members were in the stockade, or to reject them and, in effect, to accept the army's position. The military's tally was 4,893 against the Daihyo Sha Kai, 4,120 for the Daihyo Sha Kai, and 228 undecided. Amidst claims of voting irregularities, the army accepted their official count, and with that vindication, on January 15, 1944, the military returned Tule Lake to the WRA, except the stockade, which it controlled until May of that year. The WRA closed the stockade in August 1944.

The Tule Lake riot, accordingly, was not really a riot but a mass protest movement on the part of Japanese Americans in that concentration camp. Their essential demand was for human dignity within the parameters of the camp and its racism and inhumanity. Those demands were met with military repression and rule, which prompted terror and physical violence to stamp out the movement and cause.

Gary Y. Okihiro

Reference

Drinnon, Richard. *Keeper of Concentration Camps: Dillon S. Myer and American Racism.* Berkeley: University of California Press, 1987.

UCHIDA, YOSHIKO (1921–1992)

Yoshiko Uchida, a writer of children's books about the Japanese American experience, was born on November 24, 1921, in Alameda, California. She was the second daughter of Japanese migrants Takashi and Iku Uchida. Her father came to the United States in 1903 and worked for the San Francisco offices of the large corporate conglomerate Mitsui and Company. Uchida's mother wrote poetry, passing on her love of literature to her two girls. Even during the Great Depression, Uchida and her family lived comfortably, for her father's job paid well and they were thrifty with their money.

While Uchida saw her home as a site of happiness and love, the other places where she spent her adolescence felt different. As a student at University High School in Oakland, she found herself ignored by many of her white classmates, who considered her a foreigner and would not invite her to any of their parties. Uchida graduated early and enrolled at the University of California, Berkeley, at the age of 16. While she still felt somewhat ostracized by her collegiate peers, she befriended several other Japanese American students and was only six months away from her graduation when Pearl Harbor was attacked on December 7, 1941.

Two months later, President Franklin Roosevelt ordered all Japanese Americans on the West Coast to leave their homes and relocate to concentration camps. Uchida and her family were no exception. The Federal Bureau of Investigation (FBI) interrogated her father, and on April 21, 1942, the Uchidas had to leave Berkeley for their new residence—a horse stall at Tanforan Racetrack in San Bruno, California. The racetrack had been converted to a civilian assembly center to house evicted Japanese Americans. Barbed wire and armed guards surrounded the facility. It was at Tanforan that Uchida received by mail a number of congratulatory graduation cards from friends, as well as her diploma from the University of California. She missed her commencement ceremony by two weeks. In a detailed scrapbook that Uchida kept during her time in camp, she pasted clippings of newspaper articles about and photos of the 5,000 students in Berkeley's Class of 1942 as they celebrated the awarding of their degrees; Uchida's caption reads: "I attend my graduation via the press."

On September 16, the family was forced to move again—this time to the Topaz War Relocation Center, a concentration camp in the arid and dusty Millard County, Utah. Within the camp's fences, Uchida taught second-grade children and thus saw not only the injustices imposed upon young Japanese Americans but also the varying interpretations these children had of their present circumstances.

Yoshiko Uchida (left), parents, and sister (right) on the day of their departure from Topaz concentration camp in 1943. (The Bancroft Library, University of California)

In the spring of 1943, Smith College accepted Uchida into, and awarded her a fellowship to attend, its master's program in education. She was therefore allowed to leave the concentration camp in May of the same year. Her sister was released with her, while her parents had to wait until autumn for the U.S. government to permit them to leave. The 13 months that Uchida spent at Topaz left a lasting impression on her consciousness, leading her to write about her wartime experiences in a number of books.

After teaching for several years at a Quaker school near Philadelphia, she came to realize that she wanted to expand her educational audience from a few classrooms' worth of students to a large number of readers. She moved to New York City to work as a secretary, and she wrote stories during her slower hours on the job, as well as in her evenings at home. Uchida soon was asked to contribute to a book about Japanese folk tales, and while working on this project (which never achieved publication) she discovered that she had a multitude of unique experiences to share with a reading public, and her work as a teacher prompted her to focus on literature specifically relevant to young people.

A trip to her parents' homeland on a Ford Foundation Fellowship in 1952 proved formative for Uchida. She came to believe that everything she loved about Japan was and always had been a part of her identity. "In my eagerness to be accepted as an American during my youth," Uchida wrote, "I had been pushing my Japaneseness aside. Now at last, I appreciated it and was proud of it. I had finally come full circle. Now it was time for me to pass on this sense of pride and self-esteem to the third generation Japanese Americans—the Sansei—and to give them the kinds of books I'd never had as a child" (*Invisible Thread*, 131).

When she returned to the United States, Uchida began to write with great prolificacy. In her lifetime, she published more than 30 books, including her celebrated *Journey to Topaz* (1971), a novel based on her experience as an internee in the Utah desert—and her collection of memoirs, *Desert Exile* (1982), which brought Uchida international attention. Most of her writings have strong historical grounding and deal with the themes of citizenship, racial identity, and interethnic relationships.

After winning acclaim in the early 1980s, Uchida traveled and lectured extensively, never ceasing to write and publish. She received more than 20 awards for her work, among them an American Library Association's Notable Book citation for *Journey to Topaz,* a New York Public Library's Best Book of the Year citation in 1983 for *The Best Bad Thing,* and the Japanese American of the Biennium award from the Japanese American Citizens League in 1988.

Uchida died in Berkeley after a stroke on June 25, 1992. Of all her writings, perhaps the one most representative of her spirit is her autobiography *The Invisible Thread* (1991), the last work she published in her lifetime. "I want each new generation of Americans to know what once happened in our democracy," Uchida wrote in the book's epilogue. "I want them to love and cherish the freedom that can be snatched away so quickly, even by their own country. Most of all, I ask them to be vigilant, so that such a tragedy will never happen to any group of people in America again" (133).

Daniel Valella

References

Uchida, Yoshiko. *The Invisible Thread.* New York: Beech Tree Books, 1995.

Uchida, Yoshiko. [Scrapbook.] Yoshiko Uchida Papers. Bancroft Library, University of California, Berkeley. BANC MSS 86/97c, 1942–1992.

"Yoshiko Uchida, 70, A Children's Author." *The New York Times*, June 24, 1992. http://www.nytimes.com/1992/06/24/obituaries/yoshiko-uchida-70-a-childrens-author.html

UNO, EDISON (1929–1976)

Activist Edison Tomimaro Uno was born in Los Angeles, California, on October 19, 1929. He was the ninth of his parents' 10 children. When Uno was 12 years old, just after the attack on Pearl Harbor, Federal Bureau of Investigation (FBI) agents took his father, Japan-born George Uno, to four different concentration camps and did not allow him to contact his family for over a year. The U.S. government soon forced the rest of the Uno family to leave their southern California home for an "assembly center" at Santa Anita Race Track. The Unos were then moved to the Amache War Relocation Center in Granada, Colorado. Four of Uno's brothers soon volunteered for military service, while his mother and the younger members of the family were transferred to Crystal City Internment Camp in Texas, where they finally reunited with Uno's father. When all Uno's family members were released except for his father, he elected to remain in the camp. He stayed in Crystal City for a whole other year, until his father persuaded him to return to Los Angeles to complete his education. The Crystal City officer-in-charge told him upon his fall 1946 departure that, after spending 1,647 days in internment, Uno was the last U.S. citizen to be released.

Outside the concentration camps' walls, Uno quickly assumed multiple leadership roles. In his senior year at Marshal High School, he was elected class president. He also served as president of the YMCA youth group Hi-Y before becoming the youngest chapter president in the history of the Japanese American Citizens League (JACL), whose East Los Angeles chapter he led at age 18. After graduating from Los Angeles State College with a degree in political science, Uno matriculated at Hastings College of Law in San Francisco. Halfway through his law school education, however, he suffered his first heart attack and dropped out after his doctors advised him to choose an alternative career.

Uno helped establish a small weekly English-language Japanese American newspaper in 1951, and for the next four years he worked as an advertising and publicity agent for five Los Angeles–based Japanese American publications. After a series of other odd jobs, Uno decided to enter the field of education and became operations manager of the University of California, San Francisco, Student Union in 1964. Five years later, he became a financial aid officer at the school—a position that allowed him to work with students and address issues of welfare and civil rights. In 1969, Uno spoke out in favor of the San Francisco State College students who held strikes that called for an increase in minority faculty, an elimination of restrictions on freedom of speech, and an implementation of ethnic studies programs.

Soon thereafter, Uno and Raymond Okamura helped organize a campaign to get the U.S. government to remove Title II of the Internal Security Act of 1950, a law that gave the president the authority to detain without trial any citizens who were suspected of espionage or sabotage during national emergencies. For 15 years, Uno tried to persuade U.S. Supreme Court Justice Earl Warren to apologize for his support of the evacuation of California's Japanese (American) families when he was the state's attorney general in 1942. Warren never made a public apology during Uno's lifetime, though he did eventually write in a memoir that he regretted his wartime support of the incarceration.

In 1970, Uno published *Japanese Americans: The Untold Story,* a children's book about the wartime mass removal and confinement. Three years later, he joined a campaign started by San Francisco pediatrician and activist Clifford Uyeda to win a presidential pardon for Iva Toguri, a Japanese American who was convicted of treason on September 29, 1949. Toguri had been one of the 13 female broadcasters collectively labeled "Tokyo Rose"—hired to host a radio program of music, comedy, and news on Tokyo Radio's "Zero Hour" show during World War II. When the war ended, the U.S. government claimed that Toguri had used her position as broadcaster to promote Japanese propaganda. She was sentenced to 10 years in prison and fined $10,000, in addition to losing her U.S. citizenship. Believing in Toguri's innocence, Uno, Uyeda, and other members of the JACL distributed

10,000 booklets with evidence demonstrating the unfairness of Toguri's trial. Major newspapers, religious organizations, and veterans groups endorsed the campaign, and eventually *60 Minutes* interviewed Toguri, bringing national attention to her case. She finally received a presidential pardon after Republican senator S. I. Hayakawa met with President Gerald Ford and convinced him to provide a full and unconditional pardon for Toguri on his last full day in office in January 1977.

Unfortunately, Uno did not live to see the results of his campaigning efforts, as he died of a heart attack mere weeks before Toguri's pardon—on December 24, 1976. A wife and two daughters survived him. More than 700 people attended Uno's memorial service in San Francisco, and his legacy lives on through numerous honors, including awards from the American Civil Liberties Union and the San Francisco Bar Association. His activism on behalf of students while an assistant dean between 1967 and 1974 led the University of California, San Francisco, to establish a Chancellor's Edison Uno Public Service Award, given each year to the student who best exemplifies Uno's selfless character.

Finally, Uno's efforts to get the U.S. government to redress Japanese Americans for their wartime confinement culminated in landmark legislation long after his death. Told repeatedly that a redress movement would rock the boat, cost millions, and lose several politicians' support for the JACL, Uno continued to fight for justice on his own. Once the Toguri pardon campaign proved successful, the fight for redress was rekindled and Congress eventually passed the Civil Liberties Act of 1988, providing each surviving detainee a national apology and $20,000 in compensation. At the ceremony celebrating the bill's passage, Japanese American leaders felt that, though Uno had been dead nearly 14 years, his spirit was powerfully present, and they paid tribute to him for sparking the ultimately successful movement.

Daniel Valella

References

Japanese American Journey: The Story of a People. San Mateo, California: Japanese American Curriculum Project, 1985.

Uno, Edison. Edison Uno Papers, 1964–1976. Department of Special Collections, Research Library, University of California, Los Angeles.

Yang, Alice. "Edison Uno." *Densho Encyclopedia.* August 28, 2012. http://encyclopedia.densho.org/Edison%20Uno/.

V

VARSITY VICTORY VOLUNTEERS

The Varsity Victory Volunteers, often called the VVV or Triple V, was a labor battalion of nisei young men in Hawai'i during World War II, formed largely in response to anti-Japanese sentiment. In the wake of Japan's attack on Pearl Harbor, some 1,500 nisei soldiers in the National Guard served in integrated regiments named the 298th and 299th Infantry. They dug trenches and went on guard details to defend the islands from a possible landing by Japan's forces. But on December 10, three days after Pearl Harbor, their commanders took away their rifles, bayonets, and ammunition, and placed them under guard and confinement to their quarters. It was clear the military had second thoughts about their loyalty. But two days later, their arms were returned to them, and they resumed their duties, stringing barbed wire and patrolling the beaches.

Some white army officers distrusted Hawai'i's Japanese Americans like a colonel who asked the commander of the 298th, "You sleep here where these Japs can slit your throat?" That skepticism prompted the army to expel the 317 Japanese American volunteers in the Territorial Guard in January 1942, and had white units "watch the local Japanese" (Okihiro, 250). Ted Tsukiyama, a member of that dismissed group, voiced his frustration, anguish, disappointment over that failure of democracy.

About a week after their expulsion, those maligned nisei wrote to the Army general, expressing their disappointment but also their loyalty to their country. "Hawaii is our home; the United States, our country," they declared. "We wish to do our part as loyal Americans in every way possible and we hereby offer ourselves for whatever service you may see fit to use us" (Okihiro, 250). The military governor accepted their offer of service, and put them to work in a labor battalion.

The army assigned those nisei civilian laborers to the 34th Combat Engineers Regiment and called them the Corps of Engineers Auxiliary, but Japanese Americans called themselves the VVV. A prominent VVV member explained their mission: to "set out to fight a twofold fight for tolerance and justice" (Okihiro, 250). Many of the men were students at the University of Hawai'i, and they were divided into 12 labor gangs under the direction of non-Japanese army staff.

Typically, the VVV worked six days each week from 7:30 A.M. to 4:30 P.M., receiving a pay of $90 per month. During the 11 months of their existence, the VVV constructed six warehouses, strung several miles of barbed wire, quarried several tons of rocks, completed one road and began work on two others, and built and repaired furniture. They made three visits to the blood bank and bought war bonds totaling $27,850. The VVV disbanded in January 1943 after it became

Banned from military service by the U.S. government, nisei volunteers joined to form a labor brigade they called the Varsity Victory Volunteers. They performed mainly manual labor to prove their loyalty. (AP/Wide World Photo)

possible for Japanese Americans to volunteer for military service in the uniform of their country.

While their leaders might have had a higher mission in mind, many of the VVV members simply joined because they were recruited or friends and others enlisted. Jackson Morisawa remembered many university students enlisting in the VVV. Most of them just joined. "Not thinking any loyalty or anything; I mean honestly, I don't think any of 'em had that in mind. If people had presented the whole Varsity Victory Volunteer adventure as a serious 'We gotta save the Japanese American population' thing. . . . Well, we had something of that sort, but we were really not seriously into that kind of thing; we didn't really think of being patriotic or any that kind of stuff. Yeah, and after you join, because everybody's doing it you wanna go in there and be part of it, okay" (Odo, 162).

The army credited the work of the VVV as instrumental in its decision to create a segregated unit of Japanese Americans, which became the 442nd Regimental Combat Team. Having proven their loyalty by establishing "a fine record," the army stated, Japanese Americans deserved the privilege of service in that new regiment. As was the case in the VVV, Japanese Americans had a variety of reasons for volunteering for the U.S. Army, including patriotism, a sense of duty, and because of anti-Japanese sentiment that forced them to demonstrate their loyalty and thereby ensure their future in Hawai'i and the United States. Indeed, many of the Japanese American leaders of the VVV served with distinction in the 100th Infantry Battalion and 442nd Regimental Combat Team and upon their return, became political leaders of a new Hawai'i.

Gary Y. Okihiro

References

Odo, Franklin. *No Sword to Bury: Japanese Americans in Hawai'i during World War II.* Philadelphia: Temple University Press, 2004.

Okihiro, Gary Y. *Cane Fires: The Anti-Japanese Movement in Hawaii, 1865–1945.* Philadelphia: Temple University Press, 1991.

WAR BRIDES

The War Brides Act of 1945 and its amendments affirm an outcome of wars of conquests involving alien lands, peoples, and women. Generally, men declare and engage in those acts of subjugation. Since the late 19th century, the United States has waged war against the Philippines, against Japan, in Korea, in Vietnam, and in West Asia (Afghanistan, Iraq, and Pakistan). And the United States, through its military might, annexed Guam and Hawai'i, and through a political agreement absorbed a portion of Sāmoa. Asian and Pacific Islander women were thereby drawn into relationships with U.S. military men whether out of romantic love or relations of power.

The 1945 War Brides Act allowed admission into the United States "alien spouses and alien children of citizen members of the United States armed forces." Those "alien spouses" were war brides. The Chinese Alien Wives of American Citizens Act (1946) amended the original act to allow the entry of Chinese wives unrestricted by the annual immigration quota of 100 Chinese set by the Immigration Act of 1924. The 1946 amendment was directed at Chinese American soldiers who married or were already married to Chinese women. Many Chinese American soldiers had wives and children in China during the war, and after its end returned to the United States with their families. These were not war brides.

Under the War Brides Act, 5,132 Chinese women entered the United States, having married U.S. servicemen, and under the Chinese Alien Wives of American Citizens Act, 2,317 additional Chinese women entered the country. Thousands of Japanese women and Filipinas (Filipino women) entered the United States each year during the decade following World War II, most of them married to U.S. servicemen, and a similar pattern developed during and after the U.S. wars in Korea and Vietnam. Unlike the Chinese women who entered the United States as war brides, most of the Japanese women and Filipinas married to U.S. servicemen entered as their dependents and not as war brides under the War Brides Act.

During the 1950s, Japanese women entering the United States as dependents of U.S. citizens ranged from 2,000 to 5,000 each year, comprising about 80 percent of all Japanese immigrants. Those numbers declined in the 1960s to 2,500 annually, and in the 1970s, to an average of 2,300 per year. Although legally not war brides, those Japanese women, like Filipinas and Korean and Vietnamese women who entered the United States as dependents of servicemen, were the outcomes of war and the continued military occupation of their countries by U.S. troops and their military bases.

For many Japanese women, social dislocation and poverty caused by the war and the apparent wealth of U.S. soldiers in Japan lured them into thinking marriage to an American was a ticket to the good life. "I thought that in America there was lots of money," a Japanese war bride recalled. "Everything is carefree, lots to eat. . . . I thought I was going to paradise" (Glenn, 58). Others married to escape the dominance of men in Japanese society, seeking a more egalitarian relationship. But both wealth and greater gender equality often eluded war brides once settled in the United States where the cost of living was higher and patriarchy prevailed. In fact, out of their culture, war brides grew even more dependent upon their husbands, and loneliness, homesickness, and difficulty with English were their daily companions.

War brides were a consequence of war, but they were also vital to the growth of Asian and Japanese American communities. Especially for Chinese Americans, the Chinese war brides helped to even the gender imbalance and the ratio between men and women. Since the 19th century, there were far more Chinese men than women. War brides reduced that discrepancy. War brides also reproduced, and their children infused an aging population with youthful energy and creativity. Since the 1924 Immigration Act, some 100 Chinese, Japanese, Koreans, and South Asians were allowed into the United States every year. The same quota applied to Filipinos after 1934. The World War II war brides escaped those restrictive quotas, and began the demographic changes that transformed Asian America in the last three decades of the 20th century.

Gary Y. Okihiro

Reference

Glenn, Evelyn Nakano. *Issei, Nisei, Warbride: Three Generations of Japanese American Domestic Service*. Philadelphia: Temple University Press, 1986.

WAR RELOCATION AUTHORITY

On March 18, 1942, President Franklin D. Roosevelt signed Executive Order 9102, creating the War Relocation Authority (WRA) to manage Japanese Americans removed under EO 9066. Milton S. Eisenhower, brother of the military commander Dwight Eisenhower, was named the first director of the WRA. Eisenhower was from the Agricultural Department, and when he called the governors of western states to a meeting in April 1942, he thought of establishing "small inland camps on the model of Civilian Conservation Corps camps which would serve as staging areas for the evacuees as they were moved into private jobs as soon as possible and could resume something like a normal life," Eisenhower wrote in his memoirs (Daniels, 226). Eisenhower saw the WRA's function as truly one of "relocating" and not confining Japanese Americans.

By contrast, all the governors of those states, with one exception, objected to having Japanese Americans moved into their territories. The most vehement of them, Governor Nels Smith of Wyoming, came close to Eisenhower and "shook his fist in my face, and growled through his clenched teeth: 'If you bring the Japanese into my state, I promise you they will be hanging from every tree,'" Eisenhower recalled. After that April meeting in Salt Lake City, Eisenhower saw no alternative to "evacuation camps" for Japanese Americans to confine them while giving them "as much self-respect as the horrible circumstances permitted" (Daniels, 226).

Eisenhower realized the injustice of the WRA camps, and in June 1942, he resigned as WRA director. In his letter of resignation, he told the president that public attitudes had to a large degree influenced the shaping of the program of removal and confinement. But he never expressed publicly his opinion of the injustice of the WRA camps, which he insisted on calling evacuation centers. "Never," Eisenhower wrote, "did we think of them as concentration camps" (Daniels, 227).

On June 17, 1942, Dillon S. Myer became the WRA director. Myer described his responsibilities as foremost caring for the some 120,000 Japanese Americans, and then, getting them out of the camps and resettling them into "normal" situations and communities. Like Eisenhower, Myer blamed public opinion and the outcry against Japanese Americans for the situation of the camps and for criticisms of the WRA.

Located in Washington, D.C., the WRA had regional offices in San Francisco, Denver, and Little Rock, Arkansas, during 1942 to facilitate the establishment of the concentration camps and handle public relations in those areas. Especially when located near white communities, the WRA camps needed the approval of the local residents, which was the main object of the public relations work. By the fall of that year, with the camps established, the WRA closed its regional offices, and later, opened relocation offices in major cities throughout the country to assist in the relocation and resettlement of Japanese Americans released from the camps. At their peak, there were 58 such relocation offices.

WRA director Myer described the initial period of moving in and settling, from May 1942 to March 1943, as one of turmoil. Japanese Americans were dazed, confused, and frustrated, he surmised, and camp conditions were primitive and unstable. The camps were 10 "abnormal cities," Myer contended, and he and his staff tried hard to provide housing, food, employment, medical care, and social welfare to the people. The WRA was organized into divisions and sections to tend to those needs. The community management division, for instance, contained sections for education, health, community enterprises, government, and women's affairs.

The army provided the basic food supplies, and Japanese Americans worked on vegetable gardens and livestock farms to supplement their diets. WRA policy imposed a limit of 45 cents per person each day for food. The military also supplied the internal security officers and their detachments to serve under the directors for each camp. A Japanese American police force handled minor offenses.

The WRA established camp councils as a form of "self-government," but restricted offices to U.S. citizens or nisei, although both issei and nisei were allowed to vote. Japanese Americans in several of the camps challenged both the concept of "self-government" and the limitation on elective office to U.S. citizens, which they saw as undemocratic. Ultimately, the WRA and its camp directors determined camp policies, they declared, and children (the nisei) ruling over their parents (the issei) contradicted Japanese culture and familial relations. In November 1942 at Poston concentration camp, the elected council resigned after expressions of no confidence by the camp's Japanese Americans, and at Manzanar, no council was elected and instead mainly issei block managers administered the camp. Because of those acts of resistance, in early 1943, the WRA ended its ban against issei elected leaders.

More than 30,000 students enrolled in WRA-run schools, which, except for Tule Lake, were accredited by state authorities. More than 7,000 graduated from camp high schools. At first, schools opened without tables, chairs, blackboards, or books and paper, and teachers were in short supply. Teachers included recruits from American Indian reservations and returning missionaries from Japan, and more than 100 Japanese Americans in the camps with some college education served as teaching assistants due to the shortage. Science equipment and supplies were generally scarce and absent.

The WRA maintained hospitals headed by a white administrator in each camp, but Japanese Americans comprised most of the staff of physicians and nurses. Hospitals were modeled on the military's "theater of operations," and equipment and medicines were accordingly modest and in short supply.

WRA director Myer listed as his most important decisions the determination to relocate Japanese Americans outside the 10 concentration camps rather than to hold them in confinement, to campaign for the nisei to serve in the U.S. military, and to seek an end to the military exclusion orders that kept Japanese Americans from returning to the West Coast. In January 1945, Myer announced the closure of all WRA concentration camps except Tule Lake, and camps began to close their doors toward the year's end. The WRA closed its offices throughout the United States in June 1946.

Gary Y. Okihiro

References

Daniels, Roger. *Asian America: Chinese and Japanese in the United States since 1850.* Seattle: University of Washington Press, 1988.

Myer, Dillon S. *Uprooted Americans: The Japanese Americans and the War Relocation Authority during World War II.* Tucson: University of Arizona Press, 1971.

WARTIME CIVIL CONTROL ADMINISTRATION

The Wartime Civil Control Administration (WCCA) was set up by the Western Defense Command under Lieutenant General John L. DeWitt on March 11, 1942, to manage the forced removal of Japanese Americans from its Military Area No. 1. The Justice Department sent Tom C. Clark to the WCCA to coordinate the activities of civilian agencies helping the army in that process. These included the Federal Security Agency, Farm Security Administration, and Federal Reserve Bank to take care of social welfare and property transfers.

Led by a War Department staff member, Colonel Karl R. Bendetsen, the WCCA divided the West Coast into 108 exclusion zones, each comprising about 1,000 Japanese Americans. The WCCA posted exclusion order notices in each exclusion zone, required Japanese Americans to report to a central location for information and registration, provided storage for their possessions, and managed the evictions and "assembly centers" for their confinement.

The Farm Security Administration reported 7,076 Japanese American farm operators on 6,664 Japanese American–owned or leased farms totaling about 258,000 acres in Military Area No. 1. Those farms were valued at $73 million. Including those in Military Area No. 2, Japanese American farm acreages reached to over a quarter of a million acres. The government's problem was to evict Japanese Americans while keeping those farms productive for the war effort. For Japanese Americans, the removal and confinement meant the loss of a lifetime of labor.

Bendetsen presented his program of forced removals as a benign act of charity. A government official recalled a briefing held by the then major. "There on the wall was a map of the Pacific Coast with a new North-South line from British Columbia to Mexico. For our Japanese neighbors, America now commenced east of that line. We Caucasians, patriots by virtue of our skin, could continue to reside

Japanese Americans report to the San Francisco Wartime Civil Control Administration's station in January 1942. Piled on the sidewalk are their belongings. (Getty Images)

west of the line. With the deftness of a surgeon and with something of the same re-assuring antiseptic quality, the young major told us of evacuation proclamations to be followed by voluntary evacuation, followed in turn by involuntary evacuation, and mild detention for three or four years in a Federal institution." The official re-marked, "Bendetsen's tones made one think of restful, bucolic retirement, not of barbed wire or bayonets" (Girdner and Loftis, 123).

The reality, by contrast, was less than restful. The army's reports found the WCCA assembly centers to be inferior to military standards. Many of them, in fact, were converted horse race tracks and county fairgrounds, which displayed animals and livestock. "The kitchens are not up to Army standards of cleanliness," reported an army document. The hospital had no cribs for children, and no baby food ex-cept bread and milk. "The dishes looked bad . . . gray and cracked. . . . Dishwash-ing not very satisfactory due to an insufficiency of hot water. . . . Soup plates being used instead of plates, which means that the food all runs together and looks un-tidy and unappetizing" (Daniels, 89).

Bendetsen made his headquarters in the Whitcomb Hotel in San Francisco while many of his wards lived in horse stalls. The WCCA kept a tight control over the assembly centers. Each assembly center director fell under the chief of the as-sembly center branch, Rex L. Nicholson, who in turn reported directly to his su-perior, Bendetsen. WCCA policies were formed in Washington, D.C. where the Office of Education oversaw the centers' schools, and Public Health, the hospitals and sanitation. In the centers, whites managed Japanese Americans, and they lived apart from them in separate, guarded quarters that were notably better built and had individual bathrooms. WCCA rules required the white staff to refrain from forming friendships with Japanese Americans.

While center administrations varied, Japanese Americans provided the labor required for the center's operation under white supervisors. Women worked in the kitchens and mess halls and in offices as stenographers and clerks, while men cooked and washed dishes and pots and in shops as mechanics and carpenters. At first, they volunteered and received no wages, but starting in June 1942, Japanese Americans received $12 to $19 per month depending upon the level of their work. The pay was given not in cash but in script, which was redeemable only in center stores. Although initially the WCCA promoted "self-government" in the centers, in June 1942, it dissolved the center councils, increased censorship, and in August, banned all Japanese literature and records except Bibles and hymnals.

That summer of 1942, the WCCA handed over Japanese Americans to the War Relocation
Authority (WRA), and by November, the assembly centers stood empty. The Fresno center was the last to close. Hiroko Kamikawa, a former college student, reported that the center's director thanked the Japanese Americans for being "good soldiers" and obeying the rules as he puffed on his cigar (Girdner and Loftis, 208).

The WCCA remained open in San Francisco and maintained a sizable staff through September 1945.

Gary Y. Okihiro

References

Daniels, Roger. *Concentration Camps: North America: Japanese in the United States and Canada during World War II.* Malabar, FL: Robert E. Krieger, 1981.

Girdner, Audrie and Anne Loftis. *The Great Betrayal: The Evacuation of the Japanese-Americans during World War II.* London: Macmillan, 1969.

WESTERN DEFENSE COMMAND

At the start of World War II, the United States resolved to defend the entire Western Hemisphere, including North and South America, Greenland, and Hawai'i, against attack. The 19th-century Monroe Doctrine asserted that U.S. interest, which considered the New World a province and sphere of U.S. concern, and the military policy to defend the entire Western Hemisphere was an extension of its pledge to defend the U.S. homeland. Plans for that defense changed with military capabilities such as the threat posed by ships at first and by airplanes in the 20th century.

The National Defense Act of 1920 provided for a military command system for the army. In September of that year, the War Department established nine corps areas, and authorized their commanders with control over those forces within their territories. By 1933, that system of command changed when the War Department established four armies without fixed areas and restricted them to war planning and field maneuvers. As the prospect of war approached, however, commanders were given more authority for battle readiness.

Lieutenant General John L. DeWitt commanded the Fourth Army and the Ninth Corps Area on the West Coast. He assumed responsibility for the defense of his area against external attack in what was envisioned as a theater of operation because the expectation were attacks along the nation's peripheries and not its interior, which constituted the zone of the interior. Indeed, on December 11, 1941, with the onset of war four days earlier, the army designated the Western Defense Command and named it a theater of operations. As head of the Western Defense Command, General DeWitt controlled all army troops and installations in Alaska, Washington, Oregon, California, Nevada, Arizona, Idaho, Montana, and Utah.

President Franklin D. Roosevelt's Executive Order 9066 signed on February 19, 1942, empowered the military to designate military areas from which "any or all persons may be excluded" and to provide "transportation, food, shelter, and other accommodations as may be necessary . . ." The military was responsible for those provisions because the Executive Order was based on the myth of "military necessity." The army, in fact, opposed the mass removal of "any or all persons," believing "mass evacuation unnecessary," according to an action taken by General Headquarters on the day President Roosevelt issued his Executive Order (Daniels, 71).

In the Western Defense Command, General DeWitt was at first opposed to the immediate removal of Japanese Americans. He saw it as a gradual process, which included German and Italian aliens. He told an army colleague his plan was to "take the Japs first, then maybe the Germans and then last the Italians" (Daniels, 81). Toward that end, DeWitt issued proclamations, the first dated March 2, 1941, which divided Washington, Oregon, California, and Arizona into two military areas. Military Area No. 1 was subdivided into a "prohibited zone," the West Coast and a strip of land along the Mexican border, and a larger "restricted zone" surrounding the prohibited zone. In addition, the proclamation designated 98 other prohibited zones, namely military installations, power plants, and other places of strategic interest. The two zones applied to Japanese, German, and Italian aliens and "any person of Japanese Ancestry," and an accompanying press release explained the eventual exclusion of all Japanese Americans from Military Area No. 1 and all prohibited zones.

On March 16, 1942, Public Proclamation No. 2 established four more military areas for Idaho, Montana, Nevada, and Utah and listed 933 prohibited zones. DeWitt planned the forced removal of all Japanese Americans from the Western Defense Command, a plan that the War Department opposed. Public Proclamation No. 3 established on March 27 throughout Military Area No. 1 and all prohibited areas enforced curfew from 8 P.M. to 6 A.M. affecting only Japanese Americans and "enemy aliens," although the latter was not generally enforced for Germans and Italians. And Public Proclamation No. 4 restricted Japanese Americans from leaving Military Area No. 1 where most of them along the West Coast lived. Military control over their lives policed Japanese American freedoms.

On March 24, 1942, General DeWitt issued the first of his Civilian Exclusion Orders, which came three days after Public Law No. 503, an Act of Congress, which criminalized violations of the exclusion orders. DeWitt's Exclusion Order No. 1 directed Japanese Americans on Bainbridge Island near Seattle to leave their homes under military guard. Although not the first affected by exclusion (the mainly fishermen on Terminal Island in southern California were the first group of Japanese Americans evicted from their homes), the Bainbridge Islanders began the mass, forcible removal of all Japanese Americans from the West Coast.

DeWitt established the Wartime Civil Control Administration (WCCA) on March 11, 1942, to manage the mass removal, and put a reassigned War Department staff member, Colonel Karl R. Bendetsen, in charge of the operation. The army set up a reception center for the removed Japanese Americans, stored some of their possessions at their own risk, and allowed them to carry only bedding, clothing, and eating utensils sufficient for each family member. The 54 Japanese American families on Bainbridge Island had a mere six days to prepare for the move, which took them to Puyallup, Washington, fairgrounds. That procedure set the norm for the mass removal. By June 5, 1942, Military Area No. 1 was "Jap-free."

From the WCCA assembly centers, the some 120,000 Japanese Americans were taken to the War Relocation Authority concentration camps. The military handled the forcible evictions and confinement in assembly centers, and the WRA managed the concentration camps. The army, however, remained responsible for security in the WRA camps, many of which were in the Western Defense Command. Its head, General DeWitt, as early as January 1942, expressed his guiding principles in managing his troops and the civilians in his command area. "We are at war," DeWitt began, "and this area—eight states—has been designated as a theater of operations. I have approximately 240,000 men at my disposal . . . [and]

approximately 288,000 enemy aliens . . . which we have to watch. . . . I have little confidence that the enemy aliens are law-abiding or loyal in any sense of the word. Some of them yes; many, no. Particularly the Japanese. I have no confidence in their loyalty whatsoever" (Daniels, 45–46).

Gary Y. Okihiro

Reference

Daniels, Roger. *Concentration Camps: North America: Japanese in the United States and Canada during World War II*. Malabar, FL: Robert E. Krieger, 1981.

WOMEN'S ARMY CORPS

Created in May 1942, the Women's Army Auxiliary Corps (WAAC) formed a branch of the U.S. Army. In July 1943, WAAC lost its auxiliary status to attain full standing as the Women's Army Corp (WAC). During World War II, over 4,000 African American women served in the WAC and Women Accepted for Volunteer Emergency Service (WAVES), and fewer numbers of American Indian, Chinese and Japanese American, and Puerto Rican women. The Army Nurse Corps drew women, and segregated from white women, African American nurses served in and tended to all–African American units. Two Chinese American women, Maggie Gee from California and Hazel Ying Lee from Oregon, were among the 1,074 who made it into the elite Women's Airforce Service Pilots Program (WASP), flight testing damaged and repaired aircraft and ferrying domestic deliveries.

The first Japanese American women were accepted into the WAC in October 1943. They entered as volunteers, unlike most Japanese American men who were drafted into the army. A majority of the women volunteers joined the WAC after having left the concentration camps while others came from Hawai'i and from states outside the Western Defense Command. Twenty-six nisei women in Hawai'i were the first Japanese Americans to train for the WAC in 1943, and on the continent, a group of seven trained at Fort Snelling, Minnesota, a year later. A total of about 50 nisei women from Fort Snelling served in the Military Intelligence Service to work as translators but not prisoner-of-war (POW) interrogators like the men. Japanese American WACs were assigned to medical units throughout the United States, in the public information office, and as typists, clerks, and researchers in occupied Japan and Germany after the war. In all, an estimated 300 Japanese American women served in the WAC during World War II, and when open to them, the U.S. Cadet Nursing Corps enlisted more than 200 nisei women.

Ruth Fujii recalled working at McKinley High School in Honolulu during the war when "my girlfriend called and said we could get silk stockings if we joined the WACs so the very next morning, we registered" (Hazama and Komeiji, 171). Her brothers were unqualified for the service "so I wanted to represent the Fujii family" in the war effort. Instead of being angry with her, Fujii was relieved to find, "my family was proud of me." She completed her basic training in 1945, and after graduating the Army placed Fujii in a typing pool, serving in General Douglas MacArthur's

Pvt. Margaret Fukuoka of the Women's Army Corps in 1943. Japanese American men and women served their country during World War II. (Library of Congress)

office in the Philippines and on General George C. Marshall's staff in Nanjing.

Participating in the war effort for Japanese Americans, both men and women, held significance beyond mere patriotism; they had to prove their worth as U.S. citizens. "I felt that the Nisei had to do more than give lip service to the United States and by joining the WACs I could prove my sincerity," said a volunteer from Heart Mountain concentration camp. "After all, this is everybody's war and we all have to put an equal share into it." Sue Suzuko (Ogata) Kato added, "I joined the WACs—and this may sound like flag-waving—to prove my Americanism." Kato trained at Fort Snelling, and was assigned to Fort Devens, Massachusetts, after her basic training. She wound up in Washington, D.C., translating Japanese-language documents for the intelligence corps (Nakano, 169, 170).

Gary Y. Okihiro

References

Hazama, Dorothy Ochiai and Jane Okamoto Komeiji. *Okage Sama De: The Japanese in Hawai'i, 1885–1985*. Honolulu: Bess Press, 1986.

Nakano, Mei T. *Japanese American Women: Three Generations, 1890–1990*. Berkeley: Mina Press, 1990.

Niiya, Brian (Ed.). *Encyclopedia of Japanese American History*. New York: Facts On File, 2001.

WRIT OF ERROR *CORAM NOBIS*

The *coram nobis* writ, from the Latin meaning "error before us," is a device of U.S. law. Derived from the ancient writs of English common law, the writs were designed to protect defendants from arbitrary and unlawful prosecution. In the cases of *Hirabayashi* (1943), *Yasui* (1943), and *Korematsu* (1944) decided by the U.S.

Supreme Court, the *coram nobis* writ was a way to challenge the original decisions to correct a fundamental error rendered in those rulings. Seldom used, the *coram nobis* writ was deployed by attorneys for Gordon Hirabayashi, Fred Korematsu, and Minoru Yasui in 1983, charging that government prosecutors failed to acknowledge that it had no evidence to sustain the justification of "military necessity" upon which Hirabayashi, Korematsu, and Yasui were convicted and, in fact, deliberately suppressed evidence that supported the loyalty of Japanese Americans.

An attorney and constitutional scholar, Peter Irons, in the course of his research discovered the evidence that formed the basis for that challenge. In 1943 and 1944, Irons found, government lawyers complained to their superiors that the cases before the Supreme Court contained lies and involved a suppression of evidence. Their warnings, however, were ignored, and the Justice Department proceeded with its prosecution of Minoru Yasui and Gordon Hirabayashi who were convicted of violating the army's curfew order, and Fred Korematsu, who had violated the military's exclusion order. The Supreme Court's decisions, thus, according to the government's own attorneys, were based upon faulty evidence or writ of *coram nobis.*

Fred Korematsu agreed to petition for a rehearing of his original decision because, he said, "they did me a great wrong" (Irons, 1989, 3). The campaign to reopen and reverse the Supreme Court decision, unprecedented in U.S. jurisprudence, began with the federal court in San Francisco that first heard Korematsu's case. The government's claim was that the military acted to remove Japanese Americans during the war because of a well-founded fear of espionage and sabotage by Japanese Americans while in fact the government had contrary evidence of Japanese American loyalty. By failing to produce that evidence and, in fact, lying before the court constituted an error and fundamental injustice.

Coincidentally and of consequence were the hearings of the Commission on Wartime Relocation and Internment of Civilians created in 1980. During his testimony before the commission the following year, Peter Irons was encouraged by William Marutani, a commission member and Philadelphia judge, to pursue a writ of *coram nobis* to allow the Supreme Court to reconsider its wartime decisions. The suppression of evidence relevant to its decision might prompt that review, Marutani suggested. That encouragement led Irons to form a legal team to undertake the rehearing campaign.

Dale Minami, a San Francisco Bay Area civil rights attorney, joined the team. Minami was an active member of the Bay Area Attorney's for Redress (BAAR), and helped draft BAAR's statement for the Commission on Wartime Relocation in 1981. In that, BAAR contended that the Supreme Court rendered its wartime decisions based on racial stereotypes and racism or guilt by ethnic affiliation and not as individuals as is required by law. Further, BAAR urged the commission to declare the Supreme Court decisions to be invalid and thus untenable as a precedent to be used against another group.

Attorneys Peggy Nagae of Portland, Oregon, and Kathryn Bannai of Seattle joined the *coram nobis* team. Besides their expertise and keen interest in the case, Nagae and Bannai, together with Minami, practiced in cities from which the original wartime cases arose. Fred Korematsu's case was first heard in San Francisco, Minoru Yasui's, in Portland, and Gordon Hirabayashi's, in Seattle. Each assumed leadership of the legal teams in their cities. Their purpose was the reverse the wartime convictions of Hirabayashi, Yasui, and Korematsu.

The research and case preparations were massive, involving over a dozen attorneys and law students. Moreover, the campaign involved public education about the cases and wartime experience of Japanese Americans. The hope was to clear the criminal records of the three Japanese Americans, and to have the entire program of mass removal and detention declared unconstitutional. It was an ambitious effort. Attorney Donald Tamaki volunteered to head the education campaign.

On January 19, 1983, the team filed in San Francisco's federal district court Fred Korematsu's appeal. Judge Marilyn Patel heard the case. Later that month, Hirabayashi's attorneys filed his appeal in Seattle before Judge Donald S. Voorhees, and Yasui's attorneys, in Portland before Judge Robert C. Belloni. The following month, the Commission on Wartime Relocation issued its report titled *Personal Justice Denied,* which blamed the Japanese American wartime experience on "race prejudice, war hysteria and a failure of political leadership." In addition, the commission scored the Supreme Court for its endorsement of racial discrimination and deference to military authority.

Judge Patel was the first to act upon the *coram nobis* appeals. In June 1983, the Commission on Wartime Relocation published its final recommendations, and on October 4, 1983, the government presented its case to Judge Patel, asking the judge to vacate Korematsu's conviction while conceding that the mass removal and confinement of Japanese Americans was "an unfortunate episode in our nation's history." What the government's lawyers thereby tried to avoid was a court trial about a decision made some 40 years earlier. The judge denied the government's position, and stated she would proceed on the merits of the petition.

During the course of that hearing, attorney Dale Minami argued that Fred Korematsu lived for 40 years carrying the burden of the conviction that had sanctioned the mass removal and confinement of an entire people. Korematsu's interest, Minami contended, was the desire of Japanese Americans as a group for justice, which had been denied them. Korematsu testified how he was handcuffed and arrested as "a criminal." "As long as my record stands in federal court," he warned, "any American citizen can be held in prison or concentration camps without a trial or a hearing." And he concluded, "I would like to see the government admit that they were wrong and do something about it so this will never happen again to any American citizen of any race, creed or color" (Irons, 1989, 26).

Judge Patel concluded the proceedings with her finding that the writ of *coram nobis* was an appropriate vehicle for contesting the wartime decisions, and although she could not reverse the Supreme Court, she declared, its judgment stands as "a constant caution that in times of war or declared military necessity our institutions must be vigilant in protecting constitutional guarantees" (Irons, 1989, 26). Patel then granted the writ of *coram nobis* without issuing a written opinion.

In Portland, Judge Belloni denied Minoru Yasui's petition in January 1984, siding with the government and refusing to render a judgment on an action 40 years after the events took place. Judge Voorhees in Seattle held his hearing on Gordon Hirabayashi's appeal in May 1984. "We can only admire his courage for standing up for his rights," Judge Voorhees stated of Hirabayashi and his petition. "What he really is seeking now is vindication of his honor, and I feel that he has that right" (Irons, 1989, 33).

The judge then proceeded to give Hirabayashi that right by holding a hearing on his appeal in June 1985. A key witness was Edward J. Ennis, then 77 years old, who recalled telling his superior in 1943 that there was a suppression of evidence in the government's case before the Supreme Court. Moreover, said Ennis, Assistant Secretary of War John J. McCloy "deliberately withheld" information from the Justice Department that showed the military's decision for mass removal was based on its inability to separate the loyal from the disloyal. Accordingly, the military opted for mass, rather than individual, removal and detention.

On February 10, 1986, seven months after that court hearing, Judge Voorhees issued his written opinion. Voorhees expressed his admiration for Hirabayashi, and charged that McCloy's deliberate suppression of evidence "seriously prejudiced" the government's case. That act, the judge stated, comprised "an error of the most fundamental character," which required vacating Hirabayashi's conviction of violating the "evacuation" order but let stand his violation of the military curfew. After an appeal of that decision, both of Hirabayashi's convictions were reversed.

The government chose not to pursue those lower court rulings before the Supreme Court so the goal of a Supreme Court reversal was not achieved. But the overall purpose of the *coram nobis* campaign of justice for Japanese Americans as a collective group was achieved with the signing of the Civil Liberties Act of 1988. The *coram nobis* cases were a part of that larger struggle for redress and reparations.

Gary Y. Okihiro

References

Irons, Peter. *Justice at War.* New York: Oxford University Press, 1983.

Irons, Peter. *Justice Delayed: The Record of the Japanese American Internment Cases.* Middletown, CT: Wesleyan University Press, 1989.

YASUI, MINORU (1916–1986)

Minoru Yasui was born in Hood River, Oregon, to issei migrants in 1916. He was the third son in a family of nine children. Like many nisei, Yasui visited Japan as a child and attended Japanese-language school in Oregon. After graduating from high school, he entered the University of Oregon and earned a bachelor's degree in 1937. During his time there, Yasui joined the Army's Reserve Officer Training Corps (ROTC), and when he graduated in 1937 earned a second lieutenant's commission in the army's Infantry Reserve. He continued into the University of Oregon's law school, and in 1939 was the first Japanese American to receive his law degree from that institution.

In 1939, Yasui passed the state's bar examination, but because of racism could not find a job with any established law firm in Portland, Oregon. So Yasui moved to Chicago to work for the Japanese consulate, which needed an American lawyer to advise them and handle their daily legal affairs. The day after Japan's attack on Pearl Harbor and heeding the advice of his father, Yasui quit his job and returned home to Oregon. His intention was to enlist in the military, but each time he tried, the army rejected his offer.

On December 13, 1941, the FBI arrested Yasui as an "enemy alien," despite his U.S. citizenship, and froze his bank account. After his release, Yasui returned to Portland to practice law, mainly to help Japanese Americans who sought his legal advice and offer assistance in their exclusion and evacuation orders. President Franklin Roosevelt's Executive Order 9066 and the military's curfew, which discriminated against all Japanese Americans, seemed an affront to the rights of citizens so Yasui decided to challenge the constitutionality of the curfew. He later wrote in his memoir, "I could scarcely blame anyone for not wanting to challenge the order, and since no one else would do it, I had to" (Yasui, 57). On March 28, 1942, Yasui deliberately violated the curfew by walking around Portland's downtown area and asking a police officer to arrest him. The police instead urged him to return home, so Yasui turned himself in at a police station.

Newspapers reported Yasui's action as "Jap Spy Arrested!!!" It described Yasui as a traitor who betrayed the United States and his Army officer's commission. Radio broadcasts claimed his father had been arrested as an agent of Japan, and that Yasui had cleverly used his U.S. citizenship to secure a law degree so he could become an agent of the Japanese government.

Yasui was indicted, and while on bail he returned home to Hood River, violating restrictions on his movement. The authorities arrested him at his family's home in Hood River, and tried him. On November 16, 1942, federal judge James Alger

Minoru Yasui was an attorney and fighter for civil rights.
(Carl Iwasaki/Time Life Pictures/Getty Images)

Fee found that laws targeting a race as Yasui had contended about the army's curfew infringed upon the constitutional rights of citizens. But he went on to rule that Yasui had forfeited his citizenship by working in the Japanese consulate and thus he was no longer a U.S. citizen. He sentenced Yasui to a year in prison and a $5,000 fine.

Yasui served time in Portland's Multnomah county jail, and Minidoka concentration camp in Idaho. While in prison, Yasui wrote: "Nights were bad, because after the lights would go out in the cells, things would become quieter, and one was left alone with one's thoughts . . ." (Yasui, 59–60). Upon appeal, the U.S. Supreme Court treated *Yasui v. United States* as a companion case to *Hirabayashi,* and on June 21, 1943, the court ruled in favor of the government's position and claim to war powers because of the national emergency. It also, in Yasui's case, reversed Judge Fee's finding that the curfew was unconstitutional and found that Yasui had not forfeited his U.S. citizenship by working at the Japanese consulate. The Supreme Court then returned Yasui's case to Judge Fee who removed the fine and decided Yasui had served enough time for his curfew violation.

In 1944, the War Relocation Authority released Yasui from Minidoka concentration camp to work at an ice plant in Chicago. He later moved to Denver. He passed the bar in Colorado, and practiced law in that state, aiding at first mainly Japanese Americans who had relocated to Denver after their release from the concentration camps. Yasui married, had a family, and served in community relations and worked for the Japanese American Citizens League. Because of his labors, Denver's community leaders established the Minoru Yasui Community Service Award in 1976. During the campaign for redress and reparations in the 1970s and 1980s, Yasui worked tirelessly for that cause.

During the 1980s, like Gordon Hirabayashi and Fred Korematsu, Yasui joined the *coram nobis* movement to secure a rehearing of his wartime conviction. New evidence showed that the government's lawyers had withheld crucial evidence from the U.S. Supreme Court, allowing for a rehearing. Yasui's attorneys filed a petition in Portland, and they urged the judge to conduct a hearing to allow for testimony on government misconduct and to render a judicial ruling. Instead, on January 26, 1984, the judge declined to rule on a case decided some 40 years earlier, and granted the government's motion to vacate the conviction and dismiss the petition. Yasui appealed, intent on securing a decision on the constitutionality of the mass removal and confinement of Japanese Americans, but he died on November 12, 1986, and his case died with him.

Minoru Yasui was buried in his hometown of Hood River, Oregon, next to his parents, brothers, and sister. Yasui's niece, Robin, read his eulogy. "We are remembered after our lives are over, not by the material possessions we accumulate, but the influences we have had on our fellow men. Min left little in material wealth, but his untiring efforts on behalf of all of us, especially the Japanese Americans, will long be remembered. His life has been forever imprinted in the history of the Japanese-Americans . . ." (Yasui, 73).

Gary Y. Okihiro

Reference

Yasui, Robert S. 1987. *The Yasui Family of Hood River, Oregon.* Edited by Holly Yasui. N.p.: Holly Yasui Desktop Publishing.

YELLOW PERIL

The idea that Asia and Asians posed a threat to Europe and Europeans, the "yellow peril" served to unite previously competing European powers on the bases of race, religion, and civilization. Although the term "yellow peril" was probably coined by Germany's Kaiser Wilhelm II in 1895, the notion that Asia and Europe formed irreconcilable oppositions, East and West, is an ancient idea derived from the Greeks and their 5th century B.C. battles against Persia and the Mongol invasions of Europe during the 13th century A.D.

In 1895, Kaiser Wilhelm II commissioned a painting that showed Austria, England, France, Germany, Italy, Russia, and other European nations represented as women all looking at an approaching calamity. Leading the group of women is the archangel Michael who stands pointing to the approaching horror. The vast plain of "civilized" Europe extends before them, and in the distance burning cities in the path of the invaders send smoke billowing to the heavens. From the threatening clouds emerge the figures of the Buddha and a Chinese dragon, representing the powers of darkness. Beneath the painting, the Kaiser inscribed the legend: "Nation of Europe, defend your holiest possession."

Despite national rivalries during the late 19th century at the height of European expansions in Africa and Asia, Kaiser Wilhelm II warned, Asian religion and civilization threatened to overwhelm Europe's "holiest possession," Christianity and European civilization. Put another way, the "yellow peril" or a common enemy served to cohere the divided nations of Europe. Moreover, named the "yellow peril," the danger involved race or the struggle between white or European and yellow or Asian.

Germany's Kaiser Wilhelm II commissioned this painting in 1895, depicting the threat posed by the "Yellow Peril" to European Christianity and civilization. (The Carnegie Library of Pennsylvania State College)

Intellectuals like the British Charles H. Pearson blamed white expansions into the tropical band for invigorating its colored peoples and teaching them to emulate white civilization. Having learned the lessons of science and industry, Pearson predicted in his *National Life and Character* (1893), those black and yellow peoples will rise up against their white masters and conquer them. Their numbers alone, he wrote, which far exceeded whites, were sufficient to overrun the world's minority race. Japan's victory over Russia in 1905, the first defeat of a white nation by a nonwhite nation in modern warfare, seemed to confirm Pearson's rendition of the "yellow peril." The American Lothrop Stoddard, in his *The Rising Tide of Color against White World-Supremacy* (1920) saw colored immigration to the United States as the inundating flood, threatening white purity and survival. Newspapers, novels, comics, and films took up the theme during the first half of the 20th century.

The U.S. federal government joined the "yellow peril" chorus following the 1920 sugar plantation strike on the island of O'ahu in the Territory of Hawai'i. Led by Filipino and Japanese workers, the strikers demanded higher wages for men and women, a nonracial wage scale for white and nonwhite workers alike, an eight-week paid maternity leave for women workers, and improved health-care and recreational facilities. The sugar planters claimed the strike was "an attempt on the part of the Japanese to obtain control of the sugar industry" and "a dark conspiracy to Japanize this American territory." A federal labor commission sent to investigate the strike, in a secret report, concluded, "Hawaii may have its labor problems . . . but *we believe that the question of National Defense and the necessity to curtail the domination of the alien Japanese in every phase of the Hawaiian life is more important than all the other problems combined.*" The commission called that danger "the spectre of alien domination," which could "sweep everything American from the Islands" (Okihiro, 65–81, 95–97).

In addition to Hawai'i's labor situation, the West Coast was endangered by the numbers of Japanese migrants and their reproduction. In a 1921 report, the Bureau of Investigation, forerunner of the FBI, described "Japan's program for world supremacy" as beginning with the "peaceful invasion" of its migrants into California. If immigration was left unchecked, the report cautioned, "the white race, in no long space of time, would be driven from the state, and California eventually become a province of Japan . . ., further, that it would be only a question of time until the entire Pacific coast region would be controlled by the Japanese." Japan's plans involved all of the earth's colored peoples, the report continued. "It is the determined purpose of Japan to amalgamate the entire colored races of the world against the Nordic or white race, with Japan at the head of the coalition, for the purpose of wrestling away the supremacy of the white race and placing such supremacy in the colored peoples under the dominion of Japan" (Okihiro, 113–18).

The military in Hawai'i planned and prepared for the coming war with Japan at least as early as 1921 when the U.S. war secretary approved a plan to intern all enemy aliens. Two years later, Colonel John L. DeWitt, who would become the head of the Western Defense Command and a key figure in the mass removal and detention of Japanese Americans on the West Coast, argued for the establishment of martial law in Hawai'i in the event of war with Japan. Thus, on December 7, 1941, when Japan attacked Pearl Harbor, the military declared martial law and forcibly detained some 1,400 Japanese Americans, both aliens and citizens, in Hawai'i. Fear of the "yellow peril," which had its beginnings in European expansions in Africa and Asia during the late 19th century was influential in the removal and detention of Japanese Americans during World War II.

Gary Y. Okihiro

Reference

Okihiro, Gary Y. *Cane Fires: The Anti-Japanese Movement in Hawaii, 1865–1945.* Philadelphia: Temple University Press, 1991.

YONEDA, KARL G. (1906–1999)

A dedicated Communist, trade unionist, antifascist, and writer, Karl G. Yoneda was born in 1906 to issei parents who migrated from Hiroshima Prefecture. Yoneda first lived in Glendale, California, where his parents worked as farmers. In 1913, he was sent to Japan where he spent 13 formative years, attending high school in Hiroshima. He read avidly, and was drawn to socialism and labor activism.

Only 16 years old, Yoneda traveled to China in search of a blind Russian anarchist, Vasily Eroshenko, whose fairy tales "deeply fascinated me" (Yoneda, 9). He returned to the United States in 1926 after participating in strikes in Osaka, Hiroshima, and Tokyo, and was detained on Angel Island in San Francisco bay.

Yoneda's father, Hideo Yoneda, began as a sugar plantation worker in Hawai'i in 1895. He left for Japan in 1903 to marry, and with his wife, Kazu, returned to the islands. Like many others, he heard opportunities were better on the continent so he and his wife joined the mass, labor migration to the West Coast. In Glendale, Yoneda's parents farmed vegetables on a small plot of land. He had two sisters, Ami and Hozumi, and an older brother who was sickly. He remembered watching his brother walk with a wooden board tied to his back presumably to keep him upright; George was frail since birth, Yoneda's mother told him, and he died in 1910. His father called Yoneda "Goso," meaning having the strength of three to compensate for his brother's weakness.

Yoneda found work as a domestic servant for $5 a day while attending Hollywood Evening High School. At the boardinghouse in which Yoneda stayed, Einosuke Yamaguchi taught him about racism and how capitalists grew rich from the labor of workers. He pointed out that the American Federation of Labor supported Japanese exclusion, and how the Industrial Workers of the World tried to organize African and Japanese American workers but were attacked by government agencies. Yamaguchi told Yoneda about the Trade Union Educational League that was organized by Communists in 1920. The league, he said, paid particular attention to the plight of nonwhite workers. Yamaguchi added that the Communist Party in the United States was founded in 1919 by, among others, Sen Katayama (1859–1933), a world famous Japanese labor leader. The Communist Party, he told Yoneda, fought for migrant and African American workers.

Yoneda attended meetings of the Los Angeles Japanese Workers' Association (JWA), and in 1927 joined the Communist Party under the name, Karl Hama. He chose the name "Karl" after Karl Marx. "Thus my over fifty-year association with the Party began with a feeling of ease among the JWA members and hundreds of whites, Mexicans, and Negroes, men, women, and children who were present at that May Day meeting [1927]." Yoneda also joined the International Labor Defense (ILD), and quickly immersed himself in workers' struggles, fighting deportation of migrant laborers, advocating for the right to political asylum, and organizing against the lynching of African Americans. Japanese American women like Yu Fujikawa, a poet and idealist, Mary Hatsuko Imada, a devoted fighter for workers' rights, and Tomo Kitabayashi joined the ILD, along with many other Asian Americans, Yoneda remembered.

After decades of organizing, beatings, and editorship of the *Rodo Shimbun,* the official organ of the Japanese Workers' Association of America, the FBI took Yoneda into custody following Japan's attack on Pearl Harbor. At the Immigration Detention Station in San Francisco, he found other Japanese American community leaders. Yoneda had been an outspoken opponent of Japan's imperial expansions in China and was well known for his advocacy of democracy over fascism and militarist Japan. Indeed, just over a day later, the FBI released Yoneda after apologizing for the "mistake." On December 10, 1941, Yoneda tried to enlist in the U.S. military but was rejected because the War Department had classified nisei as "enemy aliens," 4C, and thus ineligible for military service.

Like other Japanese American radicals and conservatives, Yoneda advocated cooperating with the government, "if deemed a military necessity that all . . . should be evacuated from military areas," he wrote, "we are ready to go" (Yoneda, 122). Only James Omura, the *Current Life* editor, Yoneda remembered, testified before the Tolan Committee against "evacuation," asking provocatively: "Are we to be condemned merely on the basis of racial origin?" (Yoneda, 121). For Yoneda and his fellow Japanese American Communists, while "evacuation" violated Japanese American civil rights, a Fascist victory would mean the loss of all rights. The war against fascism, hence, took precedence over nisei constitutional liberties.

In March 1942, Yoneda volunteered to help get Manzanar assembly center ready in advance of Japanese Americans destined for the camp. After sleeping on army cots in a crowded barracks, Yoneda woke up the next morning for his first glimpse of the camp. There were no toilets or washrooms, he discovered, and the outdoor faucets were frozen. Building materials were littered throughout, and "we saw GIs manning machine guns in the watchtowers. The barbed wire fence which surrounded the camp was visible against the background of the snow-covered Sierra mountain range. 'So this is the American-style concentration camp,' someone remarked" (Yoneda, 127). The next day, they began to clean the camp to make the place as hospitable as possible.

On April 1, 1942, Yoneda's white wife, Elaine Black, and their son, Tommy, arrived at Manzanar reuniting the family. Black did not have to go, but she insisted on joining her husband at Manzanar. Tommy had to go because he had a drop of "Japanese blood." At first, the family had to share their room with strangers because of crowding, but later they had their own apartment. The Yonedas set to work in the camp, Elaine at the library and camouflage net factory and Karl as block leader. Karl worked for a season harvesting sugar beets in Idaho, and he volunteered for the Military Intelligence Service (MIS) Language School.

Yoneda and the other Manzanar MIS recruits left for Minnesota in December 1942. At Camp Savage, they underwent Japanese-language training, graduating in June 1943, and then went to Camp Shelby, Mississippi, to undergo basic training. "During our short stay in Mississippi," wrote Yoneda, "we had a glimpse of the oppressed lives of Negroes and poor whites to whom we talked. . . . They asked, 'Why are you fighting for Roosevelt's country?'" (Yoneda, 151). In January 1944, Yoneda's unit shipped out to Calcutta, India, and in India they worked with Chinese, Burmese, and other language translators deciphering documents and translating propaganda leaflets for distribution over enemy lines. They gathered and translated captured documents, and interrogated Japanese prisoners of war, including Korean women who were enslaved sex workers for the Japanese Army. After Japan's surrender and the war's end, Yoneda returned to the United States in November 1945.

His days at Manzanar and service in the MIS, Yoneda remembered in his autobiography, were among "the most anguishing and crucial days of my life" (Yoneda,

165). While most praise the patriotism of the nisei soldiers for their service to the U.S. nation, he reminded his readers, few remember the equally brave and heroic deeds of Japanese Americans who fought, as internationalists, for democracy against fascist tyranny.

Gary Y. Okihiro

Reference

Yoneda, Karl G. *Ganbatte: Sixy-Year Struggle of a Kibei Worker.* Los Angeles: UCLA Asian American Studies Center, 1983.

CAMPS, CENTERS,
AND PRISONS

ASSEMBLY CENTERS

President Franklin Roosevelt's Executive Order 9066 signed on February 19, 1942, set off a train of events that led to the mass, forcible eviction of some 120,000 Japanese Americans and their confinement. The order authorized the military to designate areas "from which any or all persons may be excluded," and to provide "transportation, food, shelter, and other accommodations as may be necessary" for those excluded persons.

The exclusion order enabled the military commander to remove Japanese Americans to temporary shelters called "assembly centers," administered by the civilian Wartime Civil Control Administration (WCCA), prior to their "relocation" to permanent concentration camps. There were 18 assembly centers hastily erected in large, open areas to accommodate the masses of displaced people in the spring and summer of 1942. Nine were fairgrounds, two were horse racetracks (Tanforan and Santa Anita), two were migrant laborers' camps (Marysville and Sacramento), one was a livestock exposition hall (Portland), one was a mill site (Pinedale), and one was a former Civilian Conservation Corps (CCC) camp (Mayer). In addition, Manzanar and Poston began as assembly centers, and later became concentration camps.

Although conditions varied one center to another, all of them were places of confinement that held a racially profiled population. Numbered tags worn on the clothing were used to identify people, not their names. Long lines, bureaucratic forms, crowded conditions, and communal baths and toilets reduced their individuality. They were herded onto trucks intended for cattle and settled into former horse stalls still reeking of manure conspired to strip them of their humanity. High fences confined and military police and searchlights patrolled the facilities, and the center's police held and enforced roll calls and curfews and conducted invasive, periodic searches. These were the assembly centers.

Beginning in May 26, 1942, Japanese Americans left the assembly centers for the concentration camps as they were being completed. By the end of October, the assembly centers stood empty, and the War Relocation Authority (WRA) ran concentration camps, filled with Japanese Americans.

Fresno

Located on the Fresno County Fairgrounds, the Fresno Assembly Center opened on May 6 and closed on October 30, 1942. It was the last center to close, and it held a total of 5,344 Japanese Americans. Most of them came from the central San

Joaquin Valley and Amador County. Their flimsy barracks stood on the infield of the fairgrounds' racetrack, aligned into four blocks of 20 barracks each. Once a week, visitors were allowed during a two-hour period, and despite its brevity, the interval was described as a happy time with excitement in the air because of the gifts and letters brought from the outside.

Teiko Tomita remembered the heat in the Fresno Assembly Center. The temperature soared in June, she recalled. There were no shade trees, and the barracks were poorly constructed with tin roofs that magnified the heat. When it got hot, she noted, the tar seeped through the floor and the bed legs would get stuck to the sticky, soft floor.

Marysville

A migrant workers' camp about eight miles south of Marysville, the assembly center opened in April 1942 and confined a total of 2,465 Japanese Americans from Placer and Sacramento counties. By July they were gone, and soldiers occupied the center, which consisted of about 100 barracks, five mess halls, and two infirmary buildings.

Mayer

The Mayer Assembly Center was located about 75 miles northwest of Phoenix, Arizona. The center was a former CCC camp, and held only 245 people, making it the smallest assembly center, and the shortest occupied, from May 7 to June 2, 1942. Most of Mayer's Japanese Americans were from southern Arizona.

Merced

Situated within the San Joaquin Valley town of Merced, the assembly center was built upon the site of the county fairgrounds. Open from May 6 to September 15, 1942, the center confined a total of 4,669 Japanese Americans mostly from northern California. A nisei mother who had exhibited flowers at the fairgrounds now found herself confined in a place that once also penned animals.

Kiyo Hirano described her first impressions of the Merced center. "Lined up properly and grouped separately in the open space were countless barracks that looked like they were covered with tar paper. Standing in that long line, I looked at the many barracks and wondered, 'Is one of these going to be our home?'" After being marched to the infirmary for physical examinations, guards went through her bags, purse, and even pockets to search for and confiscate knives and other forbidden objects. Hirano was then assigned a room, which had a high ceiling and open space allowing conversation to cross from one room to another affording little privacy. She was fortunate, Hirano wrote, because she was not in a horse stall, which still reeked of manure. Those, she said, "suffered from the unsanitary conditions and terrible odor" (Hirano, 7, 9).

Meals were regimented and served at seven for breakfast, noon for lunch, and six for supper. "With the signal of the bell all from each block went in lines and ate at the tables." Those who really suffered, Hirano observed, were the elderly and the infirm. "During this time," she recalled, "the weak, the elderly, and the sick died one after the other. The flag flying half-mast in front of the office meant that once again someone had passed away that day." At the same time, while the hospital was full, the diseased, pregnant, and sick were fortunate because there were so many Japanese American physicians in the center (Hirano, 8).

In Merced, a young couple met, got engaged, and married. "To fall in love and move into marriage within three months of internment was impressive speed," Hirano commented. Rumors spread in the center about moving to a concentration camp somewhere in Colorado, she wrote. The target date was August, and packing would be easy because they had such few possessions. She began feeling optimistic and looked forward to the two-day train ride. "But," Hirano wondered, "what was a hot Colorado desert without even a simple tree going to be like?" (Hirano, 9).

In Merced Assembly Center, Wataru Ishisaka observed, "People acted just like dumb sheep, because life was so disrupted and confused. They lost their human dignity and respect" (Sarasohn, 202).

Pinedale

Located near Fresno, California, Pinedale Assembly Center was on vacant land near a mill-workers housing area. When it opened on May 7, 1942, Pinedale held a total of 4,823 Japanese Americans mostly from Sacramento and El Dorado counties. The assembly center closed on July 23, 1942.

Japanese Americans called Pinedale "hell's acre" because of the incredible heat, which soared to 120 degrees in the shade. "It was a terribly hot place to live," remembered Hatsumi Nishimoto. "It was so hot that when we put our hands on the bedstead, the paint would come off! To relieve the pressure of the heat, some people soaked sheets in water and hung them overhead." Others threw water on the concrete floor and lay there as the water evaporated. Besides the heat and tight and uncomfortable sleeping quarters, Tei Endow reported there was no privacy in the barracks, which had flimsy or no walls and in the toilets, which stood in a long row without partitions. And the meals, recalled Miyoshi Noyori, often consisted of strange and unappetizing foods and combinations that left one hungry after eating. "Frequently our meal was a plateful of white beans, four or five fresh spinach leaves, a piece of bread, and sometimes a couple of wienies," she reported. "That was all we were served, so we had to eat it" (Tamura, 175, 176).

Some of Pinedale's Japanese Americans were from Oregon. From the train's window, they caught glimpses of their place of confinement. "I remember seeing a large cactus when our train stopped at a field near Pinedale, so I guessed that we had arrived at a hot place," said Itsu Akiyama. "We were completely fenced in, and there were watchtowers with soldiers bearing rifles." Misuyo Nakamura added, "I saw a soldier with a rifle who was stationed on one of those high towers outside the fence. I was very frightened! I was sure he had designs on shooting us!" (Tamura, 173–74). Center officials told the Japanese Americans never to use the word "camp" to refer to Pinedale because the facility was an "assembly center" and not a "concentration camp." But the barbed-wire fence, guard towers, and armed soldiers showed Pinedale to be a concentration camp. And most Japanese Americans like Itsu Akiyama and Misuyo Nakamura viewed it as a camp and not as an assembly center.

Pomona

Los Angeles County Fairgrounds was the site for the Pomona Assembly Center, which confined Japanese Americans from May 7 to August 24, 1942. The center held a total of 5,514 persons who were mainly from San Francisco and Los Angeles.

Shizu Hayakawa left San Francisco by train to go to the Pomona Assembly Center. The journey took two days because the train had to wait every time another train passed, and the train's windows were covered so she could not see where they were going. At Pomona, she remembered, everyone complained about the food, which was so poorly cooked and prepared.

Portland

Located on the site of the Pacific International Livestock Exposition Pavilion, the Portland Assembly Center held a total of 4,290 Japanese Americans from Oregon and Washington State between May 2 and September 10, 1942.

"What really surprised me was to enter the Portland center which, you know, was a former stockyard," Masaji Kusachi recalled. "My family of ten was assigned a small room that had no doors—just curtains hung over the doorway." Without ceilings, he continued, you could hear everything your neighbor was saying, and "the odor was so bad!" The stable floor, Kusachi explained, was simply covered over by boards, and the smell rose through the cracks. After all, he said, horses had just left the place. In addition to the stench, there were lots of flies attracted by the manure. A health inspection would certainly condemn the place for human habitation, Kusachi concluded (Tamura, 177).

Puyallup

Located about 35 miles south of Seattle, Washington, Puyallup Assembly Center was built on the Western Washington State Fairgrounds to hold a total of 7,628 Japanese Americans from Washington State and Alaska between April 28 and September 12, 1942. Besides the usual grandstand, stables, racetrack, and other buildings common to fairgrounds, Puyallup had a rollercoaster, which made it distinctive as an assembly center. Also, fences sliced the center into four separate units to keep the Japanese Americans divided and hence more easily controlled.

A contemporary observer described the barracks, because of their uniform, flimsy appearances, as rabbit hutches. Some Japanese Americans were housed in converted pigpens, and a Japanese American upon first seeing the barracks from the bus window thought the Puyallup center was a chicken farm. Ted Nakashima, an architectural draftsman, called the center a "concentration camp, U.S. style."

While at the Puyallup Assembly Center, Yoshito Fujii observed, "Everybody gave up and accepted the situation as a wartime misery" (Sarasohn, 180).

Sacramento
The Sacramento Assembly Center, also known as Walerga, was built at a migrant workers' camp some 15 miles northeast of Sacramento, California, to hold a total of 4,770 Japanese Americans from May 6 to June 26, 1942. Most of them came from Sacramento and San Joaquin counties.

Salinas
Located on the fairgrounds at the north end of Salinas, California, the Salinas Assembly Center confined a total of 3,608 Japanese Americans from April 27 to July 4, 1942. Most came from the Monterey Bay area. After Japanese Americans left for the WRA concentration camps, the Salinas Assembly Center was used to train an army unit of Filipino soldiers to fight against the Japanese.

Santa Anita
Located on the grounds of a famous horse racetrack, Santa Anita was the largest and longest occupied assembly center, holding a total of 19,348 Japanese Americans from March 27 to October 27, 1942. Most came from Los Angeles, San Diego, and Santa Clara counties. Horse stalls were converted into housing units, the grandstand became living quarters for bachelors, and new barracks were built. The horses left three days before the Japanese Americans arrived.

"Have you ever slept in a stable?" Ernest Fukuda asked. "Many of us did at Santa Anita, and believe me, they need more than clean straw." Japanese Americans named the rows Bridle Path for the racetrack and Seabiscuit Avenue after the famed horse, Seabiscuit, whose stall, barrack 28, units 24 and 25, became an apartment of honor for its Japanese American occupants (Girdner and Loftis, 151).

Half-an-hour visits by those outside the center were allowed once a week. When notified that friends were at the center's front gate, Japanese Americans walked from their barracks to a gate, across a half-mile clearing to a second fence, then past another clearing to the fence where their friends awaited on the other side. "You stick a foot over the line, and you get a bawling out from the M.P. [military police]," a nisei college girl wrote. "One man got a bottle of beer from one of his friends, and the M.P. came along and took it from him and emptied the bottle at his feet . . ." (Girdner and Loftis, 156).

On May 30, 1942, the army directed the WCCA to recruit 800 to 900 Japanese Americans at Santa Anita to begin camouflage net production within a week. Recruitment began in earnest, and rumors of a WCCA blacklist of those who refused to work created resentment and fear. The WCCA urged the nisei, especially women, to work on the nets as their patriotic duty and warned them this would be their only opportunity to work and earn wages. In addition, individuals received notices to appear at the employment office and with that, the WCCA forced them

A line of armed soldiers greet Japanese Americans at the Santa Anita Assembly Center, April 5, 1942. (National Archives)

to make a decision. Some refused to work because confinement violated their civil liberties, others claimed they opposed war and would not contribute to war making, and a few cited hay fever and the dust associated with net manufacturing. Still, sufficient workers showed up, and before long Santa Anita was producing 250 to 260 large camouflage nets each day.

Japanese Americans worked a 44-hour week, and many took pride in their work. But after lunch in mid-June, a laborer stopped working. The foreman demanded he return to work, but the Japanese American insisted he was hungry and had to get a bite to eat. Soon, others stopped working, and in all some 800 workers walked off the job. The spontaneous strike shut down Santa Anita's entire net production. Later that afternoon and during the following day, representatives met with the administrators to settle their differences. The workers complained about the center's food, about the dust and fumes that irritated the eyes and lungs, about the long hours they spent at work on hard cement floors that wore on the feet, and the hot weather and stifling conditions of work. With concessions from the center's administrators, the Japanese Americans returned to work within days of the initial strike.

But after a June 18 meeting, the WCCA arrested six men and later five more for having attended that gathering, which was held to discuss general center conditions and ways to improve them. Clearly, the administrators did not want the camouflage net strike to spread among the center's Japanese Americans and to challenge some of the center's rules like speaking in Japanese during meetings and not having a policeman present at any gatherings. The men were first confined to a jail cell, then released by the California attorney general, and seized again by the military police. Two of them, Ernest and Toki Wakayama, were released when the southern California branch of the American Civil Liberties Union (ACLU) secured a writ of habeas corpus for the couple. The ACLU's plan was to use the Wakayama case to test their imprisonment without a hearing or trial, contending discrimination based solely upon their race or ancestry. The ACLU later dropped the Wakayama for other cases, which challenged more directly the constitutionality of the concentration camps.

The Santa Anita strike is notable for being the first mass act of resistance by Japanese Americans while under confinement during the war. It also foreshadowed a larger act of rebellion over military abuses.

On August 4, 1942, Santa Anita's security police instituted a center-wide search for contraband. "Overzealous" and "overbearing" officers, in the words of the Army commander, entered Japanese American quarters and seized anything they chose, including preparation for baby formulas and special food for the sick. The search angered the center's Japanese Americans, and by the afternoon crowds gathered and a suspected inu or informer was beaten. The army called in 200 troops to quell the rebellion, and martial law lasted for three days.

Masses of people filled the streets before the soldiers arrived. Mrs. Takaichi spotted some officers who had searched the barracks overwhelmed by the numbers of Japanese Americans who cornered them. "And their eyes were green," she said. "They were absolutely terrified, because they suddenly realized, they could have one little gun, you know, but there was nothing to keep the tremendous horde of people from tearing them limb from limb." But the army arrived to save them. Their trucks with mounted machine guns sped into the center, and the soldiers piled out wearing helmets and holding rifles with bayonets. Between them and the masses stood an old, Japanese American woman, Mrs. Takaichi recalled, who stared down the troops and walked slowly with her cane keeping the soldiers at bay. The sight broke the tension, and the people dispersed laughing.

In the aftermath of the uprising, the army apprehended young men and a few women without notice or apparent reason, and sent them to destinations unknown. A nisei wrote to her former schoolteacher about the military crackdown. "People have had to put up with so much here, most of which was unnecessary: the ban on Japanese literature; Japanese records; and the denial of free speech, assembly, press, freedom of religion . . . the search, and many other things. I feel that the sooner everyone is relocated the better it will be for everyone concerned. If things continue like this, I fear that there will be something that will make August 4 look silly" (Girdner and Loftis, 193–94).

Stockton

Located on the San Joaquin County Fairgrounds, the Stockton Assembly Center confined a total of 4,390 Japanese Americans from May 10 to October 17, 1942. Most of them came from San Joaquin County.

Tanforan

The Tanforan Racetrack in San Bruno, California, about 12 miles south of San Francisco was the site of the Tanforan Assembly Center. The center opened on April 28 and closed on October 13, 1942, and it held a total of 8,033 Japanese Americans from the San Francisco Bay area.

"As the bus pulled up to the grandstand," Yoshiko Uchida wrote of her first impression of the Tanforan Assembly Center, "I could see hundreds of Japanese Americans jammed along the fence that line the track. These people had arrived a few days earlier and were now watching for the arrival of friends or had come to while away the empty hours that had suddenly been thrust upon them." Uchida and her family got out of the bus, and were directed under the horse track's grandstand to stand in line and fill out forms. Their bags were searched, they had a brief physical examination, and they walked over muddy ground before reaching their quarters, which was a horse stall. Called an apartment, Uchida wrote, the "euphemism was so ludicrous it was comical" (Uchida, 69, 70).

Osuke Takizawa reported of his horse stall: "It was terrible. The government moved the horses out and put us in. The stable stunk awfully. I felt miserable, but I couldn't do anything. It was like a prison, guards were on duty all the time, and there was barbed wire all around us. We really worried about our future. I just gave up." His wife, Sadea Takizawa, added of that first night in Tanforan, "Though I was tired, I couldn't sleep because of the bad smell. It was hell" (Sarasohn, 183).

Ten by twenty feet, the stall was empty except for three folded Army cots lying on the floor, Yoshiko Uchida noted. "Dust, dirt, and wood shavings covered the linoleum that had been laid over manure-covered boards, the smell of horses hung in the air, and the whitened corpses of many insects still clung to the hastily white-washed walls." Two small windows high over the entrance were the only source of sunlight. There was nothing they could do but sweep the room, and stuff their mattresses with straw. Scrounging through the assembly center for scraps and other necessities became a valuable skill, Uchida wrote (Uchida, 70).

At dinnertime, Uchida and her family stood in line for their meal. "When we arrived," she recalled, "there were six long weaving lines of people waiting to get into the mess hall. We took our place at the end of one of them, each of us clutching a plate and silverware borrowed from friends who had already received their baggage. Shivering in the cold, we pressed close together trying to shield Mama from the wind. As we stood in what seemed a breadline for the destitute, I felt degraded, humiliated, and overwhelmed with a longing for home. And I saw the unutterable sadness on my mother's face" (Uchida, 70–71).

The lack of privacy in the latrines and showers was "an embarrassing hardship," and many tried to partition off each toilet and shower with newspapers and sheets. In addition, everything was in short supply, including hot water, which appeared sporadically, and toilet paper, which people stole and hoarded. It was "everyone for himself or herself," Uchida wrote. Survival required that. Women had to wake up at three or four in the morning to wash their dirty laundry, and still there were long lines. As a consequence, Uchida observed, most learned to rush to everything. "They ran to the mess halls to be the first in line, they dashed inside for the best tables and then rushed through their meals to get to the washtubs before the suds ran out" to wash their plates and utensils (Uchida, 77).

Every weekend, Uchida wrote, the grandstand visiting room was crowded with friends from the outside. They brought especially food, which those in the assembly center missed. Visitors were laden with cookies, cakes, candy, potato chips, peanut butter, and fruit, she reported, and those gifts "gladdened our hearts" and supplemented "our meager camp diet. Some friends came faithfully every week, standing in line from one to three hours for a pass to come inside the gates." These were mainly white neighbors and friends who undertook this great act of courage, in the face of anti-Japanese hatred, and charity. (Uchida, 84).

Japanese Americans organized churches in Tanforan, established a library of over 5,000 books with the help of outside donations, and set up education and recreation programs. Hundreds of players joined softball teams, and hobby shows and Saturday night dances attracted many participants. People sat on the floor to watch movies. "Hundreds were willing to put up with the discomfort in order to be entertained for an hour or two," Uchida reported. Japanese Americans built trays, chests, ashtrays, and bookends, and cultivated flowers and miniature trees, which they exhibited at hobby shows. They got so popular, Uchida noted, that a separate exhibit for garden and flower enthusiasts had to be organized to accommodate the crowds (Uchida, 87).

In June 1942, Uchida explained, the center's administrators instituted a twice-daily roll call, once before breakfast and the other at 6:30 in the evening. "It seemed an unnecessary irritation to add to our lives," she commented, "unless it was designed to impress on us the fact that we were under surveillance, for there was little opportunity or inclination for anyone to escape." Also that month, the FBI launched center-wide searches for contraband, turning some stalls inside out and making people feel violated and insecure. Rumors began circulating of an impending move to a concentration camp. Three months of communal living, wrote Uchida of Tanforan, wore on the nerves. "There was no place to cry and no place to hide. It was impossible to escape from the constant noise and human presence. I felt stifled and suffocated and sometimes wanted to scream" (Uchida, 93, 96).

Tulare

Located on county fairgrounds in the town of Tulare, California, the assembly center held a total of 5,061 Japanese Americans from April 20 to September 4, 1942. Most of those came from Los Angeles and Sacramento counties. The center had over 150 barracks, eight mess halls, and eight communal buildings for toilets, showers, and laundries. The military police occupied the northern end of the fairgrounds.

Her daughter, Hatsuye Egami remembered, told her once she entered Tulare Assembly Center she would never come out. The war would have to end first, she declared. The barracks, Egami reported, were built of rough boards with small windows and a concrete floor. Eight people occupied each room. The toilets and showers, she noted, relegated them to a state of nakedness. "Polished civilized taste and fine sensitivity seem to have become worthless here." The mess hall held 160 persons while 500 waited their turn in line. The food was simple, though adequate. The issei, she reflected, in the United States for 40 or 50 years pursuing their gigantic dreams tilled the soil that was "a mother to them, and their life was regulated by the sun. They were people who had worked with all they had, until on their foreheads, wave-like furrows were harrowed. Every time I see these oldsters with resigned, peaceful expressions, meekly eating what is offered them, I feel my eyes become warm" (Gorfinkel, 27, 30–31).

On May 18, 1942, Egami played the piano at the funeral of Michiko Toguri, the first death in Tulare. She was a stranger, Egami wrote, but they were together in the assembly center, having boarded the "same ship of destiny . . . to live, to die." That fate bound them together. So she played the piano for Toguri, whose coffin bore "a pitifully small amount of flowers" because they were not found in the center. Words of condolence were uttered, touching Egami's heart, and others offered sympathy and prayers. It was, she confessed, "truly an unforgettable funeral," despite the rough setting and meager flowers (Gorfinkel, 37, 38).

Turlock

Located at the Stanislaus County Fairgrounds in Turlock, California, the Turlock Assembly Center held a total of 3,699 Japanese Americans mainly from the Sacramento River delta area and Los Angeles. The assembly center opened on April 30 and closed on August 12, 1942. Later that year, the assembly center became a prison and rehabilitation center for military convicts.

Gary Y. Okihiro

References

Girdner, Audrie and Anne Loftis. *The Great Betrayal: The Evacuation of the Japanese-Americans during World War II.* New York: Macmillan, 1969.

Gorfinkel, Claire (Ed.). *The Evacuation Diary of Hatsuye Egami.* Pasadena, CA: Intentional Productions, 1995.

Hirano, Kiyo. *Enemy Alien.* San Francisco: JAM Publications, 1983.

Sarasohn, Eileen Sunada (Ed.). *The Issei: Portrait of a Pioneer: An Oral History.* Palo Alto, CA: Pacific Books, 1983.

Tamura, Linda. *The Hood River Issei: An Oral History of Japanese Settlers in Oregon's Hood River Valley.* Urbana: University of Illinois Press, 1993.

Uchida, Yoshiko. *Desert Exile: The Uprooting of a Japanese-American Family.* Seattle: University of Washington Press, 1982.

DEPARTMENT OF JUSTICE CAMPS

Most Japanese Americans were held in War Relocation Authority (WRA) concentration camps, but several thousand were confined in Department of Justice (DOJ) camps run by the department's Immigration and Naturalization Service (INS). On the continent the day after Pearl Harbor, the Federal Bureau of Investigation (FBI) apprehended 1,212 Japanese and 559 German and Italian "enemy aliens" who fell under the jurisdiction of the DOJ. Both the FBI and INS were at the time within the DOJ. By March 1942, the INS held over 4,000 "enemy aliens" in its internment camps mainly in Fort Missoula, Montana and Fort Lincoln, North Dakota. In addition, the U.S. government pressured Mexico, Panama, Costa Rica, Nicaragua, Bolivia, Colombia, Ecuador, and Peru to hand over 2,264 of their Japanese to the United States. Germans and Italians were also among those expelled. Those also fell under the authority of the DOJ and were placed in its INS camps. The United States intended to use the Japanese as hostages in exchange for its prisoners of war held by Japan in the Pacific conflict.

The "enemy aliens" or those residing in the United States were first held in temporary detention centers scattered throughout the country, from Ellis Island in New York harbor to Angel Island in San Francisco Bay. Others included detention centers in San Pedro, Sharp Park, and Tuna Canyon, California and detention centers in Seattle, Cincinnati, and Boston. In all the DOJ maintained nine permanent internment camps and 18 temporary detention centers. In addition to the Japanese, German, and Italian "enemy aliens" were confined and interrogated about their sympathies for or ties to Nazi and Fascist organizations. At the Ellis Island immigration station, for instance, there were 279 Japanese, 248 Germans, and 81 Italians under custody in December 1941. The U.S. Army used a portion of the abandoned immigrant detention center on Angel Island together with other internment camps to confine and interrogate its Japanese and German prisoners of war.

There were eight DOJ camps for Japanese Americans, three in Texas (Crystal City, Kenedy, and Seagoville), two in New Mexico (Fort Stanton and Santa Fe), and one each in Idaho (Kooskia), Montana (Fort Missoula), and North Dakota (Fort Lincoln). Generally, the DOJ separated men from women, except for the internment camps in Crystal City and Seagoville, Texas, which held families and single women. The DOJ deployed its INS Border Patrol guards to patrol its internment camps.

As early as September 1939, the FBI drew up lists of suspicious or "disloyal" aliens to be taken into custody in the event of war, classifying them into A, B, or C based upon the supposed degree of danger they posed. On June 28, 1940, Congress passed the Alien Registration or Smith Act, which required every alien over 14 years old to register and have their fingerprints taken by the government. By the end of that year, the DOJ maintained the registrations of nearly five million resident aliens. The government's authority over enemy aliens allowed it to arrest and confine them without due process or charges and a jury trial. Instead, Alien Enemy Hearing Boards, consisting of three civilian members, determined the fate of those arrested by the FBI. They were presumed to be guilty unless proven innocent. Those were the bases for the World War II "enemy aliens" program.

Besides German and Italian "enemy aliens" or those living in the United States, the government held nonresident German and Italian nationals even before the United States declared war on Germany and Italy. During World War II in Europe but before the United States entered the war, German and Italian seamen caught in U.S. waters or stranded in U.S. ports fell into the DOJ alien registration and detention program. In 1939, the United States held the German crew of a ship abandoned off the coast of Cuba as "distressed seamen paroled from the German Embassy." Those unfortunate civilians were sent, after FBI investigations and alien board hearings, to DOJ camps like Fort Lincoln and Fort Stanton.

Several shiploads of "enemy aliens" made the transit from Latin America to the United States. The first, the *Etolin*, reveals the process. Sailing from Callao, Peru, on April 5, 1942, with 173 Germans, 141 Japanese, and 11 Italians, all men, the *Etolin* made its way up the Pacific coast. Following instructions from the United States, Peru had made no charges against them, gave them no hearings, confiscated their passports, and issued them no visas. In Ecuador, the *Etolin* picked up 38 Germans and 10 Japanese, in Colombia, 149 Germans, and 3 Italians. When the ship landed in San Francisco, the INS informed the men that they were entering the United States illegally because they had no passports or visas. Of course, the U.S. government had schemed to set that trap. They were thus placed within INS custody, and taken by train to the DOJ internment camps in Texas. Later shipments included families, men, women, and children.

Over 80 percent of the Japanese from Mexico, Panama, and Latin America were from Peru. The United States interned approximately 1,800 Japanese Peruvians, all of them in Texas at Crystal City, Kenedy, and Seagoville. Japanese had been living in Peru since 1899 when the first boatload of labor recruits arrived in Callao. As migrant laborers, they contributed to the country's agricultural development, but after World War II Peru refused to accept them back. In the United States, they were "illegal immigrants" who could not be released from DOJ custody. After the war, between November 1945 and June 1946, nearly 100 returned to Peru because they were married to Peruvians or had Peruvian citizenship, while 750 were shipped to Japan. As the fate of the rest was being determined, the Peruvians remained in Crystal City until August 1946 when they were given jobs at Seabrook Farms in New Jersey. Many other Japanese Americans had gone before them from the WRA camps to Seabrook Farms, which was a transition center, like a halfway house, from complete confinement to freedom.

Key to that release as "restricted parolees" into "relaxed internment" was San Francisco civil rights attorney Wayne M. Collins who fought for the reinstatement of the renunciants to U.S. citizenship. During a visit to Crystal City to consult with some of his clients, Collins was told about the situation of the Peruvian Japanese. On June 25, 1946, Collins filed in San Francisco a writ of habeas corpus on behalf of the 364 Japanese Peruvians. The federal circuit court accepted his petition, and thereby allowed the 364 to remain in the United States provided they had employment guarantees, which the Seabrook Farms, partially enclosed with a high, chain-link fence, supplied. German prisoners of war supplied the labor for Seabrook's frozen food plant, and by September 1946, Seabrook employed about 3,000 workers, most of them Japanese and African Americans.

Crystal City

Originally a Farm Security Administration migrant labor camp for 2,000 people, the DOJ expanded the Crystal City camp to hold 3,500 and placed a fence and guard towers to secure the 290-acre grounds. Before the first Japanese Americans arrived in March 1943, Crystal City held 35 German and one Italian aliens and their families temporarily until the facilities intended for them were built. For a time, the Germans overlapped with the Japanese, and the camp was divided into two sections for those two groups. At its peak, there were approximately 4,000 women, men, and children in Crystal City, two-thirds of that total were Japanese Americans with about 660 from Peru and 600 from Hawai'i.

Peruvian businessman Seiichi Higashide left behind his wife and five children to board the U.S.S. Cuba in March 1944 for Panama. Other Japanese Peruvians and many Germans and several Italian families were also among the ship's passengers. The men were kept below deck separated from their families. After passing through the Panama Canal and stops in Panama and Cuba, the Cuba docked in New Orleans. The INS greeted the men, had them shower, and baptized them with DDT powder, an insecticide but also cancer-producing. So much DDT was sprinkled over the men that "brushing out our white powdered hair and putting on clothes, we looked as though we had climbed out of a flour bin." The INS then put nametags on each, and put them on a train. On board, the men rejoined their families (Higashide, 157).

Single men, including Higashide, were deposited in Kenedy, which was small but had the same features as the other internment camps with barbed wire and barracks. Other single men, Higashide noted, were sent to Santa Fe, and families to Crystal City. In June 1944, after a few months in Kenedy, Higashide rejoined his family in Crystal City, which, he observed, was much larger than Kenedy. In Crystal City, Japanese, Germans, and Italians from Central and South America lived together but in their own sections with Japanese from Hawai'i and single, Japanese Americans from the WRA concentration camps. A hospital, post office, schools, churches, and stores served the confined people, and there were a baseball field, volleyball and tennis courts, and a swimming pool. Although a town, wrote Higashide, Crystal City, with its barbed wire fence, still made its people feel like "birds in a cage" because they had to make "incalculable material and spiritual sacrifices before being forced into it [the camp] against their will" (Higashide, 166, 168).

As the war ended and the WRA concentration camps and DOJ camps began to close, Crystal City became a major site for those transfers from other camps. From Santa Fe and other camps came Japanese Peruvians, people without a country, to await their final disposition. In March 1946 when Tule Lake concentration camp closed, the approximately 400 renunciants from that camp were sent to Crystal City. In late 1947, with the final departure of the Japanese Peruvians, the camp closed. A monument erected in 1985 and dedicated to "the sons, daughters, and friends of the families who were interned in this camp" refers to the DOJ camp at Crystal City as a World War II concentration camp.

Fort Lincoln

Often called Bismarck after the town five miles south, Fort Lincoln was built by the U.S. Army in the early 20th century, and during the 1930s served as the headquarters of North Dakota's Civilian Conservation Corps (CCC). During World War II, buildings were added and a fence erected to imprison mainly German seamen who were stranded in U.S. waters and ports, starting in 1939 when the war in Europe began. Japanese Americans arrived in 1942, but they were transferred, leaving the camp to German internees until February 1945 when 650 Japanese Americans were sent to Fort Lincoln. These were the so-called troublemakers from Tule Lake and Santa Fe and renunciants who asked for repatriation to Japan after the war's end.

Iwato Itow was one of those classed as a troublemaker at Tule Lake. After spending about 10 months in Poston concentration camp where, he said, he was "a nervous guy" wasting his life away, Itow received a permit to work in Cleveland at a factory making parts of military equipment. But after about five months, the WRA recalled him, and sent him to Tule Lake concentration camp. There he joined a Japanese group that performed morning exercises to keep in shape but which the WRA considered to be nationalistic and "pro-Japan." As a member of that group, Itow recalled, he got up "early in the morning and made those noises, exercise you know. So they got tired of that and sent us to Bismarck, North Dakota. Guess I was identified as pro-Japan and a militant" (Tateishi, 144).

At Fort Lincoln, according to Itow, "nobody made any trouble there, and everybody was quiet. It was all fenced in and we could move around, but our letters were censored. Some of my friends wrote me a letter; it was all cut out." When the sun came out in the spring, men sunbathed because there was nothing to do. They merely shuttled between their barracks and the mess hall. Interrogators tried to determine if he entertained Japanese loyalties, and the government eventually sent Itow, a U.S. citizen, to Japan. He later returned to his native land, but remains "bitter" because of how the United States treated Japanese Americans during the war and the lost opportunities. "I am still bitter about that, and I don't think I'll ever forget . . ." (Tateishi, 145).

Fort Missoula

Located adjacent to the town of Missoula, Montana, Fort Missoula was built in 1877 for U.S. Army troops in their conquest of the Flathead Indians. During World War I, the fort was a military training ground, and in the 1930s the Civilian Conservation Corps (CCC) took over the camp. The DOJ took control of the property in 1941, and converted it into an internment camp for Italian nationals, mostly seamen, and Italian and Japanese resident aliens. The Italians arrived first in the spring of 1941, and the Japanese, in December. By April 1942, there were approximately equal numbers of Italian and Japanese men among the total of 2,003 in Fort Missoula.

The internment camp consisted of 30 army-style wooden barracks, each accommodating up to 38 men. Cots lined the barracks walls, and the men received two woolen blankets, a comforter, a pillow, and sheets. The camp also had a mess hall, kitchen, assembly hall, storehouse, and canteen. Surrounding the camp was a barbed wire fence, floodlights for surveillance, and a guardhouse at the front gate. A fence separated the Italians from the Japanese. Outside the camp was a hospital with a pharmacy and dental office that served the Italians and Japanese.

Fort Missoula served principally as a holding pen for Japanese Americans. There, the men were given cursory hearings after which most were transferred to other internment camps or to the WRA concentration camps. Several died soon after their arrival, a few "volunteered" to work on local farms, and by the end of 1942 there were only 29 Japanese left in the camp while the numbers of Italians rose to over 1,200. In March 1944, 258 Japanese from Hawai'i entered Fort Missoula before being transferred to Santa Fe, New Mexico. In July 1944, the camp was officially closed.

Although they were not prisoners of war, the Japanese were interned enemy aliens who fell under the protections of the Geneva Convention of 1929, which guaranteed food, hygiene, health, and religious freedom while in captivity. They could be forced to maintain the camp without pay but other work must be voluntary and for a salary. In early 1942, the 633 Japanese complained the United States violated the Geneva terms by exacting compulsory labor and the guards subjecting them to verbal and physical abuse. Their spokesman, Taoka, alleged the Japanese were required to clean the stables of the Border Patrol's four horses and maintaining areas outside their living quarters, immigration officials kicked and beat several Japanese and withheld food to extract confessions, and being subjected to insulting treatment from Korean Japanese-language translators. Taoka was also threatened with solitary confinement if he continued to intervene on behalf of the

Japanese. After a DOJ investigation, two Border Patrol officers were fired and their superior was reassigned.

Alien enemy hearing boards, comprised of civilians, were set up to determine the fate of the Japanese. Most hearings required translators, including Korean and Japanese Americans and white missionaries, and they were usually superficial and arbitrary. Guilt by association was the practice, such as speaking Japanese, working for a Japanese firm, and membership in a Japanese American organization. In 1942, some 673 were "paroled" to assembly centers and concentration camps. The others were given over to the army custody. In April 1942, 346 left Fort Missoula by train for internment at Fort Sill, Oklahoma, and in August, another 172 were sent to Camp Livingston, Louisiana.

A few Japanese chose to remain in INS-run Fort Missoula. A pharmacist, No-buichi Tsutsumoto, who feared transfer to an army camp, led that group. He petitioned Fort Missoula's supervisor to allow the remaining Japanese, totaling 28, to stay if they supplied garden crops for the Italian kitchen. They would feed themselves and the Italians, and Tsutsumoto offered to undertake any work for the camp. The supervisor agreed, and the Japanese compound remained open until the camp's closing.

Iwao Matsushita arrived at Fort Missoula in December 1941. Despite a famous Montana blizzard and temperatures that dipped to 52 degrees below freezing, he wrote to his wife that he was comfortable thanks, in part, to the heavy underwear and ski clothes that she had packed for him in his suitcase. The food was excellent and plentiful, he reported, and, he gleefully noted, it included rice. At the same time, his typical weekly menu reveals an odd mixture of foods, such as on Monday, creamed potato and jam for breakfast, sandwich, lettuce, rice, and applesauce for lunch, and pork and beans, radish, salad, and raisins for dinner. By contrast and not mess hall fare, his friend shared sushi and sashimi with him one day, which Matsushita called his "taste of freedom" (Fiset, 115, 128).

To occupy his days, Matsushita wrote poetry, read the *Readers Digest* and *New York Times*, and like many others, gathered stones to polish and fashion into pendants. In the summer of 1942, the Japanese played against the Italians in a softball game that was "real fun" with the Japanese winning easily, 27 to 7, over an Italian team that "did not know the rules & made many errors." But as the onset of winter approached and nearly a year apart, Matsushita grew anxious. "Your letters are overdue," he scolded his wife. "Nor have I heard that you got my stones, so I'm a bit worried that you might have caught a cold. . . . The snow has started to fall in earnest. . . . I've learned to appreciate my past freedom" (Fiset, 158, 206).

On the anniversary of their separation, Matsushita informed his wife that the U.S. government had classified him, after his hearing, "potentially dangerous to the public safety." He was, accordingly, sentenced to internment for the war's duration. "You'll probably be terribly disappointed having waited a lonely year with hopeful expectations, but please don't cry," he urged. "Keep your chin up." He planned to appeal the ruling, Matsushita told his wife. "The point is we need to be together as soon as possible." It was not until January 1944, however, that

Matsushita was able to rejoin his wife, not in freedom, but in the Minidoka concentration camp where she was being held (Fiset, 213, 215).

Fort Stanton

A former army outpost in the U.S. war against the Apache nation and later, a tuberculosis sanatorium, Fort Stanton was in an isolated part of New Mexico 35 miles north of the town of Ruidoso. Before the United States entered World War II, the government used Fort Stanton's abandoned CCC camp to detain German seamen. But after nine unsuccessful escape attempts the DOJ converted Fort Stanton into an internment camp with barbed-wire fences and INS border patrol agents. After the war, the state used Fort Stanton as a minimum-security prison for women.

The camp's first internees were German seamen who had abandoned their ship off Cuba's coast in 1939, and were placed in the deserted CCC camp at Fort Stanton. When the DOJ converted Fort Stanton into an internment camp, it interned seaman from the German merchant ship, *S.S. Columbus,* which the men had scuttled off New Jersey in December 1939. Those seamen were interned at Ellis Island and then, across the continent on Angel Island, and in January 1941, 410 of them entered the camp at Fort Stanton. Later, the WRA established at Fort Stanton a Japanese Segregation Camp #1 for so-called troublemakers from WRA concentration camps, and by October 1945, Fort Stanton's segregation camp, like the WRA run isolation centers at Moab and Leupp, held 58 Japanese Americans.

Kenedy

Formerly a Civilian Conservation Corps (CCC) camp, Kenedy internment camp was the result of a lobbying effort by the adjacent Texas town of Kenedy. A high fence and watchtowers surrounded the camp, and Japanese worked in its 32-acre vegetable farm while Germans ran a slaughterhouse. The first contingent of 464 Germans, 156 Japanese, and 14 Italians from Central and South America arrived in April 1942. By 1943, there were about 2,000 internees, including over 700 Japanese. After the Japanese were transferred into other camps like Santa Fe, Kenedy became a camp for German prisoners of war in September 1944, and after July 1945, several hundred Japanese prisoners of war.

In Camp Kenedy, Seiichi Higashide wrote, "we were given food and clothing, and all of our basic, survival needs were met. We had more than enough free time and, indeed, passed much of our time aimlessly. All we could do was gather in small groups to engage in foolish conversation, gamble, or participate in sports to keep us from boredom." Despite the government's name for the camp, relocation center, Higashide declared, "we simply perceived it as no more than a 'concentration camp'" (Higashide, 158).

The camp's director instituted two roll calls daily, one at 9 A.M. and the other, at 4:30 P.M. when the siren sounded. Men were required to assemble, stand in line, and answer when their names were called. There were three, sometimes four bed checks each night, and mounted patrols augmented the guards at night. Touching the perimeter barbed-wire fence activated an electric alarm, and there was just one escape attempt recorded during Kenedy's first 18 months. A devastating hurricane in August 1942 destroyed buildings, downed electric power lines, broke gas mains, and weakened many structures. The Germans, led by a ship captain, refused to help in the cleanup, knowing the terms of the Geneva Convention.

The Japanese were less informed and organized than the Germans who were young, understood English better, and were organized as seamen. Taiichi Onishi, a merchant from Lima, Peru, attempted suicide four times. He clearly needed help, which the INS felt incapable of providing. The War Department, despite experience handling mental illness among soldiers, refused to accept Onishi, so finally, the state of Texas admitted Onishi into one of its mental institutions. About the same time, Yukihiko Kobashigawa died of pulmonary tuberculosis.

Kooskia

Located in north-central Idaho, Kooskia was a remote highway construction camp 40 miles east of the town of Kooskia. Between May 1943 and May 1945, the Kooskia internment camp held 256 Japanese Americans, their interpreter, and 27 white civilian employees. At least 28 of the internees were from Peru and two from Mexico and two, from Panama. Most of the all-male Japanese Americans served as highway construction workers.

The INS recruited men from its camps like Fort Missoula and Kenedy where "volunteers" offered to work at Kooskia. In need of construction workers, the Public Roads Administration used Japanese internees to help build the Lewis and Clark Highway beginning in 1943. Men like Arturo Shinei Yakabi and his friend, Seiho Inamine, left Fort Missoula to work on drilling and blasting rock to clear the route for the highway. They, like the Chinese who helped build the transcontinental railroad in the 19th century, clambered over rocks and ridges held by ropes to drill holes for dynamite. For that arduous and hazardous labor, they were paid $55 per month. After four and a half months of that work, Yakabi, Inamine, and others from Fort Missoula were recalled for their transfer to Kenedy.

A second contingent, recruited from Kenedy and comprised of 17 from Peru, included men who were barbers, chauffeurs, cooks, restaurant workers, merchants, and mechanics. Others followed them, some serving several terms in Kooskia. Many of the men were transients between camps. Peruvian Samatsu Uema, for instance, spent his 33 months in confinement at Kenedy, Fort Missoula, Kooskia, and Santa Fe.

Santa Fe

The DOJ acquired the Santa Fe camp from the New Mexico State Penitentiary that once included a CCC camp. At an elevation of 7,000 feet, the camp experienced mild temperatures in the summer but cold extremes and snow during winters. The DOJ expanded the camp, and by March 1942, Santa Fe internment camp had a capacity of 1,400. The first internees were 826 Japanese Americans, all men from California. The DOJ saw Santa Fe as a temporary place where five

Alien Enemy Hearing Boards considered the cases of the Japanese Americans. One of them died in Santa Fe, 523 were assigned to WRA concentration camps, and 302 were turned over to U.S. Army custody. The last Japanese American left Santa Fe in September 1942, and the camp was deactivated. After February 1943, the camp was expanded, and by June 1945 there were 2,100 Japanese American men in Santa Fe. Many were renunciants from Tule Lake and leaders of the camp's so-called pro-Japan faction, according to the WRA.

Santa Fe included the standard barracks, barbed-wire fence, and guard towers and searchlights at intervals. Mess halls, kitchens, a bakery, canteen, laundry room, recreation hall, library, and medical facilities dotted the camp. There were also gardens, a 19-acre farm, and a poultry farm. In December 1943, some 350 men threatened to petition Japan to forcibly separate families of U.S. prisoners of war if they were not reunited with their families in other DOJ and WRA camps. On November 10, 1945, there was only one unsuccessful escape attempt. Oto-matsu Kimura scaled the perimeter fence, and when guards ordered him to get down, Kimura reportedly dared the guards to shoot him. He climbed the light pole to the top of the watchtower, and jumped to the road below, possibly fracturing his pelvis and vertebrae. Kimura was hospitalized.

The Tule Lake alleged troublemakers arrived in Santa Fe during and after the period of martial law at Tule Lake. Between December 1944 and March 1945, the army and WRA identified and removed the men they considered to be pro-Japan to Fort Lincoln and Santa Fe. When the Santa Fe administrators attempted to expel a few of the leaders of the Tule Lake transfers to the isolation center at Fort Stanton on March 12, 1945, a crowd of about 250 gathered and demanded that they too be removed to Fort Stanton's Segregation Camp #1. The administration called upon the INS border guards, and then directed the Japanese Americans to disperse, which they refused. The guards fired tear gas into the crowd, and charged wielding clubs as the rioters threw stones at them. In about 10 minutes, the melee was over, and four Japanese Americans were hospitalized with injuries and 360 were confined to a stockade inside the Santa Fe camp.

The camp's population fell and rose with transfers during 1945 and 1946. Santa Fe's administrators removed over 17 alleged leaders to Fort Stanton, and in June 1945 a group of 399 arrived from Tule Lake. In November 1945, after Japan's surrender, 894 Japanese Americans left Santa Fe for Seattle and 330 more, in December. Those were destined for Japan. In March 1946, some 200 men from Fort Lincoln arrived, and in April, 135 were sent to Crystal City and 89, to Terminal Island, California for "repatriation" to Japan. By May 1946, only a dozen Japanese Americans remained in Santa Fe, and the camp closed shortly thereafter.

Seagoville

Located about 20 miles southeast of Dallas, Texas, the Seagoville camp was originally a DOJ prison for women. In 1942, the Bureau of Prisons transferred the prison to the INS, which converted it into an internment camp. In May 1942, Seagoville held 319 "enemy aliens," mostly from Latin America, including 119

Japanese and the rest, Germans and Italians. For a while, the Bureau of Prisons maintained a presence in Seagoville where 15 women prisoners were held for several months along with the "enemy aliens." The internment camp closed in June 1945, and after the war, Seagoville became a low-security prison for men.

Gary Y. Okihiro

References

Fiset, Louis. *Imprisoned Apart: The World War II Correspondence of an Issei Couple* Seattle: University of Washington Press, 1997.

Higashide, Seiichi. *Adios to Tears: The Memoirs of a Japanese-Peruvian Internee in U.S. Concentration Camps.* Seattle: University of Washington Press, 2000.

Tateishi, John. *And Justice for All: An Oral History of the Japanese American Detention Camps.* New York: Random house, 1984.

FEDERAL BUREAU OF PRISONS

During the course of the forcible eviction and detention of Japanese Americans during World War II, Japanese Americans as individuals and groups, including draft resisters, disobeyed laws they deemed to be in violation of their civil liberties. The U.S. government prosecuted those violators, notably individuals whose cases reached the U.S. Supreme Court. Those rulings became legal pillars of presidential powers during national emergencies. Already in the U.S. Army, a group of nisei soldiers refused combat training while their families were being confined in concentration camps. Those who were convicted were sentenced to terms in federal prisons. In 1947, President Harry Truman pardoned all of the war's draft resisters.

Catalina Federal Honor Camp

Located in the Santa Catalina Mountains northeast of Tucson, Arizona, the Catalina Federal Honor Camp was originally established in 1939 to house convicts who worked on a nearby highway. Like the concentration camp, the honor camp had barracks, a mess hall, a laundry, shops and classrooms, an area for the administrators, and a vegetable, chicken, and turkey farm. The honor camp, however, had no barbed-wire fence or guard towers, and instead had painted rocks marking the camp's borders. During World War II, the honor camp held draft resisters and conscientious objectors (those who violated the draft law because they refused to participate in all wars), including for a time Gordon Hirabayashi who was a Quaker and a conscientious objector.

Gordon Hirabayashi deliberately violated the military curfew because he wanted to test the legality of the government's forced removal and confinement of Japanese Americans. The U.S. Supreme Court ruled in May 1943 that the military had the right during wartime to impose restrictions like curfews on Japanese Americans. After his arrest, Hirabayashi was held in Washington State's King County jail for several months, and after the Supreme Court decision against him, three months at the Catalina Federal Honor Camp.

Japanese American draft resisters from Granada and other concentration camps spent time at the honor camp. The United States at the start of World War II classified Japanese Americans as ineligible for military service, but in need of men for the war, changed that classification making the nisei eligible to the draft. Many Japanese Americans volunteered and others were drafted, but more than 300 refused to serve in the U.S. military on the grounds that their civil liberties had been violated and those rights had to be restored before serving their country. Heart Mountain concentration camp was the center of that draft resistance movement but young men at other camps also joined in with mixed outcomes.

A judge dismissed the case against 26 draft resisters from Tule Lake concentration camp because, he stated, it was "shocking to the conscience" that U.S. citizens were confined allegedly because of "disloyalty" and then compelled to serve in the military. Another judge fined the some 100 draft resisters at Poston a penny because confinement in a concentration camp was sufficient punishment. But the judge who ruled on the cases of the draft resisters at Heart Mountain sentenced 63 of them to three years imprisonment and he questioned their loyalty. In addition, the judge sentenced the seven leaders of the Heart Mountain resistance movement to prison terms in Leavenworth Federal Prison. Later, 22 more from Heart Mountain were tried and convicted of violating the draft law. About 45 Japanese American draft resisters, mostly from Granada concentration camp, served their sentences in Catalina Federal Honor Camp.

During the war, then, the honor camp held convict laborers, Japanese American resisters, and other draft resisters and conscientious objectors. They broke rocks with sledgehammers, cleared bushes and trees, drilled holes for dynamite, and worked at the farms to produce food. After the highway was completed in 1951, the honor camp became a facility for juvenile offenders, and later, a youth rehabilitation center. As a part of the Coronado National Forest, the former honor camp was named the Gordon Hirabayashi Recreation Site in honor of the wartime Japanese American resister.

Leavenworth Federal Penitentiary

Located about 15 miles northwest of Kansas City, Kansas, Leavenworth was built in 1897 by U.S. Army prisoners who were the first to be incarcerated there in 1903. The prison was completed in the 1920s, and it held military and civilian convicts in separate quarters.

The seven Japanese American draft resistance leaders from Heart Mountain served time in Leavenworth, together with 28 nisei soldiers from Fort McClellan, Alabama, who in March 1944 refused to undergo combat training while their families were being held in concentration camps. After a court martial, the 28 were sentenced to 5 to 30 years in prison.

McNeil Island Federal Penitentiary

Located on McNeil Island in Puget Sound about 10 miles southwest of Tacoma, Washington, McNeil Island Federal Penitentiary was built in the 1920s and 1930s. Like the Catalina Honor Camp, McNeil Island was a work prison where inmates canned fish, cleared land, and farmed.

Heart Mountain draft resisters as well as Gordon Hirabayashi spent time at McNeil Island. More numerous than the Japanese Americans, however, were the war's conscientious objectors such as members of the Jehovah's Witness church.

Gary Y. Okihiro

U.S. ARMY INTERNMENT CAMPS

The U.S. Army maintained at least seven internment camps for Japanese Americans during World War II on the continent, including those listed below and possibly, Fort Florence, Arizona and Fort Meade, Maryland. In addition, the army maintained one internment camp in Alaska, and at least nine in Hawai'i. Lordsburg was the only camp built especially for Japanese Americans. Most were on military bases.

Alaska
Fort Richardson

Japanese Americans, including biracial American Indians, were held by the U.S. Army in Fort Richardson, about nine miles north of Anchorage, Alaska, before being removed to Puyallup Assembly Center in Washington State.

Continent
Camp Forrest

Camp Forrest, Tennessee, was a large military facility used during World War II as a training ground for the U.S. Army. A fenced off portion with guard towers and dogs served as an internment camp for Hawai'i's Japanese Americans transferred from Camp McCoy. Although located at about 2,000 feet above sea level, during the summer months, Camp Forrest was hot, and the men shed their Wisconsin winter clothes for Tennessee weather.

Camp Livingston

Camp Livingston, Louisiana, held over 800 Japanese Americans, including 400 from the West Coast, 354 from Hawai'i, and 184 from Panama and Costa Rica. Those from Hawai'i came by way of internment facilities at the immigration station in Honolulu, Sand Island, internment camp, Angel Island in San Francisco bay, Camp McCoy, Wisconsin, Fort Sill, Oklahoma, and finally, Camp Livingston in June 1942. The summer heat was staggering, and the earth was sandy. Some men dug holes in the sand to cool their bodies.

Camp McCoy

A former Civilian Conservation Corps (CCC) camp, the Camp McCoy internment camp was located nine miles west of Tomah, Wisconsin. In February 1942, 170 Japanese Americans from Sand Island internment camp on O'ahu were sent to a corner of Camp McCoy for confinement behind barbed wire. At another corner of the camp, Japanese American soldiers also from Hawai'i trained to fight in the U.S. Army in defense of freedom. Also at Camp McCoy were German and Italian "enemy aliens." From Camp McCoy, Hawai'i's Japanese American internees were sent to Camp Forrest.

Fort Sam Houston

Fort Sam Houston internment camp in Texas served as an assembly center for reassignment to Lordsburg and Fort Sill. Several groups of Japanese Americans from Hawai'i were sent there along with transfers from Fort Missoula and about 300 indigenous peoples from Alaska.

Fort Sill

Located near Lawton, Oklahoma, Fort Sill held approximately 350 Japanese Americans, including those from the West Coast and Hawai'i, previously confined in Fort Missoula. Japanese from Nicaragua, Panama, Bolivia, and Peru joined the U.S. Japanese in Fort Sill. After the Japanese Americans left Fort Sill, the camp probably confined German prisoners of war.

On May 12, 1942, Kanesaburo Oshima, a barber from the island of Hawai'i, climbed the outer barbed-wire fence in broad daylight reportedly shouting, "I want to go home!" A guard barked out a warning, while another shot Oshima dead in front of his friends who had urged they be allowed to help him get down from the fence and return to the camp. Oshima was depressed, his friends revealed. He had been forced to leave his wife and 12 children who had little means of support. Since his internment, Oshima constantly worried over their well-being, he confided to his priest and friend. Now he was dead. Hozui Nakayama, his priest, presided over Oshima's funeral, which was attended by all of Fort Sill's Japanese Americans. Also present were Army guards with machine guns pointed at the mourners because of they feared an uprising. Oshima was buried in Oklahoma, but years later his oldest son claimed his remains to bring them home for reburial in Kona, Hawai'i.

Lordsburg

The army began camp construction in February 1942 just east of the town of Lordsburg, New Mexico. At an elevation of over 4,000 feet, Lordsburg was hot in the summer and freezing during winter. The limestone ground supported only sparse vegetation, and the wind whipped up punishing sandstorms. By July there were 613 Japanese Americans in the Lordsburg camp, transfers from Fort Lincoln, North Dakota, from Alaska, including biracial American Indians, and some 250 from Hawai'i, arriving between June and October 1942. Most, though, were from the West Coast. In all, some 1,500 Japanese Americans passed through Lordsburg between July 1942 and July 1943 when all of them were gone and approximately 4,000 Italians replaced them. In February 1946, the internment camp closed.

On July 27, 1942, an army sentry shot and killed two internees, Toshiro Obata and Hirota Isomura, on their way to Lordsburg. The guard who shot them testified the men were trying to escape. Both men had a high fever, were too ill to walk from the station to the camp, and were waiting for a ride when they were shot. Two Japanese American physicians asked for an autopsy, which was denied and the army only investigated the case over two months later. Isomura was 57 years old and was a fisherman, and Obata was active in Buddhist church activities. Their deaths cast a pall over the camp.

When Japanese Americans complained about hard labor, which, they said, the Geneva Conventions disallowed, the camp authorities cut off the newspapers, turned off the lights earlier at nights, banned listening to the radio, and reduced canteen privileges. The men petitioned the Spanish embassy in New Orleans (Spain represented citizens of Japan in the United States during the war), and when the ambassador and a U.S. state department official arrived in Lordsburg to investigate the men's claims, the camp director told them the work was entirely voluntary. The men asked the investigators who would voluntarily work in 110 degree heat especially elderly men who were priests and office workers and not used to outdoor, manual labor. They were forced to perform inhumane labor, the Japanese Americans testified. When the investigators left, the army dispensed more punishment on the men.

A third incident reinforced the men's contention that the army mistreated and abused them. About 30 Japanese American men followed a tractor shoveling dirt and removing stones for a road outside the camp when the tractor broke down. The driver stopped to get replacement parts, and asked the men to return to camp to await his return. When a sentry saw the workers returning to camp early, he assumed they had gone on strike and raised the alarm. A few hours later, a military police captain confronted the men and accused them of striking. He then fired a shot at the feet of the work gang's leader, scolding him and the men. When it was clear the men were innocent of the charge, the army explained that the captain's actions were justified and refused to apologize.

Stringtown

A state prison near Strington, Oklahoma, the internment camp during World War II held mainly Japanese American "enemy aliens" but also German naval prisoners of war. It later became a state hospital for patients with venereal disease, and then a medium security prison.

Hawai'i
Ha'iku

On the island of Maui, Haiku Camp served as an internment site for Japanese Americans such as Toraji Yano, a plantation worker and store employee. Japanese song books in his possession and his brother-in-law's photograph in a Japanese naval officer's uniform condemned him. At Haiku, Yano met leaders of Maui's Japanese American community, including Shodo Kawamura, Shoten Matsubayashi, Shigeru Terada, and Tetsuji Hanzawa. Many were transferred to camps on O'ahu but Yano remained in Haiku for several months. There were 51 Japanese Americans interned on Maui in January 1942, 56 the next month, and only nine in September 1942, four in August 1943, and one in December 1943. Most were transferred to camps on O'ahu or released.

Honouliuli

Located amidst sugarcane fields at Honouliuli gulch, near Waipahu on the island of O'ahu, Honouliuli internment camp opened on March 1, 1943, replacing the camp at Sand Island as the principal site for internment in the army-ruled territory. A Swedish vice-consul visited Honouliuli shortly after it opened and found some 250 Japanese Americans housed in frame cottages each with eight to 10 occupants sleeping on double-deck beds. The camp had a medical dispensary and hospital, dental clinic, canteen, and kitchen. On his second visit in May 1943, the vice-consul found that electricity had been installed, and the internees had planted trees and gardens. He counted 84 issei and 154 nisei in the camp.

That periodic visitor failed to capture the true feelings of the internees by describing Honouliuli's physical plant. Dan Nishikawa recalled with anger his forcible internment, and credited his interest in crafts for preventing him from going mad. He told how during the first three months white internees received fresh fruits and vegetables and even pumpkin pie for Thanksgiving, while Japanese Americans ate only canned foods like pork and beans and chili con carne. Only after they protested did the Japanese Americans receive fresh fruits, vegetables, and eggs. U.S. pilots, Nishikawa testified, flew low over the camp, and practiced bombing runs, buzzing the internees' shacks. When he complained, Nishikawa was told that in the event of another attack by Japan, U.S. planes would bomb the Honouliuli camp first.

Sam Nishimura compared Sand Island with Honouliuli, and preferred the latter camp because he enjoyed the family type internment with nine men sharing his cabin. Several of Nishimura's housemates worked in the kitchen, he explained, and they returned at night with pastries and coffee for snacks before lights out at 9 o'clock. Still, Nishimura noted, daily life was regimented around roll calls in the morning and evening, and surprise inspections kept them on edge. Confinement was stressful, Nishimura agreed, and some broke down and "lost their minds." He described a Japanese American who rolled a rock in his hand constantly smoothing out its rough edges until the four-inch-square rock became a perfect baseball. When asked what he intended to do with the rock, he replied he was saving it for his sweetheart. The man, Nishimura said, was "just going at it everyday. Nothing else. Nobody talked to him" (Okihiro, 249).

Honouliuli was built to hold up to 3,000 internees, and barbed-wire fences divided the camp to separate men from women and Japanese from Germans and Italians. In addition, Japanese and Korean prisoners of war captured in the Pacific were confined in "hell valley" or jigoku dani, a name given to the place by the Japanese American internees. The valley trapped the sun's heat, and the camp boiled with humidity. From 1943 to 1945, approximately 2,700 Korean prisoners of war, nearly all civilian laborers and a few soldiers were interned in Hawai'i. Imperial Japan conscripted Korean men to serve in its military, and forced Korean workers to build its military bases throughout the Pacific. Japan also forced Korean women to serve their men as prostitutes. After the war ended, the Korean prisoners of war returned to Korea in December 1945.

The number of Japanese Americans held in Honouliuli internment camp reached a peak of 324 in January 1944, but by September 1945, there were only 25 Japanese Americans. The lifting of martial law in Hawai'i on October 24, 1944, made the internment of U.S. citizens difficult. The army, thus, removed many to concentration and internment camps on the continent where President Franklin Roosevelt's Executive Order 9066 remained in force. The end of martial law, however, did not terminate the military's control over Hawai'i. On October 18, 1944, before the lifting of martial law, President Franklin Roosevelt signed Executive Order 9489, which authorized the Pacific Ocean commander to declare Hawai'i a military area, regulate travel, maintain press censorship, and exclude and intern "enemy aliens" and all those considered security risks. In that way, the military maintained control over Hawai'i until the war's end.

Kalāheo

The Kalāheo Stockade on the island of Kaua'i was used as an internment camp for Japanese Americans. Paul Shizuo Muraoka was a U.S. citizen who lived in Japan from 1932 to 1934 and worked at the Japanese Consulate in Honolulu for six months. The Federal Bureau of Investigation (FBI) picked him up, and held him in solitary confinement for a month in the gymnasium shower room on Lihue sugar plantation. He was later transferred to the Kalāheo Stockade where he joined others like Shinobu Taketa, a plumber, Mr. Senda, a photographer, Hisashi Fujimoto, and Kazuto Yokota. After a year in the stockade, Muraoka and his wife and Taketa and his wife were sent to Jerome concentration camp in Arkansas.

Kīlauea

On the island of Hawai'i, Kīlauea Military Camp served as an internment site for that island's Japanese Americans. Myoshu Sasai, a Buddhist priest, was taken by a Hilo police officer and two soldiers from his wife and young child on December 8, 1941. Sasai knew the police officer, and was his marriage counselor. "They would have an argument, the husband and wife," explained Sasai, "and I would call them over and have a meal with them and make them shake hands." Pearl Harbor changed that, and Sasai now sat in a "sampan bus" that made about a dozen stops picking up internees before depositing them at Kīlauea Military Camp.

A large hall lined with beds and lockers greeted the men. Throughout the night, a constant stream of buses emptied their load, and by morning, there were more than a hundred internees. To get to the mess hall, internees had to walk between two lines of soldiers with bayonets. As he walked that gauntlet, Sasai recalled, he was shocked by the starkness of the camp. Inside, however, food was plentiful and nutritious. "They really fed us well," reported Sasai, "but outside, around the mess hall, soldiers surrounding us." Even when going to the toilet, soldiers accompanied the internees. When an internee tried to escape by climbing the fence, Hishashi Fukuhara remembered, the soldiers shot the man. "They killed him; they shot him dead," testified Fukuhara (Okihiro, 219–20).

In February 1942, at the Hilo post office, a hearing board of soldiers, attorneys, and a local "haole big shot" interrogated the internees as family members strained to catch a glimpse of the proceedings. "While at the hearings, friends and family would crowd the corridors to peer through the windows to get a view," Sasai wrote. Sasai's greatest enjoyment was to see his wife and child during the two or three times he appeared before the panel. Two FBI agents informed Sasai that he was destined for internment on the continent. Family members were allowed to enter the Military Camp to bid their final farewells but, recalled Sasai with great sadness, "we really didn't have too much to say besides take care of yourselves and stay well. The talks were long, but that's what it boiled down to."

The men were loaded onto Army trucks and driven to Hilo harbor where they boarded the *Waialeale*. Japanese American internees were confined to the upper deck, bound for Sand Island internment camp, and below them were their sons, nisei volunteers for the U.S. Army. Sasai reflected upon that sad irony. "Boys born in Hawaii, young boys from Hawaii are going. Even though their citizenship may be different, they are on their way. We are going someplace too. I thought we were all being forced to go." Japanese Americans, in disregard of their citizenship, were "being forced to go," Sasai understood. "Normally the ocean is pleasant," he observed, "but in wartime, the ocean is scary. You don't know what is in it" (Okihiro, 220).

There were 85 Japanese American internees on the island of Hawai'i in January 1942, 110 in February 1942, six in September 1942, and two in June 1944. Most were transferred to O'ahu and later, the continent, and others, released.

Sand Island

The army, under martial law, evicted the Public Health Service from Sand Island to convert its facilities into an internment camp. The station's medical director received word of that intention on December 7, 1941, as the smoke still billowed over Pearl Harbor. The following day, the army began work on the island and camp. Situated in Honolulu harbor, Sand Island served as an immigration quarantine station, which had houses, kitchens, and administrative buildings that could readily serve as an internment camp. The island could also be easily guarded to prevent escape attempts.

The army divided the camp into sections, a compound for up to 250 Japanese men and another, for white men, 25 Germans and Italians, and a third compound for 40 women, including Japanese and whites. Each unit had its own kitchen and mess hall and recreational facilities. For the first six months, the camp's internees slept in tents while the barracks were being built. Yasutaro Soga described Sand Island's beginning. After a strip search, the Japanese Americans were led outside in the rain and ordered to erect 20 tents. Because most of the men were elderly and not used to physical labor, they found the task exhausting and frustrating because they had to work in the rain and gathering darkness. "We were soaking wet from rain and perspiration," Soga remembered, and the men completed the job around nine o'clock at night. They then slept in those tents with their wet clothes (Okihiro, 215).

In addition to the trying physical conditions, the army instituted practices to tax the mind. Roll calls each morning and evening regimented the day, and searches, including strip searches, were common and reduced privacy and a sense of self-control. A former internee exclaimed, "They stripped us down and even checked the anus. We were completely naked. Not even undershorts. They even checked our assholes." Once the guards lined up a group of men against a wall and threatened to shoot them. "With that threat," another internee remarked, "there was no need to say anything more" (Okihiro, 217).

Men and women worried over the fate of their families, and, Soga wrote, "we grew desolated more and more," and "we were insecure and impatient." A Japanese American attempted suicide by slicing his wrist with a razor, and a priest insisted he was pregnant. Many suffered depression, and some became insane. The army heightened that sense of insecurity by conducting surprise raids and searches of the internees' tents, holding frequent interrogations, and picking random individuals for confinement in an isolation cell with only water and hard crackers. Kokubo Takara from the island of Kaua'i died on Sand Island, perhaps from conditions in the camp and from the lack of proper medical care (Okihiro, 216).

At least 18 Japanese women and ten German and Italian women were held in the women's compound on Sand Island. The wife of the camp's commander, Carl Eifler, oversaw the women. The Japanese American women arrived at Sand Island, like the men, through jails, military camps, and Honolulu's immigration station. They were community leaders, again, like the men, including Japanese-language school teachers, Buddhist and Shinto nuns, and a few, like Umeno Harada, because of their connection with their husbands. Harada's husband, Yoshio, helped a downed Japanese pilot involved in the Pearl Harbor attack on the island of Ni'ihau, and both were killed while trying to elude capture. Umeno Harada, newly widowed and a mother of three young children, was interned as an accomplice.

On February 17, 1942, two days before President Franklin Roosevelt's Executive Order 9066 that authorized the mass removal of Japanese Americans on the West Coast, the army selected 172 Japanese Americans from the Sand Island internment camp for shipment to internment camps on the continent. These, the army said, were the "troublemakers." On the morning of February 20, military trucks, escorted by jeeps mounted with machine guns, sped the men out through the back gate of the immigration station past family members who had come to catch a last glimpse of their men. Once on board the *Ulysses Grant,* the men were confined below deck until the ship arrived a week later at Angel Island in San Francisco bay.

One of those men, Suikei Furuya, recorded his continental odyssey. From Angel Island, which once detained Chinese and Japanese migrants, Furuya was sent to Camp McCoy, Wisconsin and then Camp Forrest, Tennessee. He wrote of conflicts among mentally strained men who shared a single barracks, of the joy of receiving letters from home, and of baseball games and an evening lecture series, the most popular activities at Camp McCoy. The huts at Camp Forrest, Furuya recalled, "were makeshift and cracks were seen all over the place," and when it rained, the roof leaked and the floors were "always flooded." The bedding was dirty, and the authorities refused to provide clean sheets and covers. "I couldn't stand the smell of them," Furuya wrote. Meals at Camp Forrest, however, were good, and in the evening the men basked in the glow of fireflies. "I felt so relaxed that I forgot the hard conditions that I was placed [in]." Just as the men began to settle in, they were moved to Camp Livingston in Louisiana.

Camp Livingston, Furuya reported, was divided by wire fences to separate Japanese from Hawai'i, Panama, and the West Coast. With many highly educated men, he wrote, the internees organized classes on Japanese culture and a curriculum for an internee college. On one occasion, the men refused to carry pine logs for a military airport being built outside the camp. The labor in aid of the U.S. military was in violation of the Geneva Convention. The army retaliated with a general lockdown, and provocatively stationed sentries with machine guns pointed at the men inside the internment camp. Thus threatened, the men relented, and carried the logs for the military.

After 11 months in Louisiana, Furuya was sent to the Department of Justice (DOJ) internment camp, Fort Missoula in Montana where he joined Peruvian Japanese, Germans, and Italians. The excitement of greater freedoms in being allowed to play baseball and golf, go fishing, see movies, and take photographs in camp was surpassed by the fervor generated among the men with the entrance of forty women internees. Christmas 1943 was memorable, reported Furuya, because of the gifts—books, green tea, shoyu, miso, medicines—sent by the Japanese Red Cross. "We were so grateful for their kindness," he recalled, "that we didn't know how to express [it] in words."

On April 3, 1944, Furuya left Montana for Santa Fe, another DOJ camp, where he joined some 800 internees from Hawai'i. "The four years of camp life," reflected Furuya, "were not after all in vain. We learned a lot. . . . We learned to appreciate our wives. . . . We found that those who were respected in our communities turned out to be completely opposite of what we expected them to be, whereas others whom we thought idles but we found beautiful personalities among them." Still, Furuya longed for freedom beyond the barbed-wire fence. "I must have been mentally exhausted from constantly living together with a mass of people," he wrote. "I had a strong desire to be alone in a quiet atmosphere . . ." (Okihiro, 260–62).

Meanwhile, back in Hawai'i, on March 1, 1943, the army closed the Sand Island internment camp, and transferred the internees to Honouliuli internment camp. Sand Island held 190 Japanese Americans in January 1942, 292 in February 1942, and 319 in September 1942.

Waiākea

Waiākea Prison Camp on the island of Hawai'i held Japanese Americans together with civil offenders such as rapists and burglars. "The Waiakea Prison Camp is the most convenient and practicable institution for confinement at hard labor on Hawaii," the army commander of Hawai'i district boasted. "The county jail is a rest house [by comparison]." The camp's internees, he reported, were employed working on the Hilo airport "where hard labor means just that." According to the camp's prison report, a sentence of one month at hard labor was given for using profane and obscene language, three months of hard labor for being a "disorderly person," six months for being a "common nuisance," and one year for possession of excessive amount of currency and unlawful possession of a Japanese flag.

Wailua

The Wailua military prison on the island of Kaua'i served as a temporary internment camp for Japanese Americans apprehended on that island. Kaetsu Furuya, a Japanese-language-school principal, was confined there together with his friend, Kokubo Takara. On the evening of December 7, 1941, Furuya was taken to the Wailua facility, which had iron bars and an iron slab for a bed. There were no toilets, only a one-gallon can that had to be called for, and the place was infested with mosquitoes. "We all got swollen faces from mosquito bites," remembered Furuya. Breakfast consisted of coffee and a cracker so hard that "it wouldn't break even if you bit it" (Okihiro, 218).

Jukichi Inouye, another Japanese-language-school principal on Kaua'i, was taken on December 8, 1941, and placed in the Waimea jail, which he described as cramped, the toilet was a bucket, and "there was no place to hide." After three days, and he and nine others were placed without an explanation in a dump truck and driven away. "We were wondering where they were going to execute us. Some thought the graveyard that we were nearing was going to be the place. But then we went by it without stopping." Instead, the men were taken to Wailua military prison where they joined Furuya and the others. There were 70 to 80 priests, language-school teachers, and community leaders, Inouye estimated.

Inouye described interrogations before an examination board, like the alien hearing boards on the U.S. continent, consisting of a military officer and three managers from Lihue sugar plantation. In February 1942, 27 internees from the Wailua military prison, Furuya and Inouye included, were transferred to the Honolulu immigration station and then, Sand Island. Haruko Inouye witnessed the men's departure from the port of Nawiliwili, Kaua'i. The men were in a truck, and the guards kept "the internees on one side and the families on the other side." That separation, she said, was like the neighbors and friends who shunned them fearing they would be picked up by the military. "They thought anything could happen to them, so they tried to avoid me" (Okihiro, 219).

Interned on Kaua'i were 41 Japanese Americans in January 1942, 53 in February 1942, nine in September 1942, one in August 1943, and two in June 1944.

Others

The army maintained internment camps for Japanese Americans on the islands of Moloka'i and Lana'i. There were four confined on Moloka'i in January and February 1942, and on Lana'i, two in January 1942, and three in February 1942. These internees were released or transferred to other camps.

Gary Y. Okihiro

Reference

Okihiro, Gary Y. *Cane Fires: The Anti-Japanese Movement in Hawaii, 1865–1945*. Philadelphia: Temple University Press, 1991.

WAR RELOCATION AUTHORITY CAMPS

The War Relocation Authority administered 10 concentration camps located in isolated parts of the country, away from large cities, industries and railroad lines, and military installations. As "security risks," Japanese Americans had to be held in places to minimize the danger they allegedly posed. Most of the camps were placed on federal or federal administered lands, including American Indian reservations run by the Bureau of Indian Affairs.

The WRA camps were sizable cities holding tens of thousands of people. As such, each had barracks to house the Japanese Americans, communal mess halls and toilets, laundries, schools, warehouses, and a hospital, sewage treatment plant, and cemetery. A fenced off area was reserved for the camp's white administrators and staff members. To keep the Japanese Americans within its confines, each camp had a security fence topped with barbed wire and at intervals and guard towers with searchlights.

The barracks were 20 feet by 120 feet divided into six apartments of three different sizes. The partitions dividing the units extended only to the eaves, leaving open the gap between the wall and roof, disallowing privacy. Exposed wood frames supported the roof and exterior walls, which consisted of boards covered with tarpaper, and raised, wooden floors that warped, revealing the ground below and allowing wind and dust into the barracks.

Each block, consisting of 10 to 14 barracks, had a mess hall, toilets for men and women, a laundry, and a recreation hall. All of the structures were based on Army designs that were low cost, used cheap and plentiful materials, and could be built quickly. Crews consisted of local workers who were often unqualified for the task of building. The term "Topaz carpenter" remains a derogatory name for any man with a hammer and little else such as those who were hired to build Topaz concentration camp. Japanese Americans were also used to construct some of the buildings like schools and churches.

All of the camps had agricultural works, including vegetable gardens and hog and chicken farms and cattle ranches, for Japanese Americans to produce food to meet their needs. Other subsistence activities operated by Japanese Americans for camp consumption were garment, mattress, and cabinet factories and a soy sauce plant at Manzanar.

Most camps were located in physically taxing environments besides having the stresses of confinement and the lack of privacy. Japanese Americans had to contend with seasonal extremes of heat and cold against which their flimsy

Japanese American internees contributed to the war effort by raising guayule plants for rubber. Manzanar concentration camp. (National Park Service)

barracks offered few protections. The soil was dry and often unproductive, and when winds whipped up dust storms frequently resulted. In the semitropical conditions in Arkansas, they experienced frequent rains that flooded the camps and with swamps and forests that surrounded them infested with poisonous water snakes and disease spreading mosquitoes.

After the last camp closed in March 1946, the original owners were handed back the lands and structures. Buildings were sold, auctioned off, or given to local residents to serve as residences, schools, and hospitals. Others were dismantled and their materials salvaged. Most lay abandoned, but today all still have remains and a few standing structures, testifying to the people who once inhabited those sites. The Arizona camps left behind useful canals and roads and agricultural fields that benefited the American Indian reservations on which they were located. The National Register of the U.S. National Park Service lists six of the 10 concentration camps for their historical significance.

Gila River

Located about 50 miles south of Phoenix, Arizona, the Gila River camp was built on Gila River Indian Reservation despite objections from the Gila River Indian nation. The location was approved by the Bureau of Indian Affairs in March 1942, and in July 1942 the first group of Japanese Americans arrived. Originally designed to hold 10,000, the camp grew to 13,348 by September 1942, making it the fourth largest city in Arizona behind only Phoenix, Tucson, and the other Arizona WRA concentration camp, Poston. In exchange for the lease of 16,500 acres, the WRA agreed to build roads and develop agricultural lands to improve conditions on the reservation. The Gila River camp actually consisted of two camps just over three miles apart. The first was called Camp No. 1 and later, Canal Camp, and the second, Camp No. 2 or Butte Camp.

Most of the Japanese Americans in Gila River were from California assembly centers at Fresno, Santa Anita, Stockton, Tulare, and Turlock. The WRA built Gila River as a model camp with its double roof to protect the residents from the heat of the desert sun with distinctive red roof shingles, lending color to an otherwise drab environment. In April 1943, First Lady Eleanor Roosevelt escorted by WRA director Dillon Myer visited the camp for six hours to inspect the facilities and conditions in the camps. Mrs. Roosevelt published a report of her visit in *Colliers Magazine,* October 16, 1943, to refute charges that Japanese Americans were being spoiled in the camps, and reported that they were enjoying life while U.S. soldiers were suffering and dying for the nation. In her article, Mrs. Roosevelt defended the camps as living up to "the American idea of justice as far as possible."

With only one guard tower for the Gila River camp, the WRA could not have been concerned about Japanese Americans escaping. In fact, within six months, the camp's perimeter fence came down along with the sole watchtower. The Gila River Japanese Americans were extremely successful in growing food not only for their camp but for other camps as well. By August 1942, nearly a thousand men and women converted 500 acres of grazing land into vegetable farms for corn, beets, carrots, and celery, and cash crops like cotton, flax, and castor beans. At its peak in 1943 to 1944, Gila River's farms produced 20 percent of the food for all 10 concentration camps, and even supplied watermelons to U.S. Army troops. And they raised thousands of cattle, hogs, and chickens for camp tables.

For those farms, the WRA built loading docks and warehouse facilities along railroad lines, bridges, and over 20 miles of roads. That infrastructure of roads and irrigation canals, the agricultural enterprises, and camp barracks and buildings have benefited the Gila River Indian nation on whose land they are located. Today, in return for Japanese American visits to and markers at the campsite, the Gila River Indian nation requires respect for its sovereignty by not, for instance, having U.S. federal intrusions in its territory such as a registered site.

The desert heat rose to 125 degrees, and at times people had to use a cloth or handkerchief to protect their hands before opening a doorknob. Some left tubs of water in the sun for hot bath water. Despite its limitations, the desert and its features provided opportunities for the inhabitants of Gila River camp. Junipers and sagebrush became Christmas trees, and Yuri Katai remembered movie nights under the stars. "We would all sit on a hill on an army blanket," Katai said. "A big cactus was sometimes in our way when we tried to see the screen. Once in a rain storm the lightning hit this cactus and smashed it to smitherines" (Girdner and Loftis, 217). On other nights, issei men went to the buttes near the camp to sing "long songs" or naga-uta, their highly trained, quivering voices settling down over the camp from their jagged perch above.

Granada

Granada concentration camp was also called Amache, which was its post office station named for the Cheyenne Indian who married the man for whom the county was named, Prowers. Granada was located in Colorado about 140 miles east of the town of Pueblo. About 3,600 feet in elevation, the ground was arid and wild grasses, sagebrush, cottonwood trees, and prickly pear cactus dotted the prairie. The WRA purchased the some 10,500 acres from private landowners, farmers, and ranchers, and construction on the camp began in June 1942 with about a thousand local and 50 Japanese American workers. Two months later, the camp opened, and by October 1942, Granada held 7,318 Japanese Americans, making it the 10th largest city in the state.

The nearby Arkansas River and wells provided water for the camp's large agricultural projects that included vegetable crops along with cattle, poultry, and hogs. Even the high school had a 500-acre farm maintained by student workers. Unlike the camp at Gila River, Granada, despite its agricultural productivity, was a secure camp with a four-strand barbed wire fence and six watchtowers along the fence and perimeter. Armed military police with searchlights manned the towers, and only in September 1945, after Japan's surrender, did the military police leave the camp. White residents of the nearby town of Lamar posted signs with "Japs Not Wanted Here" on them.

Kiyo Hirano remembered that the train taking her and others from the Merced Assembly Center to Granada had blinds over the windows. When a man near her tried to pull them up to look outside, an armed soldier barked, "Hey you! No one looks outside!" Forbidden to look out, Hirano said, was disorienting, and the only hints of their destination were the occasional station stops and the heat that kept increasing as the train proceeded. They were heading for a hot place, she felt. When they tried to sleep, Hirano wrote, another soldier ordered them to sleep with their seats upright, and when someone muttered "Goddamn!" to that demand, the guard pointed his rifle and yelled, his eyes glaring, "Who said that?" They finally arrived at Granada, exhausted and covered with soot from the train (Hirano, 11).

Kay Uno attended school in Granada. "The school was in English," she said. "Pledge of allegiance and everything. We were Americans. We participated, and we were proud to sing, especially patriotic songs. We were very patriotic in camp," she concluded. "I was too young to see the irony of it." Ernest Uno realized he was in a concentration camp. "You could see life going on as usual right outside the fence," he noted of the contrast inside and outside the camp. "People in their cars, driving back and forth. I definitely thought of myself as a prisoner. We were just a fence away from freedom" (Levine, 55, 69).

Kiyo Hirano's sons attended the camp's schools, and everyone seemed to share an interest in beautifying their bleak surroundings. People planted trees and flowers, and in a few months, she recalled, the desert seemed to disappear amidst the foliage and splash of colors. But summer ended, and winter set in. Winds blew and snow fell. "As soon as one went outside," she wrote, "one's nose felt a sharp pain as though pricked by a needle." And as winter progressed, Hirano observed, "people were becoming tired of their fenced-in lives, so that emotions became violent. As indications, there were ugly fights between adults, and also sexual problems between men and women. I prayed that winter would end and spring would come soon" (Hirano, 17).

Japanese Americans worked, Hirano noted, to earn a meager salary and to keep busy. As the war continued and local farmers experienced a labor shortage, they tried to recruit Japanese Americans from the camp to harvest sugar beets and perform other hard manual labor. One of her sons signed up, she wrote, and after a day at work his back ached and his hands were covered with blisters. The camp's administrators pushed farm and factory work for nisei over 18 years of age, Hirano noticed. Apparently, the wartime need for labor overrode the "military necessity" concerns that had established and justified the camps. As those workers left Granada, the camp's population declined steadily.

Hirano wrote about life in Granada as a wife and mother but mainly as a mother. She, as wife, received a 10-day pass to visit her brother-in-law in the Topaz concentration camp because he was near death. Shortly after she arrived, he passed away. Hirano worried over her oldest son when he reached 18 years old and became eligible for the draft. He instead moved to Cleveland having been recruited from the camp to work in a factory. When she received word he had been injured on the job and had to have surgery to repair his finger, Hirano worried over his recovery. "My breast was filled with a mother's love for her child," she wrote from Granada. And when a neighbor's son was killed fighting for the United States, Hirano went to console the young man's parents. "The parents were seated blank-faced on the benches, their eyes puffed from tears," she recalled. "I felt I should say something, but words would not come out, so we just cried together holding onto each other's hands. I bowed deeply, feeling great sympathy for them" (Hirano, 24).

As the months passed, Hirano observed, more and more Japanese Americans left the camp to serve in the army, attend college, or work. Some went to Denver while others, to Chicago. A man recruited workers to start a "Japanese colony" at Seabrook, New Jersey, where a frozen food factory served as a transition camp to freedom. A few families agreed to leave Granada for Seabrook. More young women than young men remained in the camp, Hirano wrote, and teenagers disobeyed their parents and got into fights with other teens. Adults, too, got drunk and fought with each other. Those days were frustrating and restless. A recruiter from a cannery in Utah approached Hirano to offer her a job in Brigham City. She left Granada on May 31, 1945, and bid farewell to her friends. "Life in camp was over," she reflected. "It had been a long three years. We were seen off by many people. They had come in the cold and dark at 6 o'clock in the morning. We promised to meet again in California and got on the truck. To camp, with many memories, and to the desert, goodbye" (Hirano, 26, 29).

Heart Mountain

Located about 12 miles northwest of Cody, Wyoming, Heart Mountain concentration camp was, like many others, built on high, sagebrush desert at about 4,700 feet elevation. A crew of about 2,000 began construction on the camp in June 1942, and the first Japanese Americans arrived in August. When full, the camp's 10,767 Japanese Americans made Heart Mountain the third largest city in Wyoming. A sentry post stood at the camp's entrance, and barbed wire and nine watchtowers enclosed the borders. Military police patrolled the grounds, and security was high especially during periods of mass protest in the camp.

Besides the usual structures within the camp, Heart Mountain had over a thousand acres of agricultural land and a system of canals to direct water to those fields. Japanese Americans added about a mile of canal to the existing system, which benefited local, white farmers in areas adjacent to the camp. They also gained when the Japanese Americans left the camp in 1945 from the buildings and the land that was cleared, leveled, and made fertile by the camp's captives.

Heart Mountain, Yosh Kuromiya recalled, "was very desolate. We felt we had been completely abandoned by civilization. But after being there awhile, I began to appreciate the beauty of the place. The mountain ranges in the distance, the bluffs. As dry as it was, it had its own unique beauty" (Levine, 52). William Hosokawa described the camp as it was being built. "Still under construction, Heart Mountain was a desolate place. There were workers everywhere putting up military type barracks, about 125 feet long, six living units per barrack. They were made out of wood and covered with black tar paper. The natural cover of the desolate countryside—the sagebrush and buffalo grass—had been torn up by the construction workers in bulldozers and trucks, and so the least little bit of wind would raise the dust—a very fine, alkaline dust" (Tateishi, 20). Most of the Japanese Americans were from southern California, Hosokawa found, although there were some from San Jose and Yakima, Washington.

One of those from San Jose was Jack Tono whose father was a strawberry grower in California. Tono worked at a produce packinghouse, and when the war came he was ready to join the army. Frustrating, thus, was the government's forced removal and confinement of Japanese Americans, because "I just couldn't understand the whole atmosphere of the whole thing, being a citizen." In addition, Tono recalled, Japanese Americans were not accused of any crime, and "yet they would commit us to a prison, in a camp, without a trial or nothing. That really got to me. To this day I'll never forget it" (Tateishi, 168, 169).

At Heart Mountain, Tono decided he would stand up for his rights as a U.S. citizen and refuse to take a backseat to anyone. He joined the Heart Mountain Fair Play Committee's call for draft resistance when the U.S. government changed its initial ruling to make the nisei subject to the draft. Tono and 62 others faced arrest for failing to report for physicals prior to enlisting in the army. About 200 to 300 young men, Tono reported, agreed with the Fair Play Committee's reasoning that their confinement in concentration camps was undemocratic and they would fight to preserve democracy only after their rights as citizens had been restored. After all, Tono, asked, "what kind of democracy is it when your parents, your brothers, and sisters are in camp and you have to die for the country?" (Tateishi, 170).

In April 1943, the FBI arrested the 63 draft resisters, and held them in three county jails in Casper, Laramie, and Cheyenne to await their trial in June. When the judge addressed them as "You Jap boys," Tono remembered, the men knew their conviction was assured. The judge sentenced them to three years in the federal penitentiary; the younger ones served time at McNeil Island near Tacoma, Washington, and the older ones, at Leavenworth, Kansas. "I think our group respected citizenship more than anybody in this country, because we were actively trying to preserve our citizenship rights, instead of just *saying* that we're citizens of this country," Tono declared of the draft resisters. "If you're treated the way we were, there's no such thing as real citizenship. You have to fight and pay your dues" (Tateishi, 174).

The Heart Mountain draft resistance movement was the largest among Japanese Americans with 85 men imprisoned for draft law violations. The total was 315 imprisoned for resisting the draft in the 10 concentration camps. Moreover, the Japanese American draft resistance movement was one of the largest in U.S. history, and it highlighted the contradiction of racism and inequality and the obligations of citizenship. A similar movement was draft resistance among African Americans during the U.S. war in Southeast Asia in the 1960s.

Heart Mountain was physically taxing. "Very often the ground was so icy people fell down," a Japanese American testified. The rain, wind, and snow marked the seasons, and many recorded the temperatures that fell to minus 30 degrees. Boots cracking and breaking ice was a familiar sound. A Japanese American wrote: "For the last few days we've been having a real taste of Wyoming winter. It started out with a blizzard—and, oh, what a blizzard! It's just like the kind we see in the movies. I never thought I'd really be in one. . . . The laundry and latrine barrack is about fifty yards away from our doorsteps. Dad wets his hair there and by the time he comes back to our barrack, his hair is frozen to ice!" (Girdner and Loftis, 228). Children in school held tins filled with hot ashes between their legs to keep warm.

The extreme cold and high altitude resulted in high rates of illness and overcrowding in the hospital. A complaint to the WRA detailed an epidemic of colds and pneumonia, heart and stomach ailments, frequent nausea, chronic arthritis and rheumatism, and a shortage of hospital beds and physicians. Inadequate diets and a rumor of white kitchen employees profiting from pilfering the camp's food supplies led to a Japanese American protest and WRA investigation. Several whites were found guilty and were fired.

The camp's farm project posed particular challenges because of the alkaline soil and the short growing season. Soil scientists, Japanese American and white, tested the soil, and experienced Japanese American farmers directed the work of transforming the desert into productive gardens. Some 700 men worked in fields of corn, potatoes, tomatoes, cucumbers, celery, cantaloupe, and watermelon, and Japanese vegetables like daikon (radish), gobo (burdock), nappa (cabbage), and karashi (mustard). Fiichi Sakauye, the farm superintendent and a farmer from

San Jose, observed: "We worked harder than we were working on our own farms. In order to get out and harvest the crop we had to be on the ball. Once we had sixty acres of sweet corn to be canned. We went to the canning company to contract for having the corn processed, and that night it froze, and that was the end of the sixty acres of corn. That's why timing was very important" (Girdner and Loftis, 230–31).

Lillian Sugita and four of her friends managed to get passes to leave the camp to spend a few hours in nearby Cody. They looked forward to the trip eager to get a soda. But when they boarded the bus, everyone seemed to stare at them as if they were "from Mars," she recalled. And when they sat at the lunch counter in Cody's drugstore, no one came to serve them. "Finally they brought this sign that says, 'We don't serve Japs.' We looked at that and we didn't know what to do. One of the girls said, 'Oh, shit,' and we all started laughing. We said we didn't want anything anyway." But "we were devastated. All we did the rest of the day was wait for the bus so we could get back to camp" (Levine, 72).

Japanese Americans farmed in Wyoming before the Heart Mountain camp was built, and, showing the falsity of "military necessity," they remained outside the barbed wire that contained their fellow citizens. These advised the newcomers about farming in Wyoming, and they provided seed for specialized crops. Many were frequent visitors to socialize with fellow Japanese Americans, including young people who felt isolated in Wyoming. Romance blossomed and at least one woman from the camp married a local, Japanese American farmer's son, a veterinarian.

For others, life ended at Heart Mountain concentration camp. Mrs. H. T. Nakamura's young son died of meningitis in that desolate place far away from home. "I had to be a tower of strength for my children," she remembered (Girdner and Loftis, 254).

Jerome

One of two concentration camps in Arkansas, Jerome, was located about 120 miles southeast of Little Rock. The camp was named for the nearby town of Jerome, which was one-half mile south of the camp. Unlike the camps of the high deserts, Jerome had an elevation of just 130 feet, and was built in the Mississippi River delta about 12 miles west of the river. The ground was swampy, and forests covered the area of about 10,000 acres managed by the Farm Security Administration. In July 1942, construction on the camp began, it opened in October, and reached its peak in November when there were 8,497 Japanese Americans from California and Hawai'i in the camp. Dollie Nagai remembered her arrival at Jerome. "They shoved us," she said, "pushed us, rammed us all in like cattle. I felt like an animal" (Levine, 52). Jerome was the last camp to open, and the first to close in June 1944. After the Japanese Americans left, Jerome became a prisoner-of-war camp for captured German officers and troops.

Jerome was the least developed of the 10 concentration camps, and had one of the smallest populations. A barbed wire fence and seven watchtowers secured the camp, although guards seemed unnecessary and the fence was not high. The swamp that surrounded the camp was filled with water moccasins and other poisonous snakes, making escape difficult and unlikely. Jerome had the distinction of being the only camp where an outsider shot the camp's Japanese Americans. A local, white farmer shot and wounded two Japanese Americans on a work detail in the woods. Their assailant said he thought they were trying to escape so he shot them. At the nearby town of Dermott, a white resident shot a Japanese American soldier who was visiting the camp. Thereafter, Dermott was off-limits for Japanese Americans.

With trees in the area, Jerome's sawmill produced firewood and lumber. Its over 600 acres produced 85 percent of the vegetables required by the camp, and its hog farm raised over 1,200 animals for food. Still, at the camp's beginning, Mary Tsukamoto recalled, people had to cooperate to survive. Shortly after arriving in October 1942, "all of a sudden cold weather arrived, and they didn't have enough wood to heat the rooms," Tsukamoto said. "We were on the edge of the Mississippi River, the swamplands of Arkansas. We had to go into the woods to chop wood. All the men stopped everything; school, everything, was closed and the young people were told to go out and work. They brought the wood in, and the women helped to saw it." Desperate and afraid, many began hoarding wood (Tateishi, 14).

Frequent rains facilitated lush vegetation, which Japanese Americans grew in profusion around their barracks. "Between the barracks," recalled Sada Murayama, "there was a trellis with morning glories, forming a tunnel of flowers. One block in particular was a showplace. Any outside visitors were taken there" (Girdner and Loftis, 219). But the rains and swampy ground also bred mosquitoes, and the danger of malaria was ever present. The army, in fact, regularly sprayed the swamp with deadly DDT to combat the problem, although later, scientists found that DDT could produce cancer in humans and was banned.

Lillian Sugita remembered Jerome's rains. "The camp was right in the thick of the swampland," she observed. "When it rained, it didn't stop. There were huge runoff ditches between the buildings for flood control, but you didn't have pathways over the ditches. They would be flooded in the summer and iced in the winter. We put down planks so we could walk across. I heard of some drownings." Dollie Nagai and her friends were spooked by their surroundings. "We were near bayous," she noted. "It was all forest, and they said, 'Don't go out there because it's dangerous.' One time my childhood friend and I were walking outside and one of those great big huge buzzards came swooping down. We ran back to 'civilization'" (Levine, 51–53).

Angie Nakashima believed that the older Japanese Americans suffered the most in the camp. "It was a hardship on my dad and mother," she noted. "My dad lost everything. He turned gray almost overnight." And Bert Nakano watched his mother's anguish. She was very lonesome, he said, and took the food home to the barracks to eat alone. "My mother had nothing to do. She felt like a failure. . . . She suffered so much." Dollie Nagai admitted even as a child, "I was angry in Jerome. Why did it happen to us? Why are we here? I'd go for walks in the camp in the evening and I'd talk to myself." Added Sumi Seo, "The worst thing about the camp was we felt we didn't have a country. We didn't know what we were, American citizens or Japanese. . . . Sitting in the camps like that didn't do us any good" (Levine, 64–67).

Japanese American and white teachers taught in the camp's school, which consisted of barracks divided into classrooms. Study hall was held in the mess hall. The curriculum included algebra, geometry, biology, civics, and Latin, remembered Dollie Nagai. The Latin teacher was very, very good, she said, but "we didn't feel the Caucasian teachers were qualified, although some probably were." Sumi Seo missed her friends. "When I got to camp," she said, "I wrote to everybody I could think of. We were so hungry for people to write to us, for some kind of news from outside." But no one returned her letters, only Charlotte Owens. "She wasn't afraid of what other people thought," Seo said admiringly. "I don't know why she was different." After her release from Jerome, Seo discovered that a mailman had told her friends writing to her was "helping the enemy" (Levine, 54–55, 59–60).

The shootings of Japanese Americans outside the Jerome camp mirrored the racism against people of color in the state. Many saw Japanese Americans as "yellow Negroes." Arkansas's governor, Homer Adkins, refused to allow Japanese Americans to work, settle, or attend college in the state, and public opinion strongly agreed with that position. Moreover, many of the state's whites disliked the presence of Japanese Americans and believed they were being "coddled" in Jerome and Rohwer, the two concentration camps in Arkansas. Ben Tagami remembered signs that read, "No Blacks, No Mexicans, No Japs, No Jews, No dogs allowed here." Those were common, he said (Levine, 63). In that climate, nisei soldiers trained at nearby Camp Shelby in Mississippi, a 15-hour bus ride, and when on leave often visited Jerome.

So active were the Japanese Americans in supporting nisei soldiers that Mary Tsukamoto and her husband Al helped set up a United Service Organizations (USO) at the Jerome camp for the young men to boost their morale. After all, many of the men came from concentration camps where their families were being held as they trained to defend the ideals of democracy and fight for their future in the United States. Mary Tsukamoto served as the Jerome USO's first director, and Mary Nakahara was her dedicated assistant. The USO held dances and baseball games, and organized a memorable fun-filled Fourth of July weekend. Each week, one to three busloads of Japanese American soldiers, each bus carrying 45 men, arrived at the Jerome camp to participate in USO activities.

Mary Nakahara who later became the widely known and respected activist Yuri Kochiyama discovered a sense of community among fellow Japanese Americans in the act of helping others. "Though we lived in dismal barracks," Nakahara said, "men would build beautiful pieces of furniture out of the most useless-looking piece of driftwood. Women would order pieces of material from Montgomery Ward mail-order catalogues and create curtains to partition the rooms, and make bedspreads and tablecloths to brighten up our living quarters. These little touches helped to make this wasteland more like a home." Men and women planted flowers around their barracks, and "we enjoyed seeing the bleakness of camp bloom with flowers and greenery." And Japanese music, performed on Japanese instruments, and dance made her proud to be Japanese. Nakahara became Japanese in Jerome (Fujino, 58, 59).

Manzanar

Located in California's Owens Valley, Manzanar was about 220 miles north of Los Angeles near the towns of Lone Pine and Independence. The valley floor is 3,900 feet in elevation and is enclosed to the west by the Sierra Nevada range and to the east by the White-Inyo range of mountains. A high desert, Manzanar was hot during summer and cold during winter. The land is dry with little precipitation, although two perennial streams flow into the valley from the Sierra's snows, supplying water to distant Los Angeles. Construction on the camp began in March 1942, and within six weeks most of the major work was completed. First run by the army's Wartime Civil Control Administration, Manzanar became the first WRA camp. Around May, there were over 7,000 Japanese Americans in the camp, and by July they totaled over 10,000. Over 90 percent came from Los Angeles.

Some Japanese protested working at the Manzanar camouflage net factory because of the meager pay and dust, which clogged their noses and lungs. (National Park Service)

A five-strand barbed-wire fence and eight watchtowers surrounded the camp, which had a unique feature called the Manzanar Children's Village. Japanese Americans built the three one-story buildings, unlike the usual barracks, in June 1942. Each building had running water, baths, and toilets, and one building housed a superintendent and a kitchen and a dining and recreation room. The village was home to Japanese American orphans from the restricted zone, including hapas or mixed race children and those, including infants, in the care of white foster homes. The girls lived in one building, and the boys, in another. Before the war, there were three homes for Japanese American orphans, the Shonien or Japanese Children's Home of Los Angeles, the Maryknoll Home for Japanese Children in Los Angeles, and the Salvation Army Japanese Children's Home in San Francisco. There were 101 children in Manzanar's Children's Village, 90 percent were from California and the rest, from Oregon, Washington, and Alaska, and nearly 20 percent were hapas.

"At Children's Village," Mary Matsuno remembered, "the grownups were very strict with us. They did it for our good, even though we might still feel that it was too much. They didn't like the ones that were mixed blood. They got rid of those kids faster than they did the Japanese. They were put up for adoption as quickly as possible." Shohei Hohri lived in the boys' ward. "I had to be sure that lights were turned off at the right time and everyone got up on time, things like that," he recalled of his responsibilities. "I made sure everyone washed, dressed, and went to breakfast. Then they went to school." Because he was older than most, Hohri told stories to the younger boys every night. Years later, remembering the Children's Village at Manzanar, Hohri declared, "In all of America's shameful, illegal internment of Japanese and Japanese Americans, the most shameful episode remains the internment of the orphanage children. Taken not only from orphanages but even from foster homes." But what was lost was gained, he concluded, in the friendships made by children in the village that have lasted a lifetime (Levine, 87–90).

The Manzanar riot of December 1942 was one of several significant acts of open resistance in the WRA concentration camps. On December 5, Fred Tayama, a well-known leader of the Japanese American Citizens League (JACL), was beaten, and a suspect, Harry Ueno, was arrested for that assault and was removed from the camp and confined in the jail at Independence. The next day at a mass meeting attended by over 2,000, the people drew up demands for presentation to the camp director by a delegation of five men. These included the unconditional release of Ueno and an investigation into general camp conditions by the Spanish consul (during the war, Spain represented the interests of citizens of Japan). When the negotiating committee, joined by about a thousand people, marched to the administration building to present their petition, military police armed with rifles, machine guns, and tear gas blocked their progress. They, however, allowed the five men through, and the camp director promised Ueno's return if the crowd dispersed, which they did, but they reassembled later that evening to demand Ueno's release.

From Harry Ueno's perspective, two jeeps filled with military police came to his barrack to arrest him the night of December 5. He had no idea about what he was charged with or why he was being arrested. He knew, nonetheless, that the authorities held him in contempt. When he asked that his family be notified about where he was, Ueno said, Ned Campbell, the WRA camp's assistant director, shot back at him "with hatred in his face": "Nobody is going to know where you are going to. I won't let anybody know where you are. And you are going to stay there for a long time" (Embrey, Hansen, Mitson, 54).

After a night in the Independence jail, much to Ueno's surprise, the police returned him to Manzanar. Looking out the window of his camp prison cell, Ueno saw military police putting on their gas masks. People outside were singing the Japanese Navy marching song perhaps to keep warm, and they did not threaten the soldiers. According to Ueno, "No Nihonjins [Japanese] I could see carried any sticks or weapons or anything. The crowd were all kinds—women, young people, Nisei, Kibei, all of them." The soldiers simply began lobbing tear gas into the crowd. Because of the wind, the "smoke just covered the whole area; people were running away. I couldn't see the movement because my view was from in front of the police station. But the campsite was all filled up with people beyond the administration building." A sergeant in charge exhorted his men, "Remember Pearl Harbor" and "Hold Your Ground,'" Ueno recalled. He repeated that several times as if to stiffen the resolve of the troops. "I could see some of the young MPs kind of shaking, scared because the crowd [was] so big there." Before the gas cleared, the soldiers started shooting (Tateishi, 199, 200; Embrey et al).

There was confusion among the troops and their commanders, according to Ueno who was inside the police station and overheard them. No one seemed to know who ordered the shooting, but it was clear that a young Japanese American, James Ito, was killed and another, Katsuji Kanagawa, was mortally wounded. Nine others lay wounded in the street. Most were shot in the back, indicating they were running away from the soldiers. At the hospital, the dead and injured arrived and placed on stretchers in the corridors. The Army tried to coerce the attending physicians and nurses to falsify their records to indicate that the bullets entered from the front to justify the military's action of firing into a confrontational mob, according to a hospital staff member. Dr. James Goto, the chief medical officer and surgeon, refused, and the next day he was dismissed and relocated to another concentration camp (Tateishi, 237).

Throughout the night bells tolled, and people held meetings while soldiers patrolled the camp. More suspected informers were beaten that night and their families threatened. The next morning, December 7, the military took over the camp and arrested the negotiating committee members and other leaders of the resistance. Despite that show of force, a new committee confronted the military commanding officer to demand Ueno's release, and they, too, were arrested. The WRA sent them to isolation centers at Moab, Utah and Leupp, Arizona. Suspected collaborators, called *inu* (dog) in Japanese, and their families were likewise removed from Manzanar for their protection.

Block managers distributed black armbands to wear while mourning for the two dead and in solidarity with the resistance movement. Between two-thirds and three-fourths of the camp population wore those armbands, showing the extent of the discontent. Camp observers described Manzanar as shaken for weeks, and long conferences and meetings between the camp director and Japanese Americans followed in an uneasy though subdued camp.

The ordeal of Harry Ueno and the others, nonetheless, continued. Crowded cells, hunger, and cold greeted the men, Ueno recalled, with occasional baskets of cheer from the camp's Japanese Americans, including Japanese foods like sushi for New Years Day. On January 9, they were taken by bus and then train to Moab, Utah. On the train and guarded constantly by military police, Ueno asked an African American porter for paper and pencil to write to his family. The porter, recognizing the circumstance, motioned with his eyes that he would secret them under the mattress when fixing the bunks. When he got off the train at Salt Lake City, Ueno slipped the porter a dollar, the only money he had left, and the letter, which his family eventually got. "That black porter," Ueno noted with gratitude, "he really take chance because even the bathrooms, they wouldn't let us shut the door. The MP was standing right there" (Tateishi, 202).

At Moab the men were cut off from the rest of the world, and their mail was censored. Military police followed them constantly, even to the bathrooms. The FBI had a special interest in Ueno because as the head of Manzanar's Mess Hall Workers' Union he had lodged complaints about WRA staff stealing from the allocations of sugar and meat for the camp's Japanese Americans. Sugar was rationed during the war, and was thus under government control. It was also sold on the black market. So FBI agents from Salt Lake City, Los Angeles, and Washington, D.C. descended on Moab to question Ueno about his accusation that the WRA was the problem, not Japanese Americans. Many in Manzanar believed that the WRA and military police arrested Ueno, in fact, because of his role in blowing the whistle on the WRA. After serving time at the Moab isolation center, the WRA sent Ueno to Tule Lake concentration camp where he remained to 1946.

Manzanar, like all the concentration camps, was a tragic disruption in the lives of tens of thousands of Americans. But the camp was also a place where people tried to maintain their human dignity and a sense of continuity and community for especially the children. Accordingly, Japanese Americans strived to create "normal" lives and conditions in an abnormal, even destructive environment. Yoshiye Togasaki spoke about life in Manzanar through her eyes as a physician. Because of crowding, she noted, precautions had to be taken to avoid epidemics such as food poisoning. The kitchen staff had to be extra careful to wash their hands and sterilize the dishes and utensils used by large numbers of people. And the white Navy officer and head of the camp's medical program had absolute power over his staff but had little knowledge or experience handling the needs of children, babies, and mothers, and the elderly. Baby formula, for instance, was made in a big vat that could easily spread infection to masses of children. Togasaki insisted that mothers make their own formula, but they lacked the capacity of boil water in their apartments.

With the warming weather, Togasaki observed, instances of whooping cough, scarlet fever, and measles rose. Without antibiotics or vaccines, lots of people got sick, and "we were getting some awfully sick children. And you try to take care of kids in a barracks with no running water and only one electric bulb above you." In addition, sand blew everywhere, making the camp unpleasant and vulnerable to illnesses like kidney infections and tuberculosis. "I am a doctor," Togasaki explained. "I understand that a lot of people who had much more tragic experiences than I did were not in a position to cope with things because of their background. And I understand why they can really be mad and feel resentful." There were whites like the president of California's Council of Churches who told her "the filthiest darn things, things like, You're just a traitor, and How do I know how to trust you? I don't know you from anything—you're Japanese, so you're not trustworthy. And there were a lot of dirty cusswords in between." But other whites, notably the Quakers, were "always very steadfast" in their support of Japanese Americans (Tateishi, 224–26).

Mary Sakaguchi could not forget Manzanar's food. "The food was so bad," she said, "we called it 'SOS' food—Same Old Slop. Everybody would get diarrhea. We called that the 'Manzanar Twins'—Diar and Rhea. Everybody had twins." Jim Matsuoka remembered a teacher in Manzanar's school who called an assembly "to speak about Pearl Harbor and she broke into tears, sobbing as she described the bombs raining down. I have no problems with that. But even as kids we knew there was an association, that somehow *we* were a part of that bombing. We didn't need to hear that. She was laying buckets of guilt on us. There we were, kids, and we were absorbing that stuff" (Levine, 53, 55).

To improve their lives, Sue Kunitomi recalled, Japanese Americans planted gardens and lawns. People wanted to beautify their bleak surroundings, she said, and to cover the dirt with foliage to reduce dust storms. Harry Ueno remembered standing in the baking sun and swirling dust when a friend suggested they build a pond. "Hey, let's dig a pond over there," he said. "Maybe there's water there or we can pipe it in, and I'll bring a lot of rocks." They got to work, and soon others joined them, including an experienced gardener who built ponds before the war. "The whole block pitched in," Ueno reported. It took nearly two months to construct, but "people sat on the rocks, and the enjoyed it" when the pond was finished. Mary Sakaguchi was so depressed she kept herself busy working in Manzanar's hospital. People organized knitting, sewing, and carving schools, including a beauty school, she reflected. "Many years later I thought I could have learned to be a beautician. Then at least I could have done my own hair" (Levine, 57–58, 59).

The psychological effects of the camps must have worn on the lives of Japanese Americans. Jim Matsuoka remembered misbehaving as a child of six or seven, and his mother chasing him to punish him. "She was a warm person," Matsuoka said, "and I never saw her cry a lot. All of a sudden she burst into tears. That really stunned me. I couldn't figure out what was wrong. Little bits of things becoming frayed. The tension and stress poking through." Mary Sakaguchi's sister, brother, and father all died within seven months of arriving in Manzanar. Her brother, a dentist, offered to serve in the U.S. Army but was rejected because he was a "Jap."

"I think that must have eaten away at him," Sakaguchi surmised. Shortly there-after, he developed "an intestinal obstruction and was sent by car to Los Angeles County Hospital from Manzanar. He died four hours after surgery. He was thirty-one years old. When all of this happened, I couldn't cry. I couldn't feel any emo-tion at all. You couldn't afford to cry. You had to hold everything together or you'd fall apart" (Levine, 64, 66–67).

Since 1969 on the last Saturday in April, Japanese Americans have organized the Manzanar Pilgrimage, an annual visit to the camp. Sue Kunitomi Embrey, one of the founders of the pilgrimage, believed that the living needed to commemo-rate the dead and to remember the past to avoid repeating its wrongs. Buses leave from Los Angeles, carrying hundreds of pilgrims who clean the campsite, bring presents, especially water, Embrey advised, to the dead, and dance, watch per-formances, and listen to speeches. The pilgrimage is a significant event in Asian American history because it helped and continues to inspire the Asian American movement and Asian American studies. For instance, after the tragedy of Septem-ber 11, 2001, and its aftermath when Muslim and South and West Asian Amer-icans were profiled and victimized, those groups have joined in the Manzanar Pilgrimage.

Today, Manzanar is a registered California historic site and is listed on the Na-tional Register of Historic Places as a National Historic Landmark maintained by the National Park Service. The landmark designation marks the site as holding "significance in commemorating the history of the United States of America." In 1992, Congress designated Manzanar a National Historic Site.

Minidoka

At an elevation of 4,000 feet, Minidoka was built on a high desert with shrubs and sagebrush typical of that ecology. Located 15 miles from Jerome and Twin Falls, Idaho, the camp was about 50 miles away from the actual town of Minidoka. Five miles of barbed wire and eight watchtowers enclosed the camp, which began con-struction in June 1942 and opened in August. At its peak, Minidoka held 7,318 Japanese Americans, mainly from Washington, Oregon, and Alaska.

On the train to Minidoka, Min Yasui remembered, African American stewards "would indicate their sympathy toward us as though to say, without speaking, that they empathized with us." When the train pulled up at an isolated siding north of Twin Falls, Yasui noted, there were no houses in sight, no trees, nothing green, just sagebrush and "mostly dry, baked earth." The place seemed so distant from the green of Oregon's Willamette Valley (Tateishi, 75–76).

Yasui continued his introduction to Minidoka. "We saw the barbed-wire fences, the watchtowers, guard houses, the MP detachments, the administration housing, warehouse areas, and block after block of black, tar-paper barracks, about 120 feet long and about 20 feet wide." Inside there were army cots with metal springs, a potbellied stove, and a bare bulb hanging from the ceiling. The cracks in the wood floors allowed one to see the earth below. Yasui soon discovered that Minidoka was on a slight rise with an irrigation canal along the camp's southern border. To

Japanese American internees collect their baggage at the Minidoka concentration camp in Idaho, August 1942. (National Archives)

emphasize that he was in a concentration camp, Yasui pointed out: "I am not certain where the MP unit was quartered, but it was obvious that access in and out of the camp was controlled by the military" (Tateishi, 76, 77).

Theresa Takayoshi remembered the difficult environment and its impact upon the people. "Minidoka was just so dusty," she said, "so dusty, and so cold in the wintertime. None of us from Seattle had clothes that were warm enough for that climate. The dust storms that would just come up without notice were just terrible. And I felt the family situation was deteriorating." As a young mother with two little children, Takayoshi worried over their welfare when her husband was away so much working and playing cards with his friends. Once, after giving her children baths, Takayoshi dumped the wash pail over the side when a gust of wind blew the water and dust back over her. "I was a mess," she laughed (Tateishi, 218, 219).

Hanaye Matsushita arrived in Minidoka in August 1942 when, she wrote, the place was "unedurably hot and dusty," making her feel tired and "worthless because of the horrible heat." "I can hear the violent winds blowing across the wide plains. In the distance I hear the sound of the sagebrush blowing in the wind, rattlesnakes, and the howling of coyotes." Matsushita admitted to her husband who had been separated from her in the Fort Missoula internment camp, "When I dwell on this situation, I have suicidal feelings, but I've got to keep myself together until your return. I imagine you're also experiencing rough times." Her husband, Iwao Matsushita, responded, "Take care of your health, that's of the primary importance" (Fiset, 168, 169).

Helen Murao was orphaned at a young age, and when she entered Minidoka she took on the responsibility of serving as surrogate mother to her two younger siblings. The three of them lived together in a small barracks unit. "It was usually for two people," Murao noted, "but since we were kids and we didn't take up so much space, three of us were put in one of those end barracks." Murao insisted that her brothers attend school, did their homework, and went to bed at a set time. She controlled those boys like a drill sergeant because she was determined to keep the family intact. "I insisted that my two brothers and I eat together in the mess hall as a family unit. I insisted that we have grace before meals. And I insisted that they be in our room at eight o'clock at night. Not because I wanted to see them but because I thought that's what we should do as a family unit—we should be together, spend our time together, and live as a family . . ." In fact, Murao determined, "*I'm going to prevail, my will is going to prevail, my own life will prevail.* I'm not going to kill myself, I'm going to prevail" (Tateishi, 46, 47).

Poston

Sometimes called the Colorado River concentration camp, Poston was about 12 miles south of Parker, Arizona. The camp was named after Arizona's first superintendent of Indian Affairs, Charles Poston, who established in 1865 the Colorado River Reservation where the concentration camp was built. Poston was only 320 feet in elevation but as part of the Sonoran desert, it was hot during the summer and cold in the winter. Like the other concentration camp in Arizona, Gila River, the reservation's Indians opposed its construction on their land but on the basis that they opposed the injustice of the camps and refused to inflict harm upon another group. Members of the Tribal Council saw a connection between their dispossession and the exclusion and confinement of Japanese Americans. The army and Bureau of Indian Affairs overruled their objection, in part, because the bureau saw this as an opportunity to improve the reservation from military expenditures and the exploitation of cheap, plentiful Japanese American captive labor.

Poston consisted of three camps set about three miles apart and called by the WRA, Poston I, II, and III, but the Japanese Americans called them Roaston, Toaston, and Duston, indicating how they experienced the camps. Construction began March 1942, and operation began by May. Because of the heat, modification included a double roof and extra wood strips to fill in the cracks between boards that shrank. Also, there were no guard towers because they were unnecessary in such an isolated, desolate place. Escape would have been difficult and hazardous, the WRA believed. At its height, Poston confined 17,814, which made it the largest of the 10 concentration camps and the third largest city in Arizona.

The WRA implemented its use of forced labor by requiring a pledge by all of Poston's Japanese Americans. "I swear loyalty to the United States and enlist in the War Relocation Work Corps for the duration of the war and fourteen days thereafter in order to contribute to the needs of the nation and in order to earn a livelihood for myself and my dependents," the oath began. It went on to declare acceptance of any pay given to them and to observe all work rules and regulations. Further, in the course of such labor, Japanese American workers promised not to hold the WRA and government liable for any injury or damages incurred. Nobu Shimahara signed the work pledge "without bothering to read it, or even caring what it said. What choice did I have?" he asked. "People just lined up and signed" (Bailey, 90). The oath made them, like prisoners, ideal laborers being virtually cost free. That condition failed, however, to control totally the thoughts and behaviors of Japanese American workers.

A Japanese American researcher, Richard Nishimoto, documented some of that rebelliousness in a report he filed on Poston's firebreak gang. Because of the ever-present threat of fire in that dry environment, work gangs cleared the grasses, shrubs, and tree stumps around the camp to create a firebreak. They also, in the early days of the camp, cleared building debris such as scrap lumber and bits of tarpaper that posed a fire hazard. Nishimoto served as the leader of one of those crews. Despite the extreme heat that soared to over 110 degrees, the WRA exhorted its work supervisors, "Don't let them ease up. Keep 'em busy." A Japanese American retorted, "How do they expect us to work without any drinking water around,'" and others shouted, "Who do they think we are? Hell, we're no slaves. We don't have to work, if we don't want to." Still another declared, "It's too hot. No use working! We're getting only six cents an hour anyway." And, Nishimoto added, "I knew that they thought of me as a white-man's 'stooge'" (Nishimoto, 45, 46).

The firebreak crew dwindled from over 100 to about 20 when it became apparent that they could not be forced to work. Most refused to acquiesce to government pressure and false promises. For instance, in July 1942, the WRA refused to pay the men for their hours of work because, according to a white supervisor, "these Japs worked as volunteers . . ." That decision prompted an angry Nishimoto to think, "My men were tricked into working by a false promise of financial return. Now this guy is refusing to pay the due compensation. That's treachery! They just wanted my men to work for nothing. They just wanted to exploit them without any intention of paying wages" (Nishimoto, 57). After protest, the WRA agreed to pay the men. But more than payment, Nishimoto soon learned, Japanese Americans worked, even on days when the temperature rose to 125 degrees, on projects that benefitted their lives and advanced the interests of their children and community.

Poston's Japanese Americans, Nishimoto understood, "were critical and suspicious toward the administration and the staff at Poston." They believed the WRA was corrupt. "They did not doubt that the hospital was killing the Japanese. . . . They thought that white men were 'slave drivers.' . . . When my crew failed to receive their wages which were due to them, they were again outspokenly suspicious and resentful . . ." When confronted with an arrogant white boss, the men nearly jumped on him. "Someone shrieked in Japanese, 'God damn it! The young punk's cocky,'" Nishimoto reported of an incident in July. "'He's arrogant! Let's beat him up. That's the only way to teach him. Come on, let's beat him up.' Others took up the chant, 'Let's beat him up!'" Only by driving away did the man escape (Nishimoto, 67, 68).

The Poston strike of November 1942 was another of the significant acts of open resistance that included the mass movements at Heart Mountain, Manzanar, and Tule Lake. Following the beating of a suspected inu or informer in Poston Unit I on November 14, 1942, the security police rounded up and questioned about 50 suspects. Two of those were detained for further questioning and to await the arrival of FBI agents. For two days, a delegation met with the camp officials seeking the release of the two men, and on November 18, some 2,500 Japanese Americans gathered in front of the jail where they men were being held to demand their release. The WRA administration assured the people that justice would prevail and urged patience. Most Japanese Americans believed that any trial outside the camp, where anti-Japanese racism prevailed, would prejudice the case against the men. In protest, the camp leaders, the community council, Issei Advisory Board, and block managers, all resigned, and that evening formed an Emergency Committee of 72, comprised of a representative from each block, and the Emergency Council of 12, the committee's leaders, who called for a general strike.

The Japanese Americans were divided on that course of action, but each block maintained discipline by threats against inu and organizing a round-the-clock vigil in front of the prison. The administrators, too, were divided, a faction favoring a hard line by calling in the military police to crush the strikers and another, advocating negotiations. The latter group prevailed, and during those meetings it became clear that the strikers had bigger objects in mind beyond the two accused prisoners. They demanded self-government within the camp, having Japanese Americans choose their leaders and political and economic activities within WRA guidelines. On November 24, the WRA camp administrators granted a measure of self-government, released one of the prisoners because of a lack of evidence, and released the other to await his trial inside the camp. The settlement led to a stable camp where before the strike a contentious atmosphere had prevailed.

The situation, nonetheless, was far from normal. The forced removal and confinement failed to promote stability and contentment. Poston was not the usual community in the U.S. Signs such as the one a barber posted in the nearby town of Parker, "Jap, Keep Out, You Rat!" reminded Japanese Americans of the racism that had prompted their confinement behind barbed wire. And from the start, Poston's administrators deployed a network of informers, inu, to keep tabs on the situation, resulting in an atmosphere of distrust, rumors, and suspicions. Threats of physical violence and beatings, thus, were common. Moreover, the WRA's policy favoring nisei because of their U.S. citizenship over issei eroded issei or parental authority over their children. The policy also fingered the nisei as the group working with the administrators, earning them privileges but making them the targets for beatings.

Physical maladies spread because of the climate, tight quarters, communal fa-cilities, and inadequate shelter, clothing, and medical supplies. Dysentery, likely spread through the kitchens, was epidemic, measles, influenza, and a lung conges-tion common to desert regions plagued Poston's Japanese Americans, stuffing the small hospital to overflowing.

Mabel Ota had her baby in Poston where at the beginning there was only one obstetrician. The day she went in to have her baby, that lone Japanese American physician was in his barracks resting because the previous day he had collapsed from heat exhaustion. But her baby was due, and its heartbeat was getting fainter as the day wore on, waiting for the physician to deliver her. The next day, the phy-sician performed the delivery without an anesthesiologist. "They took me to the delivery room and gave me a local and I could see the knife to cut me," recalled Ota. "Then he used these huge forceps, and I kept watching the clock. He really had a hard time yanking her out, but I was conscious all the time. So it was really a horrible experience." He finally succeeded but the baby, Madeline, suffered brain damage from the ordeal, and was developmentally very slow (Tateishi, 110).

Ota's mother and father were in the other Arizona camp at Gila River where the high starch diet brought on a diabetic attack, which the camp physicians, despite having been told he was a diabetic, misdiagnosed his ailment as melancholia or depression. They failed to administer a blood test, which was standard for diabet-ics. Instead, the WRA transferred him to the Phoenix Sanitarium for shock treat-ment to cure his presumed melancholia. After about six weeks of shock treatment, her father died. "But his death certificate definitely says, 'Died from diabetes,' so he went into a diabetic coma, that's what it was, and then he died. If he didn't go to camp I'm sure he would have lived to a ripe old age, because he was very careful watching his diet," Ota noted sadly (Tateishi, 111–12).

The first death at Poston occurred just over two weeks after the first group ar-rived in May. Because the camp lacked the facilities, arrangements for the body and funeral were difficult. Adding to the gloom was the concentration camp itself and the losses suffered as a result. Bodies had to be shipped to Yuma and then to San Diego for cremation, so an enterprising undertaker in Yuma offered to handle all the mortuary work in Poston. The WRA approved, and he proposed to set up shop adjacent to the hospital until Japanese Americans protested. Having a crema-tory next to the hospital might not send the right message to patients, they pointed out. So the undertaker set up shop next to the warehouse area in October 1942, and business included supplying urns for the ashes of the deceased because the WRA could only offer paper cartons.

From Hawai'i came the educator, Miles Cary, former principal of McKinley High School in Honolulu, derisively called "Tokyo High" because of its large numbers of Japanese American students. Cary volunteered to become Poston's director of edu-cation. In the islands, Cary had directed nisei education toward an academic track when plantation schools tried to steer the second generation toward manual labor and a return to the plantations. At Poston, he tried to inspire the nisei and their parents, under the trying conditions of the camp, to dream in disregard of the lim-itations of race. "I believe that most of you want your boys and girls to be helped to live rich, significant lives in America," Cary told the parents. "I believe, too you want them helped to learn how to have a part to share in building the better world of the future. What would a better world be like?" he asked, and answered "A world in which a man, regardless of pigmentation, would be treated with respect. A world in which each individual, according to his powers, would be encouraged to make his special contributions toward improving the common life" (Bailey, 96).

Japanese American labor put over 2,000 acres under cultivation, producing vegetables and field crops. They raised chickens at all three campsites, and had a hog farm between units I and II. They built warehouses, an ice storage facility, a butcher shop, and a plant nursery, and they dug ditches and an irrigation system to water their fields. Their labor made the desert bloom.

The last Japanese Americans left Poston on November 28, 1945. Before all of them departed, however, a few Hopi Indian families moved into the camp to join the remaining Japanese Americans to help maintain the farms and fields, which became a part of the reservation.

Rohwer

Rohwer was named for the nearby town of Rohwer, and located about 110 miles southeast of Little Rock and 27 miles north of Jerome, the other concentration camp in Arkansas. The Mississippi River flowed a few miles away and like Jerome, Rohwer sat in a low-lying swampland among creeks, canals, and bayous managed by the Farm Security Administration. During spring, about half of the land given over to the camp sat under swampy bayou water. As a consequence, wooden sidewalks and drainage ditches with bridges crisscrossed the camp. Construction began July 1942, and by September, Rohwer was open to the 8,475 Japanese Americans, most from California. Barbed wire enclosed the 51 blocks, and a patrol road and eight guard towers secured the camp's perimeter.

"We pulled in at Rohwer, Arkansas, late at night," Miyo Senzaki said. "I remember getting off the train and getting in the Army trucks and then we came to a spot and they let us off and that was the campsite. They had the barracks set up, but then everything wasn't completed." A friend showed her a pile of lumber, which was guarded by men on horseback. One of them warned them that if they stole the lumber they would be shot on sight. Despite that, Senzaki admitted, "we grabbed the lumber and ran." Her husband made furniture with it because the barracks were empty except for cots that served as beds.

"Being at Rohwer was just a lonely feeling that I can't explain," Senzaki continued. "I thought to myself, I never ever dreamed that I would come to live here. I had this really sad feeling, never thinking you're going to be in there. You couldn't run anywhere. It was scary because there was no end to it. You could run and run and run but where are you to go? It was just nothing but water and then there were rattlesnakes. We felt like prisoners" (Tateishi, 102–3).

Medical care at Rohwer was impossible, Senzaki noted. There was only one physician, and there were outbreaks of measles, mumps, and food poisonings. Thus, despite suffering severe headaches and bleeding, her husband had to wait nearly a month before he could see Dr. Ikuta. During the operation, they discovered a blood clot behind his ear bone, which a visiting army physician diagnosed as fatal. But her husband survived, and in gratitude Senzaki and her husband's mother tried to give Dr. Ikuta all of their savings, 25 dollars. Senzaki waited at the hospital, and when Dr. Ikuta arrived she "grabbed him and thanked him for saving my husband's life." But the physician refused the money, and took instead the bottle of whiskey, which she had also offered, saying "I'll take the drink" (Tateishi, 103–4).

Work at Rohwer involved clearing the land of trees and undergrowth. One day, a work crew of Japanese Americans in the woods was surprised by a group of armed white men who apparently believed the group to be Japanese paratroopers, making a beachhead in their neck of the woods. The posse marched their prisoners to town, paraded their catch through the streets, and deposited them in the city jail. The WRA had to bail the Japanese Americans out of that predicament.

The intense heat and humidity and frequent rains made Rohwer unpleasant at best and difficult to farm. After they drained the swamps, an unexpected drought that summer required diverting water from a nearby bayou for the fields. In the spring, contrarily, heavy downpours flooded the crops and made the earth muddy. The soil was fertile, nonetheless, and with careful cultivation, weeding, and crop rotation, Japanese American farmers were eventually rewarded with good yields of soy and mung beans.

A unique feature of the Rohwer camp remains its cemetery, which was located just outside the fence with its entrance facing the concentration camp. The cemetery holds 24 burial spots marked by headstones and two large monuments, one dedicated to those who died in the camp and the other, to the men of the 100th Battalion and 442nd Regimental Combat Team. The monument marking Rohwer's dead was erected in October 1944. Its inscription in Japanese reads, "May the people of Arkansas keep in beauty and reverence forever this ground where our bodies sleep." In 1974, the camp's cemetery was listed on the National Register of Historic Places, and in 1992 was designated a National Historic Landmark.

Topaz

Located in west-central Utah, Topaz sits about 140 miles southwest of Salt Lake City. Called the Central Utah Relocation Center at first, the camp acquired the name of the nearby Topaz Mountains that distinguished an otherwise flat landscape. The camp lay in the Sevier Desert at an elevation of 4,600 feet. High desert temperatures, rainfall, and vegetation typified life in Topaz for the 8,130 Japanese Americans who lived there after the camp's opening in September 1942. Most of the people were from the San Francisco Bay Area, and their first impressions were of a dry waterless place, dust and the alkaline soil that could sting the eyes and skin, and the absence of greenery. Recalled Morgan Yamanaka, "There seemed to be a wall way out there; to see the blue sky and then the more you look at it, the wall seems to be moving. It was a dust storm rolling in, and it just engulfed you, and before you knew it, you could not see anything." Caught in a dust storm, Miné

Okubo remarked, "When we finally battled our way into the safety of the building we looked as if we had fallen into a flour barrel" (Taylor, 91). The writer Yoshiko Uchida called Topaz "the city of dust."

Upon their arrival, Uchida remembered, Japanese Americans were given instructions on the proper use of terms within the camp to dress up the nakedness of the place. Topaz's officials directed Japanese Americans to say, dining hall and not mess hall, safety council, not internal police, residents, not evacuees, and mental climate, not morale. "After our long and exhausting ordeal," she commented, "a patronizing sheet of instructions was the last thing we needed." Instead, Uchida and her fellow Japanese Americans were more concerned with the two or three inch deep "great mass of loose flour-like sand" that sent up swirls of powder by simply walking over it, the cracks in the walls and floors that let in the every-present dust, and the empty barracks with only army cots and no mattresses (Uchida, 109).

Confronted with those conditions, Japanese Americans busied themselves to make Topaz livable and as comfortable as possible. They plugged the holes in their units, cleaned the toilets, dug irrigation ditches, farmed agricultural fields and chickens, turkey, hogs, and cattle, and they planted thousands of trees and other vegetation. "It was inhumane and unnecessary to subject the internees to such discomfort," Yoshiko Uchida observed. A woman suffered second-degree burns from hot tar that dripped from the roof onto her face as she slept, and at first many suffered from food poisoning and diarrhea because of unsanitary conditions in the mess halls. The people worked, thus, to improve the quality of their lives. As the artist Miné Okubo put it, "Comfort was uppermost in the minds of the people" (Okubo, 137).

With temperatures that varied by as much as 50 degrees in a single day, Yoshiko Uchida noted, water in their barracks could be frozen in the morning and in the afternoon, her sister and her could return home after a day in the sun "covered with dust, and feeling like well-broiled meat." The days could be harsh and unkind, but the evenings could be pleasant. "The sand retained the warmth of the sun, and the moon rose from behind dark mountains with the kind of clear brilliance seen only in a vast desert sky," Uchida wrote. "We often took walks along the edge of camp, watching sunsets made spectacular by the dusty haze and waiting for the moon to rise in the darkening sky. It was one of the few things to look forward to in our life at Topaz" (Uchida, 110).

Walking along the fence at the camp's edge, however, could be dangerous as was shown by the fatal shooting of James Hatsuaki Wakasa on April 11, 1943. On an evening stroll, 63-year-old Wakasa wandered too near the fence when a guard, after several verbal warnings, shot and killed him. Wakasa was facing the soldier when he was killed. Before this incident, there were eight previous warning shots fired at Japanese Americans near the barbed-wire fence. Without witnesses, there was only the guard's account and speculations that Wakasa might have been distracted or did not hear the warning (he was hard of hearing) before the sentry shot him from a watchtower some 300 feet away. Whatever the cause, Wakasa was dead.

Wakasa was an issei bachelor. A graduate of Tokyo's Keio College, Wakasa went on to two years of postgraduate study at the University of Wisconsin, which he completed in 1916. He was thus highly educated, although he worked primarily as a cook. That was typical of his generation when service work was the only occupation open to Japanese Americans because of racism. Wakasa also served in the U.S. Army during World War I. The evening of his death, a friend had dinner with Wakasa, and instead of returning to his barracks, said he was going for a walk. About 30 minutes later, the friend heard Wakasa had been shot.

Nervous over the shooting, Topaz's administrators called a general alert, and for two days military police armed with machine guns, gas masks, and tear gas terrorized the camp's population. The funeral preparations added to the tension, with the administrators fearful that the occasion might prompt a mass protest and riot. Even the place of the funeral was debated. Japanese Americans wanted it held on the spot where Wakasa died, while the WRA wanted it held elsewhere because of the disturbing symbolism of the bloodstained earth near the fence and under the guard tower. Japanese Americans held a general work stoppage before the funeral to protest the killing and demonstrate their outrage at what was a senseless and needlessly cruel act. Women made huge wreaths of paper flowers, and on April 20 a crowd of up to 2,000 Japanese Americans attended the Protestant service held in an open space near but not at the site of Wakasa's death.

Michiko Okamoto was deeply disturbed by the killing, which formed the most lasting memory of her time in Topaz. "We were totally vulnerable," she said of the lesson she learned from Wakasa's death. "We were helpless. There was no way of defending ourselves from anybody who just got trigger-happy and wanted to shoot us" (Taylor, 145). About a month later, on May 22, 1942, a guard from the southeast watchtower fired a warning shot at a couple walking too near the fence. This time, the soldier refrained from shooting to kill. Many Japanese Americans, including some WRA camp administrators, believed the military police were "Jap-haters" or recently returned soldiers from the Pacific war front and were thus trigger happy.

Amy Akiyama remembered the lines at Topaz. "Lines to go to the bathroom, lines for this, lines for that. Lines for everything you did." And the bathrooms, she said, had no partitions so "the women were so vocal about it, they did put some in, but not doors. A lot of people brought something they'd hang" to give them privacy. Many busied themselves collecting seashells from the lake bed on which Topaz was built, and made pins and jewelry with them. Morgan Yamanaka's father fashioned armchairs from tree limbs, a Japanese display case, and swords from old car springs. Akiyama's mother enjoyed going to the theatre to see films that flickered like home movies and stopped when the reel tape broke. "I don't remember any movie going smoothly," Akiyama noted (Levine, 53, 56–57, 58–59).

In addition to the schools for children and evening "Americanization" classes for the adults, noted Miné Okubo, there was a canteen, dry-goods store, barbershop, beauty parlor, and a dry cleaning and shoe repair shop. The canteen, she explained, was like a country store where people gathered to gossip and discuss family and community concerns. Art and hobby classes were popular, and exhibits showed the handiwork of the camp's Japanese Americans. People participated in and attended baseball, basketball, and football games, and some practiced golf and organized ping pong, badminton, and tennis tournaments. Sumo or wrestling and talent shows and movies entertained audiences, and Buddhists celebrated Hanamatsuri or flower festival on the anniversary of Buddha's birth. Gradually, Okubo observed, Japanese Americans improved the conditions of life in Topaz.

Amy Akiyama's grandfather died in the camp. "My mother said she thinks he died of a broken heart," said Akiyama. The old people had nothing to do; they had no future and lost the zest for life. "We all went to the funeral. It was a Buddhist funeral, and they burned a lot of incense. I can still smell it." Thereafter, whenever she smells incense it brings back that memory, Akiyama confessed, of "hearing the Buddhist priest chanting and seeing the profile of my grandfather in the casket" (Levine, 62). The cemetery at Topaz, Miné Okubo noted, lay empty; no one was buried there. Families sent the bodies to Salt Lake City for cremation, and they kept the ashes for a final resting place in the hope of returning home to the San Francisco Bay Area.

Tule Lake

Situated in Modoc County, California, near the Oregon border, Tule Lake concentration camp has a rich and varied history. The land once belonged to the Modoc nation, but white settlers, hunters and traders, and gold miners occupied the valley in the 19th century. Because of that dispossession and the Modoc refusal to be uprooted and confined to a reservation, the United States waged a war against them. A small band led by Kintpuash of about 74 men and 85 women and children made their last stand against the U.S. Army of over 600 troops on the Lava Beds just south of the concentration camp. About 70 years later, the U.S. government removed and confined Japanese Americans near the site of the Modoc nation's demise.

Construction on the camp began on April 1942, and by May the first group of Japanese Americans arrived from Oregon and California. Nearly from its start, Tule Lake saw Japanese American resistance to conditions in the camp. Before the end of the year, there was a mess hall strike in July to protest inadequate food, a campaign for higher wages in August, and two labor strikes in August and September.

In 1943, the U.S. government issued a "loyalty" questionnaire to Japanese Americans in the ten WRA concentration camps. Question 27 asked about a willingness to serve in the U.S. armed forces, and Question 28, foreswearing loyalty to the Japanese emperor. To the WRA, those questions indicated the loyalty of those who answered the questions "Yes" and "Yes." But it was more complicated than that. The nisei were U.S. citizens by birth, and they never swore loyalty to Japan's emperor. Accordingly, if they answered "Yes" to Question 28, they might be suspected of having harbored loyalty to Japan. For issei who could not become U.S. citizens by law, answering "Yes" would make them, in effect, people without a country. Who, then, would protect their rights? As for Question 27, many nisei, like the draft resisters at Heart Mountain, believed that answering "Yes" endorsed the loss of their civil liberties. They would gladly serve their country once their rights as citizens were restored. After all, following Pearl Harbor, the United States classified all nisei as "aliens" and made them ineligible to volunteer or liable for the draft.

Many answered conditionally, "Yes, if my rights as a citizen are restored." Of the nearly 78,000 who filled out the questionnaire, about 6,700 answered "No" to Question 28. Approximately 2,000 more qualified their "No" answer, which the WRA classed as a "No." The WRA labeled all of them as "disloyal," and began the process of segregation or the removal of the so-called "No-No Boys" from their camps to the designated segregation center at Tule Lake. The camp at Tule Lake was chosen for that purpose because it had the highest percentage of "No-No's." At other camps, the average was 10 percent who refused to answer or answered "No," but at Tule Lake, the figure was 42 percent. Some 6,000 moved out of Tule Lake to other camps, leaving 8,500 behind. "Disloyals" from other camps moved into Tule Lake, and by the spring of 1944, there were over 18,000 Japanese Americans in that camp, making it the largest of the 10 concentration camps.

In anticipation of that move, in the summer of 1943, the WRA converted Tule Lake into a maximum-security camp for "disloyals." A man-proof, six-foot high chain link fence topped with barbed wire surrounded the camp, spiked with watchtowers at intervals along the perimeter manned by soldiers with machine guns. For a time in 1943, an enhanced military presence with eight tanks occupied the camp to ensure the homeland security.

As was the case in all the other camps, Tule Lake administrators encouraged the Japanese to produce on vegetable, hog, and chicken farms for their subsistence. In October 1943, Japanese farm workers struck in protest over the death of a fellow laborer, Kashima, who died in a truck accident. The day following Kashima's death, in elections held for a representative body called the Daihyo Sha Kai, Japanese who were critical of the WRA and its policies won, but the camp's director, Raymond Best, ignored them and their negotiating committee, casting them as troublemakers.

When the national WRA director Dillon Myer visited Tule Lake on November 1, 1943, the Daihyo Sha Kai insisted on meeting with him by massing thousands of Japanese around the administrative building in which Myer was meeting with Best. George Kuratomi, the protesters' spokesman, outlined for Myer the people's grievances that included Best's dishonest dealings with them, white racism among several WRA staffers, and inadequate food and overcrowding. At base, Kuratomi explained, the Japanese asked that they "be treated humanely from this Government, this Government of the United States." Myer expressed confidence in Best and his dealings, and offered Kuratomi and the protesters no encouragement or promise of redress. To adjourn the meeting, military police on jeeps mounted with machine guns swept into the camp, and with tear gas dispersed the protesters. Soldiers then proceeded to single out and apprehend the suspected leaders.

White WRA administrators feared for their personal safety, having witnessed the Japanese demonstration. The next day, November 2, after Myer and Best failed to reassure them, they went directly to Lt. Col. Verne Austin, head of the military detachment that comprised an entire battalion of some 1,200 troops, to get his promise that Army troops would guarantee their safety. Best, angered over that vote of no confidence, fired two of his most outspoken critics, and within a week 20 staff members resigned. Meanwhile, white settlers in the Tule Lake basin complained that Best, Myer, and the WRA coddled the Japanese, and the local and national press took up the mass protest of November 1 mounted by the Japanese "enemy." White WRA staff members added to those criticisms, which were either hysterical or uncovered quite vicious attitudes toward "those Japs," according to Emily Light, a schoolteacher. After a minor scuffle between a small group of Japanese and several white administrators, Best called in the military as if to placate his critics.

Tanks rolled into the camp on November 4, and the army declared military rule and its determination to stamp out the protest by removing troublemakers. The army imposed a 6 A.M. to 7 P.M. curfew and arbitrarily apprehended and detained Japanese without recourse to charges or hearings. Austin disbanded the Daihyo Sha Kai and arrested its members, required identification badges of everyone 12 years and older, and mounted a comprehensive sweep of the entire camp to take into custody agitators and confiscate weapons. On November 26, three groups of about 150 men, each soldier carrying full field equipment and a gas mask and all officers bearing side arms, clubs, and gas grenades, marched through the camp to carry out their order. The troops netted 25 tons of rice and other grains, 22 barrels of saké mash, 400 boxes of canned goods, 20 crates of dried fruit, 20 cartons of cereal, 2 saké stills, a Japanese-language printing press, 500 knives, 400 clubs, 2 public address systems, and 500 radio receivers.

To segregate their catch from the rest of the camp, the army erected in late November a stockade surrounded by barbed wire fence and guard towers, and within the stockade built two to five barracks and tents called the "bull pen" to chill out the incorrigibles. The bull pen, then, was a prison within the stockade within the concentration camp. The authorities drew up lists, methodically hunted down their quarry, and seized over 350 of them and tossed them into the stockade. Matsuda Kazue's brother, Yamane Tokio, was one of those who were arrested, beaten, denied medical attention, and locked in the bull pen for nine months. Flimsy and unheated, the tents offered scant protection from the elements that reached freezing temperatures in winter. With bunks set in the frozen ground and no extra clothing or blankets, living in the bull pen was "a life and death struggle for survival," Yamane testified. Matsuda pleaded with the authorities to release him, to transfer her husband who was being held in the Justice Department camp at Santa Fe, New Mexico, so he could see his dying mother and then, to attend her funeral all to no avail. The military transferred Yamane from Tule Lake to the Santa Fe alien detention center, despite his U.S. citizenship. He was among some 1,200 sent by the military from Tule Lake to Justice Department internment camps.

Beatings, such as the one administered to Yamane, were common in Tule Lake's interrogation rooms where fists and baseball bats were the preferred instruments of reason. A former security officer recalled with delight the night of terror on November 4, the day the tanks rumbled into camp. "None of the three Japs were unconscious but all three were groggy from the blows they received, especially the one . . . hit with the baseball bat," he began. These, the officer explained, had been picked up and taken to the administration building where they were ordered to lie on the floor. When they refused, "I knocked my Jap down with my fist. He stayed down but was not unconscious. [Q] hit his Jap over the head again with the baseball bat . . ." Later, during questioning, the officer had an "itching to take a sock at the Jap so I . . . hit a hard blow to the jaw with my fist. [He] went down and out. I reached down and shook him hard in an effort to revive him. I even grabbed him by the hair and shook his head. After about three minutes he came to." Meanwhile, screams could be heard coming from the back rooms. That night in all, 18 Japanese were "severely beaten with baseball bats," according to a deposition, and some required "hospitalization for several months and the mentality of one was impaired permanently as the result of the beating he had received" (Drinnon, 142–43).

Despite the military's repressive rule, an overwhelming number of Japanese continued to express confidence in the Daihyo Sha Kai through December 1943 even though the army refused to recognize them and held most of them in the stockade, segregated from the camp population. Toward the end of December and the start of January 1944, a series of events brought the standoff to a head. On the morning of December 30, Lt. Schaner, the stockade's warden, arbitrarily pulled two men, Tsuda and Yoshiyama, and ordered them to the bull pen. A few days earlier, Schaner had chosen them to be the spokesmen for the others in the stockade, and his actions seemed to demonstrate his absolute powers over the fates of his charges. In protest against Schaner's highhandedness, the men refused to assemble for the 1 P.M. roll call. If the men cleaned the stockade area and assembled for the evening roll call, Schaner promised, he would release Tsuda and Yoshiyama from the cage. The Japanese fulfilled their part of the bargain but by the next morning the pair had not been freed. So the men again refused to assemble for the morning roll call, but were forced from their barracks by armed troops later in the day.

Facing the assembled men, Schaner pointed to Uchida, and commanded that he join Tsuda and Yoshiyama in the bull pen. Then he challenged the Japanese. "Now if there are any more of you who would like to go with him, just step up towards the gate." After a moment's pause, one of them, Todoroki Koji, stepped forward and, according to an army eyewitness, there was a murmur among the men, followed by the entire group breaking ranks and moving in the direction of the gate. Frustrated, Schaner left the men standing in the snow for about three hours while he consulted with his commander, Austin, about his next step. "I was just waiting for that," Schaner told the men. "You men will be put on bread and water for twenty-four hours. You men will have to learn that we mean business and will not tolerate such a demonstration." Trucks then entered the stockade compound, and removed all stores of food. In addition, Schaner ordered a search of the stockade's barracks, which was undertaken "in a most unnecessary destructive method," in the words of a military observer. As a result, many personal items such as radios, pens, watches, cigarettes, and cash were stolen from the Japanese.

Provoked, the men vowed to go on a hunger strike until the release of everyone from the stockade. Tsuda explained, "The reason the men . . . are on this hunger strike is because they know not the reason they are in the stockade. They feel they have been unjustly confined and the reason given to them is that they are the potential troublemakers and strong arm men of the colony, which they feel is not true. This is the manner in which they are trying to prove their sincerity and show that they should be vindicated" (Okihiro, 78–79). The hunger strike lasted from January 1 to January 6, 1944 over the Japanese New Year, which carried religious and cultural significance, with no tangible concessions from the administrators. News of the hunger strike leaked out to the camp population on its third day, and instead of a general protest in support of the stockade hunger strikers, sentiment appeared to turn toward a swift compromise to reverse and bring to an end the escalating hostilities.

Some in the camp favored accepting the army's demand that the Daihyo Sha Kai must be disbanded and a new body elected to negotiate the end of martial law. Others argued supporting the Daihyo Sha Kai as the only and true representative of the people. Both supported their positions with appeals to Japanese, not American values, and both regretted the split in the ranks of an otherwise united people. The Daihyo Sha Kai had not shown a "true Japanese spirit," one argument went, by not resigning when they failed to dislodge the military from the camp. "We have no other desire than to exist as a true Japanese and to return to Japan unashamed," the appeal concluded. The other faction supported the Daihyo Sha Kai for exhibiting a "true Japanese spirit" by refusing to compromise with the army. "I surely hate to see the Japanese divided," said a stockade leader Inouye, "and hate to see them fighting with each other." Shimada explained the thinking on the outside: "Let me repeat this, the Army would not give a chance to talk about [the] release of you people [those in the stockade], unless normal condition was first returned." To which Inouye replied, "We realize all the things you people are going through and have told the men in the stockade that you people are working so hard for the common goal. We are just as worried as you people are" (Okihiro, 81).

On January 11, 1944, Tule Lake's Japanese voted, according to the official tally, 4,893 against the status quo, 4,120 for the status quo, and 228 undecided. The status quo meant retention of the Daihyo Sha Kai. The voting might have been influenced by the army's rounding up of Daihyo Sha Kai sympathizers the morning of the vote, and some claimed voting irregularities. A Japanese report claimed a true count of 31 blocks (a residential unit of barracks) for status quo, 29 against, four blocks undetermined, and one block abstained. Whatever the final tally, the vote showed a reluctance to repudiate the Daihyo Sha Kai and to concede the occupying Army's position despite the prospect of an end to martial law and the release of the men in the stockade. On January 15, the army returned the camp, except the stockade, to the WRA, and on May 23, 1944, control of the stockade reverted to the WRA, but tensions remained high. The following day, a Japanese was shot and killed by a guard following a minor altercation, and in June Tasaku Hitomi, a suspected collaborator, was found murdered. In August 1944, the stockade was closed. The WRA and Army, the U.S. state, had failed to extinguish completely the people's spirit of resistance.

Morgan Yamanaka remembered moving from Topaz to Tule Lake and noticing the difference. Although the fence and guard towers surrounded both camps, Yamanaka said, at Tule Lake the presence of the military was much more evident. Whenever something happened, he noted, "you came up against them . . . you felt the physical presence of the MPs." Yamanaka and his brother ended up in the stockade. He described the procedure for admittance into that prison within a prison. "We were herded into army trucks, and we were shoved into a room in the military barracks and we waited interminably. We were just squatting on the floor, no furniture. We were jam-packed on the floor for hours on end, and every so often one of us would be called." When he was finally called, Yamanaka was led down the hall and "placed in a dark room, shoved into a chair, and all of a sudden the light went on—classic third degree" (Tateishi, 114–15).

After his questioning, Yamanaka found himself sitting again on the floor in a crowded room. When they needed to go to the bathroom, the guard disregarded their pleas. "We called the MP and said we had to go," he recalled, "and his attitude was just, fuck you, don't pee on the floor" (Tateishi, 116). Someone offered him a boot to urinate in but he and the others simply held it. There were constant raids in the stockade barracks, Yamanaka remembered, to harass them. Once, he said, a young soldier pointing a submachine gun at his belly was quaking in his boots, scared stiff of the "troublemakers" in the stockade. Yamanaka thought he might pull the trigger out of fear, which then made him scared. At another time, the MPs ordered them out in the snow, standing only with underwear and flip-flops for three or five hours. The stood in a line facing a jeep with a machine gun pointed at them. That is when the men decided to go on a hunger strike, Yamanaka concluded.

Ben Takeshita, like Morgan Yamanaka, was transferred from Topaz to Tule Lake during segregation. He noticed at Tule Lake a greater stress on Japanese culture, including Japanese-language classes, which his older brothers started. Children learned Japanese ethics, respect for parents, and the history of Japan. During the "food riots, because there was not enough food," Takeshita said, a neighbor, Okamura, was shot. "He was a big guy, but so gentle," he remembered. A guard apparently felt he was being threatened when Okamura walked toward him, so "the guard shot him from about five feet away and killed him. The guard was charged with misuse of military property and fined fifty cents for the bullet. There was a court-martial, but he wasn't convicted of anything. There was tension because of this type of thing," Takeshita noted (Tateishi, 246–47).

His oldest brother, Takeshita said, was under suspicion because he promoted sports tournaments, which the WRA considered to be militaristic. They took him in, and questioned him for several days. They reached a point when they said, "'Okay, we're going to take you out.' And it was obvious that he was going before a firing squad with MPs ready with rifles." They asked him if he wanted a cigarette; he said no. They asked if he wanted a blindfold; he refused it. They stood him up, and went as far as saying, "'Ready, aim, fire,' and pulling the trigger, but the rifles had no bullets. They just went click . . ." When he heard that story, Takeshita recalled, "I really got mad." It was torture, he declared, "like the German camps" (Tateishi, 247). After the war, that brother left the United States and went to Japan to live.

Not content with the concentration camps as a solution to "disloyal" Japanese Americans, Attorney General Francis Biddle drafted legislation to allow a U.S. citizen to renounce that citizenship during wartime upon approval of the attorney general. Anti-Japanese groups like the Native Sons of the Golden West lobbied for such law, and on July 1, 1944, President Franklin Roosevelt signed Public Law 405 that legislated renunciation. It was difficult, especially during wartime, for citizens to renounce their U.S. citizenship, so Public Law 405 was unusual. Although 5,589 Japanese Americans took advantage of the law to renounce their U.S. citizenship between December 1944 and July 1945, with few exceptions, all of them were from Tule Lake where about 70 percent of the nisei over 18 years old renounced. Segregation was relevant to renunciation as well as conditions in the camp especially during the period of martial law and military repression.

Department of Justice teams visited Tule Lake in early 1945 to facilitate the process of renunciation. Japanese Americans who feared a future in the United States because of the prevailing anti-Japanese hatred and those who had lost faith in the nation and its promise of equality under the law were inclined to petition for renunciation. And parents who sought repatriation to Japan pressured their children to renounce their U.S. citizenship. As Morgan Yamanaka said, renunciation was a way of keeping the family together. As the year moved on, however, most of those who renounced their U.S. citizenship sought to withdraw their applications. They had second thoughts about that. San Francisco attorney Wayne M. Collins worked for the Tule Lake Defense Committee to stop the deportation of the renunciants because they signed under duress, Collins claimed. For 22 years those cases remained active in the courts, and of the 5,978 Japanese Americans who sought to invalidate their renunciation and have their U.S. citizenship restored, 5,409 won their suit. The last case was decided on March 6, 1968, long after the end of World War II and the alleged claim of "military necessity." Racism was surely evident in the campaign to remove U.S. citizenship from Japanese Americans and deport them from the United States.

Graffiti scribbled on a Tule Lake camp warehouse wall in Japanese offered a critique of the U.S. government's program of forced removal and confinement.

The world is not governed fairly.
Not a land of God, nor of Buddha, nor of the stars.
Longing for the stars.

And on the stockade wall, in English and Japanese:

Show me the way to go to home. (Burton, 300, 310)

Gary Y. Okihiro

References

Bailey, Paul. *City in the Sun: The Japanese Concentration Camp at Poston, Arizona*. Los Angeles: Westernlore Press, 1971.

Burton, Jeffery F. et al. *Confinement and Ethnicity: An Overview of World War II Japanese American Relocation Sites*, National Park Service, U.S. Department of the Interior, Publications in Anthropology 74. Tucson, Arizona: Western Archeological and Conservation Center, 1999.

Drinnon, Richard. *Keeper of Concentration Camps: Dillon S. Myer and American Racism*. Berkeley: University of California Press, 1987.

Embrey, Sue Kunitomi, Arthur A. Hansen, and Betty Kulberg Mitson (Eds.). *Manzanar Martyr: An Interview with Harry Y. Ueno*. Fullerton: Oral History Program, California State University, 1986.

Fiset, Louis. *Imprisoned Apart: The World War II Correspondence of an Issei Couple*. Seattle: University of Washington Press, 1997.

Fujino, Diane C. *Heartbeat of Struggle: The Revolutionary Life of Yuri Kochiyama*. Minneapolis: University of Minnesota Press, 2005.

Girdner, Audrie and Anne Loftis. *The Great Betrayal: The Evacuation of the Japanese-Americans during World War II*. Toronto: Macmillan, 1969.

Hirano, Kiyo. *Enemy Alien*. San Francisco: JAM Publications, 1983.

Levine, Ellen. *A Fence Away from Freedom: Japanese Americans and World War II*. New York: G. P. Putnam's Sons, 1995.

Nishimoto, Richard S. *Inside an American Concentration Camp: Japanese American Resistance at Poston, Arizona*. Tucson: University of Arizona Press, 1995.

Okihiro, Gary Y. "Tule Lake Under Martial Law: A Study in Japanese Resistance." *Journal of Ethnic Studies* 5:3 (1977): 71–85.

Okubo, Miné. *Citizen 13660*. New York: Columbia University Press, 1946.

Tateishi, John. *And Justice for All: An Oral History of the Japanese American Detention Camps*. New York: Random House, 1984.

Taylor, Sandra C. *Jewel of the Desert: Japanese American Internment at Topaz*. Berkeley: University of California Press, 1993.

Uchida, Yoshiko. *Desert Exile: The Uprooting of a Japanese-American Family*. Seattle: University of Washington Press, 1982.

WAR RELOCATION AUTHORITY (WRA) CITIZEN ISOLATION CENTERS

The War Relocation Authority (WRA), following the Manzanar riot of December 1942, set up an abandoned Civilian Conservation Corps (CCC) camp at Dalton Wells near Moab, Utah, to serve as an isolation center for "troublemakers." Japanese Americans chosen for isolation depended solely upon the discretion and whim of each WRA concentration camp's director.

Moab

The Moab isolation center opened in January 11, 1943, when 16 men from Manzanar concentration camp arrived. The isolation center had no fence, and was divided into an administration area, support buildings, and barracks. Within a few months, the WRA sent others from Manzanar and other camps to the isolation center. A dozen or so came from concentration camps at Gila River, Arizona, others from Jerome and Rohwer, Arkansas, and about 15, from Tule Lake, California. At its peak, the Moab facility held 49 men. Moab closed on April 27, 1943, when its Japanese Americans were taken by bus to Leupp, Arizona.

A Moab guard, called by the Japanese Americans "Seamy" because his first rule was "see me" before doing anything, was especially overbearing. He made rules such as no Japanese language permitted, English only, and no talking with others across barracks. Japanese Americans could only speak with those in their barracks. He then said that anyone violating his rules would be jailed for three months. That threat prompted 20 Japanese Americans to challenge the guard by daring him to put them all in jail. The guard hesitated, and later, he arbitrarily picked a handful of men to put in the Moab county jail.

Special punishment was meted out to the five or six held in Moab's Grand County jail, which included Harry Ueno, the central figure of the Manzanar uprising. The six were locked in a four-by-six-foot box with a two-by-two-foot hole for air on the back of a pickup truck for the 13-hour ride to Leupp that passed through Utah, Colorado, New Mexico, and Arizona. The road was "pretty rough," Ueno said, and it was "Hot! Humid! We really had a hard ride!" The truck made about ten stops before arriving at Leupp on April 28, 1943 (Embrey et al., 74).

Leupp

An abandoned American Indian boarding school on the Navajo Reservation supplied the facilities for the WRA isolation center at Leupp, Arizona. A fenced off area in Leupp was devoted to the "incorrigibles" who were held in an isolated area of the camp. A few, including Harry Ueno, were placed in the Winslow town jail for three or four days. The days were hot but the nights were freezing, Ueno noted, and they had to ask for additional blankets. From the Winslow town jail, the men were removed to the jail in Leupp where at one time about 150 military police guarded 45 to 50 Japanese Americans whose numbers rose and fell. Unlike Moab, Leupp had a barbed-wire fence and four guard towers.

After hearings, Ueno and about five others were sent to Tule Lake concentration camp. Others returned to Manzanar, and FBI agents spirited a few away to other camps. Even Leupp's head of internal security wrote that the WRA's classification of the men as dangerous was certainly questionable. The Leupp camp was closed on December 2, 1943, and a train took the remaining 71 Japanese Americans to Tule Lake concentration camp.

Gary Y. Okihiro

Reference

Embrey, Sue Kunitomi, Arthur A. Hansen, Betty Kulberg Mitson (Eds.). *Manzanar Martyr: An Interview with Harry Y. Ueno.* Fullerton: Oral History Program, California State University, Fullerton, 1986.

PRIMARY DOCUMENTS

Document 1

"MY LAST DAY AT HOME": A STUDENT WRITES OF JAPANESE INTERNMENT

A Japanese American student writes of being removed to a concentration camp during World War II.

Chieko Hirata
Period II, English I

My Last Day at Home
The month of May when I was attending school, all the residents of Hood River county, as well as the people of the whole western coast was surprised to receive such an unexpected order of evacuation.

Promptly after hearing about the order I with my folks went to register and then for a brief physical examination. Then I helped my folks pack and prepared to leave my dear home on May 13, 1942.

On May 8, 1942 I withdrew from Parkdale Grade School, where all my friends and teachers bid me farewell with sorrowful face and tears. Our packing never seem to cease, we kept on packing then finally we were finished. Then came May 13th, my most dreaded day which I shall never forget the rest of my life. On the afternoon of the 13th, I board the train headed for Pinedale, California.

On the night of the 15th we arrived. The weather was pretty hot. In Pinedale I lived in the D-section which had forty barracks, which had vie apartments to a barrack.

I stayed at the Pinedale Assembly Center about two months. Then around July 15, 1942 we received our order to evacuate for Tule Lake. Then on July 18th we evacuated for Tule Lake and spent a night on the train. I arrived in Tule Lake. At present I am living in Block 58. The residents of this block is most Tacoma folks which I am not very much acquainted with as yet. Being that my cousin lives in Block 57 I am always visiting them.

I am always hoping that this war will end, so that I will be able to go back to Parkdale, my home town and see all my old friends, and live to my dying days in my old home in Parkdale, Oregon.

Herbert Yoshikawa
Japanese and the Post War Period

When we came to this camp it was still a period of confusion and uncertainty. Now, after settling down, one of the questions uppermost in our minds is that of finding jobs after the war.

Source: "My Last Day at Home," by Herbert Yoshikawa, n.d. [National Archives]

Document 2

THE RINGLE REPORT

Kenneth D. Ringle was a naval intelligence officer who was the Navy's leading spe-cialist on Japanese Americans. Ringle spent from 1928 to 1931 in Japan learning the Japanese language, and in 1940 was assigned to Los Angeles where he investigated the "Japanese question." His report, the Ringle Report, was addressed to the chief of Naval Operations, and bore no date but must have been written after January 20, 1942. Ringle's report agreed with other intelligence reports of the time, and it contends, before the mass eviction of Japanese Americans from the West Coast, that the removal and detention of some 120,000 Japanese Americans was unjustified on the basis of "mili-tary necessity."

That within the last eight or ten years the entire "Japanese question" in the United States has reversed itself. The alien menace is no longer paramount, and is becoming of less importance almost daily, as the original alien immigrants grow older and die, and as more and more of their American-born children reach matu-rity. The primary present and future problem is that of dealing with these Amer-ican-born United States citizens of Japanese ancestry, of whom it is considered that [at] least seventy-five per cent are loyal to the United States. The ratio of these American citizens of Japanese ancestry to alien-born Japanese in the United States is at present almost 3 to 1, and rapidly increasing.

That of the Japanese-born alien residents, the large majority are at least pas-sively loyal to the United States. That is, they would knowingly do nothing what-ever to the injury of the United States, but at the same time would not do anything to the injury of Japan. Also, most of the remainder would not engage in active sab-otage or insurrection, but might well do surreptitious observation work for Japa-nese interests if given a convenient opportunity.

That, however, there are among the Japanese both alien and United States citi-zens, certain individuals, either deliberately placed by the Japanese government or actuated by a fanatical loyalty to that country, who would act as saboteurs or agents. This number is estimated to be less than three per cent of the total, or about 3500 in the entire United States.

That of the persons mentioned . . . above, the most dangerous are either already in custodial detention or are members of such organizations as the Black Dragon Society, the Kaigun Kyokai (Navy League), or the Heimusha Kai (Military Service Men's League), or affiliated groups. The membership of these groups is already fairly well known to the Naval Intelligence Service or the Federal Bureau of Inves-tigation and should immediately be placed in custodial detention, irrespective of whether they are alien or citizen.

That, as a basic policy tending toward the permanent solution of this problem, the American citizens of Japanese ancestry should be officially encouraged in their efforts toward loyalty and acceptance as bona fide citizens; that they be accorded a place in the national effort through such agencies as the Red Cross, U.S.O., civilian defense, and even such activities as ship and aircraft building or other defense production activities, even though subject to greater investigative checks as to background and loyalty, etc., than Caucasian Americans.

That in spite of paragraph . . . above, the most potentially dangerous element of all are those American citizens of Japanese ancestry who have spent the formative years of their lives, from 10 to 20, in Japan and have returned to the United States to claim their legal American citizenship within the last few years. These people are essentially and inherently Japanese and may have been deliberately sent back to the United States by the Japanese government to act as agents. In spite of their legal citizenship and the protection afforded them by the Bill of Rights, they should be looked upon as enemy aliens and many of them placed in custodial detention. This group numbers between 600 and 700 in the Los Angeles metropolitan area and at least that many in other parts of Southern California.

That the writer heartily agrees with the reports submitted by Mr. Munson . . . . [N.B. Curtis B. Munson was a businessman who served as an intelligence agent for the White House. His report of November 1941 was submitted to President Franklin Roosevelt, who received a summary, and Secretary of War Henry Stimson, who received the entire report. Munson agreed with Ringle's assessment of Japanese American loyalty, except to contend a few were disloyal and could sabotage vital installations like dams, bridges, and power stations.]

That, in short, the entire "Japanese problem" has been magnified out of its true proportion, largely because of the physical characteristics of the people; that it is no more serious than the problems of the German, Italian, and Communistic portions of the United States population, and, finally that it should be handled on the basis of the individual, regardless of citizenship, and not on a racial basis.

[In retrospect, on February 21, 1952, Ringle wrote: "The service intelligence services, local police, immigration and other Federal agencies had been observing these people for many years and compiling records on many individuals. In the Los Angeles area, where there was the greatest concentration in the United States, some four hundred and fifty dangerous persons, including all the pro-Japanese leaders so far as was known, were arrested as individuals before midnight on 7 December 1941 and were interned. Where then was the potential danger that made it necessary to intern every other person of Japanese ancestry in the Spring of 1942? This I can say with authority. In later careful investigations on both the West Coast and Hawaii, there was never a shred of evidence found of sabotage, subversive acts, spying, or fifth column activity on the part of the Nisei or long-time local residents . . . . I reported officially in 1941 that it was my considered opinion that better than 90% of the Nisei and 75% of the original immigrants were completely loyal to the United States." (Cited in Roger Daniels, Asian America: Chinese and Japanese in the United States since 1850, 210–11. Seattle: University of Washington Press, 1988.)]

Source: Lieutenant Commander K. D. Ringle to The Chief of Naval Operations. Subject: Japanese Question. Japanese Internment and Relocation: The Hawaii Experience. University of Hawai'i, Hamilton Library, Special Collections, Box 1.

Document 3

EXECUTIVE ORDER 9066

On February 19, 1942, President Franklin Roosevelt signed Executive Order 9066, which authorized the mass removal and confinement of Japanese Americans from the West Coast. He, according to his assistant secretary of war, instructed the military to "go ahead and do anything you think necessary," but, he admonished, "be as reasonable as you can."

EXECUTIVE ORDER
AUTHORIZING THE SECRETARY OF WAR
TO PRESCRIBE MILITARY AREAS

WHEREAS the successful prosecution of the war requires every possible protection against espionage and against sabotage to national-defense material, national-defense premises, and national-defense utilities. . . .

NOW, THEREFORE, by virtue of the authority vested in me as President of the United States, and Commander in Chief of the Army and Navy, I hereby authorize and direct the Secretary of War, and the Military Commanders whom he may from time to time designate, whenever he or any designated Commander deems such action necessary or desirable, to prescribe military areas in such places and of such extent as he or the appropriate Military Commander may determine, from which any and all persons may be excluded, and with respect to which, the right of any person to enter, remain in, or leave shall be subject to whatever restrictions the Secretary of War or the appropriate Military Commander may impose in his discretion. The Secretary of War is hereby authorized to provide for residents of any such area who are excluded therefrom, such transportation, food, shelter, and other accommodations as may be necessary, in the judgment of the Secretary of War or the said Military Commander, and until other arrangements are made, to accomplish the purpose of this order. The designation of military areas in any region or locality shall supersede designations of prohibited and restricted areas by the Attorney General under the Proclamations of December 7 and 8, 1941, and shall supersede the responsibility and authority of the Attorney General under the said Proclamations in respect of such prohibited and restricted areas.

I thereby further authorize and direct the Secretary of War and the said Military Commanders to take such other steps as he or the appropriate Military Commander may deem advisable to enforce compliance with the restrictions applicable to each Military area hereinabove authorized to be designated, including the use of Federal troops and other Federal Agencies, with authority to accept assistance of state and local agencies.

I hereby further authorize and direct all Executive Departments, independent establishments and other Federal Agencies, to assist the Secretary of War or the said Military Commanders in carrying out this Executive Order, including the furnishing of medical aid, hospitalization, food, clothing, transportation, use of land, shelter, and other supplies, equipment, utilities, facilities, and services.

This order shall not be construed as modifying or limiting in any way the authority heretofore granted under Executive Order No. 8972, dated December 12, 1941, nor shall it be construed as limiting or modifying the duty and responsibility of the Federal Bureau of Investigation, with respect to the investigation of alleged acts of sabotage or the duty and responsibility of the Attorney General and the Department of Justice under the Proclamations of December 7 and 8, 1941, prescribing regulations for the conduct and control of alien enemies, except as such duty and responsibility is superseded by the designation of military areas hereunder.

[Franklin Delano Roosevelt, signature]

THE WHITE HOUSE,
February 19, 1942.

Source: Code of Federal Regulations, title 3, sec. 1092 (1938–1943).

Document 4
PUBLIC LAW 503

Public Law 503, enacted by the Congress in March 1942, implemented Executive Order 9066.

Seventy-seventh Congress of the United States of America;
At the Second Session
Begun and held at the City of Washington on Monday, the fifth day of January, one thousand nine hundred and forty-two
An Act
To provide a penalty for violation of restrictions or orders with respect to persons entering, remaining in, leaving, or committing any act in military areas or zones.
Be it enacted by the Senate and House of Representatives of the United States of America assembled, That whoever shall enter, remain in, leave, or commit any act in any military area or military zone prescribed, under the authority of an Executive order of the President, by the Secretary of War, or by any military commander designated by the Secretary of War, contrary to the restrictions applicable to any such area or zone or contrary to the order of the Secretary of War or such military commander, shall, if it appears that he knew or should have known of the existence and the extent of the restrictions or order and that his act was in violation

thereof, be guilty of a misdemeanor and upon conviction shall be liable to a fine not to exceed $5,000 or to imprisonment for not more than one year, or both, for each offense.

Sam Rayburn
Speaker of the House of Representatives

Carter Glass
President of the Senate pro tempore

Approved, March 21, 1942

Source: Public Law 503, March 21, 1942. National Archives

Document 5

LETTER FROM TEACHER TO STUDENT

Letter from a teacher to a student and her family that had been forcibly removed in 1942.

EMERSON JUNIOR HIGH SCHOOL
1650 Selby Avenue
West Los Angeles, California
April 6, 1942

Dear Mrs. Honda and Family:

I do wish to thank you for your lovely gifts that you have sent through Rose. It seems so difficult at this time to express ourselves as we really feel. We understand how difficult it must be to give up all you have accumulated here in West Los Angeles, both as to friendships and as to material belongings.

However we can remember all the gracious things that you have done. It has reaped its reward in our school as it has helped build up a fine spirit in our Japanese pupils. We can only hope, further, that although they will be dispersed in various states they will still continue to be Emersonians loyal to all our ideals.

Thank you again. We wish that you may not have to stay away long. Rose was doing so well. It must be that she can come back soon to do the things that a girl of her ability and personality is able to do.

Sincerely yours,
Ruth Brockhouse

Source: Letter from Ruth Brockhouse of Emerson Junior High School to the Honda family. April 6, 1942. National Park Service.

Document 6

INSTRUCTIONS TO ALL PERSONS OF JAPANESE ANCESTRY

Under the authority granted by EO 9066, the army established military zones, and informed their Japanese American residents of their forcible removal. These signs were posted in public places in the spring of 1942 as "Instructions to All Persons of Japanese Ancestry," which included men and women, young and old with a drop of "Japanese blood."

[The first part of "Instructions" specifies the area or neighborhood from which "all persons of Japanese ancestry" had to vacate. It also gave the address to where all Japanese Americans had to report.]

The Following Instructions Must Be Observed:

1. A responsible member of each family, preferably the head of the family, or the person in whose name most of the property is held, and each individual living alone, will report to the Civil Control Station to receive further instructions. This must be done between 8:00 A.M. and 5:00 P.M. on Monday, May 4, 1942, or between 8:00 A.M. and 5:00 P.M. on Tuesday, May 5, 1942.

2. Evacuees must carry with them on departure for the Assembly Center, the following property:

    (a) Bedding and linens (no mattress) for each member of the family;

    (b) Toilet articles for each member of the family;

    (c) Extra clothing for each member of the family;

    (d) Sufficient knives, forks, spoons, plates, bowls and cups for each member of the family;

    (e) Essential personal effects for each member of the family. All items carried will be securely packaged, tied and plainly marked with the name of the owner and numbered in accordance with instructions obtained at the Civil Control Station. The size and number of packages is limited to that which can be carried by the individual or family group.

3. No pets of any kind will be permitted.

4. No personal items and no household goods will be shipped to the Assembly Center.

5. The United States Government through its agencies will provide for the storage, at the sole risk of the owner, of the more substantial household items, such as iceboxes, washing machines, pianos and other heavy furniture. Cooking utensils and other small items will be accepted for

storage if crated, packed and plainly marked with the name and address of the owner. Only one name and address will be used by a given
family.

6. Each family, and individual living alone, will be furnished transportation
to the Assembly Center or will be authorized to travel by private automo-
bile in a supervised group. All instructions pertaining to the movement
will be obtained at the Civil Control Station.

Go to the Civil Control Station between the hours of 8:00 A.M. and 5:00 P.M.,
Monday, May 4, 1942, or between the hours of 8:00 A.M. and 5:00 P.M., Tuesday,
May 5, 1942, to receive further instructions.

J. L. DeWITT
Lieutenant General, U.S. Army
Commanding

Source: Unrau, Harlan D. *The Evacuation and Relocation of Persons of Japanese Ancestry during World War II: A Historical Study of the Manzanar War Relocation Center.*
United States Department of the Interior, National Park Service. 1996.

Document 7
LETTERS OF A COUPLE INTERNED APART

*Iwao and Hanaye Matsushita were issei (first generation Japanese Americans) who were
separated by the doctrine of "military necessity" during World War II. Iwao Matsushita
was interned by the Immigration and Naturalization Service as an "enemy alien" at Fort
Missoula, Montana while his wife, Hanaye Matsushita, was confined in the War Relocation Authority's Minidoka concentration camp in Idaho. Their letters reveal the pain of
that separation instigated and enforced by the U.S. government. Iwao Matsushita was
born on January 10, 1892, to Christian parents, while Hanaye was born on March 9,
1898, and because of poverty, her parents left her at an orphanage. Her adoptive parents
reared her in the Christian faith, and sent her to a private, Christian school in Tokyo.
Hanaye married Iwao on January 22, 1919, and they sailed for Seattle, Washington, in
August of that year. At the time, Japanese Americans totaled about 3 percent of Seattle's
population, and Iwao worked as a cook, lodging house manager, and Japanese-language
schoolteacher. He landed a job with the Japanese firm Mitsui and Company, and prospered with the interwar business boom with the Asian trade accounting for over 70 percent of Seattle's total import and export business. The couple bought a house in 1927, and
Iwao taught Japanese-language classes at the University of Washington. Matsushita was
a wealthy man on the eve of World War II. After 20 years with Mitsui and Company, he
tendered his resignation in 1940, citing his original passion to study English and English
literature at the University of Washington. In his resignation letter, Matsushita wrote: "I*

enjoy my life in Seattle. I have so many happy memories with nice people—both Japanese and Americans. Especially I enjoy photography and mountain climbing. I have visited Mt. Rainier, my lover, more than 190 times. I cannot leave Seattle when I think of the beautiful views of Mount Rainier."

[Note: These letters were censored. Forbidden and removed were details of the camp, names of internees, and words and phrases, which censors believed contained hidden messages. Japanese American letter writers knew of that practice, and they wrote their letters with the censors' eyes in mind.]

[The letters begin on December 11, 1941 with Iwao Matsushita's apprehension and detention at Seattle's Immigration Station from where he writes: "We are very comfortable here at the Immigration station . . . . We have many friends here & not very lonesome at all." On December 28, 1941, Matsushita writes to his wife to inform her of his arrival at Fort Missoula in Montana following a train ride. "The ground is covered with patches of snow & surrounding mountains are salt-and-peppery. The temperature is freezing & very dry. Please don't worry & take good care of yourself."]

[On January 3, 1942, Iwao Matsushita writes to "My dear wife":]

We had a famous Montana blizzard on the 30th evening, but the next day, we had spotless blue sky & bright sunshine. The surrounding undulating hills covered with powder snow were really tempting. Toward evening the full moon was high in the eastern mountains, which was made purple by the setting sun. What a magnificent view it was! I wished I could have seen this scenery with you.

The New Year's day was again bright, but the temperature registered 20 below zero, which means 52 below freezing point. But don't lose your heart, because we really don't feel so cold as you might when you hear about this in Seattle.

We are now accustomed to the temperature here, & when it snows it usually is *warm*—around 10 above zero. . . .

So please don't worry about my life here, but pray for our happy meeting in the future. Take good care of yourself, & write me sometimes.

Your loving husband Iwao Matsushita.

[On January 8, 1942, Hanaye Matsushita writes:]

My dear husband:

I have received your letters on January 2nd, Friday morning. Am glad to hear from you and thankful to the people who are very kind to you over there. I wish you to be healthy and to trust in God. Keep calm and be in good spirit. This coming 10th is your birthday. Wish you many happy returns from all my heart, especially this year.

I am living fine and healthy. Since you have left, I gained 3 pounds. I am still taking daily cod liver oil which doctor gave to me. Don't worry about me please. I can manage myself no matter what happens. I am doing things businesslike little by little. I hope peace will come all over the world very soon. Everybody are very kind to me. Pray God day and night. If you want money let me know without hesitate.

Wishing you good health.
Lovingly, Your wife

[In August 1942, Hanaye Matsushita was forcibly removed from her Seattle home and confined in the assembly center at Puyallup, Washington. Later, she was taken to Minidoka concentration camp. She wrote to her husband on August 20, 1942, "My dear husband":]

On the 15th we left Puyallup and arrived here around four in the afternoon on the 16th. The doctors will stay in Puyallup until the 28th or 29th of next month. Or, at the worst, they'll be sent somewhere else. I'm resigned to try living a bachelor's life. Aunt Kaneko and I are doing well living together. I owe a lot to her. Two or three single women will move in nearby since there are not enough living quarters to go around. . . .

It's unendurably hot and dusty, though eventually I'll get used to it. My body is weak and can only stand so much. I pray to God for strength and tolerance. At times like this I wish day and night for your quick return. . . .

I have many things to tell you, but in the afternoons I am worthless because of the horrible heat. When I dwell on this situation, I have suicidal feelings, but I've got to keep myself together until your return. I imagine you're also experiencing rough times. I have come to understand what it's like to live alone in this world. People tease me, calling me the Montana widow. . . .

I can hear the violent winds blowing across the wide plains. In the distance I hear the sound of sagebrush blowing in the wind, rattlesnakes, and the howling of coyotes.

I'm thankful to this country that we can live here in safety. The soldiers stand guard day and night. I shed tears of sympathy for them standing in the scorching afternoon heat and the evenings that are so cold as to require lighting a fire, for each soldier is someone's son. At night a crescent moon shines brightly, the grandiosity of nature brings tears to my eyes. I need to focus my mind on something. I'll ponder God's benevolence.

The house we are living in now is built for winter and equipped with a new coal stove so we won't die of the cold. We eat at the cafeteria.

Our boxes have yet to arrive, so we have no tables or chairs. I am writing this letter on my lap. We should be settled in a few days. I anxiously await your next letter and pray that your day of return comes soon. Take care of your health. I'll write again.

Hana

[A concerned Iwao wrote back to his wife on August 25, 1942.]

Dear Hanaye,

I was happy to receive word of your safe move. I studied the map the other day and learned that you were located far south of us. I imagine it's very hot there. Once you've become used to it, it shouldn't be too bad. Take care of your health, that's of the primary importance.

The number in the camp is gradually diminishing as people are transferred or released to the "outside." It probably won't be long now. My fate is entirely unknown. Be prepared for the worst, should that happen. [censored] is being transferred, too.

As I have said many times, if you remember that there are many others who are worse off, we'll be able to give thanks no matter what may befall us. If we trust in the Lord, even if we are left alone in the wilderness, we'll not feel any loneliness.

With the lessening population, my chore days come almost daily. However, meals continue to get better. For example, for breakfast we have hot cakes, corn flakes, bologna, and pears, and for dinner miso salmon, cucumber pickles, miso pork, and mixed rice. It's sumptuous. We have movies twice a week. I was reminded of the old days when I saw *Sun Valley Serenade* and *Charley's Aunt.*

Reports from other camps indicate that apparently there aren't places that are as good as Missoula. No word can describe the air of the highlands. Snow is still left on Mount Lolo. To be sure, they say there are lots of fireflies in the forest of Louisiana.

My regards to Aunt Kaneko. I'll write again. Please take care.
Iwao

[Hanaye wrote on September 1, 1942:]

My dear husband:

I received your letter and postcard and am happy to hear that you're doing well. We've finally settled in. It's been cold enough in the mornings and evenings to use the stove. . . .

Aunt has been of great help.

The place where we currently stay has a good view. At night I can hear the rush of the Snake River. It flows rapidly and is apparently quite dangerous. I can see the green grasses on the riverbank. The mornings are especially tranquil.

Uncle should arrive around Friday together with patients. . . .

I feel safe and assured that you'll return soon. Whatever happens, I'll remain calm, so please don't worry. Everyone moving here from Puyallup should be here by Friday. This is going to be a big place. They're constructing a large hospital and building houses throughout the day in preparation for the winter. The well water is drinkable though it's a bit hard. Since last week I've been able to boil water for laundry.

It seems like only yesterday when we went picking *matsutake* mushrooms at the end of August last year. It all seems like a dream. . . .

Hiroshi Tada has been sent to a Tacoma hospital with a head-related illness that may be a result of depression. It's really too bad. I am praying for his quick revival. When I feel hopeless and that all is lost, I think of your homecoming to boost my spirits.

Sorry to be using a pencil but I gave Uncle my ink. I hear that snow has fallen in the mountains. I reminisce and wait expectantly for the day when we can sit together in peace and quiet. Peaceful days will return. I pray for everyone's happiness. Take care of yourself. I pray for your safety until the day we can see each other again.

Hana

[Hanaye and Iwao Matsushita were finally reunited at Minidoka concentration camp on January 11, 1944. There they remained until August 7, 1945, when Iwao returned to Seattle to reestablish a home and job while Hanaye stayed at Minidoka because of her fragile health. Hanaye left Minidoka on October 2, 1945, and rejoined her husband in Seattle. Hanaye believed her ill health, her thinning hair, and the onset of cancer was in part due to the longstanding anxiety caused by her wartime experience. Hanaye passed away on February 3, 1965, at the age of 66. Iwao followed Hanaye when he died quietly on December 17, 1979.]

Source: Fiset, Louis. *Imprisoned Apart: The World War II Correspondence of an Issei Couple.* Seattle: University of Washington Press, 1997, pp. 25, 113, 114, 117, 118, 167, 168.

Document 8

"THE FENCE" BY AN EVACUEE (1943)

A firsthand account of living inside the fenced compound at a Japanese American concentration camp during World War II.

HEART MOUNTAIN RELOCATION CENTER
Community Analysis Section

August 11, 1943

The Fence By an Evacuee
"The barbed wire fences are to keep cattle outside." a man who was eating at my side in a mess hall said. "So I would not sign the petition to Washington".

But most everybody else signed the petition asking no fence be erected around the center. There appeared at that time in the Sentinel a strong editorial condemning the fence. The petition was forwarded to Washington. No answer. No explanation by our WRA officials either. The barbed wire fence was erected in spite of such a protest—without any explanation. Yet some kept on believing the fence was to keep the cattle out, until they saw watch towers being built and soldiers in them. Then even their creditity was dashed to pieces.

"Why these fences when we never think of leaving the center?" some asked.

When the evacuees were moved from Pomona Assembly Center and from the one at Santa Anita where their freedom was nil, they were made to believe that at the Relocation Center which is located outside of the western military zone their freedom of action will be mostly restored. So their disappointment was indeed acute when they first found out that they could not go to the towns of Cody and Powell even for shopping, then saw the barbed wire fences going up and the watch towers at strategic places built.

99 out of 100 wondered "Why all these restrictions." Then resentment followed.

I think the above took place in November some time 1942. Then one day, a group of women crept outside of the fence on the southern side and ventured to the dump yard to pick up old wires to use them for artificial flower making. (They could not buy wires at the stores. The Heart Mountain center having been opened in a desert that had been bare of any junk piles, wires or any metallic materials. Artificial flower making was at its height and there were about 3 instructors to teach women folk the art.) Well, these few women were busy in picking wires from old lettuce crates etc. when suddenly a jeep approached and M P. put them in it and took them to the guard house and they were kept there some time (some say over night, I do not know whether it was so). People were indignant.

One day a group of children, some of whom were as young as four years old, approached the watch tower (in broad daylight) at the north-western corner of the center and passed it a few steps and were indulged in playing there. After several whistle blowing to caution the children to trace back inside the tower which they apparently did not understand, M.P. came and hustled the children in a jeep and took them to the guard house and kept them there until Mr. Robertson came and rescued them (I think our clock chairman reported the incident to a block meeting).

Then a shooting of an evacuee by a M.P. at Topaz was reported in newspapers because the evacuee approached the wire fence too closely. Then it downed on even very credulous souls that the army meant business when they set up the fence. When young children go too close the fence, mothers would shout at the top of their voice "Don't go there. Come back".

Sometime in February 1943 Mr. Barber, the former Community Service Dept. Head, came to visit our center. (He works in the Washington WRA office). Surrounding him, we—block chairmen and a few leaders—had a tea party. Everyone asked Mr. Barber one and the same question: "Why this restriction? At Amache relocation center, evacuees could go to a neighboring town very freely. Why the same freedom not given to us in H.M.?" "Well," Mr. Barber answered "someone in Cody overheard a couple men were saying 'if I see a Jap in the town, I will shoot and kill him". "We are cautious. Hence this restriction etc."

Late in May the Victory Garden on the western side of the center was opened. Then Mr. Todd announced that Victory gardeners could stay outside the fence till sundown. Everyone was eager to take advantage of the extended time limit and went out in evenings. The towers around the center are now empty until about nine o'clock P.M. Guards in day time were removed to outer towers. Now people seem to have forgotten that the wire fences still stand. They do not seem to mind. The fences are lost from gossiping lips.

A few Japanese-Americans visited this center the other day. They said "These watch towers are bad. The relocation centers at Poston and Gila have no fences even. What are these menacing guard towers for?"

In going to Cody and Powell, evacuees will be questioned by M.P. and mist show passes. As far as the evacuees are concerned, this procedure is not very humiliating to comply with. But American people passing on the scene come to think of the evacuees more and more in the terms of internees. No wonder that the city councils of Cody and Powell have passed the resolutions limiting our visiting of their cities. The fact evacuees are under the glaring lights of watch towers and they are questioned by M.P. every time they go out of the camp must make outsiders think we are internees. There is no question of this interfering with the relocation of the evacuees, because people outside think we are dangerous characters. This interferes with the carrying out of the main purpose of the Relocation Center—relocation.

I am one of the residents and am familiar with psychological movements of the fellow residents. And I think there will be no trouble inside the center in future big enough to need the presence of military police. Let Japanese police assume all the responsibility the military police is now functioning. It will remove the stigma of concentration camp from our relocation center. It will relieve many soldiers from here to an active service. Neighboring towns would open their doors wide for the evacuees.

If Japanese-American boys are good to serve the U.S. army, (and they are) they should be good enough to assume the duty of police works in the WRA camp (my opinion).

In connection with this assumption of duties by the Nisei, I want to say further—that all the important duties now assumed by the Administrative officers (Caucasian), should be transferred to the Niseis (except the positions of the project directors and a few others). The evacuees are criticized for being irresponsible, negligent, and not quite honest in discharging their duties in the center. Why? because we evacuees are depended on the Government. Our psychology is "Let Uncle Sam do it". Way down in our psychology is that consciousness that injustice was done to the Japanese-Americans in evacuation and relocation. That is perhaps the reason why boys on the Agricultural project is not efficient. Carpenters and plumbers are not efficient. Now Caucasian supervisors assume responsibilities for their being inefficient.

The center will be better in every respect.

Source: Essay, "The Fence," by an evacuee, August 11, 1943. National Archives.

Document 9
BEAUTY SCHOOL PROGRAM

Program from a show put on by the Manzanar Beauty School, April 21, 1944. They may have lost their freedom and privacy, but many women at Manzanar never lost pride in their appearance. To encourage female internees to sign up for its new spring term, the Manzanar Beauty School, presented a program called Today's Coiffure, showcasing the current hair styles from Career Girl, to High School to Sports looks.

MANZANAR
BEAUTY SCHOOL
HAIR STYLE SHOW
TIME 730 PM ADM 10¢
APRIL 21 1944 FLOOR 2
MANZANAR BEAUTY SCHOOL
announces a new school
term beginning May 15,
1944
Register at 7- 1-1
Adult Education Department
The Program of training provides theory and practice in:
Manicuring
Hand and Arm Bleach
Hand and Arm Massage
Marcelling and all Iron Curls
Permanent Waving
Shampooing and All
Wet Curls
Facials
Scalp Treatments
Dye and Bleach
Hair Cutting
Oral, Written and Practical Tests
Instructions and Lectures on Sanitation, Sterilization and Skin
and Scalp Diseases
Ethics, Salesmanship,
Courtesy and Conduct
Enroll now for the new term!!!
MANZANAR BEAUTY SCHOOL
PRESENTS
TODAY'S COIFFURE
Greetings..Dr. Genevieve W. Carter
The Beauty School............................ ..Dorothy Yamamoto
Commentator......................................Toshiko Nakamura

Vocal Number
Models and Today's Coiffure—
Spring Parade.....................................Mary Jean Kramer
Margaret Yamane
Hideko Minabe
Natsuko Fujimoto
Elizabeth Yamane
Echo Coto
Mey Kakehashi
Children... Arlene Kurokawa
Kinuyo Okamoto
Virginia Ann Carter
Nancy Feil
Junior High School...............................Yoko Ando
Naomi Inouye
High School.....................................Junko Yoshimoto
Rosie Hanawa
Mitoso Kuramoto
Sports...Yoshiko Kusunoki
Elizabeth Moxley
Alice Hama
Natsu Nishimori
Career Girl.......................................Oma Umhey
Masako Matsuo
Echo Coto
Mother and Daughter.........................Mesako Kurokawa and Daughter
Florence Kawasumi and Daughter
Sub-Debs.......................................Lilliam Uyemura
Rosie Maruki
Matrons...Masako Kinoshita
Chiyo Yato
Bessie Murray
Formals...Natsuko Fujimoto
Kiyo Kusunoki
Karie Shindo
Michiko Sakamoto
Diane Tani
Jane Tsuda
Mary Wada
Sachi Yamada
Teruko Yonai
Kiyo Yoshida
Hideko Matsuno
Masako Kimura
Skit...High School Drama Class

Bridal Procession
Flower Girl......................................Emy Okamoto
Bridesmaids....................................Riyo Nakamura
Jane Tsuda
Maid of Honor................................Mary Aoki
Bride...Lily Yokota
****
Vocalists.......................................Henry Kano
Mary Kageyama
Accompanist..................................Joan Umeda
Music...High School Orchestra
Conducted by Mr. Louis Frizzell
Judges..Mrs. Hazel Feil
Miss Sachiko Tashima
Mr. Clyde L. Simpson
Mr. Edward Chester
Mr. Frank Yasuda
Our appreciation to the electricians and others who helped us.

Source: Manzanar National Historic Site, MANZ 017 //01-003a. National Park Service.

Document 10

CAMPUS NEWSPAPER

Published by the journalism class, The Campus Pepper *and* The Spot *kept students informed on scholastic activities, sports, and social gossip. In October 1944,* The Campus Pepper *reported on a speech by Dillon Myer, national War Relocation Authority director, to a student assembly urging them to keep their chins up and "make the most out of your time in high school."*

CAMPUS PEPPER

Oct. 13, 1944

Leadership
Not long ago I overheard a young man in Manzanar make a remark about leadership. It was, "I would not want to be a leader here. It's just sticking your neck out for trouble."

That same day I heard a girl make a similar remark, "I don't like to be a chairman of a committee; that's being too forward for a girl. "

These two remarks made me think about Nisei leadership and wonder how these young people could ever develop into leaders if they passed by all opportunities for getting experience in leadership.

We all know that the Nisei were lacking in leadership before evacuation at a time when experiences political and social leadership were critically needed.

The Nisei are again taking their places in normal American communities. Let us hope that they are realizing the importance of finding a place for themselves where they can develop leadership and have a voice in community and national affairs.

There is a need for leadership in every age group. Without student leaders, there is no school spirit or morale. The Church, industry, politics, social reform—all need leaders for progress.

Learning to be a leader or learning to follow a leader comes only with practice. Your school life is the best place for this first training.

Dr. Carter

Learning How

Yesterday, after a successful fire drill the Manzanar Secondary Student Body witnessed a demonstration on the use of various fire extinguishers east of the auditorium.

Fire Chief Hon opened the assembly by addressing the students. In his address he related several incidents regarding fire. One was the large fire in Chicago in 1871, and another was the setting aside of fire prevention week sometime in October by President Wilson in 1913. Each year at least five hundred million dollars is lost through fires. Something burning every minute means the loss of more than one million dollars a day.

The demonstration started with a sizzle when Mr. Smith was drafted to demonstrate a pump extinguisher used for ordinary fires. The use of the foamide was demonstrated by Mr. Rogers. This foam is to blanket the flame and used usually on oil fires.

Mr. Dykos demonstrated the Pyrono Extinguisher but this is not so highly recommended. Mrs. White demonstrated the carbon dioxide extinguisher and Mr. Inouye finished the demonstration with the fog spray.

Staff

    Editor in Chief...........Teddy Hayashi
    Assistant Editor..........Seizo Tanibata
    News Editor..............Yuki Shiba
    Feature Editor............Marian Uyomatsu
    Exchange Editor.........Virginia Kikuda
    Business Manager........Roy Muto
    Make-up Editor..........Ken Yamamoto
    Assistant Make-up.......Henry Nakano
    Boys' Sports Editor......Shorty Hashimoto
    Girls' Sports Editor......Rosie Tamai
    Reporters................Alice Nakahama, Lily Yoshino, Lawrence Honda,
                            Mary Honda, Rosio Honda, Sue Ioki, Kazuko Kedota,

Florence Kikura, Aiko Miyaki, Toshiko Korishita, Kiyo Nishi, George Sakamoto, Kuniaki Sakamoto, Sumiko Yamaka, Yuri Yamazaki, Kazy Yoshimura

This, The Third Year

You have just commenced your third year at Manzanar Secondary School. This should be your best year so far, not only at Manzanar but at any school which you have attended.

As you look back over the development of the high school and is progress since Evacuation, it is evident that our students have come a long way in working out educational opportunities that compare favorably with those of the schools from which they came and the schools to which we believe they will go before long.

In our classes, on the school grounds, and with our student council, our clubs, and with other organized groups you all have an opportunity to get the same kind and the same quality of education that you can get elsewhere. To do this we need all "hands" working together to achieve good scholarship, a fine spirit, a high type of character, and well developed extra class activities.

The staff of the CAMPUS PEPPER this semester is organized as a club. The size of the paper will be smaller at first, but the quality of the finished job should be and can be of the highest. Let us all pledge our support to the staff in giving us a school paper that will serve the needs of our students in promoting the things that we believe are most worthwhile.

Rollin C. Fox
Principal

Junior Council

At a recent Junior Council meeting a Seventh Grade Initiation was discussed. Closing the initiation period, a party has been suggested, a party of which will be devoted to a Court of Consequences. This Court will "try" the Seventh Grade violators of "Initiation Week."

Dillon S. Myer

Last week, at the first assembly held in the new auditorium, the Manzanar High School Student Body was honored to have as their guest speaker, Dillon S. Myer director-in-chief of the W.R.A.

Mr. Myer began his address with the statement that people on the whole have two things to fight, ignorance and fear. To help overcome these two factors, there is nothing better than a good education.

Ending his speech he said, "Keep your chin up! Get the most out of your time in High School. Education is not everything, but it is basic. We must have it to fight ignorance, fear, and those feeling of insecurity which are caused by not being adequately prepared. Manzanar is making its contribution to the services of the United States through the fellows who have volunteered or have been drafted through the Selective Service."

"Students of Manzanar, I am proud of you."

Prevention Week

Fire-prevention week, a nationwide observance, is being commemorated in Manzanar, October 8–14, by a seven-day program. This program includes demonstrations of fire extinguishers and equipment to the kitchen crews and hospital staff, fire drills at both Elementary and Secondary schools, movies for the public, and a general clean-up.

Besides this program, an essay and poster contest was sponsored by Community Activities and the Fire Department. The winners will be announced at a public assembly on Friday, October 13, at 8:00 p.m. Fire Prevention movies will be shown tonight at the auditorium. Tickets are available at the Block Offices.

Dedications

1. I'LL WALK ALONE—Sumi Nomoto

2. IS YOU IS OR IS YOU AIN'T—Rosie Honda

3. TOGETHER—Shorty and Teddy

4. HOW MANY HEARTS HAVE YOU BROKEN?—Yuri Yamazaki

5. TIME WAITS FOR NO ONE—All late students

6. SWINGING ON A STAR—Seventh Grade

7. IT HAD TO BE YOU—Jiro Iwata

8. I'LL BE SEEING YOU—Mary Toguchida

9. LET ME LOVE YOU TONIGHT—Miyo Nishi

Getting Personal

Hello, GILA: Guri "Harriet" M., how's your "Ideal"?

Wondering who "Green Eyes" is? Just ask Jiro Iwata or Tsutomu Toma—they'll be sure to know.

I wonder why Tamotsu Nakahara gets so red when he's called "Brooklyn". It couldn't have anything to do with a certain K.Y. who went to New York, could it?

It seems that Tosh M. can't make up her mind about who her "a-re" is. Come on, Tosh, tell us. Is it K.M. or T.M.?

Why is Sumi Nemoto so sad these days? It couldn't be because someone has left camp, could it?

Isn't it a coincident, Yoshiko N., that "I'll Walk Alone" seems to fit you and your M.S.

T. Amano, your favorite class seems to be 5th period English. Could it be S.H.?

Why is T. Hayashi called "Shorty"? Is it because she is so tiny? Wonder how she takes it?

Do you notice the "light" in Tom Izuhara's eyes when a certain Y.N. is mentioned?

Sport Bits

Mr. Fox has sent a letter to our neighborhing High Schools asking for games with Manzanar Hi. Let us all hope that the answer will be "YES."

***

Glancing in the boys' stock room, we can see so many lavender trunks that we think they might go around the whole project.

***

We have some football equipment, a part of which came from Jerone. The trouble may be that the equipment is so big that we cannot fit the boys into them.

Girls Elect

The officers of the girls' Physical Education classes elected at the beginning of term now have the classes running smoothly. They are as follows: Period I, President, Kazy Yoshimura; Vice-President , Gladys Natsumoto; Secretary, Kiyou Nishi; Period II, President, Kei Ono; Vice-President, Mas Yogo; Secretary, Ryo Yano; Period VII, President , Yuki Shiba; Vice-President, Teddy Hayashi; Secretary, Tasie Kitagawa.

Mr. Smith

Our coach, Mr. Smith, prefers Huntington, West Virginia, but since he is here he doesn't mind the weather too much, except for the sand and dust.

He has attended Marshall college in Huntington and received his degree from Alderson-Broaddus college, Philippi, West Virginia, which is about the size of the Manzanar High School.

After arriving here, he was offered a job at Rivers, Arizona, but he is satisfied here because all the students tell him it is worse down there.

He has a sense of humor a mile long with his "corny" jokes. Don't worry, because we have an experienced instructor.

Intramural

Intramural football games are just around the corner with Coach Smith as the director. The teams were formed in gym classes; therefore, all the teams will have stiff competition.

Some games will be played during the class period and others will be played after school. It is anticipated that awards will be given to the winning teams.

Source: The Campus Pepper, Manzanar Secondary School Newspaper, 1944, Page 1 of 6. National Park Service.

Document 11

KOREMATSU V. UNITED STATES (1944)

Korematsu v. United States *(1944) was a landmark Supreme Court case that upheld the constitutionality of the internment of Japanese descent persons during World*

War II. Following the bombing of Pearl Harbor on December 7, 1941, President Franklin D. Roosevelt wasted little time in issuing Executive Order 9066, which sought to severely restrict the civil liberties of those of Japanese descent residing in the western United States, including Arizona, California, Oregon, and Washington. Under EO 9066 exclusion zones were established, requiring Japanese (issei and nisei) to relocate to the interior of the United States on the grounds that they posed threats to national security. Fred Toyosaburo Korematsu, who resided in San Leandro, California, refused to relocate on the grounds that the executive order violated his civil rights. A divided court sided with the federal government in a 6–3 decision with Justice Frank Murphy arguing that internment violated the Constitution and was clearly racist.

Mr. Justice Black delivered the opinion of the Court.

The petitioner, an American citizen of Japanese descent, was convicted in a federal district court for remaining in San Leandro, California, a "Military Area," contrary to Civilian Exclusion Order No. 34 of the Commanding General of the Western Command, U.S. Army, which directed that, after May 9, 1942, all persons of Japanese ancestry should be excluded from that area. No question was raised as to petitioner's loyalty to the United States. The Circuit Court of Appeals affirmed, and the importance of the constitutional question involved caused us to grant certiorari.

It should be noted, to begin with, that all legal restrictions which curtail the civil rights of a single racial group are immediately suspect. That is not to say that all such restrictions are unconstitutional. It is to say that courts must subject them to the most rigid scrutiny. Pressing public necessity may sometimes justify the existence of such restrictions; racial antagonism never can.

In the instant case, prosecution of the petitioner was begun by information charging violation of an Act of Congress, of March 21, 1942, 56 Stat. 173, which provides that

> . . . whoever shall enter, remain in, leave, or commit any act in any military area or military zone prescribed, under the authority of an Executive order of the President, by the Secretary of War, or by any military commander designated by the Secretary of War, contrary to the restrictions applicable to any such area or zone or contrary to the order of the Secretary of War or any such military commander, shall, if it appears that he knew or should have known of the existence and extent of the restrictions or order and that his act was in violation thereof, be guilty of a misdemeanor and upon conviction shall be liable to a fine of not to exceed $5,000 or to imprisonment for not more than one year, or both, for each offense.

Exclusion Order No. 34, which the petitioner knowingly and admittedly violated, was one of a number of military orders and proclamations, all of which were substantially based upon Executive Order No. 9066, 7 Fed. Reg. 1407. That order, issued after we were at war with Japan, declared that the successful prosecution of the war requires every possible protection against espionage and against sabotage to national defense material, national defense premises, and national defense utilities. . . .

One of the series of orders and proclamations, a curfew order, which, like the exclusion order here, was promulgated pursuant to Executive Order 9066, subjected all persons of Japanese ancestry in prescribed West Coast military areas to remain in their residences from 8 p.m. to 6 a.m. As is the case with the exclusion order here, that prior curfew order was designed as a "protection against espionage and against sabotage." In *Hirabayashi v. United States,* . . . we sustained a conviction obtained for violation of the curfew order. The Hirabayashi conviction and this one thus rest on the same 1942 Congressional Act and the same basic executive and military orders, all of which orders were aimed at the twin dangers of espionage and sabotage.

The 1942 Act was attacked in the *Hirabayashi* case as an unconstitutional delegation of power; it was contended that the curfew order and other orders on which it rested were beyond the war powers of the Congress, the military authorities, and of the President, as Commander in Chief of the Army, and, finally, that to apply the curfew order against none but citizens of Japanese ancestry amounted to a constitutionally prohibited discrimination solely on account of race. To these questions, we gave the serious consideration which their importance justified. We upheld the curfew order as an exercise of the power of the government to take steps necessary to prevent espionage and sabotage in an area threatened by Japanese attack.

In the light of the principles we announced in the *Hirabayashi* case, we are unable to conclude that it was beyond the war power of Congress and the Executive to exclude those of Japanese ancestry from the West Coast war area at the time they did. True, exclusion from the area in which one's home is located is a far greater deprivation than constant confinement to the home from 8 p.m. to 6 a.m. Nothing short of apprehension by the proper military authorities of the gravest imminent danger to the public safety can constitutionally justify either. But exclusion from a threatened area, no less than curfew, has a definite and close relationship to the prevention of espionage and sabotage. The military authorities, charged with the primary responsibility of defending our shores, concluded that curfew provided inadequate protection and ordered exclusion. They did so, as pointed out in our *Hirabayashi* opinion, in accordance with Congressional authority to the military to say who should, and who should not, remain in the threatened areas.

In this case, the petitioner challenges the assumptions upon which we rested our conclusions in the *Hirabayashi* case. He also urges that, by May, 1942, when Order No. 34 was promulgated, all danger of Japanese invasion of the West Coast had disappeared. After careful consideration of these contentions, we are compelled to reject them. . . .

It is said that we are dealing here with the case of imprisonment of a citizen in a concentration camp solely because of his ancestry, without evidence or inquiry concerning his loyalty and good disposition towards the United States. Our task would be simple, our duty clear, were this a case involving the imprisonment of a loyal citizen in a concentration camp because of racial prejudice. Regardless of the true nature of the assembly and relocation centers—and we deem it unjustifiable to call them concentration camps, with all the ugly connotations that term implies—we are dealing specifically with nothing but an exclusion order. To cast this case into outlines of racial prejudice, without reference to the real military dangers which were presented, merely confuses the issue. Korematsu was not excluded from the Military Area because of hostility to him or his race. He was excluded because we are at war with the Japanese Empire, because the properly constituted military authorities feared an invasion of our West Coast and felt constrained to take proper security measures, because they decided that the military urgency of the situation demanded that all citizens of Japanese ancestry be segregated from the West Coast temporarily, and, finally, because Congress, reposing its confidence in this time of war in our military leaders—as inevitably it must—determined that they should have the power to do just this. There was evidence of disloyalty on the part of some, the military authorities considered that the need for action was great, and time was short. We cannot—by availing ourselves of the calm perspective of hindsight—now say that, at that time, these actions were unjustified. . . .

Mr. Justice Murphy, dissenting.

The judicial test of whether the Government, on a plea of military necessity, can validly deprive an individual of any of his constitutional rights is whether the deprivation is reasonably related to a public danger that is so "immediate, imminent, and impending" as not to admit of delay and not to permit the intervention of ordinary constitutional processes to alleviate the danger. . . .Civilian Exclusion Order No. 34, banishing from a prescribed area of the Pacific Coast "all persons of Japanese ancestry, both alien and non-alien," clearly does not meet that test. Being an obvious racial discrimination, the order deprives all those within its scope of the equal protection of the laws as guaranteed by the Fifth Amendment. It further deprives these individuals of their constitutional rights to live and work where they will, to establish a home where they choose and to move about freely. In excommunicating them without benefit of hearings, this order also deprives them of all their constitutional rights to procedural due process. Yet no reasonable relations to an "immediate, imminent, and impending" public danger is evident to support this racial restriction, which is one of the most sweeping and complete deprivations of constitutional rights in the history of this nation in the absence of martial law. . . .

Racial discrimination in any form and in any degree has no justifiable part whatever in our democratic way of life. It is unattractive in any setting, but it is utterly revolting among a free people who have embraced the principles set forth in the Constitution of the United States. All residents of this nation are kin in some way by blood or culture to a foreign land. Yet they are primarily and necessarily a part of the new and distinct civilization of the United States. They must, accordingly, be treated at all times as the heirs of the American experiment, and as entitled to all the rights and freedoms guaranteed by the Constitution.

Source: Korematsu v. United States, 323 U.S. 214 (1944).

Document 12

COMMENCEMENT PROGRAM

Annual commencement program from Manzanar High School at Manzanar Relocation Center, California, June 2, 1945.

Annual Commencement
Manzanar
High School
Community Auditorium
MANZANAR, CALIFORNIA
Saturday evening, June 2, 1945
Following the Commencement program
the graduating class and their parents
will be honored by the Parent-Teacher
Association at a reception and dance in
the auditorium.
***

Grateful acknowledgement is herewith
given to the staff at the Music Hall for
their generous contribution in time and
effort in making available the numbers
by the orchestra.
PROGRAM
Presiding, Ralph P. Merritt
Project Director
PRELUDE—"The White Queen"................by O. Metra
*PROCESSIONAL................................"Pomp and Circumstance"
*INVOCATION.................... ....Rev. Yukichi Naito
 Manzanar Christian Church
WELCOME..Roy K. Muto
 President, Class of 1945
GREETINGS......................................Rev. Shinjo Nagatomi
 Manzanr Buddhist Church
"GOD OF OUR FATHERS".......................Ensemble
 Graduating Class
GREETINGS TO CLASS OF 1945...............Lyle G. Wentner
 Assistant Project Director
TROMBONE SOLO—"Ave Maria," by
Gounod...Roy Nagawaka
COMMENCEMENT ADDRESS..................Dean Edwin A. Lee
 University of California, Los
 Angeles
VOCAL SOLO—"Through the Years"...........Yukio Ogawa

PRESENTATION OF THE CLASS OF 1945....Rollin C. Fox
                                                                     Principal
AWARD OF DIPLOMAS..........................Genevieve W. Carter
                                                                     Superintendent of Education
                                                                     Howard K. Murakami
                                                                     Parent-Teacher Association
RESPONSE FOR GRADUATING CLASS........Teruko Hayashi
*"STAR SPANGLED BANNER"..................Audience
*BENEDICTION...............................Father Leo Steinbach
                                                                     Manzanar Catholic Church
*RECESSIONAL.................................."Victorious Legions March"
—
*Audience Standing
Class Officers
PRESIDENT..Roy K. Muto
GIRLS' VICE-PRESIDENT.........................Kiyoko G. Nishi
BOYS' VICE-PRESIDENT.........................Hisao Hashimoto
SECRETARY...Yuriko Yamazaki
TREASURER...Seizo Tanibata
HISTORIAN...Ryoko R. Yano
GIRLS' ATHLETIC MANAGER....................Virginia T. Kikuda
BOYS' ATHLETIC MANAGER....................Masaru Kusaba
                                                                     Advisors
Mrs. Virginia A. Hayes   Mrs. Beatrice H. White
THE STAR SPANGLED BANNER
Oh say! can you see, by the dawn's early light,
What so proudly we hailed at the twilight's last gleaming?
Whose broad stripes and bright stars, thro' the perilous fight,
O'er the ramparts we watch'd, were so gallantly streaming?
And the rockets' red glare, the bombs bursting in air,
Gave proof thro' the night that our flag was still there,
Oh, say, does that Star Spangled Banner yet wave
O'er the land of the free and the home of the brave?

Source: Manzanar National Historic Site, MANZ 0170/-016. National Park Service.

Document 13

MEMOIRS OF SHIGEO KIKUCHI

Shigeo Kikuchi was the wife of Buddhist priest, Chikyoku Kikuchi, who ministered mainly on the Big Island of Hawai'i. They were Buddhist missionaries, and Shigeo Kikuchi taught at the Na'alehu Hongwanji Japanese Language School since 1907. Her husband served as the school's principal, and both served at the Pahala Hongwanji temple until Reverend Kikuchi's retirement in 1953. Originally written as Kaikyō shoki no omoide, *Shigeo Kikuchi's text was translated and published as* Memoirs of a Buddhist Woman Missionary in Hawaii *by the Buddhist Study Center Press in 1991.*

[The Kikuchis, like the rest of their neighbors, were shocked at the news of Japan's December 7, 1941, attack on Pearl Harbor. Shigeo Kikuchi recalled the events of that night in her memoirs.]

At midnight, someone knocked at the door. My husband got up to answer the knock and found a Hawaiian police officer friend standing at the door. "Rev. Kikuchi, I want you to come to the office for a minute." My husband left with him but soon after returned home. The policeman told him "I want you to go to Volcano [a military camp on the island of Hawai'i] and because it was cold there you should take come warm clothing. You may have to stay there two or three days." I borrowed the policeman's flashlight [the military had ordered a blackout] and in the darkness, gathered some warm clothing and put them into a bag. After changing his clothes, he picked up the "Shinshu Seiten" from the bookcase and put it into his pocket. As he left he said, "There is nothing to worry about, I will return in two or three days. But I want you to inform the resident Japanese that we are now in an unexpected situation. Because we are governed by the United States everyone must respect and obey the law of the government and continue to work earnestly. Whatever happens, be patient, control yourself, and never argue or fight with people of other ethnic groups. As for me, nothing to worry about because I have done nothing wrong. After this investigation is over, I will come home." Then he disappeared into the darkness with the officer.

The war had changed our friendly climate overnight. We were now considered enemies. It cause me great pain to face members from other ethnic groups.

As soon as the investigation was over, I had hoped that my husband would be home, but I waited a week, then two weeks, and yet he did not return. Perhaps by Christmas, I thought. Maybe by New Year's. My hopes and expectations were in vain. I received no word from him.

As an enemy alien, my bank savings account and my checking accounts were frozen, and I suffered a great deal.

[Over the weeks that followed, U.S. soldiers increased in numbers while those worshipping at the Buddhist temple declined. There were rumors of arrests, and of FBI searches of homes. As a result, Japanese Americans lived in fear.]

Since my arrival in Hawaii, I had continued to keep diaries but now I burned these also. I burned the record books of names of donors who had contributed for [in Japan] the Kanto earthquake relief fund and for flood victims' relief fund. I later realized how foolish it was for me to do so, but at the time I was in a panic-stricken state. The local police supervisors were very strict and kept a close watch on us. While the temple was a gathering place for people before the war, no one would come anymore because of the fear of the F.B.I. It was only natural for them to feel this way, but it left me with an empty and sad feeling.

In this way the new year of 1942 passed. One day in February, an unexpected news was released saying, the internees will be allowed to see their families. The members of the families were very excited and happy and began preparing favorite foods day and night, for their fathers, husbands or brothers. On that day there were people who had left their homes before dawn with carloads of children to travel a hundred miles to visit their loved ones. As usual I had a ride with Mrs. Suzuki's family. As I got down from the car and walked together with a large crowd across a spacious area, a building surrounded by wire mesh fence became visible. As I approached closer to the wire-fence, I could see the internees' faces fastened to the fence as they eagerly awaited the arrival of their family members. "Mrs. Kikuchi, sensei is here," I heard a voice. After three months of insecurity and a feeling of uneasiness due to our separation, we were finally allowed to see each other. Holding each other's hands there was no word necessary to express the joy of reunion.

Through the kindness of the officer-in-charge, the internees' families were relaxed and they spread out their homemade lunch on the lawn and enjoyed eating, chatting, and laughing. There was no end to their conversation. The MP's showed no sign of concern in the families' conversations and furthermore they even over-looked the time limit in the visiting hours. They were very generous and friendly. The first thing I handed out to my husband was a letter that I brought with me from Akira. For my husband, that letter from his son was his greatest concern. In this letter, Akira says, "I am always with Buddha so please do not worry about me. Although you do not send me money I'll work as a school boy and study." Reading Akira's letter my husband was relieved and extremely happy.

Finally, the time of departure arrived. Volcano towards the evening is rather chilly. We do not know when we will be able to meet again. Perhaps this might be the last time! Those remaining, those leaving, both said reluctant farewells to each other. There was a scene where a little child waved his hand crying, "Daddy bye-bye." There were other scenes of mothers or wives, with tears in their eyes, waving their hands, loathing to part. I can still see these scenes vividly before my mind's eye. This moment of farewell was very, very sad indeed.

[On January 18, 1943, the Pahala Hongwanji temple and language school was burned to the ground. No one knew the cause of the fire, but the military was at the time occupying the language school building.]

The people who gathered to watch the fire together with the Caucasian soldiers who were there suggested that the school building which was aflame should be destroyed in order to keep the fire from spreading to the temple. For some unknown reason the plantation manager failed to heed that suggestion. The temple, which might have been saved, also burned to the ground.

[Chikokyu Kikuchi returned from internment camps on the U.S. continent on November 13, 1945. Shigeo Kikuchi remembered that moment or reunion.]

Seeing my husband at first glimpse, I was surprised at seeing him so thin, but he had a happy smile on his face and he exchanged greetings in high spirits. I was relieved. I took a deep breath. How grateful I felt to see him once again. We paid homage together at Hilo Betsuin [Buddhist temple] then, at Hilo Inn, twenty to thirty people welcomed us. Mr. Shirakawa, Mr. Hamada, Mr. Fujioka, Mr. Takaki, and Mr. Miyahara were together in one car. As we approached Pahala, members of the temple turned out to welcome my husband who had returned after four years of absence. As soon as we arrived there my husband kneeled down in front of the temporary altar of Amida Buddha, reciting nembutsu as he shed his tears.

After the four years of absence, there were many urgent matters waiting for my husband that had to be accomplished right away. Among them were the reopening of the Japanese Language School and the rebuilding of the Pahala Hongwanji Temple. This had to be rushed by all means. During the war, Naalehu Japanese language school had been taken over by the Army, therefore, the minister's residence was used as the classroom. Because no school building remained in Pahala the minister's home had to be used as a classroom when we reopened our Japanese Language School in 1946.

Compared to the enrollment before the war, the attendance of pupils was very small. With such minimal income, a teacher could not be hired, and so only my husband and I taught them. Since the outbreak of the war, the Japanese language had not been in use, so we had to start the teaching of Japanese from scratch. It was very difficult to try to return to a normal pre-war level.

[The Kikuchis retired, and moved to Honolulu where they lived until their deaths. In closing, Shigeo Kikuchi expressed gratitude for her life and the "many people who helped me in so many ways."]

Presently, my body has become weaker. I am now living at the nursing home, but many people come and visit me and I am overwhelmed. Besides, I am at ease because my only son Akira stays with me everyday.

My day is getting closer to return to the Pure Land and I have asked Reverend Kawaji for a favor about this book. After ninety odd years in this world, I owe many thanks to many people who helped me in so many ways. I would like to dedicate this book to everybody, with many thanks.

Source: Kikuchi, Shigeo. *Memoirs of a Buddhist Woman Missionary in Hawaii.* Buddhist Study Center, 1991, pp. 35, 36, 37, 40, 43, 44, 51, 68, 69, 72.

Document 14

MEMOIRS OF SEIICHI HIGASHIDE

Seiichi Higashide was born on the island of Hokkaido in northernmost Japan in 1909. "There," he wrote in his memoirs, "I spent the greater part of my youth in quiet discontent, yearning for greater opportunities than my remote village in the wooded mountains could provide." During the Great Depression, Higashide managed to escape to Tokyo, which was larger than his remote village but still he found it to be confining. He thus left Japan, his first motherland, for Peru in 1930. There, Higashide put down roots, married, had five children, and extended his horizons. Peru, he wrote, was his second motherland. But in 1941 when Japan warred on the United States, Peru severed relations with Japan and hounded Japanese Peruvians as "enemy aliens." Police kidnapped Higashide and others in broad daylight, and deported them to the United States for detention in internment camps. Higashide found himself in the Crystal City, Texas, internment camp run by the Immigration and Naturalization Service. His family joined him there in July 1944. After the war, Higashide chose to remain in the United States, which became his third motherland, became a U.S. citizen, and settled in Chicago and then, Hawai'i. Higashide fought for redress and reparations for Japanese Latin Americans, and as a consequence of that struggle 145 Japanese from Latin America received compensation under the Civil Liberties Act (1988). Seiichi Higashide died in 1997.

[These excerpts from Higashide's memoirs begin in Peru about a year after Japan's attack on Pearl Harbor. After a tip from an acquaintance on February 22, 1943, Higashide eluded arrest. He remained at home but in hiding. Under the floorboards, he dug an underground hideout about six feet square. He furnished it with a bed, small desk, food and water, and radio. Whenever the police came to get him, he went underground.]

For several months our lives continued without incident. The war was still on, so some uneasiness remained in the back of my mind. In general, however, I did not pay particular heed and began to conduct myself in a more open manner, not much different than the time before the war. But, one day, I was suddenly reminded of the fact that Japan was still at war. I can never forget . . . it was January 6, 1944.

It was a Sunday, and we had taken the family out for a picnic at Lake Huacachina. Lake Huacachina was a small expanse of water located at the lowest point of a basin that looked like an ancient volcanic crater. It was known for its cold, green waters that had some salt and sulfur content. Above its waters rose exquisite sand dunes, where people enjoyed a form of sand skiing. It was a wonderful, peaceful Sunday. We had leisurely spent the entire day there and returned home late that evening.

We had just sat down at the table for a late supper when it began. There was a knock on the front door. Previously, if it was not a special pattern of knocks, we would not have opened the door until I entered the underground cubicle. But we had enjoyed many months of an open and peaceful life, so we had forgotten those precautions. One of our employees, Victor, opened the door without hesitation. It was a fatal mistake.

Instantly, five men entered our home and one said, "We are from Lima Police Headquarters. Seiichi Higashide is under arrest." There was no opportunity to feign ignorance. Among the five was a detective from the Ica police office who knew me well. As I had been concerned about earlier, the central police headquarters in Lima had requested the cooperation of the Ica provincial police.

All the avenues had been cut off. I was to be taken immediately to the Ica police headquarters. It is said that even rats in desperate circumstances fight back; I also needed to put up some resistance. "I will not hide or try to escape, so please wait outside," I said calmly. "We are having our supper." We finished our meal in a proper way and, after a change of clothing, I went out.

[The next day, after tearful farewells to his family and his pregnant wife, Higashide was taken to Lima, the capital, where he was held in a jail.]

My cell was a concrete box about six feet wide and about 10 feet deep. The entry, facing a walkway, had a movable framework of iron bars. During the day, the gate-like framework of iron bars was raised and we could go out onto the walkway and into other cells. At night, however, the bars were lowered and locked. If we had to eliminate bodily wastes we were told to do it "wherever you want" in our cells.

It was completely disgusting. The wastes that accumulated during the night were hosed out with water every morning, but because this had been repeated over many years the stench had permeated the concrete and remained permanently. When I was pushed into the cell my first reaction was to that powerful smell.

[On January 18, 1944, Higashide was put on board a ship at the port city of Callao.]

Surrounded by American soldiers carrying rifles with fixed bayonets, we were lined up four abreast and marched over to the gangway to board. M.P.'s were on all sides of us and it was clear that elaborate precautions had been taken. It was then that I truly came to understand that I was a "prisoner of war." The ship was a small freighter that had been hastily militarized with the placement of a number of cannons on it.

When we were all on board the ship, we were made to strip naked and everything that we had brought on board was examined. Then, an officer appeared and began a long and detailed explanation in Spanish of the rules and regulations we were to follow. He ordered complete compliance and repeated that any infractions would be met with severe punishment. It was quite a long presentation but no one made a sound; not even a cough or a shuffle came through the intent silence. Eventually, his speech ended. As ordered, we went down into the hold of the ship and were locked in.

[The ship sailed with the men in the hold below deck.]

We were not allowed to even step out of the hold of the ship. We had no way even to confirm the position of the sun or stars, so we had no way of determining where the ship was heading. We assumed that it was heading northward toward the United States, but we had no way of confirming it. Then, three days after we began our journey, the ship suddenly slowed and eventually stopped.

It was too soon, even on a direct route, to have reached the United States. Had something happened? In the hold of the ship speculation ran rampant. The ship did not move for a long time. Then, from somewhere, a touch of raw, warm air began entering the hold. In two or three hours the hold became unbearably warm. It must be Panama! I felt sure we were in Panama.

Later, the steel door was opened and we were ordered to disembark. Holding our hands up to shade our eyes, we climbed onto the deck. I took in a deep breath of fresh air. The air was warm but was nevertheless a refreshing respite from the stale air breathed by so many people in the hold of the ship. It was truly delicious, I thought. I looked out in all directions. Our surroundings were clearly in a tropical area. I was sure it was Panama.

[The ship carried some Germans and 29 Japanese Peruvians. They were confined in a military camp in Panama where they were treated like soldiers, following their daily routine. Besides forced assemblies and roll calls, the men were directed to clear bushes with armed soldiers standing guard. It was "truly hard and painful labor," Higashide testified, especially for elderly men who spent their lives in offices. "Everyone was physically and spiritually exhausted." After several weeks in the military camp in Panama, on March 6, 1944, the men were loaded onto another ship for the passage to New Orleans. From New Orleans, Higashide and others boarded a train to Texas.]

Those of us who were removed from the train at that small depot were taken to Camp Kenedy, a camp for single men in southern Texas. Of the 27 detention camps that had been built in the United States, it was one of the smallest. Yet, basically, it was no different from the other detention camps.

It was fenced in on four sides with barbed-wire and within it were jerry-built barracks where detainees lived. The camp was, literally, for men who were alone. Married men such as I, who had not been able to be reunited with their families, were assigned to it. From what I heard, those who had been reunited with their families were almost all sent to Crystal City. Earlier, unmarried men and those who had left their families behind in Peru had been sent in random manner to camps built for U.S. residents of Japanese ancestry. After some time had passed, however, such "single men" were placed in specific camps, most notably that at Santa Fe, New Mexico and Camp Kenedy.

Here, there were a number of others like myself who were waiting to be reunited with their families, but the great majority were young, high-spirited, unmarried males. It was in such an environment that I began my "second term" as a detainee. Here, everyone called the facility "the camp." The U.S. government agencies formally called it a "relocation camp," but we simply perceived it as no more than a "concentration camp."

Source: Higashide, Seiichi. *Adios to Tears: The Memoirs of a Japanese-Peruvian Internee in U.S. Concentration Camps.* Honolulu: E&E Kudo, 1993, pp. 7, 135, 136, 139, 141, 142, 143, 145, 157, 158. Used by permission of the University of Washington Press.

Document 15

LAST WITNESSES

In a collection of essays titled Last Witnesses, *Japanese Americans were asked to recall the World War II past for present-day readers. Each generation, the book's editor writes, "must find its own way into this painful chapter of our history, one that has yet to be closed." Published in 2001, some 60 years after the forced, mass removal and confinement, the collection contains writings by Japanese Americans who were asked to remember the past for future generations as the last remaining witnesses to the events that changed forever the lives of some 120,000 people. The book's editor writes in her introduction: "We witnesses and writers make an implicit compact with the young: you will read our stories and hear our voices—but not in silence. If the history of the incarceration is to influence the future, you must constantly renew its stories with dialogue, reflection, active engagement with the issues, and conscience. Only by honoring this trust will you succeed in making the event outlive its witnesses and outwit the eternal return of myth."*

[Sue Kunitomi Embrey was a pivotal figure in the historic, Manzanar pilgrimage. She was the daughter of Gonhichi and Komika Kunitomi, and grew up in Little Tokyo, Los Angeles. Embrey recalled life in Little Tokyo during the 1920s. "It was a segregated Asian ghetto of poor working people, small businesses, churches, temples, and Japanese language schools. It was a tightly knit community in which life was always busy, and cultural activities filled the evenings and weekends of those who longed for their homeland. For the young people growing up in Little Tokyo, there was a sense of strength and protection from a hostile world." Embrey graduated from Lincoln High School shortly before the war, and following Executive Order 9066 on February 19, 1942, and the mass removals of that summer, Embrey and her family were sent to Santa Anita assembly center and then, to Manzanar concentration camp. There, Embrey witnessed the Manzanar riot of December 1942, and she wrote for the Manzanar Free Press, *a camp newspaper begun by nisei. Embrey received clearance to attend nursing school in Madison, Wisconsin, in 1943 with sponsorship from the YWCA but could not attend the University of Wisconsin because the institution was not open to nisei students. The following year, Embrey moved to Chicago where she found a job at the Newberry Library through the American Friends Service Committee. Embrey worked at the library until 1948, after the war, when she returned to Los Angeles to live with her mother. There she met and married Garland Monroe Embrey, attended college, and received her master's degree from the University of Southern California. As an older, returning student, Embrey got involved in student activism and the fight for Asian American studies and justice for Asian Americans. Her concentration camp experience proved valuable in that demand for civil rights. Embrey joined the repeal campaign of Title II of the Internal Security Act (1950), which authorized the attorney general to put dissidents into concentration camps, and she worked on having Manzanar concentration camp declared a state historical landmark. It was under those banners that Embrey and others organized the first Manzanar pilgrimage.]*

It was a cold and windy December day in 1969 when several hundred of us huddled together against the biting wind at the site of Manzanar to commemorate the human tragedy that had played out on the desert floor of the Owens Valley more than twenty-seven years earlier. The event, the first of what were to become annual pilgrimages to the camp's site, was meant to publicize the beginning of a campaign to repeal Title II of the Internal Security (McCarran) Act of 1950. Under Title II, the president was empowered to exclude and detain anyone considered a threat to national security. It was appropriate that survivors of the camps be in the forefront of the campaign to repeal a law that would threaten the civil liberties of all Americans.

The Manzanar Committee celebrated our thirtieth anniversary pilgrimage in April 1998. At our request, each camp reunion and pilgrimage group raised a banner of its own creation in a roll call held before the interfaith religious services. It was a fitting memorial on the eve of the millennium.

My narrative ends here, but my journey continues. In the more than three decades of my involvement with Manzanar and my other community activities, I have reaped benefits I never expected. I have met extraordinary ordinary people and participated in wondrous events while traveling across America. Numerous individuals also involved with the preservation of Japanese American history have been my friends and mentors. I have been recognized for my support of working men and women and was one of thirty-five White House delegates to the United Nation[s] Mid-Decade Conference on Women, held in Copenhagen in 1980. During President Jimmy Carter's term in office, I was invited to a breakfast at the White House.

It has been a long journey of hard work, patience, and endurance, but it has also been one of fun and companionship. As I meet earnest young men and women who feel strongly about our nation and the ideals on which it was founded, I am optimistic about our future. With the vision of these young people, human and civil rights are being strengthened for future generations so that all Americans can share equally in the bounties of our country.

Source: Harth, Erica (Ed.). *Last Witnesses: Reflections on the Wartime Internment of Japanese Americans.* New York: Palgrave, 2001, pp. 14, 15, 168, 177, 184. Reproduced with permission of Palgrave Macmillan.

Selected Bibliography

ANTI–ASIANISTS

Flowers, Montaville. *The Japanese Conquest of American Opinion*. New York: George H. Doran, 1917.

Hynd, Alan. *Betrayal from the East: The Inside Story of Japanese Spies in America*. New York: Stratford Press, 1943.

Irwin, Wallace. *Letters of a Japanese Schoolboy*. New York: Doubleday, Page & Company, 1909.

Irwin, Wallace. *Seed of the Sun*. New York: George H. Doran, 1921.

Kyne, Peter B. *The Pride of Palomar*. New York: Cosmopolitan Book, 1921.

McClatchy, Valentine Stuart (Ed.). *Four Anti-Japanese Pamphlets*. New York: Arno Press, 1978.

Marquand, John P. *Your Turn Mr. Moto*. New York: Popular Library, 1935.

Steiner, Jesse Frederick. *The Japanese Invasion: A Study in the Psychology of Inter-Racial Contacts*. Chicago: A. C. McClurg, 1917.

Stoddard, Lothrop. *The Rising Tide of Color against White World-Supremacy*. New York: Charles Scribner's Sons, 1920.

JAPANESE AMERICANS

Azuma, Eiichiro. *Between Two Empires. Race, History, and Transnationalism in Japanese America*. New York: Oxford University Press, 2005.

Boddy, E. Manchester. *Japanese in America*. Los Angeles: E. Manchester Boddy, 1921.

Chuman, Frank F. *The Bamboo People: The Law and Japanese-Americans*. Del Mar, CA: Publisher's Inc, 1976.

Connor, John W. *Tradition and Change in Three Generations of Japanese Americans*. Chicago: Nelson-Hall, 1977.

Conroy, Hilary. *The Japanese Frontier in Hawaii, 1868–1898*. Berkeley: University of California Press, 1953.

Conroy, Hilary and T. Scott Miyakawa. *East Across the Pacific: Historical and Sociological Studies of Japanese Immigration and Assimilation*. Santa Barbara, CA: Clio Press, 1972.

Creef, Elena Tajima. *Imaging Japanese America: The Visual Construction of Citizenship, Nation, and the Body*. New York: New York University Press, 2004.

Daniels, Roger. *The Politics of Prejudice: The Anti-Japanese Movement in California and the Struggle for Japanese Exclusion*. New York: Atheneum, 1970.

Duus, Masayo Umezawa. *The Japanese Conspiracy: The Oahu Sugar Strike of 1920*. Berkeley: University of California Press, 1999.

Glenn, Evelyn Nakano. *Issei, Nisei, War Bride: Three Generations of Japanese American Women in Domestic Service*. Philadelphia: Temple University Press, 1986.

Grodzins, Morton. *Americans Betrayed: Politics and the Japanese American Evacuation*. Chicago: University of Chicago Press, 1949.

Gulick, Sidney L. *The American Japanese Problem: A Study of the Racial Relations of the East and West.* New York: Charles Scribner's Sons, 1914.

Harden, Jacalyn D. *Double Cross: Japanese Americans in Black and White Chicago.* Minneapolis: University of Minnesota Press, 2003.

Hosokawa, Bill. *JACL: In Quest of Justice.* New York: William Morrow, 1982.

Hosokawa, Bill. *Nisei: The Quiet Americans.* New York: William Morrow, 1969.

Hosokawa, Bill. *Thirty-Five Years in the Frying Pan.* New York: McGraw-Hill, 1978.

Hunter, Louise H. *Buddhism in Hawaii: Its Impact on a Yankee Community.* Honolulu: University of Hawaii Press, 1971.

Ichihashi, Yamato. *Japanese in the United States: A Critical Study of the Problems of the Japanese Immigrants and Their Children.* Stanford: Stanford University Press, 1932.

Ichioka, Yuji. *Before Internment: Essays in Prewar Japanese American History.* Stanford, CA: Stanford University Press, 2006.

Ichioka, Yuji. *The Issei: The World of the First Generation Japanese Immigrants, 1885–1924.* New York: Free Press, 1988.

Inouye, Daniel K. *Journey to Washington.* Englewood Cliffs, NJ: Prentice Hall, 1967.

Iwata, Masakazu. *Planted in Good Soil: A History of the Issei in United States Agriculture,* 2 vols. New York: Peter Lang, 1992.

Iyenaga, T. and Kenoske Sato. *Japan and the California Problem.* New York: G. P. Putnam's Sons, 1921.

Kawakami, Kiyoshi K. *Asia at the Door: A Study of the Japanese Question in Continental United States, Hawaii and Canada.* New York: Fleming H. Revell, 1914.

Kawakami, Kiyoshi K. *The Real Japanese Question.* New York: Macmillan, 1921.

Kikumura, Akemi. *Through Harsh Winters: The Life of a Japanese Immigrant Woman.* Novato, CA: Chandler & Sharp, 1981.

Kimura, Yukiko. *Issei: Japanese Immigrants in Hawaii.* Honolulu: University of Hawaii Press, 1988.

Kitagawa, Daisuke. *Issei and Nisei: The Internment Years.* New York: Seabury Press, 1967.

Kitano, Harry H. L. *Generations and Identity: The Japanese American.* Needham Heights, MA: Ginn Press, 1993.

Kitano, Harry H. L. *Japanese Americans: The Evolution of a Subculture.* Englewood Cliffs, NJ: Prentice-Hall, 1969.

Kurashige, Lon. *Japanese American Celebration and Conflict: A History of Ethnic Identity and Festival, 1934–1990.* Berkeley: University of California Press, 2002.

Lind, Andrew W. *Hawaii's Japanese: An Experiment in Democracy.* Princeton, NJ: Princeton University Press, 1946.

Matsumoto, Valerie. *Farming the Home Place: A Japanese American Community in California, 1919–1982.* Ithaca, NY: Cornell University Press, 1993.

Maykovich, Minako K. *Japanese American Identity Dilemma.* Tokyo: Waseda University Press, 1972.

McWilliams, Carey. *Prejudice: Japanese-Americans: Symbol of Racial Intolerance.* Boston: Little, Brown, 1944.

Millis, H. A. *The Japanese Problem in the United States.* New York: Macmillan, 1915.

Miyamoto, Kazuo. *Hawaii: End of the Rainbow.* Rutland, Vermont: Charles E. Tuttle, 1964.

Miyamoto, Shotaro Frank. *Social Solidarity among the Japanese of Seattle.* Seattle: University of Washington, 1939.

Modell, John. *The Economics and Politics of Racial Accommodation: The Japanese of Los Angeles, 1900–1942.* Urbana: University of Illinois Press, 1977.

Ogawa, Dennis M. *Jan Ken Po: The World of Hawaii's Japanese Americans*. Honolulu: University Press of Hawaii, 1973.

Ogawa, Dennis M. *Kodomo no tame ni, For the Sake of the Children: The Japanese American Experience in Hawaii*. Honolulu: University Press of Hawaii, 1978.

Okimoto, Daniel I. *American in Disguise*. New York: Walker/Weatherhill, 1971.

Petersen, William. *Japanese Americans: Oppression and Success*. New York: Random House, 1971.

Smith, Bradford. *Americans from Japan*. Philadelphia: J.B. Lippincott, 1948.

Strong, Edward K. *The Second Generation Japanese Problem*. Stanford: Stanford University Press, 1934.

Takabuki, Matsuo. *An Unlikely Revolutionary: Matsuo Takabuki and the Making of Modern Hawai'i*. Honolulu: University of Hawai'i Press, 1998.

Takahashi, Jere. *Nisei/Sansei: Shifting Japanese American Identities and Politics*. Philadelphia: Temple University Press, 1997.

Tamura, Eileen H. *Americanization, Acculturation, and Ethnic Identity: The Nisei Generation in Hawaii*. Urbana: University of Illinois Press, 1994.

Van Sant, John E. *Pacific Pioneers: Japanese Journeys to America and Hawaii, 1850–80*. Urbana: University of Illinois Press, 2000.

Wilson, Robert A. and Bill Hosokawa. *East to America: A History of the Japanese in the United States*. New York: William Morrow, 1980.

Yanagisako, Sylvia Junko. *Transforming the Past: Tradition and Kinship among Japanese Americans*. Stanford, CA: Stanford University Press, 1985.

Yoo, David. *Growing Up Nisei: Race, Generation, and Culture among Japanese Americans of California, 1924–49*. Urbana: University of Illinois Press, 2000.

WORLD WAR II

Ahn, Hyung-ju. *Between Two Adversaries: Korean Interpreters at Japanese Alien Detention Centers during World War II*. Fullerton: Oral History Program, California State University, 2002.

Armor, John and Peter Wright. *Manzanar*. New York: Times Books, 1988.

Arrington, Leonard J. *The Price of Prejudice: The Japanese-American Relocation Center in Utah during World War II*. Logan: Utah State University, 1962.

Austin, Allan W. *From Concentration Camps to Campus: Japanese American Students and World War II*. Urbana: University of Illinois Press, 2004.

Bailey, Paul. *City in the Sun: The Japanese Concentration Camp at Poston, Arizona*. Los Angeles: Westernlore Press, 1971.

Bosworth, Allan R. *America's Concentration Camps*. New York: W.W. Norton, 1967.

Broom, Leonard and John I. Kitsuse. *The Managed Casualty: The Japanese-American Family in World War II*. Berkeley: University of California Press, 1973.

Chang, Gordon (Ed.). *Morning Glory, Evening Shadow: Yamato Ichihashi and His Internment Writings 1942–1945*. Stanford, CA: Stanford University Press, 1997.

Chang, Thelma. *"I Can Never Forget": Men of the 100th/442nd*. Honolulu: Sigi Productions, 1991.

Christgau, John. *"Enemies": World War II Alien Internment*. Ames: Iowa State University Press, 1985.

Collins, Donald E. *Native American Aliens: Disloyalty and the Renunciation of Citizenship by Japanese Americans during World War II*. Westport, CT: Greenwood Press, 1985.

Crost, Lyn. *Honor by Fire: Japanese Americans at War in Europe and the Pacific*. Novato, CA: Presidio Press, 1994.

Daniels, Roger. *Concentration Camps, U.S.A.: Japanese Americans and World War II*. New York: Holt, Rinehart and Winston, 1971.

Daniels, Roger. *The Decision to Relocate the Japanese Americans*. Philadelphia: J. B. Lippincott, 1975.

Daniels, Roger. *Prisoners Without Trial: Japanese Americans in World War II*. New York: Hill and Wang, 1993.

de Nevers, Klancy Clark. *The Colonel and the Pacifist: Karl Bendetsen, Perry Saito, and the Incarceration of Japanese Americans during World War II*. Salt Lake City: University of Utah Press, 2004.

Duus, Masayo Umezawa. *Tokyo Rose: Orphan of the Pacific*, translated by Peter Duus. Tokyo: Kodansha International, 1979.

Duus, Masayo Umezawa. *Unlikely Liberators: The Men of the 100th and 442nd*, translated by Peter Duus. Honolulu: University of Hawaii Press, 1987.

Fugita, Stephen S. and Marilyn Fernandez. *Altered Lives, Enduring Community: Japanese Americans Remember Their World War II Incarceration*. Seattle: University of Washington Press, 2004.

Fujita, Frank. *Foo: A Japanese-American Prisoner of the Rising Sun*. Denton: University of North Texas Press, 1993.

Fujitani, Takashi. *Race For Empire: Koreans as Japanese and Japanese as Americans during World War II*. Berkeley: University of California Press, 2011.

Gardiner, C. Harvey. *Pawns in a Triangle of Hate: The Peruvian Japanese and the United States*. Seattle: University of Washington Press, 1981.

Gesenway, Deborah and Mindy Roseman. *Beyond Words: Images from America's Concentration Camps*. Ithaca, NY: Cornell University Press, 1987.

Girdner, Audrie and Anne Loftis. *The Great Betrayal: The Evacuation of the Japanese-Americans during World War II*. New York: Macmillan, 1969.

Gordon, Linda and Gary Y. Okihiro. *Impounded: Dorothea Lange and the Censored Images of Japanese American Internment*. New York: W.W. Norton, 2006.

Grodzins, Morton. *Americans Betrayed: Politics and the Japanese Evacuation*. Chicago: University of Chicago Press, 1949.

Harris, Catherine Embree. *Dusty Exile: Looking Back at Japanese Relocation during World War II*. Honolulu: Mutual Publishing, 1999.

Harth, Erica (Ed.). *Last Witness: Reflections on the Wartime Internment of Japanese Americans*. New York: Palgrave, 2001.

Hayashi, Ann Koto. *Face of the Enemy, Heart of a Patriot: Japanese-American Internment Narratives*. New York: Garland, 1995.

Hayashi, Brian Masaru. *Democratizing the Enemy: The Japanese American Internment*. Princeton, NJ: Princeton University Press, 2004.

Higa, Karin M. (Ed.). *The View from Within: Japanese American Art from the Internment Camps, 1942–1945*. Seattle: University of Washington Press, 1994.

Hirabayashi, Lane Ryo. *The Politics of Fieldwork: Research in an American Concentration Camp*. Tucson: University of Arizona Press, 1999.

Hohri, William. *Repairing America: An Account of the Movement for Japanese-American Redress*. Pullman: Washington State University Press, 1984.

Ichinokuchi, Tad (Ed.). *John Aiso and the M.I.S.: Japanese-American Soldiers in the Military Intelligence Service, World War II*. Los Angeles: Military Intelligence Service Club of Southern California, 1988.

Ichioka, Yuji (Ed.). *Views from Within: The Japanese American Evacuation and Resettlement Study.* Los Angeles: UCLA Asian American Studies Center, 1989.

Inada, Lawson Fusao (Ed.). *Only What We Could Carry: The Japanese American Internment Experience.* San Francisco: California Historical Society, 2000.

Irons, Peter. *Justice at War: The Story of the Japanese American Internment Cases.* New York: Oxford University Press, 1983.

Irons, Peter (Ed.). *Justice Delayed: The Record of the Japanese American Internment Cases.* Middleton, CT: Wesleyan University Press, 1989.

Ishigo, Estelle. *Lone Heart Mountain.* Los Angeles: Anderson, Ritchie and Simon, 1972.

Ishizuka, Karen L. *Lost & Found: Reclaiming the Japanese American Incarceration.* Urbana: University of Illinois Press, 2006.

James, Thomas. *Exile Within: The Schooling of Japanese Americans, 1942–1945.* Cambridge, MA: Harvard University Press, 1987.

Kashima, Tetsuden. *Judgment without Trial: Japanese American Imprisonment during World War II.* Seattle: University of Washington Press, 2003.

Kiyosaki, Wayne S. *A Spy in Their Midst: The World War II Struggle of a Japanese-American Hero.* Lanham, MD: Madison Books, 1995.

Leighton, Alexander H. *The Governing of Men: General Principles and Recommendations Based on Experience at a Japanese Relocation Camp.* Princeton, NJ: Princeton University Press, 1945.

Mackey, Mike. *Heart Mountain: Life in Wyoming's Concentration Camp.* Powell, WY: Western History Publications, 2000.

Mackey, Mike (Ed.). *Remembering Heart Mountain: Essays on Japanese American Internment in Wyoming.* Powell, WY: Western History Publications, 1998.

Maki, Mitchell T., Harry H. L. Kitano, and S. Megan Berthold. *Achieving the Impossible Dream: How Japanese Americans Obtained Redress.* Urbana: University of Illinois Press, 1999.

Martin, Ralph G. *Boy from Nebraska: The Story of Ben Kuroki.* New York: Harper & Brothers, 1946.

Masuda, Minoru. *Letters from the 442nd: The World War II Correspondence of a Japanese American Medic.* Seattle: University of Washington Press, 2008.

Matsumoto, Toru. *Beyond Prejudice. A Story of the Church and Japanese Americans.* New York: Friendship Press, 1946.

McClain, Charles (Ed.). *The Mass Internment of Japanese Americans and the Quest for Legal Redress.* New York: Garland, 1994.

Moore, Brenda L. *Serving Our Country: Japanese American Women in the Military during World War II.* New Brunswick, NJ: Rutgers University Press, 2003.

Muller, Eric L. *American Inquisition: The Hunt for Japanese American Disloyalty in World War II.* Chapel Hill: University of North Carolina Press, 2007.

Muller, Eric L. *Free To Die For Their Country: The Story of the Japanese American Draft Resisters in World War II.* Chicago: University of Chicago Press, 2001.

Murata, Kiyoaki. *An Enemy among Friends.* Tokyo: Kodansha International, 1991.

Murphy, Thomas D. *Ambassadors in Arms: The Story of Hawaii's 100th Battalion.* Honolulu: University of Hawaii Press, 1954.

Murray, Alice Yang. *Historical Memories of the Japanese American Internment and the Struggle for Redress.* Stanford: Stanford University Press, 2008.

Murray, Alice Yang (Ed.). *What Did the Internment of Japanese Americans Mean?* Boston: Bedford/St. Martin's, 2000.

Myer, Dillon S. *Uprooted Americans: The Japanese Americans and the War Relocation Authority during World War II.* Tucson: University of Arizona Press, 1971.

Nagata, Donna K. *Legacy of Injustice: Exploring the Cross-Generational Impact of the Japanese American Internment.* New York: Plenum Press, 1988.

Nelson, Douglas W. *Heart Mountain: The Story of an American Concentration Camp.* Madison: State Historical Society of Wisconsin, 1976.

Ng, Wendy L. *Japanese American Internment during World War II: A History and Reference Guide.* Westport, CT: Greenwood Press, 2002.

Odo, Franklin. *No Sword to Bury: Japanese Americans in Hawai`i during World War II.* Philadelphia: Temple University Press, 2004.

Okihiro, Gary Y. *Storied Lives: Japanese American Students and World War II.* Seattle: University of Washington Press, 1999.

Okihiro, Gary Y. and Joan Myers. *Whispered Silences: Japanese Americans and World War II.* Seattle: University of Washington Press, 1996.

Okubo, Mine. *Citizen 13660.* New York: Columbia University Press, 1946.

Pak, Yoon K. *Wherever I Go, I Will Always Be a Loyal American: Schooling Seattle's Japanese Americans during World War II.* New York: RoutledgeFalmer, 2002.

Personal Justice Denied. Report of the Commission on Wartime Relocation and Internment of Civilians. Washington, D.C.: Government Printing Office, 1982.

Robinson, Greg. *A Tragedy of Democracy: Japanese Confinement in North America.* New York: Columbia University Press, 2009.

Robinson, Greg. *By Order of the President: FDR and the Internment of Japanese Americans.* Cambridge, MA: Harvard University Press, 2001.

Shibutani, Tamotsu. *The Derelicts of Company K: A Sociological Study of Demoralization.* Berkeley: University of California Press, 1978.

Spicer, Edward H., Asael T. Hansen, Katherine Luomala, and Marvin K. Opler. *Impounded People: Japanese-Americans in the Relocation Centers.* Tucson: University of Arizona Press, 1969.

Suzuki, Lester E. *Ministry in the Assembly and Relocation Centers of World War II.* Berkeley: Yardbird Publishing, 1979.

Takezawa, Yasuko I. *Breaking the Silence: Redress and Japanese American Ethnicity.* Ithaca, NY: Cornell University Press, 1995.

Tanaka, Chester. *Go For Broke: A Pictorial History of the Japanese American 100th Infantry Battalion and the 442nd Regimental Combat Team.* Richmond, CA: Go For Broke, 1982.

Tateishi, John. *And Justice for All: An Oral History of the Japanese American Detention Camps.* New York: Random House, 1984.

Taylor, Sandra C. *Jewel of the Desert: Japanese American Internment at Topaz.* Berkeley: University of California Press, 1993.

tenBroek, Jacobus, Edward N. Barnhart, and Floyd W. Matson. *Prejudice, War, and the Constitution.* Berkeley: University of California Press, 1954.

Thomas, Dorothy Swaine. *The Salvage.* Berkeley: University of California Press, 1952.

Thomas, Dorothy Swaine and Richard S. Nishimoto. *The Spoilage.* Berkeley: University of California Press, 1946.

Uchida, Yoshiko. *Desert Exile: The Uprooting of a Japanese American Family.* Seattle: University of Washington Press, 1982.

Van Valkenburg, Carol Bulger. *An Alien Place: The Fort Missoula, Montana, Detention Camp, 1941–1944.* Missoula: Pictorial Histories Publishing, 1995.

Wax, Rosalie H. *Doing Fieldwork: Warnings and Advice.* Chicago: University of Chicago Press, 1971.

Weglyn, Michi. *Years of Infamy: The Untold Story of America's Concentration Camps.* New York: William Morrow, 1976.

Yenne, Bill. *Rising Sons: The Japanese American GIs Who Fought for the United States in World War II.* New York: St. Martin's Press, 2007.

Yoshida, Jim. *The Two Worlds of Jim Yoshida.* New York: William Morrow, 1972.

Yoshitsu, Masao. *My Moments in the Twentieth Century: An Immigrant's Story.* New York: Vantage Press, 1987.

About the Editor and Contributors

THE EDITOR

Gary Y. Okihiro, PhD, is professor of international and public affairs at Columbia University in the City of New York. His latest books are *Pineapple Culture: A History of the Temperate and Tropical Zones* (2009); and *Island World: A History of Hawai'i and the United States* (2008). Okihiro holds a doctorate in history from UCLA.

THE CONTRIBUTORS

Jenny M. James
Columbia University

Kassandra M. Lee
Columbia University

Jasmine Little
Columbia University

Carrie M. Montgomery
Columbia University

Daniel Valella
Columbia University

Kia S. Walton
Columbia University

Autumn Womack
Columbia University

Belle Yan
Columbia University

Index

Note: Page numbers in **boldface** reflect main entries in the book.